Spinning
a Sacred
Yarn

Spinning

Women Speak

a Sacred Yarn

from the Pulpit

THE PILGRIM PRESS
NEW YORK

Library of Congress Cataloging in Publication Data
Main entry under title:

Spinning a sacred yarn.

1. Women in Christianity—Sermons.
2. Sermons, American.
BV639.W7S64   252′.0088042   82–569
ISBN 0–8298–0604–0 (pbk.)   AACR2

The Pilgrim Press, 132 West 31 Street, New York, New York 10001

Acknowledgments

The publisher acknowledges with appreciation permission to use the following copyrighted material.

Scripture quotations marked TEV are from the *Good News Bible: Today's English Version;* Old Testament: © American Bible Society, 1976; New Testament: © American Bible Society 1966, 1971, 1976; used by permission. Scripture quotations marked JB are from THE JERUSALEM BIBLE, copyright © 1966 by Darton, Longman & Todd, Ltd. and Doubleday & Company, Inc; used by permission of the publisher. Scripture quotations marked NAB are from *The New American Bible,* copyright © 1970 by the Confraternity of Christian Doctrine, Washington, D.C.; used by permission of the Confraternity of Christian Doctrine. Scripture quotations marked NEB are from *The New English Bible,* © The Delegates of the Oxford University Press and The Syndics of the Cambridge University Press 1961, 1970; reprinted by permission. Scripture quotations marked RSV are from the *Revised Standard Version of the Bible,* copyright 1946, 1952, and © 1971 by the Division of Christian Education, National Council of Churches, and are used by permission.

Lines on page 34 from "The Everlasting Mercy" are reprinted with permission of Macmillan Publishing Company, Inc. from *Poems* by John Masefield. Copyright 1912 by Macmillan Publishing Company, Inc., renewed 1940 by John Masefield. Poem on page 44 is "There Is Pain," from *A Book of Eve* by Catherine de Vinck (Allendale, PA: House of Poetry) and is used by permission. Poem on page 76 is "Indifference," from *The Sorrows of God,* by G.A. Studdert-Kennedy. Copyright © 1924 by Harper & Brothers. Reprinted by permission of Hodder & Stoughton Ltd. "The Enigmatic God" by Carter Heyward is reprinted with permission of *The Witness* (April 1978, pp. 4–7), Box 359, Ambler, PA 19002. Poem on page 189 is from *Cricket Song,* by Winston Abbott. Copyright © 1971 by Inspiration House Publishers. Reprinted by permission.

Contents

Preface

For a long time, women were not allowed official positions of power in religion. There are many theories about why this was so. At last, the situation is gradually changing and women are being given the pulpits they deserve. It is a slow process, with continual setbacks, and it takes a pioneering strength to persevere. They have that strength.

This collection represents an important moment in time for these women: Protestants, Catholics, Jews, speaking from pulpits all over the country, they lend a new dimension to religion. Enthusiastic, fresh, hopeful, they provide excitement, energy and insight that is apparent in the way they handle the broad range of subject matter present in these sermons: from Mary to Ishmael, from liberty and justice to singing songs, cooking, thinking about an enigmatic God. These women represent a loud, strong, clear and important new set of voices. They are voices that we welcome.

The Editors

Spinning a Sacred Yarn

Unbinding for Life
ANN GREENAWALT ABERNETHY

There was a man named Lazarus who lived in the village of Bethany with the two sisters, Mary and Martha, and he was ill. . . . The sisters sent this message to Jesus, "Lord, the man you love is ill." On receiving the message, Jesus said, "This sickness will end not in death but in God's glory, and through it the Son of God will be glorified."

Jesus loved Martha and her sister and Lazarus, yet when he heard that Lazarus was ill he stayed where he was for two more days before saying to the disciples, "Let us go to Judaea. . . . Our friend Lazarus is resting, I am going to wake him." The disciples said to him, "Lord, if he is able to rest he is sure to get better." The phrase Jesus used referred to the death of Lazarus, but they thought that by "rest" he meant "sleep," so Jesus put it plainly, "Lazarus is dead; and for your sake I am glad I was not there because now you will believe. But let us go to him." . . .

On arriving, Jesus found that Lazarus had been in the tomb for four days already. . . . When Martha heard that Jesus had come she went to meet him. Mary remained sitting in the house. Martha said to Jesus, "If you had been here, my brother would not have died, but I know that, even now, whatever you ask of God, he will grant you." "Your brother" said Jesus to her "will rise again." Martha said, "I know he will rise again at the resurrection on the last day." Jesus said: "I am the resurrection. If anyone believes in me, even though he dies he will live, and whoever lives and believes in me will never die. Do you believe this?" "Yes, Lord" she said "I believe." . . .

When she had said this, she went and called her sister Mary, saying in a low voice, "The Master is here and wants to see you." . . . Mary went to Jesus, and

3

as soon as she saw him she threw herself at his feet, saying, "Lord, if you had been here, my brother would not have died." . . .

Still sighing, Jesus reached the tomb: it was a cave with a stone to close the opening. Jesus said, "Take the stone away." Martha said to him, "Lord, by now he will smell; this is the fourth day." Jesus replied, "Have I not told you that if you believe you will see the glory of God?" So they took away the stone. Then Jesus lifted up his eyes and said: "Father, I thank you for hearing my prayer." . . . When he had said this he cried in a loud voice, "Lazarus, here! Come out!" The dead man came out, his feet and hands bound with bands of stuff and a cloth round his face. Jesus said to them, "Unbind him, let him go free."

—JOHN 11:1–44, JB

If you have spent time with the theater section of your news-paper over the past month, you have discovered some movie titles which pick up themes from this morning's scripture lesson. Three of them are: *Jesus, The Awakening,* and *Resurrection.* The advertisement for the movie *Jesus* pictures a lone pair of sandals in the desert and says, "The man you thought you knew . . . stripped of myth and mystery." The ad for *The Awakening* shows a mummy wrapped in strips of cloth and says, "They thought they had buried her forever." And the tagline for the film *Resurrection* says, "It is not supposed to happen. Be there when it does."

I have seen none of these films, and only know what has been communicated to me about them through the newspaper. I am struck, however, by Hollywood's use of these religious titles and themes. Whenever the secular world begins to take religious material and reshape it, we, in the church, need to take notice. Whenever the Christian story becomes commercialized and reinterpreted through a popular medium, we, in the church, need to sharpen our understanding of our biblical heritage and faith. We cannot afford to let Hollywood do our work for us—because chances are good that Hollywood has other mes-sages to communicate—nor can we afford to let Hollywood interpret the Christian faith to this society. We have already had too much use of Jesus' name to defend selfish and idolatrous political rhetoric over the past months. Just as we cannot abdicate our understanding of the Gospel to small-minded clergy and politicians, so we cannot remain mute and unin-formed in the face of Hollywood scriptwriters and producers.

The theater section of our morning newspaper calls us back to our lifelong quest to study, understand, proclaim, and live out our Christian story. When we have better understood the messages of the Lazarus story, then we should be better interpreters of our sacred script to those about us who will see and hear only the Hollywood version.

The raising of Lazarus is a difficult story for our modern minds to comprehend. It has been a difficult story from the time of its happening and through all the generations of its telling. Probing and hearing its messages is a far more important activity than questioning or affirming its historical accuracy. In John's Gospel, the raising of Lazarus is the last straw. It was the event which solidified the Pharisees' determination to do away with Jesus. For Jesus, it was his last chance to communicate the power and radicalness of his message. This was the final scene in a drama of signs, miracles, and words chosen by Jesus to give flesh to God's marvelous love and unbelievable graciousness.

The stage curtain opens. The drama is familiar to each of us. Someone we love is ill, desperately ill, ill unto death. We reach out for the best healer we know, hoping frantically that he or she will come in time to start the one we love back to life and health. We are anxious, burdened by responsibility, afraid of our own insufficiencies, hoping, hoping for help, in time. So Martha and Mary send a message to Jesus: "The man you love is ill"; and in that message is another: "The man we love is ill—come, come quickly and help!" But Jesus cannot come, not for several days, and Lazarus' life gives way to death. For Martha, for Mary, for you, and for me, nothing seems so final as death. It is frightening, and fracturing, and foreign; it is the bottom line on the human experience. Our loved one is dead. Lazarus is dead. Hope is finished. And we move through the ritual of burial, wrapping and putting the body away, weeping, remembering, and saying good-bye. Into this scene, in its fourth day, Jesus arrives. Both Mary and Martha make clear their disappointment that their friend-healer didn't arrive sooner when they say, "Lord, if you had been here, my brother would not have died." Mary's tears allow Jesus to share his own tears, but Jesus has not come to this place to celebrate death. He has come to celebrate life!

Before he even left for Bethany, Jesus had tried to tell his disciples that they would find Lazarus dead but that Jesus would bring him to life. All the disciples could understand was awakening, that Jesus would call Lazarus out of a restful, healing sleep. Jesus also tells Martha that Lazarus will rise again, but Martha believes he is speaking of some far-off resurrection at the end of time. She can affirm that he is the Messiah, but she has no way of understanding his words, "I am the resurrection." The idea was too radical, totally incomprehensible, fitting into no frame of understanding that Martha or the disciples had ever known before. They might have said, "If you speak about an awakening or the traditional Hebraic understanding of a final resurrection —that we can understand. But your words about resurrection, about reversing death—that is too much, the very idea sails right over our heads! Death is death, and that is all." Jesus stands at the end of his ministry, and those who should have understood him the best hear and do not understand. So Jesus gets on with the work of enfleshing his words and of incarnating God's love, just as he has done throughout his ministry.

With Martha, with Mary, with the disciples, and with the mourners who have come to Bethany to grieve, Jesus goes to the tomb where Lazarus has been laid. "Take the stone away," he says. And Martha, speaking for the whole crowd, cries out, "Lord, . . . this is the fourth day." For four days and nights the sisters and the mourners had been trying to live beyond this death, to say good-bye, to lay Lazarus to rest and to get on with their lives; and now Jesus was asking them to look again at the horrible, stinking reality of death.

What Martha could not understand before she saw it happen is that God does break into human life precisely where it is most rotten and painful. God's love, God's gift of new life, is not a future reality. It is here and now, breaking into the present, bursting into history through the man Jesus, the Christ. God's love turns the tables on illness and poverty, on injustice and oppression, on imprisonment and—yes, yes, even on death. The blind see, the lame walk, chains fall from the captives, the oppressed dance, and the dead are raised to life.

So Jesus stands at the tomb of Lazarus and, after praying, cries in a loud voice, "Lazarus, come out!"—and Lazarus does come out! And all the power and grace of God are released for new life to happen there in that place—or here in this place. The kingdom of God is here. The kingdom of God is now. Life with God is not a future promise, but a gift here and now, within time and space, within human history, within your life and my life. And Jesus comes from God and Jesus is God, so we see afresh that ours is a God of compassion, a God of tears, a God committed to give life to decaying existence, and a God compelled to make even lifeless bones dance.

Lazarus does come out, and we see him stand before us. But wait—he is all bound up. His feet and his hands, his head and his torso are wrapped with strip upon strip of cloth. He cannot participate in life until he is freed from the bondage of the wrappings which bind his being. To the crowd gathered around the tomb Jesus says, "Unbind him, let him go free!" The crowd will not be bystanders to the wonder and work of resurrection. Jesus commands them to participate with him in that life-giving act. We are in the crowd, as well. The command of Jesus comes to us: "Unbind them, unbind all of your brothers and sisters, let them go free! You may, you must, participate in the work of resurrection. This your brother is bound, this your sister is unfree. Come and unwind the wrappings which keep them from wholeness and freedom and new life."

There are times when we are all bound in strips of cloth and someone comes to us and helps unwind the bandages which keep us from fullness of life. One strip is depression and another is grief. One strip is jealousy and another is insecurity. One strip is anger and another is loneliness. One strip is illness and another is fear. One strip is emptiness, another self-hatred. On and on the strips go, encircling our beings, destroying our freedom, deadening our lives. We understand Lazarus' bondage, for each of us has been there too.

To live together in resurrection life, to be faithful to families and friends and church communities, we need to unbind one another. In the church we are the givers and the receivers of pastoral care. Together, for each other, we participate with God in unwinding the strips that keep us in captivity. The spirit of God is present in each resurrection moment, but just as Jesus counted on the onlookers of long ago to release Lazarus from bondage, so God counts on us to share in the work of resurrection with those who are near to us and those who are far off.

Hear how one group of people called Vernon Jordan back to life after his nearly fatal shooting last May [1981]:

> Ten weeks after a deer-hunter's rifle placed a wound the size of a fist an inch from his spine, Jordan arranged for the local executives of the Urban League to come to the hospital. Still painfully weak, but eager to disprove the rumors of his incapacitation, he got out of the wheelchair at the meeting room door and walked in, wearing his blue pajamas and matching robe.
>
> The sound of 118 pairs of hands clapping matched his steps. Leaning over the lectern, the effort stinging, but the act exhilarating, Jordan spoke. "I've been waiting three months for that," he said, with his million-dollar smile. "Why don't you do it again?" [Boston *Globe*, October 31, 1980.]

At the beginning of this sermon we spoke of a movie entitled *Resurrection,* which carried the tagline, "It is not supposed to happen. Be there when it does." That is wrong. It is supposed to happen. It happens over and over again as God breaks into the human scene with life. Do be there when resurrection happens. God needs you to unbind the strips which keep another from walking and dancing free. Do be there when resurrection happens.

ANN ABERNETHY *is minister of Pastoral Care of Wellesley Congregational Church in Massachusetts. She is a member of the UCC Coordinating Center for Women and has been a consultant for the Massachusetts Conference. She is a Union Theological Seminary graduate and is married and the mother of four children.*

America—Finished or Unfinished

CAROLE CARLSON

And now, Israel, what does the Lord your God require of you, but to fear the Lord your God, to walk in all his ways, to love him, to serve the Lord your God with all your heart and with all your soul, and to keep the commandments and the statutes of the Lord, which I command you this day for your good? . . . For the Lord your God is God of gods and Lord of lords, the great, the mighty, and the terrible God, who is not partial and takes no bribe. . . . You shall fear the Lord your God; you shall serve him and cleave to him, and by his name you shall swear. He is your praise; he is your God, who has done for you these great and terrible things which your eyes have seen. Your fathers went down to Egypt seventy persons; and now the Lord your God has made you as the stars of heaven for multitude.

—DEUTERONOMY 10:12–22, RSV

He also told this parable to some who trusted in themselves that they were righteous and despised others: "Two men went up into the temple to pray, one a Pharisee and the other a tax collector. The Pharisee stood and prayed thus with himself, 'God, I thank thee that I am not like other men, extortioners, unjust, adulterers, or even like this tax collector. I fast twice a week, I give tithes of all that I get.' But the tax collector, standing far off, would not even lift up his eyes to heaven, but beat his breast, saying, 'God, be merciful to me a sinner!' I tell you, this man went down to his house justified rather than the other; for everyone who exalts himself will be humbled, but he who humbles himself will be exalted."

—LUKE 18:9–14, RSV

Yesterday was All Saints Day, a time when the Catholic Church celebrates the memory of its members who are in heaven. In the ancient church calendar, today was celebrated as All Souls Day, a time when the church focused on the souls of ordinary people rather than on the saints and martyrs. And because most ordinary people went to purgatory, the prayers of the faithful on All Souls Day were designed to intercede for departed ones in purgatory in order to shorten their time in that unpleasant place.

In thinking about today's sermon and the upcoming election, and putting that idea together with the image of all those souls in purgatory, I decided there *must* be some connection between the two. I'm not sure exactly what the connection is—maybe many of us feel like *we* are languishing in purgatory, waiting to be released when this interminable election process ends. Never in our history has there been a presidential contest where people were so uninterested, indifferent, or outright negative.

Why do we feel such a sense of hopelessness about Tuesday? Why is it that, as we become better educated, fewer and fewer people bother to vote? Why is it that the jokes about the election all have to do with rejecting all the candidates? We've all heard many stories which express that general dissatisfaction; my favorite is the one about the boat: Carter, Anderson, and Reagan were all in a boat together. It tipped over and sank, and you know who was saved—the American people! All such jokes reflect a deep cynicism about the electoral process.

I'd like to suggest that the primary reason we feel dissatisfied, the reason we sigh and look forward to the end of this process, is that we know—at a very deep level—that we have reached the deplorable situation in this country where the *ability to get elected has absolutely nothing to do with the ability to govern.* The gap between the characteristics which win elections and the characteristics which enable one to govern wisely becomes wider each time we go through an election process. And we know we—not the candidates—are the losers.

We know why. We can give all the good sociological explanations. We have allowed television to dominate our lives, and we now know that the media do indeed dominate our national destiny. The focus of each candidate's campaign staff is the creating of a *marketable image*. All the energy goes into tailoring statements so they will fit precisely what the pollsters think the people want to hear. All the basic issues are distorted, and the entire process seems superficial and empty. Being marketable has little to do with being wise and skillful in the leadership role, and we know it.

Once we longed for wise and skillful leaders. We even thought they were important enough to invest something of ourselves in their election. But we also understand enough of the election process today to know that the marketable image game has encouraged the breakdown of our two-party system. In the past, *before 1980*, think of the times many of you have worked to help elect a candidate—local, state, or national —addressing envelopes, passing out leaflets, or raising money. Now think about how few of us are involved this year. We all can recount the horror stories of the abuses of our party system— whether it is the Longs of Louisiana or the reign of Mayor Curley in Boston, it has had many weaknesses. But people did count—even if only because someone was trying to buy their votes! Area workers were valued. People knew their neighborhoods and worked in their precincts. Many of us spent time because there was human investment and human contact in that political process. We felt we counted. Today it is only the media ads which count, and we feel left out.

Because of the media pressure, the candidates who are presented all too often seem like the Pharisees of 1980. Like today's candidates who are certain of what the people want to hear, the Pharisee knew what God wanted to hear. He was so confident of his own righteousness that he really was praying to himself, not to God. All too often our candidates seem to be talking to themselves, not to us. But we also know from the comments Jesus made about this story that the Pharisee only *thought* he knew what God wanted to hear. God, in fact, wanted something quite different. So, too, I wonder if the candidates only think they know what the people want to hear—they really don't know the deep roots of our dissatisfaction.

What, indeed, is the substantive message that the pollsters ignore but many of us want to hear? I think we want to hear

something besides the rhetoric about weapons and inflation,
something besides self-centeredness. *We long to hear someone
addressing the concerns which come down to us from the people of Israel,*
concerns for the outcast, the hungry, the alien. The response to
human suffering and human need was the primary ethical test
for Israel. The author of Deuteronomy is absolutely certain
about that fact. God is God over all powers, including all
governments. God shows that power through justice and compassion and mercy, and these are the traits by which governments and the people are to be judged.

But what candidates in our midst can survive by focusing on
these issues? Our communion offering this month is for abused
children. Where are the candidates who advocate children and
their needs? One example of incredible need is health care. The
Child Health Assurance Program is a comprehensive national
bill which has received strong bipartisan support with no major
opposition. The program would provide preventive medical
care for 18 million children who presently have no coverage. No
one argues with its benefits. Health expenditures for children
are reduced by 40 percent when the children receive preventive
care. The investment of small sums is far preferable to substan-
tial investments necessary when illnesses become serious and
require extensive treatment or institutionalization. During the
first 10 years after the measles vaccine was introduced, the cost
savings was estimated to be $1.3 billion.

And yet the health program does not pass Congress. For
more than a year and a half it has been shuffled around in the
Senate. In the House it was passed, but in a form so bogged
down with abortion restrictions that its implementation seems
questionable. It proves the absurdity of our system when anti-
abortion people—who profess to care so much about children—
again and again are able to block legislation which would benefit
children. And in the meantime the children of our nation suffer.
One out of every seven children in the United States has no
regular source of health care. One out of every three children
under the age of seventeen has never seen a dentist. And a black
infant who might be born this morning while we are worshiping
together is twice as likely to die during its first year of life as a
white infant.

Health care for children is only one example; we could list dozens of areas of human need which have been neglected in this campaign.

We know that caring for children—for all who are in need—is *God's* priority during this election week. And I also believe at some level it is our priority. We worship here today not because it is a nice thing to do, not because we enjoy seeing our friends, but because we have made a commitment to follow a Savior who came to bring good news to the poor. But we hesitate to act. We know that talking about such issues in the context of an election is a foolish idea. Imagine the naiveté of suggesting that we make the forgotten ones a political priority! It certainly doesn't fit with "marketable image politicians." Yet remember, two weeks ago Clyde Miller stood in this pulpit and summoned us—as a congregation—to be fools for Christ.

Jay Forrester, a futurist who teaches at MIT, believes that it is inherent in a system like ours that leaders don't lead, they really follow. True leaders follow—but they do not follow this week's polls, they follow the deep desires and longings of the people. *The most satisfactory leadership we have had in our nation's history has emerged when the people demanded it.* In times of war and acute internal crisis, we *have* raised up capable leaders. When we settle for less, when we do not demand qualified leadership, when we do not speak up for the unpopular causes, then we are the ones who have failed—not our candidates. And I think we must admit that we have indeed failed. Perhaps we deserve to be tipped out of that boat!

But does admitting our failures mean we are finished as a nation? Faced with an unworkable congressional system, a media game presidency, and a sense of priorities which invests money in weapons and faulty computers which may destroy us, rather than in human beings who need health care and food and housing—do we conclude we are finished?

Or can we again ask the question Moses asks in Deuteronomy: What does the Lord require of us? What does the Lord require of us as we come to the end of this election process? To dream, and pray, and work, and believe in an unfinished America—unfinished enough to continue welcoming immigrants and refugees, unfinished enough to care for the neglected, to raise up compassionate leaders because its people are foolish enough to believe that compassion is important.

The God who meets us at this table reminds us that our greatness lies in our concern for the lost ones in our midst, that our power comes from service, and that joy and hope *can* replace despair and discouragement when we commit ourselves to the Christ who shared himself with us in the breaking of the bread and the pouring of the wine. Come and share with him, remembering his priorities and daring to be foolish—even as he was.

THE REV. CAROLE CARLSON *is senior pastor of Christ Congregational Church in Denver. She is a member of the Executive Committee of the UCC Coordinating Center for Women in Church and Society.*

The Wait of Pregnancy

PATRICIA A. CARQUE

In those days Mary arose and went with haste into the hill country, to a city of Judah, and she entered the house of Zechariah and greeted Elizabeth. And when Elizabeth heard the greeting of Mary, the babe leaped in her womb.

—LUKE 1:39–41, RSV

During a time of preparation for visiting relatives, my daughter, Erin, became very impatient. She was ready to go to see her grandparents and was unhappy about the delay as I tried to tie up some last-minute details before leaving. I explained to her that we needed to do a few more things before we could leave and that she would simply have to be patient and wait. Upon hearing that, she quickly rushed out of the room. Within a few minutes, she once again called to me, informing me that she was ready. Again I expressed the need for her to wait, and this time she informed me that she *had* waited and that we could go now. I went to see what she was up to and found her in the bathroom, sitting on the bathroom scale—"weighting." She had gone to the quickest place she knew to "wait," that place where you stand and instantly know what your weight is—in pounds, anyway. And then the process of waiting is over and done with. Her impatience moved her to find a way to make the waiting go a little quicker, to let it be a little easier. For Erin, waiting for something as important as a visit to her grandparents was truly a

15

burden, and she sought a quick answer. And what could be more symbolic of this burden than those pounds of weight which tie us down to the reality while our flights of expectation and anticipation move us impatiently forward?

On this final Sunday in Advent, we begin to draw to a close our season of waiting. It is a season in our church year during which we prepare for the celebration of the birth of a child who is our Lord and Savior. For many of us it is a time full of burdens, full of pressure. Whether it be the burden of finishing up Christmas shopping, church responsibilities, schoolwork, preparation for the holidays and visits from families and friends, or the heavy burden of being alone during a time of families or being poor when the world seems affluent, the days before Christmas always seem to be full and heavy ones. Many of us are so weighted down during this time that we just try to rush through it, looking for the event at the end of this busy time. Some of us rush so quickly that Advent is hardly a season at all for us, but instead an obstacle which must be surmounted (and, we hope, as easily and quickly as possible) before getting to Christmas. We do our Christmas shopping. We make our plans. We may close our lonely eyes and our poor hearts and hope that the season to rejoice will soon be over. The wait before Christmas is often a burden. And the arrival of Christmas, and the time following, is the time when some of those burdens become lifted.

Waiting is heavy. Waiting ties us down to some place when we'd rather be elsewhere. Waiting makes us impatient. Our whole lifestyle is one in which waiting means wasting time. We have microwave ovens which cook dinner in one hour instead of four. We have a Concorde which flies us to our destination in almost half the time of jet airplanes. We hate to wait on lines. We hate to wait for people. We hate to be put on hold when we're talking on the telephone. One of the most often heard reflections on waiting seems to be "Won't it be nice when this waiting is over?"

Today's scripture lesson from Luke eventually spoke to me on the subject of waiting. Both Mary and Elizabeth are pregnant, and no doubt experiencing the period of waiting before the birth of a child. And this particular situation of waiting

speaks directly to our Advent message. It is the experience of
anticipating the coming of new life—the experience of being
pregnant with life, being filled with hope and looking forward
to possibilities.

This Gospel story tells us that during her pregnancy Mary
went to visit Elizabeth, who was pregnant with the great forerunner of Christ, John the Baptist. When Elizabeth heard
Mary's greeting, the babe leaped in her womb. It is not uncom-
mon for babies to move about in their mothers' wombs, and this
would certainly supply our quick and easy answer to this
particular experience. It is simply a shifting of a mass of weight
within its enclosure. Yet it would seem that the Gospel account
tries to express more than a biological fact of the moving of
weight. Upon hearing Mary's greeting, Elizabeth's baby leaps for
joy, and she becomes filled with the Holy Spirit.

The word used by the Gospel writer to illustrate the
experience of this leaping is a verb, *skirtan,* which can be
translated to express an exultant delight before the Lord, who
liberates. It has an eschatological meaning, as it looks to the
future with joy in the presence of the Lord, who frees.

These leaps of joy appear in other places in the Bible. In
Psalm 114, the mountains skipped like rams and the little hills
like young sheep. In Wisdom: "like lambs they leapt in praising
you, O Lord, their liberator." And in Malachi: "But for you who
fear my name, the sun of righteousness shall rise with healing in
its wings. You shall go forth leaping like calves from the stall."

Elizabeth's baby leaps with joy as together they experience a
moment pregnant with hope and the promise of liberation. This
is the leap of joy which recognizes hope—the possibility, the
fulfillment of a promise. This leap comes during a time of
waiting. But this time of waiting does not appear to carry with it
the weight or burden which causes one to rush through to the
event that means the wait will be over. This seems rather to be a
time of listening, a time of adjustment. Adjusting eyes to a
darkness to see more clearly, adjusting all of the senses to listen
to the depth of the moment. It is not a time for running, but for
walking. A time full of sensitivity, full of deep experience, full of
awe, full of wonder, full of liberation. This period of waiting
defies the laws of gravity and weight, as mountains and hills

symbolically leap in celebration and joy. This waiting is full, but it is not heavy. It is full of life. It is full of the Holy Spirit. It is the wait of pregnancy.

When I was pregnant with my daughter, Erin, I found myself suddenly tied to life in a deeper way. It was surely a physical experience, but also a spiritual one, as my sensitivity toward the miracle of life increased. As surely as my weight in pounds increased, so too did my awareness of the moment-to-moment experience of being full of life. In some ways it was a burden. I became heavier; I became clumsier. And at times I became overwhelmed by the fears associated with the responsibility of carrying and caring for a life. In some ways, it was truly a weight to be carried. Yet there was also the sense in which my pregnancy somehow liberated a part of me and allowed me to grow closer to God, my Creator. To understand a little more clearly that life is truly a gift, and also to understand a little more deeply that there is an awe and mystery to life that defies reasonable and weighty explanations.

Everywhere I went during this time of pregnancy, Erin went with me. My hands became her hands. My feet became her feet. My nourishment, my actions became intricately linked with her life. This time of waiting during my pregnancy with Erin became much more than a burden or a space to rush through to the event of the birth of my child. This very time of waiting was a deep experience of life for me.

And our Gospel lesson speaks to us of two other women experiencing life in a similar situation. Elizabeth carries the life of the prophet John; Mary carries the life of our Savior, Jesus. And as Mary travels to see Elizabeth, everywhere she goes, Christ goes with her. Her hands became his hands. Her feet became his feet. Her nourishment, her actions became intricately linked with his life.

And at one moment during these many moments of pregnancy, Elizabeth and Mary share an awe and wonder at the life which is filling them both. And this life is seen through the presence of God, which is experienced in a time of waiting.

It is this time of waiting into which the season of Advent has called us. It is a season of remembering that a simple woman bore a child who would save the world, and surely this memory is a time for great celebration. But it is also a season for experiencing life in the midst of waiting.

And this waiting can make us sensitive to a deeper meaning of life. This deeper meaning speaks to us of a living communion with Christ. As Mary became the temple of the physical body of Christ, so too do we, as members of the body of Christ, the church, become the temple of the presence of God. Paul asks us in Corinthians, "Do you not know that you are God's temple and that God's spirit dwells in you [1 Cor. 3:16, RSV]?" As surely as Mary physically experienced childbearing, so we experience Christ-bearing. Christ forms in us mystically, as he formed in Mary physically. Our hands become Christ's hands. Our feet become Christ's feet. Our nourishment, our actions become intricately linked with the life of Christ.

As members of the church, we are part of the body of Christ, and our body is pregnant. We are pregnant with the hope of liberation, with the fulfillment of a promise. We are full of life; we are filled with the Holy Spirit.

We need to be able to wait during this pregnancy. To be patient, and to open ourselves up to experience the miracle of life. To look at a moment and recognize the fullness of hope. To see this time only as a burden and something which needs to be rapidly rushed through is to lose a depth of our Christian message.

In those days, Mary arose and went to the hill country to greet Elizabeth with the message of the good news of her pregnancy. In these days, we need to arise and greet the world with the message of our good news. We are bearing life. And this life is one of liberation. It is one of promise. It is one pregnant with hope. And as forerunner of what is to come, it can cause us to leap with joy.

PATTI CARQUE, *M. Div., was brought up in the Roman Catholic Church, has been a member of the United Church of Christ, and has recently graduated from Lancaster Theological Seminary. She lives in Solanco with her daughter, works with the Community Action Program, and attempts to discern what it means to be a reformed nun.*

A Homily for the Feast of Teresa of Avila, Doctor of the Church

MAUREEN P. CARROLL

Yes, we know that all creation groans and is in agony even until now. Not only that, but we ourselves, although we have the Spirit as first fruits, groan inwardly while we await the redemption of our bodies. In hope we were saved. But hope is not hope if its object is seen; how is it possible for one to hope for what [one] sees? And hoping for what we cannot see means awaiting it with patient endurance.

The Spirit too helps us in our weakness, for we do not know how to pray as we ought; but the Spirit . . . makes intercession for us with groanings that cannot be expressed in speech. [And the One] who searches hearts knows what the Spirit means, for the Spirit intercedes for the saints as God . . . wills.

—ROMANS 8:22–27, NAB

"As to you, avoid the title 'Rabbi.' One among you is your teacher, the rest are learners. Do not call anyone on earth your father. Only one is your father, the One in heaven. Avoid being called teachers. Only one is your teacher, the Messiah. The greatest among you will be the one who serves the rest. Whoever [exalt themselves] shall be humbled, but whoever [humble themselves] shall be exalted."

—MATTHEW 23:8–12, NAB

Several years ago, while working on weekends at an Air Force base hospital, I had occasion to visit a young woman—a girl, really—who was nearing the time of the delivery of her first child. The chaplain had requested that I go to her especially that day: I, another woman, and at the time not much older than she was; and she, the daughter of a high-ranking officer, transported out of state by her parents, to give birth to her child anonymously, without a husband, without a family, and—it was hoped—without notice.

But on that last count the plan fell just short of perfect execution. For, although I never even learned her true name, nor saw her face distinctly as she lay in the darkened room, and although I could barely converse with her at all, so painful and shocking to her small body was the onset of labor, we held each other's hands constantly for nearly an hour. And it is her grasp, at once desperate and hopeful, that I have never forgotten. She crushed my fingers in hers and pressed her nails into my palms as if to transmit some of her sheer physical terror and agony to me. She had no words with which to release some of her psychological anguish and loneliness to me, but only long sobs and deep groans erupting from her inarticulate depths. However young, however unnaturally abandoned, she was a woman in the pangs of childbirth.

The experience of giving birth physically is one not available to nor chosen by all of us. Moreover, even on a cultural plane, the technological society has managed largely to obscure from our view the primal connection between birth and death, as well as the universality of each to human experience. It strikes us, then, as all the more daring for the Apostle Paul to rely on it—on the very throes of labor pains—to convey to his listeners something of what the world, human destiny, and one's personal history mean to the believer. How urgent it becomes for us to attend with care to our own particular labor, to our own struggle to bring something to birth, lest we shy away from the task he enjoins on us and reduce it to mere metaphor! This task, whose lines we seek to trace in our own experience, is the dying and the being born that is the stuff of sainthood in this ambiguous present.

I am referring, of course, to the threefold groanings—of the universe, of Christians themselves, and of the Spirit within us—groans in which Paul hears the anguished but sure onset of another kind of world and of another sort of human experience available in it because of Christ. The English expression "groans and is in agony," found in the first reading, fails to do justice to the full Greek connotations of these "groanings." For these groans are precisely those which overtake a woman who is literally "writhing in travail," "groaning in the pain of childbirth." Close to death in this apparent breaking and rending of herself, the expectant woman delivers up, and in that sense loses, some of the life within her for the sake of the emergence of what she hopes will be another new life.

It is not surprising that Jewish and early Christian apocalyptic found in this natural, yet ever-mysterious interplay of death and life an apt analogue for the in-breaking of the New Age, the coming of the Messiah, and the era of his Spirit. Though long desired—as Paul notes, from the beginning of time even up to the present moment—though awaited intensely as if by people "straining their necks" to peer into what cannot yet be seen, nevertheless, this day, this hour, this vision itself always arrives with the suddenness of that first sharp pang which signals to a woman that her time is near.

In the "now" of this travail, there is death and there is life, and the two are mixed indiscriminately in our experience. Thus, the groanings of human history cannot interpret themselves; and the plans and analyses—economic, political, psychological, social, religious, scientific—the schemes by which we can and must try to bring these groans to clearer articulation partake of this ambiguity. Our visions for a new heaven, new earth, new society, new church, new relations between the sexes, between nations, between classes of peoples—we know that these themselves await a deeper liberation.

To discern and articulate the truth, the kind of truth that sets humanity free, is the business of teachers, of doctors. They are persons who, like Teresa and like ourselves in this densely academic community, must school themselves in interpreting at least a few of the inarticulate groans of the human project itself. It is the wise who can expound and bring to birth the dreams latent in others. Teresa's own letters are filled with the practical details of her religio-social reformation: her activist's vision of a possible transformation of the human spirit. How marvelously unexpected, then, is the Gospel which the church chooses for today, cautioning us to call no one "doctor" and urging us to rank the erudite and even the genuinely wise together with ourselves in the great mass of learners. All wisdoms, even hers, are relativized by God's future, not yet fully born.

We might say, "Well and good." Creation's and history's groans do evade our thorough deciphering of them. But might it not be that the Christian believer, the saint, or the religious genius—mightn't she or he grow so attuned to the presence of the Spirit that, at least in the arena of personal choice, of self-construction, and of the sense of how to move oneself into a transformed future, in that realm, anyway, the ambiguities would lift?

But Paul will not have the gift of the Spirit used so facilely. Even though the Holy Spirit does provide our real entrée into another sort of existence, the Christian must still groan for a rebirth that is ultimately free from threat, for a conversion that surpasses the ever-precarious present. And it is this groan that lies at the inner core of his or her experience. Rather than being neutralized, this yearning is intensified and rendered more poignant by the simultaneous presence of the eschatological Spirit within the person of faith. Paul's counsel to "patient endurance" is misinterpreted if viewed as an exhortation to benign passivity. In fact, implied here is the energetic resistance to whatever is impeding the vision. It is an active stance of facing current difficulty, a dogged straining to see, though without ever clearly seeing, a refusal to give up hope. The deepest inner region of the self, then, cannot understand its own groanings, cannot regenerate itself completely, not even with the courage that comes from the active presence of the Spirit. Too much remains incapable of articulation and clarity; and the conversion of a total human lifetime—the very birth of the person—is slow, even if always surprising, sudden, and powerful.

Thus, the inability of the saint and even of the "doctor" to express herself wholly is a weakness which must be borne by the inarticulate groanings of the Spirit of God. Even our prayer, perhaps especially the prayer of a saint and a mystic, is deceptively ambiguous: much less something which we bring to birth, much more that one, ineffable groan of the Spirit which in time brings us to birth. Our pangs of giving birth—both in universal human history and in our personal histories—are fraught with as much miscarriage and loss as they are with coming to full term. It is the Spirit's groanings alone that are successfully and permanently creative. But we must not be naive. The proximity of the *Pneuma* of God neither illuminates the course of cosmic history nor clarifies the direction of our personal destinies. It is not we who hear and understand the murmurs of the Spirit within us, but God alone who is fluent in that language.

We take in this Eucharist today the food of pilgrims, the strength for the journey of our lives in which we must give birth to a vision. This food is sustenance in the body and in the spirit of Christ for the endurance of this labor which is inescapably ours, collectively and most personally. But the Eucharist is as well that holy communion which is already the creation of the Spirit. In the crucified and risen Christ, the one who is "the firstborn of many brothers and sisters," we begin to recognize the contours of our own visions and the shape of our own coming-to-birth. And it is in the Spirit that we—inarticulately, mutedly, deafly, and dumbly, perhaps—try to express those visions to each other and to appropriate that process of birth for ourselves. This triumph of the Spirit is what we celebrate today in Teresa of Avila, teacher, writer, saint. How timely, how fortunate for us that it has become possible to find in her an image of a woman's labor, of her painful, hopeful bringing to birth of truth and wisdom: Teresa, the first *Mater* Spiritualium acknowledged by the entire church.

MAUREEN P. CARROLL, O.P., *is a member of a Dominican women's religious community in Columbus, Ohio. She has spoken and written on the ministry of preaching by women in the church. She is a doctoral candidate in systematic theology at Catholic University of America and is completing her dissertation on a theology of Christian conversion.*

"The Day's Own Trouble"
LINDA CLARK

Let the day's own trouble be sufficient for the day.
—MATTHEW 6:34, RSV

In each of the Scripture lessons read today, a contrast exists between unfaithfulness and faithfulness. In Jeremiah (31:31–34), the old covenant is set against the new, in which God will write God's law on the hearts of the people of the House of Israel, and everyone will know God. In 2 Corinthians (4:1–15), the unbelievers whose minds have been blinded by the god of this world provide a contrast to those who have been given "this ministry by the mercy of God." And in Matthew (6:24–34), Jesus cries out against the unfaithfulness of those whose lives are spent fretting about tomorrow and about things of little consequence in the eyes of God. He says, "Seek first God's commonwealth [kingdom] and God's righteousness, and all these things shall be yours as well. Therefore do not be anxious about tomorrow, for tomorrow will be anxious for itself. Let the day's own trouble be sufficient for the day."

When we collect all the images of the life of faithfulness presented in these readings, we come up with an interesting guide for what it means to be a Christian. The Christian life is a life embedded in dailiness, not one in which the uncertainties of the future overshadow the tasks of the present. It is also one in which the signs of battle are carried on the body. The stance of a Christian is not that of a detached observer but one of an active participant, afflicted but not crushed, perplexed but not in despair, persecuted but not forsaken—in short, somewhat worn around the edges but undaunted. What keeps the Christian going, cheek to jowl with the stuff of everyday existence, is the knowledge of God written on his or her heart. In one sentence, a life of faith is this: Avoiding the very real, very human propensity to let the worries of the indeterminate tomorrows divert us from what we have to do today, we dive into the day's own trouble, seeking in it justice and God's commonwealth, firm in the knowledge of the love of God for us.

There are other images of the life of faithfulness in the Good Book which might contradict this one I've just constructed, but for a sermon delivered at the ordination of a woman to the Christian ministry, *this one suits*. It suits not only because these are troubled times and ministers are in the business of seeing to trouble, but because women in ministry are today's form of trouble. By ordaining women to the ministry, the church has given public authority to what the culture at large deems trivial, uncontrollable, irrational, and taboo—and that spells trouble. You walk into a room with your collar on, Jackie, and you are trouble. Before you open your mouth, before anyone knows what you think or that you *can* think, you are trouble. The fact of your very existence is troublesome, even if you never utter a word about sexism in the church. And when you do that, you are going to have more trouble. Yet you have chosen to take this on, as I have and many of our sisters have. So I'd like to speak to you, your friends and parishioners about the trouble posed by women who are called by God to the ministry. "To be forewarned is to be forearmed."

There are many things that could be said on this topic; I will focus on two. One of the reasons why women ministers are troublesome is because they upset the coventional wisdom about the natural order of things. This wisdom states that God is on top, men underneath God, women underneath men, children under women, animals under children, and plants under animals. Recently women have stepped out of their place in this hierarchy and, what is even more troublesome, are questioning the "naturalness" of hierarchies at all. This attack on the system inevitably leads up the ladder to God—and that causes a lot of trouble. "If God is not on top, where is God? And where are we?" Those are unsettling questions but important ones, I think. The image of a lofty God high on top of a ladder of being is no longer an adequate metaphor for God, the human community, and the relationship between them. True, it is a scriptural metaphor for God, but one among many in the Good Book, and I think we need to begin to use others at this juncture in the history of the church. Once we manage to entertain the idea that God might have other attributes than distance from us, somewhere up there, away, we see the other images for God in the Bible, including the one we've read today about God shining in our hearts (2 Corinthians 4:6).

Ordaining women to the ministry has caused us to reexamine some of our ideas about God. It is also shifting the dynamics in the human community. Let me use a story to make this point: a friend of mine was working in a Presbyterian church in Rye, New York, and was asked to preach one Sunday. It was the first time that a woman had ascended the steps of that pulpit to do anything but clean it. Afterwards, she was standing, greeting people at the door, and a friend of hers, a woman, came up to her and said, "When I saw you up there, Judy, my first thought was, 'Why, I bet I could do that!'" It took a woman preaching to enfranchise another woman to take responsibility for her own talents and religious wisdom. Preaching—the task of saying things about the nature of the life of faith—had become thinkable to that woman because she had seen one of her own kind up there doing it. The role of preacher had lost some of its loftiness in the process, some of its otherworldliness, perhaps, but the woman had gained some of her own loftiness. And she probably didn't even know she had been disenfranchised until that morning when she was furnished a role model that she could identify with at the core of her being.

All these shifts are troublesome for everyone concerned. They are accompanied by self-consciousness, guilt, anger, hesitation, self-delusion, speechlessness. Yes, in the midst of the struggle about sexism and the church we see the real insight in the saying, "Let the day's own trouble be sufficient for the day."

Another reason why women ministers are troublesome is because they bring the taint of human sexuality into the church. In our culture the woman carries the symbol of sexuality, as a glance at the advertisements screaming at us on the TV and in print will tell you. Through the power of a "force" emanating from the female of the species, all kinds of products are sold to everyone, women and men alike. There is something uncontrollable about the power of women's sexuality; many of the social conventions and taboos of our culture concern it. And now the segment of the population that has always symbolized sexuality demands public recognition and power in the church. This spells trouble.

Sexuality is and has been for centuries problematic for the church, and that goes for men ministers, women ministers, and lay people too—all of us. We would prefer to disembody God, making God into pure spirit, sending God off to the nether regions, as far away as possible from the mess of human flesh. Distance, total otherness are much more comfortable attributes of a deity than closeness and incarnation. Yet God lived among us; God was embodied, and sexuality is the stuff of embodiment. Sexuality is not just intercourse; it is the energy of self-establishment in a body here on earth. It is the basis for building human communities. It pushes us out of isolation and makes us reach out to one another.

It is easy to see how distrust of human sexuality and irresponsibility in human community are correlates of a God who is only distant and totally other. Worshiping a God who is perfection and totally separate from humanity naturally leads to despising what is imperfect and embedded in humanity—mainly ourselves and our brothers and sisters. And the glue which sticks us together—which is what sexuality is—becomes the focus of much of that despising. Yes, ordaining women, who carry the symbol of sexuality in our culture, means trouble, and in the midst of trying to come to terms with it we see the real insight in the saying, "Let the day's own trouble be sufficient for the day."

The act of ordaining women to the church's ministry *is* giving public authority to those among us whom *we* all have labeled trivial, uncontrollable, irrational, and taboo. At the same time it acknowledges that women are made in the image of God, as men are, and therefore images for God might come out of the lives of women. God may be transcendent and totally other, but God is also here among us, in the dirt and sweat of our daily lives, which is what women's work has always been. God is a housekeeper who raises children and loves us in anger and passion. God is a church secretary who manages without fanfare and recognition to hold the whole irrational, uncontrollable place together by working miracles every day.

Yes, ordaining women to the ministry means trouble, but it also holds out the promise of growth and transformation for the church, provided we don't bring to the task of dealing with the trouble yesterday's notions about God and the human community and tomorrow's fretful anxieties—which leads me back to the Gospel lesson for today.

We are called, by the mercy of God, to the ministry of *today*'s troubles. When tomorrow comes, we will have another batch of trouble. If we do not work with today's troubles today, tomorrow will have double trouble. In that predicament there is little room for growth and transformation. Secondly, *we* are called. This passage from Matthew—and the one from Corinthians, too— contradicts the comfortable notion that at the Judgment Day all of this mess will be cleared up by God, so we can just lie around and let God take care of it. No, faithfulness means taking human existence with utmost seriousness and seeking righteousness in everything we do. Thirdly, we are called to work with today's *troubles*. This ministry of yours, Jackie, and of ours, rests on the firm foundation of God's love for us, which means that troubles are opportunities for change and growth, that good can emerge from evil, and that we can transform our lives, that we are not defeated by circumstances before we begin. What an indescribably beautiful gift to have had that love engraved on our hearts!

So, this morning, let's all sing at the top of our lungs, praising God with every fiber of our beings—but this afternoon, Jackie, into the breach!

LINDA JANE CLARK *is director of the Master of Sacred Music program at Boston University, where she also teaches music and worship. She continues to ask questions of the Judeo-Christian tradition which, she feels, encompasses both the fact of oppression and the promise of liberation for women.*

"What Do You Want Me to Do for You?"

MARGARET W. CROCKETT-CANNON

And they came to Jericho; and as he was leaving Jericho with his disciples and a great multitude, Bartimaeus, a blind beggar, . . . was sitting by the roadside. And when he heard that it was Jesus of Nazareth, he began to cry out and say, "Jesus, Son of David, have mercy on me!" And many rebuked him, telling him to be silent; but he cried out all the more, "Son of David, have mercy on me!" And Jesus stopped and said, "Call him." And they called the blind man, saying to him, "Take heart; rise, he is calling you." And throwing off his mantle he sprang up and came to Jesus. And Jesus said to him, "What do you want me to do for you?" And the blind man said to him, "Master, let me receive my sight." And Jesus said to him, "Go your way; your faith has made you well." And immediately he received his sight and followed him on the way.

—MARK 10:46–52, RSV

Recently I was talking with a friend whose body is marked with the losses and scars of many radical operations. When she learned I was serving as a chaplain in a hospital, she told me of a time when she was very ill and thought she was going to die. She was frightened and felt very much alone, so when a young chaplain came into her hospital room, she reached out to him for help. There was anger in her voice as she blurted out to me,

"And do you know what he asked me? He asked, 'What do you want me to do for you?'"

For her, his question was insensitive. I don't know the tone of his voice, but he could have been asking her, "Do you want me to sit beside you, or would you rather be left alone? Do you want me to talk to you, or listen while you talk? Do you want me to pray with you, or would you prefer that we just be quiet?" She didn't answer the chaplain; she was too angry because, as she said, "He didn't do his job." But she hadn't done her job. She didn't know what she wanted. In fact, she didn't really want help. She still doesn't want help, and she is still a very angry and very sick woman.

The same thing happened to the beggar Bartimaeus, who sat beside the road outside the gates of the city of Jericho. He was blind. He couldn't see, but he could *hear* the excited voices of a large crowd of people who were approaching him, coming out of the city and heading up the road to Jerusalem. He could feel the vibrations from their footsteps, smell the dust they scuffed up in his nostrils, taste it on his lips, feel the grit between his teeth. He could feel the coolness of their shadows as they passed between him and the sun. They jostled him, and he pulled back and drew up his knees, afraid they would trample him. He felt rejected, frightened, left out.

For there was a time when he might have been a part of the crowd. He had not always been blind. The Greek word used here to indicate that he asked to receive his sight, ἀναβλέψω, carries the prefix which implies "again." The New English Bible more accurately translates it: "I want my sight back." So Bartimaeus was especially miserable because he knew what it was to be a part of the crowd—not to be passed by and in the dark, but to walk in the light. When he heard that it was Jesus who was the center of this crowd, Bartimaeus realized that he was the one who, it was said, had healed so many, and he recognized this as the chance of his lifetime. So he cried out in his misery, "Jesus, Son of David, have mercy on me!" Those nearby told him to be quiet, but he persisted, "Son of David, have mercy on me." Bartimaeus was blind, but he must have been endowed with some inner sight. Jesus' apostles were not totally aware of who he was, even as they walked beside him on this his final trip to Jerusalem, but blind Bartimaeus, the beggar, bestowed upon him the Messianic title.

Jesus stopped and said, "Call him." Bartimaeus was blind, but he was not crippled. He threw off his mantle and jumped up and ran to Jesus. With his voice, Jesus stopped him. "What do you want me to do for you? If you can see again, you will no longer be able to beg from others. You must take the responsibility for yourself and for the support of your family. Are you ready? What do you really want? What are your hopes and plans? What do you want me to do for you?"

We can relate to Bartimaeus. Often we are alone, frightened, sick, confused, in the dark. We reach out to someone near to us, saying, "I'm miserable. Help me." The person may not ask the question, but each of us must know the answer to the question: What do you want me to do for you? Each of us has to decide: What do I really want?

Do I want help? Do I want to feel better?

Do I want to be included, or would I rather feel sorry for myself?

Do I want to assume the risk and responsibility of a relationship, or would I rather stay alone?

Do I want to love and be loved? Can I let go of my anger? Can I forgive?

Do I want to get well? Am I willing to give up the power of pain?

A young woman who is very ill was asked by her doctor, "What is your life like since you have been sick?" She gave him an embarrassed little smile. "Why, I have everything I ever wanted. My husband was running around, but now I have him back. In fact, he has to come home every three hours to give me a shot for pain. And the children—they were disrespectful and disobedient and were always bickering. Now they are much more thoughtful and pleasant because Mother is so very sick." The doctor looked her directly in the eyes and said, "You are using your illness to maintain love and peace in your home. You'll have to find a better way if you want to get well again."

Finally, in prayer we cry to God for help. But do we know

what we want? We think we want to feel better and to be well, but we may not be ready. Again, each of us must answer.

Am I ready to let go of inner sickness and inner blindness?

Am I ready to let go of attitudes that keep me unhappy and paralyzed with anger and bitterness?

Am I ready to forgive so that the inner eyes of my heart are opened to another's love and goodness?

Am I ready to stop punishing myself because of a sense of guilt? Can I forgive myself?

Am I ready to stop feeling sorry for myself so that I can step out of my dark corner into the light?

Am I ready to risk entering God's loving presence and to get close to him?

Jesus does with us as he did with Bartimaeus. Jesus asks us to look at our true hopes and express them, to profess our faith so that he can act on that faith. "What do you want me to do for you?" Bartimaeus had inner sight as to who Jesus was. Probably he had inner healing too, had given up possible anger and bitterness over becoming blind. He was ready; he knew what he wanted. He wanted to be whole.

Bartimaeus answered, "I want to see again. I want things to be as they used to be. I want to move from the darkness into the light." God, the Creator, wants his creatures to be whole. Jesus likewise wanted Bartimaeus to be whole. Bartimaeus was ready, and he believed. Jesus was able to say to him, "Your faith has made you well."

We cry out to God for help. When he calls to us in answer, we must, as did Bartimaeus, draw near in headlong response. We must decide: Are we ready to be whole? If not yet ready, we must ask for inner healing, inner sight, and finally for outer adjustment and healing. We must believe in order that we can receive strength, wholeness, and vision, so that we, like Bartimaeus, can follow Jesus in the Way of Light.

Then, with John Masefield, we can say:

> O glory of the lighted mind,
> How dead I'd been, how dumb, how blind. . . .
> Out of the mist into the light,
> O blessed gift of inner sight.

THE REV. MARGARET W. CROCKETT-CANNON, *D.Min., is minister of Edwards Church, UCC, in Framingham, Massachusetts. She graduated from Harvard Divinity School in 1978 and from Andover Newton Theological School in 1979. She is a mother and grandmother, has lectured professionally for over 20 years, and worked with her first husband, the late James Underwood Crockett, horticultural writer and television gardener.*

Women: Living Wholly/Holy in a Fractured World

SALLY CUNNEEN

Friends, sisters, I am happy to be with you today, not only because you share my own long-term concerns and hopes and those of many women elsewhere, but also because I believe your conference reflects an understanding of how we as women are church in a way that speaks to the needs of the present moment. As a visitor from the backward East, I would like to share with you my perceptions of the meaning I see embodied in this meeting—something a visitor can do perhaps more easily than those of you who have worked long and hard to bring it about and are today filled with particular hopes and agendas.

First of all, your title, "Living Wholly/Holy in a Fractured World," reflects the profound change in understanding of the relation of faith to our lives that has occurred within the church in our lifetime. What we left has been summed up by theologian Richard McBrien as a Ptolemaic conception of creation: heaven above and earth below, two layers. Certainly much of what I absorbed of Catholic practice as a child reflected this sense of separation between church and world. A vocation was a call to become a priest or nun, to "leave the world" and seek "a higher life." Being good was largely an attempt to avoid things—bad movies, books, ideas, and the pleasures of the flesh—in order to seek out the things of the spirit.

But in our lifetimes the church itself has rediscovered, in the words of theologian Monika Hellwig, that

> The Bible and Christian tradition give us a different understanding of reality. . . . The sacred and the secular are not two different sectors of life, or two different areas in space or time; they are two different ways of seeing and responding to the whole of reality. In the burning bush story in Exodus 3, Moses is told to take off his shoes because the ground on which he stands is holy. But it turns out that that does not mean any one place. It means that any ground is holy, because God is everywhere—not only in places officially designated for worship but in homes, streets, offices, factories [*The Meaning of the Sacraments*].

Mystics and poets like Gerard Manley Hopkins have always known that the world is charged with the grandeur of God, but in the highly technological and sensate culture in which we live, it has been necessary for us to rediscover this truth. For this technological culture, now spreading round the world, is the first in human history to deny the very presence of the sacred within itself as it attempts to dominate the earth's limited resources. Human beings, nevertheless, cry out for this presence. So it has become necessary for those of us who do believe that God's grace penetrates all our internal and external landscapes to help create the conditions so that others may see it as well. Your panels indicate that you realize this may mean work for change in many public as well as private arenas, that we are each of us called in this atmosphere, to unique, lifelong vocations.

Nor do I believe that it has been "wholly" chance, in your first usage of the word, but rather in the second, that these decades of changing consciousness and renewal we have experienced within our church have coincided with a change in consciousness on the part of women, for many of whom these challenges were something new. I learned in the mid-sixties that many Catholic women were undergoing a profound and creative—if often painful—change in consciousness because I asked a large number of them as part of the research on my book. The passivity advocated as an ideal model of feminine behavior seemed to contradict and hamper my own ability to carry out the tasks morally required of me as a wife, mother, and citizen. Motivated by the tension in which I felt caught, I began to ask other women if this was true for them. The lengthy and passionate response I received from all over the country in 1963—the year Betty Friedan's book appeared—convinced me that many Catholic women were emerging from their own form of the feminine mystique in response to the needs of a suffering world which seemed to them potentially holy.

A single woman from New York summed up the direction of this concern: "I wonder whether the Church has squarely faced the fact that we are living in an age of revolution and that its mission is to serve living, breathing human beings and not just to organize a structure." The response to make to this reality was suggested by a married woman from Chicago: "We should start our meditation on our Christian obligations by simply listening, attending to the world around us, so that we may find out what its problems really are."

Though these women often felt isolated, they did not think they were simply following their own independent opinions. Their attitude of responsible obedience is revealed in the response of one sister, who wrote:

> I've noticed myself shuddering when people say, why is *the church* like that? Why don't *they* do it otherwise? For heaven's sake, *we* are the church. "It" doesn't do anything that we don't (at least not truly and effectively), and it can't do what we want until we stand up, acknowledge our role and speak out. "I believed, therefore I spoke out." That's what royal priesthood means. Total hierarchical direction leaves too much room for misunderstanding and disobedience. Let's open ourselves to the dangers of true equality.

This step has not been easy for many women, however, because cultural influences as well as the earlier, two-tier mentality in the church had stressed the rejection of the flesh and denial of the self. Women in particular were supposed to be unselfish servants of others: was it not especially wrong for them to place emphasis on the self? My own experience and observation convinced me, however, that only women with a strong sense of self, like Mother Teresa or Dorothy Day, were *able* to be unselfish. I have since come across two written testimonies by

Catholic women that establish from their experience the necessity of self-love in order to move on to respond to the Christian vocation to love others. The first is an article by Joan Bel Geddes called "Charity Really Does Begin at Home—with the Self," and the second is the testimony given by a San Antonio widow, Sra. Gregoria McCumber, to the bishops in the hearings they held prior to their Call to Action meeting here in 1976.

She began by introducing herself and offering the bishops present a statue she had made in ceramics class of the Blessed Mother pregnant with the baby Jesus. She admitted:

> It is not the statue we usually see. It is not the Blessed Virgin. It is the Blessed Mother. I have always wanted to see a statue like this because I can identify with a blessed mother because I am a married woman. I have had children. . . . I had a poor image of myself as a mother and as being married because so much emphasis was put just on the Blessed Virgin, something so far out of my reach I could never be like her, and I also could not identify with the celibate clergy and nuns. How can I be able to live a Christian life when in my own environment I cannot find it? How can there be a universal church if the root of the tree that is to give fruit is not a priority in the church? . . .
>
> If the church could see what I see in the environment, then I think it would put more emphasis on building basic Christian communities. We have gone to rural towns where . . . there have been people who didn't know how to read. But . . . they have gotten together in community and reflected on the Bible, because we do have grassroots theologians, we really do.

This woman's experience illuminates the inner process of change that accompanies the ability of each of us to see and respond to God's presence everywhere—and especially in others—in our daily encounters. To find first of all that all things are good: bread, bodies, and especially the particular people we are, made in God's image despite all our peculiarities and limitations. The Bible, after·all, asks us in its profound wisdom to love others as ourselves.

And this widow's self-acceptance led her to see potential powers in others that could be encouraged and developed when they were asked to respond to need. Her style of service is not

that of the bureaucrat or the expert, though she knows a good
deal about community organization, enough to know that often
the expert who has the answer may not quite understand the
problem. Her approach is that of the human person sharing a
common problem with other persons—here one of illiteracy
and poverty among minority groups—who together discover
and share resources they did not realize they had before they
were asked.

As a teacher of adults who return to college after many
years away from school, I have discovered just how fruitful such
an approach can be. I have continued to learn a great many
unexpected and important things from my students that I might
never have come to know if I had merely talked at them instead
of encouraging them to ask questions, make criticisms and
suggestions, even conduct their own seminars. Sometimes we go
astray—it gets out of hand—but in the long run the spirit,
direction, and achievement of each class is remarkable because it
touches off the unique talents and experiences of the individuals
involved—from jaded twenty-one-year-olds who at first find
everything "boring," to the eager, excellent students of seventy-
nine whose excitement never flags.

This same method of exploratory sharing with others of a
common problem is, I believe, a method of being church
wherever we are, one in which we share our fallible, creative
personal selves with each other and find that God inspires us. It
is a method I have heard advocated by many women of faith in
recent years in varied forms. I think of Virginia Mollenkott's
suggestion in her paperback *Men, Women and the Bible* that
mutual submission of persons is the biblical model for all
relationships. Or of Sister Marie Augusta Neal, that tireless and
visionary sociologist, who points out that the domination-
submission model of interaction so characteristic of our economy and politics is despoiling the earth's resources and threatening the future of humanity itself with its inequitable distribution
of them, so that it flies in the face of the Gospel injunction to
share God's creation with all his creatures.

And finally I recall the careful statement prepared by a
group of Catholic laywomen and sisters in response to the
request by the Bishops' Task Force on Women. Its findings were

strongly affirmed in many of the proposals passed at the Detroit Call to Action Conference. Here, however, I want to point to the language, the mission, and the method embodied in their view as it is revealed in their introduction:

> The church must affirm a new order based on certain basic faith convictions regarding the person, the mission of the ecclesial community, and the gifts of the Spirit. Every human being is caught up in the "one great act of giving birth" which leads to the fullness of "freedom of the children of God" (Rom. 8: 21–22). . . . Since every person is called to this liberation of the spirit, she/he possesses an inherent right to these opportunities, goods and services—be they material, relational, psychological, spiritual —necessary for full development as a person.
>
> While the person is thus called to wholeness, the church—the communion of persons gathered to remember and follow Jesus —is itself responding to a mission: to proclaim the reign of God, to help every person discover the reign within, and to prepare the way for its full blossoming in justice and peace.

The language and thinking of this statement by American Catholic women mirror the traditional, biblical sources of faith and mission. They use the organic imagery of birth found in the bible but grown distant to our technological era. Yet they relate the traditional thought and imagery to the social concepts of peace and justice relevant to the global mission today, and combine it with the most modern notions of the development of the human person. This document breathes the need for interdependence which respects the differences of things and people. And it bears the sense of "we" rather than "me" which is so necessary if human beings are to gain control of the nonhuman powers they have created.

Women of faith, then, have been moving in the direction of a new and personal assumption of responsibility in their desire to respond to God's fractured creation. You are the heirs of this tradition, called on to make it live in your city and as a sign for the rest of us. Ultimately you confirm each other and provide us with the awareness that our most personal attitudes, commitments, and relationships are significantly, if not always visibly, related to a new set of global relationships. Women of faith like yourselves are in fact mapping out a mission and a method that is not merely for or by women, but, through the movement of history that is "holy chance," the Spirit speaking through women as representatives of humanity today.

Furthermore, your meeting today is evidence that the Catholic women whom I found involved but isolated from each other fifteen years ago are now beginning to move together, to support one another in their response to a broken world. You also know as well as I that we live in very dangerous times, that most people feel powerless and all the more susceptible to the emotional release of escalated military posturing that is no solution but only increases the problems. Our economic system creates victims, then makes a business out of taking care of them—each part of the process dehumanizing.

You should have courage despite the difficulties, knowing that your personal response is called for and that it matters. One of the best sermons I ever heard on this subject was by a Capuchin friar who told us what he had learned from an old lady in Harlem whom he had helped rescue from a mugging. She turned, looked him in the eye, and said, "God sent you to me." What, the friar asked, would our lives be like if we felt this about every situation in which we found ourselves? They would be transformed. But the fact is, it is true. And if you can remember it, no matter what difficulties or setbacks you experience, this conference and all of you will grow in ways you cannot now guess.

But isn't this all too new a path? Has anyone gone this way before? It may surprise some of you that in recent years I have begun to see the Blessed Mother in a new way and believe that in taking this direction we are in fact following her human example. The more I hear about the few facts known of her life, the uncertainties and the limitations of her role during Jesus' lifetime, the better I understand why she is a good model for believers and indeed for all human beings. She was, first of all, really one among us, a poor, hardworking woman all her life. As a sheltered and religiously committed Jewish girl, she showed remarkable independence in her realistic and wholehearted acceptance of a totally unexpected vocation. And at each step of the way, from her visit to her cousin Elizabeth, to her rebuke of her son when he stayed behind at the temple, her request to her son to heed the needs of the wedding couple at Cana, and at the crucifixion, she did what she thought was right, even when it led to disagreement with her son. Imagine. Biblical evidence suggests that as a mother she too had the painful experience of not fully understanding or accepting her son's mission in his lifetime, even of being reminded by him publicly that his work came ahead of natural ties. She struggled with pain and doubt as a mother, but when her son had been put to death and she did come to understand and accept his mission, she joined his followers in their disgrace and fear.

When I recently asked a group of Catholics if they too saw Mary differently than they had when they were young, perhaps the most striking response came from a priest who replied, "Yes. I used to see her as a pretty porcelain statue. Now she seems more like Golda Meir." We could seek no better reminder of the connection of personal mission with social commitment than Mary's "Magnificat," for it sums up the Lord's concern for all his children, but particularly the poor. Nor could we find a better example of loving self-acceptance as part of the ability to give for others:

> Tell out, my soul, the greatness of the Lord,
> rejoice, rejoice, my spirit, in God my saviour;
> so tenderly has he looked upon his servant,
>   humble as she is.
> For, from this day forth,
> all generations will count me blessed,
> so wonderfully has he dealt with me,
>   the Lord, the Mighty One.
>   His name is Holy;
> his mercy sure from generation to generation
>   toward those who fear him;
> the deeds his own right arm has done
>   disclose his might:
> the arrogant of heart and mind he has put to rout,
> he has brought down monarchs from their thrones,
>   but the humble have been lifted high.
> The hungry he has satisfied with good things,
>   the rich sent empty away
>   —LUKE 1:46–53, NEB

I believe you know now why I am happy to be here today. I believe God sent all of us to each other. And I wish you enlightenment, joy, and perseverance in your attempts to develop your goals, programs, and networks. In conclusion, I would like to read the final stanza of a poem written by a little-known American Catholic poet, Catherine de Vinck, whose whole work—including a liturgy and a passion play—seems to me to capture the essence of that incarnational grace working through women's experience that you show here today:

Sisters
   do not look for symbols
   for second prints of truth:
   open your eyes, let
   ray-beams of sight pierce
   the shell of space, cut a path
   through the darkest night.
   Dive in, enter the multifolds
   of first and primal things
   and from your blood, spin these great filaments,
   these strands of love
   to wrap and hold the cosmos in.

SALLY McDEVITT CUNNEEN, PH.D., *is a founding editor of the quarterly,* Cross Currents, *author of* Sex: Female, Religion: Catholic *(Holt, Rinehart & Winston, 1968), and assistant professor at Rockland Community College (SUNY).*

"Sisterhood" Is Powerful

ANNETTE DAUM

Tonight's Torah portion, the concluding chapters of Leviticus, is particularly appropriate for examination, for probing, as we consider the future for women in "sisterhood." The last word appears in quotation marks because the focus of my sermon will be on the ways all women can and should act together as "sisters" in the broad context of that term, in common cause.

The *sidra* for the week begins with a description of the sabbatical year, the seventh year, when the land is to rest—neither to be plowed, sown, nor reaped. According to tradition, during this time all the Israelites were assembled—the men, women, children, even the stranger—to hear, to learn, and to observe the words of Torah. Certain themes are consistently reiterated: The Hebrew God is a God of freedom, who brought the Jewish people out of the house of bondage, out of slavery to freedom, and that freedom is for a purpose—to serve God in very specific ways, both in worship, including the laws of sacrifice, and in the way we treat other people, so that all may be free from slavery, poverty, and oppression. Nowhere is this more gloriously pronounced than in the decree that the fiftieth year shall be a jubilee year. On Yom Kippur, a blast of the shofar shall "proclaim liberty throughout the land to all the inhabitants thereof," a theme we see repeated in American history, for these

45

are the same words that are carved into the Liberty Bell. The jubilee year, described in today's Torah portion, was a time when the slave went free and the land was returned to those who were forced to sell their inheritance out of economic necessity. In principle, the land was not to be sold in perpetuity, for the land belongs to God. This practice also ensured that the family was not permanently deprived of their land and thus served to protect people from a never-ending cycle of poverty. We were to see those twin themes of emancipation and social justice echoed in American society as well.

Yet, ironically, we are forced to remember that most of the poor within the Jewish community, as well as the rest of American society, are women, who are denied a proper economic inheritance because of a different kind of bondage, being bound by the stereotyped image of their "proper" role in society.

The closing verses of the Torah portion indicate how pervasive the problem is, for while it existed—unsurprisingly—in biblical days, it persists even to this day. The concluding portion deals with voluntary contributions for the upkeep of the sanctuary. The amount of the offering to be made was based on the valuation of the members of the family by age and sex. At best, a woman was valued at no more than two-thirds of a man, and she had to wait till age sixty and over to achieve this exalted status. Between the ages of five and twenty, she was worth half the valuation of the male. Most of her life, from twenty to sixty, her valuation was three-fifths of a man's. Some interpreters insist that this was because a woman was not as strong physically as a man, and therefore was not worth that much. But this is hard both to follow and to swallow, since the differential already occurs in the cradle. For the male baby, one month old, is worth five shekels—the female, only three.

This evaluation is perpetuated in subtle ways today, for psychologists inform us that male and female babies are treated differently—stereotyped—from the minute they are born. It is interesting to note that in the United States the problem of how to count slaves when determining population for the purposes of representation was resolved by the founding *fathers* when they arrived at what is known as the three-fifths compromise: each slave was to be counted as three-fifths of a person.

Returning to Torah, a more reasonable interpretation of the differential in valuation could be, simply, that a woman did not earn money and that therefore her services to the synagogue and society were devalued, an attitude about women that persists to this day among women as well as men. While these values were understandable in a patriarchal society, where women's role was limited, but where Torah indicates that special care was also taken to protect the widowed and the orphaned, they are less understandable in modern society. Historically, women have been instrumental in providing the upkeep of the sanctuary since its origin. Women brought free-will offerings of gold—their jewelry, brooches, earrings, pendants, etc. They made gifts of fine materials, yarns, and skins to help build the tabernacle. And then they provided the free labor to weave the yarns and the goats' hair—evidently a skilled task—into fine cloth to beautify the sanctuary. We are still doing that today. What Sisterhood is not involved in projects to decorate the synagogue—especially at holiday times—or provide the fine needlepoint for the *Bimah* or serve on the decorating committee, or raise funds to support the purchase of the fine ritual objects? Yet how many women participate in the ritual ceremonies on the same *Bimah* built with the work of their hands?

How many women who have moved into leadership positions have achieved access to the powers that determine how the funds they raised should be spent, despite the fact that equality for women is a basic principle of Reform Judaism?

While it is true that increasing numbers of women are moving into leadership positions in local congregations and on the regional and national level, most have received their leadership training through Sisterhood. They move up the Sisterhood ladder first, then onto the congregational board, serving a longer apprenticeship than men do. Ironically, even where greater opportunities are presented, women are reluctant to assume unaccustomed roles, especially in ritual matters—probably as a result of centuries of conditioning which placed them outside the synagogue.

Many women are now working full time. Congregations are losing their volunteer services, for they are reluctant to restructure their home responsibilities. They do not think of suggesting that their husbands assume a greater share of the work in the home; they merely add new responsibilities to their old ones.

In American society, women have formed the backbone of the "volunteer" free labor market as the bearers and rearers of children. American society, like the temple, is built on the foundation of the free-will offerings of women, for which they receive no economic compensation. No wonder, then, that the woman's services are devalued. What is society's reward? The "total woman," marketed by other women as the antidote to feminism, is being totaled by this same society. What happens to the happy homemaker when the man disappears from the picture? Whether widowed or divorced, if these women are not employed, they are left without support. If there is an inheritance, it may be painfully inadequate in the light of the rate of inflation. If divorced, only 14 percent of these women receive any alimony, and of these less than half receive payments on a regular basis. Such women do not qualify for unemployment benefits. Their work has had no economic value. If divorced, they may not even qualify for Social Security benefits based on husbands' earnings. The wife's contribution has no value.

Resistance by women to the thrust for justice for women is, alas, not new. Women fought suffrage, using the same lame excuses now employed by this generation's women who do not see the necessity for ERA. In employment and in the synagogue, when women have "made it," they do not necessarily help advance the position of other women.

No one needs ERA more than the homemaker. Women should know what their rights are in the state in which they live, for without a national ERA, women's rights differ from state to state.

The Commission on Social Action of Reform Judaism has made equality for women in society and in the synagogue a priority issue. Their newly created Task Force on Women and Minorities served as a catalyst to unite all women in their determination to move the UAHC Biennial away from a non-ERA state. While we did have support from men on the commission and on the UAHC board, we were successful only after the women united to speak out in favor of such a move. The Reform movement is the only branch of Judaism that has an official committee devoted to obtaining equality for women within the movement. A special task force was created which has undertaken to free women from the bondage of ancient myths and stereotypes that prevent us from developing to the fullest potential as people created by God in the image of God. We are demanding a more accurate account of the contribution of Jewish women to Judaism and American society, so that our involvement in the fields of social work, education, politics, the movement for the abolition of slavery, for suffrage, and in the labor movement can be recognized. Who died in the Triangle Fire? Who walked the picket lines? Men assumed the positions of power in the labor movement, but it was women who died in that fire, largely women who walked that picket line.

The task force just produced a *Haggadah* which includes recognition of the crucial role played by women in the Exodus experience, in gaining and maintaining freedom throughout Jewish history. This *Haggadah* was developed specifically to help heads of single-parent families, usually women, learn how to conduct a Seder, lead and participate in the ritual, in unaccustomed roles. Unless we do this, these families will have no Seder at all and will also be deprived of participation in other rituals of our rich heritage.

We are living in exciting times, when much that is possible was not even dreamed of a decade ago. It is possible today to eliminate role-stereotyping from the religious-school curriculum, and our task force has established guidelines and developed courses to help congregations accomplish this. We have also held sensitivity training sessions for religious-school teachers to help them deal with sexist educational material in the classroom, so our daughters will not learn to "devalue" themselves. A series of synagogue consciousness-raising programs has been prepared to help women develop greater appreciation of themselves—greater understanding of opportunities available to them.

We also discovered that fresh insight into Torah commentary was needed from a woman's perspective. We need fresh

insights too into the role of women in society. If we are truly
concerned about family stability and the declining Jewish population, then the Jewish community must take serious steps to
make the option of raising children attractive. We must be
supportive, sponsor day-care centers where children can begin
to get a Jewish education; sponsor more after-school programs
for Jewish youth; fight for Social Security benefits, as well as
health insurance, for homemakers; and develop widow-to-
widow programs.

And we must ensure that freedom to choose abortion
according to her own moral conscience is maintained for every
woman, for no woman should be forced to bear more children
than she can responsibly care for.

We must reject the claim that survival of our religion and
our society depends on maintaining second-class status for
women. Our survival depends on expanding options, on encouraging the use of *all* talents of *all* people, women as well as
men. That requires a change of attitude regarding the valuation
of a woman's services, on the part of women as well as men.

This devaluation of the worth of women is perpetuated
even in the language we use, not only in texts but in liturgy as
well. It must be acknowledged that language both transmits and
fosters the prejudices of society. The Task Force on Equality of
Women in Judaism has issued guidelines for the elimination of
masculine-biased language in liturgy. Whether referring to
humanity in general or to God, such language leads us in the
wrong direction, for women as well as men are people created in
the image of God, who, in Judaism, is beyond sexuality.

We have begun to see the dimensions of the work ahead of
us, the reasons why our National Commission on Social Action
of Reform Judaism is determined to remove whatever barriers
remain to equality for women.

As "sisters" in the true sense of the word, we must unite to
proclaim the right of all women to be free from the bondage of
the past, to be free to put to the highest use all of our God-given
talents and abilities, to be free to obtain justice, to gain equal
rights in both the synagogue and society. "Liberty and justice for
all" must include women. Nothing less will do.

ANNETTE DAUM *is coordinator of the Dept. of Interreligious Affairs at Union of American Hebrew Congregations. She staffs the Task Forces on Equality of Women in Judaism and on Women and Minorities, both associated with the Reform movement. She has a Principal's Certificate in religious education and has written several education manuals for both Christian and Jewish religious educators.*

The Best Is Yet to Be

PATRICIA E. DAVIS

> For the Lord sets a father in honor over his children;
>   a mother's authority he confirms over her sons.
> He who honors his father atones for sins;
>   he stores up riches who reveres his mother.
> He who honors his father is gladdened by children,
>   and when he prays he is heard.
> He who reveres his father will live a long life;
>   he obeys the Lord who brings comfort to his mother. . . .
> My son, take care of your father when he is old;
>   grieve him not as long as he lives.
> Even if his mind fail, be considerate with him;
>   revile him not in the fullness of your strength.
> For kindness to a father will not be forgotten,
>   it will serve as a sin offering—it will take lasting root.
> —SIRACH (ECCLESIASTICUS) 3:2–6, 12–14, NAB

Because you are God's chosen ones, holy and beloved, clothe yourselves with heartfelt mercy, with kindness, humility, meekness, and patience. Bear with one another; forgive whatever grievances you have against one another. Forgive as the Lord has forgiven you. Over all these virtues put on love, which binds the rest together and makes them perfect. . . . You children, obey your parents in everything as the acceptable way in the Lord. And fathers, do not nag your children lest they lose heart.

—COLOSSIANS 3:12–21, NAB

When the day came to purify them according to the law of Moses, the couple brought him up to Jerusalem so that he could be presented to the Lord. . . . There lived in Jerusalem at the time a certain man named Simeon. . . . It was revealed to him by the Holy Spirit that he would not experience death until he had seen the Anointed of the Lord. He came to the temple now, inspired by the Spirit, and when the parents brought in the child Jesus, . . . he took him in his arms and blessed God in these words:

> *"Now, Master, you can dismiss your servant in peace;*
> *you have fulfilled your word.*
> *For my eyes have witnessed your saving deed*
> *displayed for all the peoples to see:*
> *A revealing light to the Gentiles,*
> *the glory of your people Israel."*

There was also a certain prophetess, Anna by name, daughter of Phanuel of the tribe of Asher. She had seen many days. . . . She was constantly in the temple, worshiping day and night in fasting and prayer. Coming on the scene at this moment, she gave thanks to God and talked about the child to all who looked forward to the deliverance of Jerusalem. . . .

The child grew in size and strength, filled with wisdom, and the grace of God was upon him.

—LUKE 2:22–40, NAB

"Growing old isn't so bad," someone has said, "when you consider the alternative." But I suspect that some elderly people would not agree with that statement. Last summer I worked as a hospital chaplain, and I remember well the elderly lady who remarked, "Being old isn't for sissies," and another who commented, "When you get old, it's a job just living."

In connection with our celebration of Holy Family Sunday, we often reflect on our own immediate families; but I'd like to suggest that today we broaden our concern to include the elderly, both those particular people closely related to us and also all the older women and men who share membership with us in the total human family.

It has been said that the quality of a civilization can be measured by the way in which it treats its elderly, and our church teaches that care and respect for the aged is a Christian duty. In a 1976 statement the bishops of the United States said, "The elderly do not forfeit their claim to basic human rights because they are old. But a brief look at the plight of many elderly people shows that they are in fact being denied those rights." And the statement went on to enumerate the elderly's rights to life, a job, a decent home, health care, food, and a decent income—pointing out that 22 percent of our older citizens have incomes below the federal poverty level.

Yet it seems to be an uphill battle. While ours is an aging society, with 10 percent of the people over 65 years old as compared to 4 percent in 1900, our culture is thoroughly youth-oriented. As an object of respect, the "older generation" has been replaced by the "Pepsi generation." Society, through its teachers—the media—stresses physical beauty and energy, vigor and activity, speed and efficiency. Age is the enemy; production and consumption are the goals, and the faster the better. One of my friends, a member of a religious community, tells of an old priest in his order who remains physically active and regularly strolls through the neighborhood each morning. Yet often in the afternoon he infuriates his younger brothers by asking to be taken on an errand to one of the stores he passed on his morning walk. For the old man, time is something to be filled; efficiency is no longer a virtue.

But society says that if you don't make and buy, if you can't keep up, you're useless—in the way, really—and that attitude is evident in the way we treat our unborn, our physically handicapped, our mentally ill and retarded. And in the way we try to put the elderly on the shelf instead of putting them to work, despite the fact that the great majority of older people want to work and that 95 percent of those over 65 do not require institutional care.

Being old has its problems, of course; and there are times when ministry to the elderly is very demanding. My own parents are dead, but both suffered lengthy, debilitating illnesses before they died—and there was great pain for them and their family. The biblical writers were nothing if not realists, and this can be seen in today's readings.

Sirach promises, to those who honor and care for the aged, riches, children, long life, even the hearing of prayers and forgiveness of sins—while clearly implying that such kindness may be tremendously demanding.

And in his letter to the Colossians, Paul indicates the many virtues needed for a close and harmonious family life: mercy, kindness, humility, meekness, patience. Unlike the romance of *Love Story*, real-life love, rather than meaning you never have to say you're sorry, means asking pardon again and again. "Bear with one another; forgive whatever grievances you have against one another." Paul's repeated use of "one another" highlights his stress on mutual responsibility, as do his culturally conditioned admonitions to wives and husbands, parents and children, in which the basic concern for two-way love and respect remains valid.

To those who know the human heart, family life is not easy, and only the decision of love makes it possible: "Over all these virtues put on love, which binds the rest together and makes them perfect." Especially is this true of the relationships between adult children and their aging parents, between the young and middle-aged mainstream of society and the growing minority of older people.

But what of the gifts of age? Are there any? Or is age to be dreaded rather than welcomed, accepted as inevitable, and tolerated only because it's better than the alternative? Or does age have its own usefulness and beauty? Is it perhaps true that "the best is yet to be, the last of life for which the first was made"? Is there a particular richness in that part of life on earth closest to our life in heaven with God?

The Gospel examples of Simeon and Anna suggest some of the possible graces of age for those steeped in the tradition of faith and yet open to the surprising and new. This famous pair of prophets manifest at least three beautiful qualities often found in the old, which should be recognized and honored— and maybe even imitated by the rest of us.

The old know how to wait. A contemplative friend took a temporary job in a supermarket with a computerized checkout system. One day as he was adding up a large order, the whole system broke down, and his customer wailed, "What am I going to do?" My friend replied, "Practice waiting." Often the elderly have learned the virtue of patience, with others and even with themselves. Perhaps we can learn from their slower ways and smaller worlds that faster and bigger are not always better, and that our worship of the gods of speed and size causes us to miss much along the way.

The old are often honest. Like children, they have a refreshing candor; they tend to "tell it like it is." The rest of us can easily stretch diplomacy to the point of deception and lose our own hold on the truth. We have such a stake in the status quo that change is automatically threatening. Many priests comment that the liturgical changes of Vatican II were accepted most easily by the elderly and least easily by the middle-aged. There's something about having seen everything which gives one a detachment and perspective and even an openness to the new and unexpected—even to salvation in the form of a baby.

The old are frequently grateful. I think there are few virtues more beautiful than that of a spirit of gratitude which asks for little and is always thankful. I remember how my grandmother appreciated the smallest kindnesses and was always filled with surprise and appreciation. One of the finest compliments I ever received was the comment of a friend who had done me an unexpected favor and, seeing my delight, remarked, "You're easily impressed." And one of the most instructive penances I ever received was to be asked, each night for a week, to thank God for each time that day God had not done my will. Perhaps from the elderly we can learn to be grateful for *all* of life's gifts—and for life.

Experts tell us that when we grow old whatever characteristics we have developed throughout life become accentuated. Those of us not yet old need consciously to begin to practice those virtues we would like to have accentuated in years to come. I was especially aware of that at a dinner given in my parish, a black inner-city parish, this past year. The dinner was given to honor all those parishioners eighty years old or more, who had given at least fifty years of service to the church—and there were sixty-three persons so honored! As I watched them, I thought: If I can live like these men and women, old age, rather than being the lesser of two evils, really will be the crown of life and the gateway to heaven.

PATRICIA E. DAVIS, *staff assistant to the Committee on the Laity of the National Conference of Catholic Bishops, worked previously in parish ministry and social justice education. She holds an M.Div. from Washington Theological Union and is the mother of three grown children.*

It's Hard to Sing the Song of Deborah

PRISCILLA L. DENHAM

And the people of Israel again did what was evil in the sight of the Lord. . . . Now Deborah, a prophetess, the wife of Lappidoth, was judging Israel at that time. She used to sit under the palm of Deborah between Ramah and Bathel in the hill country of Ephraim; and the people of Israel came up to her for judgment. She sent and summoned Barak . . . and said to him, "Does not the Lord, the God of Israel, command you, 'Go, gather your men at Mount Tabor. . . . And I will draw out Sisera, the general of Jabin's army, to meet you by the river Kishon with his chariots and his troops; and I will give him into your hand.'" Barak said to her, "If you will go with me, I will go; but if you will not go with me, I will not go." And she said, "I will surely go with you; nevertheless, the road on which you are going will not lead to your glory, for the Lord will sell Sisera into the hand of a woman." Then Deborah arose, and went with Barak to Kedesh. . . .

And Deborah said to Barak, "Up! For this is the day in which the Lord has given Sisera into your hand. Does not the Lord go out before you?" So Barak went down from Mount Tabor with ten thousand men following him. And the Lord routed Sisera and all his chariots and all his army before Barak at the edge of the sword; and Sisera alighted from his chariot and fled away on foot. And . . . all the army of Sisera fell by the edge of the sword; not a man was left.

But Sisera fled away on foot to the tent of Jael, the wife of Heber the Kenite; for there was peace between Jabin the king of Hazor and the house of Heber the Kenite. And Jael came out to meet Sisera, and said to him, "Turn aside, my lord,

58

turn aside to me; have no fear." So he turned aside to her into the tent, and she covered him with a rug. And he said to her, "Pray, give me a little water to drink: for I am thirsty." So she opened a skin of milk and gave him a drink and covered him. And he said to her, "Stand at the door of the tent, and if any man comes and asks you, 'Is anyone here?' say, No." But Jael the wife of Heber took a tent peg, and took a hammer in her hand, and went softly to him and drove the peg into his temple, till it went down into the ground, as he was lying fast asleep from weariness. So he died. And behold, as Barak pursued Sisera, Jael went out to meet him, and said to him, "Come, and I will show you the man whom you are seeking." So he went into her tent; and there lay Sisera dead, with the tent peg in his temple.

So on that day God subdued Jabin the king of Canaan before the people of Israel.

—JUDGES 4:1–24, RSV

In 1898, a book called *The Woman's Bible* was published. Written by Elizabeth Cady Stanton and "The Revising Committee," it was the forebear of the attempts being made today to examine scripture to understand what it *really* says about the role of women. That the Bible is a product of many patriarchal societies was nothing to be disputed. That it was/is interpreted in a sexist way was (and is) the double injustice which Elizabeth Cady Stanton was trying to address. She observed, "When those who are opposed to all reforms can find no other argument, their last resort is the Bible. It has been interpreted to favor intemperance, slavery, capital punishment, and the subjection of woman." So at eighty years old and "deserted by the professionals" (those women Greek and Hebrew scholars who refused to join in the effort because it might risk their reputations as scholars), Elizabeth Cady Stanton began. Her plan was to publish a series of essays by women on sections of the Bible where women were the principal characters or where women were glaringly excluded. The result is a small volume dealing with the Pentateuch and "Judges, Kings, Prophets, and Apostles." It is filled with technical errors and a Victorian mindset. At points, it is uneven in its treatment of the passages and has verses interpreted out of context. However, this small book also often provides insight about the women in the scripture. It raises questions which surely would have challenged its readers to question further. It is a book written with wit, an active curiosity,

and courage. The very fact of its being written encouraged
people to rethink their traditional interpretations. Elizabeth
Cady Stanton began a task for which she was ill-equipped
because no one else would even try.

One of the passages with which she deals is the Song of
Deborah. I'd like to read two paragraphs from her essay:

> Deborah was a woman of great ability. She was consulted by the
> children of Israel in all matters of government, of religion and of
> war. Her judgment seat was under a palm tree, known ever after
> as "Deborah's Palm." Though she was one of the great judges of
> Israel for forty years, her name is not in the list, as it should have
> been, with Gideon, Barak, Samson and Jephthah. Men have always
> been slow to confer on women the honors which they deserve. . . .
>
> We never hear sermons pointing women to the heroic virtues of
> Deborah as worthy of their imitation. Nothing is said in the pulpit
> to rouse them from the apathy of ages, to inspire them to do and
> dare great things, to intellectual and spiritual achievements, in real
> communion with the Great Spirit of the Universe. Oh, no! The
> lessons doled out to women, from the canon law, the Bible, the
> prayer-books and the catechisms, are meekness and self-
> abnegation; ever with covered heads (a badge of servitude) to do
> some humble service for man; that they are unfit to sit as a
> delegate in a Methodist conference, to be ordained to preach the
> Gospel, or to fill the office of elder, of deacon or of trustee, or to
> enter the Holy of Holies in cathedrals.

As I was preparing for today I looked over many possibilities. I reread this story in Judges and passed over it. But as I
looked at other scriptures, I kept coming back to Deborah. I was
a little annoyed with myself because I didn't want to preach on
this, but I was somehow hooked. Finally I realized the only way I
was going to be free of my mind snag was to work my way
through it. I began to research.

Historically, I know there is the prose version and the poetic
version of this story. The poetic version, which is in Judges 5, is
one of the oldest passages in the Bible. It is generally agreed that
the poem is by a firsthand, authentic witness of the battle,
written about 1125 B.C. The prose version, which I used, is a bit
more recent. The double version is one indication of how
important this battle was to the Israelites. The basic details of the

two are the same. The Canaanites controlled the Valley of Jezreel. The Israelites were trying to wrest this control from them. The Canaanites were exceptional warriors because of their "iron chariots," an advanced form of weaponry. This Valley of Jezreel was the Israelites' economic lifeline, and the Canaanites were trying to choke it off. In response to this tense situation, Deborah, a Judge, called the tribes to unify to do battle. (A Judge, I would note parenthetically, was a bit different from our "judge." A Judge was one who was a military champion as well as one who was a legal arbitrator. The authority of the Judge extended beyond the locale of his/her immediate clan and was recognized by the entire tribal confederacy. The office of Judge was a charismatic one, not based on heredity but on the recognition of a special endowment of Yahweh's spirit.) Back to the battle. Deborah appointed Barak to command the forces of the Israelites. Barak refused unless Deborah went with him. She agreed, but with the wisdom that made her the Judge, she told him that he would not get the credit for the victory, although he was the renowned warrior—a woman would be the one who was celebrated. It may be that she saw that in his need for her immediate presence he would not be aggressive enough to win on his own, or it may have been that she saw him beginning to preen even before he reached the battle and she wanted to confront him with who he was and what his limitations were. We are not given the reasons. We only know her prediction. On the field of battle a torrential rain came, flooding the river Kishon. The overflowing river turned the plain into sticky clay, thus trapping the Canaanite warriors in their chariots. Sisera, the general, fled on foot to the tent of Heber the Kenite. Heber was gone, but his wife, Jael, welcomed Sisera in, assuring him of safety. She gave him milk, offered him a place to sleep, then put a tent peg to his temple and murdered him. When Barak came past, she told him to enter to find the man he sought. As a footnote, I would add that in the desert one was bound by honor to protect the life of one's guests. Jael's deed was in gross violation of the desert code, particularly in view of the note that "There was peace between Jabin [the Canaanite king] and the house of Heber the Kenite."

So I did all my research, put together the historical material, and still was not comfortable with this passage. I didn't like a war story. I didn't like Jael's graphic killing. I didn't like— Then, with an unhappy flash of insight, I realized what I really disliked about this story. Just as Deborah confronted the strong Barak with his military limitation, her song confronts me with my limitation, my own sexism. And I am confronted on several levels.

The first level I call simple sexism, that attitude that men and women are somehow two different types of human with different roles to play in life. As a pacifist, I don't like this story because women are the initiators of the violence. It blows my condescending myth that women are more peaceful than men, that if women were put in positions of authority there would be less competition, less fighting, fewer wars in the world. In this story one woman calls her people to war; the other woman does the specific act of killing Sisera. Tied in with the peaceful-woman myth is my own particular division-of-labor myth. Although I think I believe in men and women doing the same tasks professionally and in the home, with this story I was suddenly confronted with that part of myself that is just as glad that men are usually the ones that have gotten stuck with the task of wars. They have also been the ones to take the credit or blame historically, and I have been delighted to have it be theirs to bear.

My second level of sexism is a bit more complex. It is the sexism of not seeing, omission. This form has to do with the process by which women are discounted by being ignored. My excuse for my "ignore-ance" is that I grew up in a time when stories of women in the Bible were not focused on, and I assumed that women were not strong characters in the scriptures. I took the easy intellectual path of relying on passages that were already familiar to me. Deborah's song, which I never heard from another's pulpit, is nonetheless available if I look—if I will have eyes to see—just as there are many other women recorded in scripture. I must discipline myself to see that women are recorded as full participants in the canon, and I must do the digging that is necessary to see how they did function instead of simply claiming that the patriarchs kept them out. Elizabeth Cady Stanton did more researching than I have done, and she wasn't theologically trained. It is too easy to blame my male professors for not raising up this material for me. It is my own sexism that keeps the material out of my reach.

The third level is the most difficult for me to break through. If the first level is that of not wanting full and equal responsibility, and if the second level is that of not seeing what can be done, the third level is that of not doing that which should be done, specifically not doing that which I cannot justify and defend beyond question. Jael broke the desert code in killing Sisera because she understood it to be the will of God. But she had to stand on the bald act itself; there was no logical, justifiable reason to support her. Elizabeth Cady Stanton wrote *The Woman's Bible* knowing she would make mistakes, that others would try to discount her work because it was not intellectually sophisticated enough. But she wrote because the intellectual sophisticates would not write it. She put herself out on a shaky limb because it was the only way to make a small step toward rectifying the glaringly imbalanced treatment of women. I am reminded of Mary, the mother of Jesus, who had to do the impossible-to-justify act of bearing an illegitimate child, and call it the son of God, because she believed it was the will of God. The Plowshare Eight moved beyond the rules and laws of our country because they too felt that to do the will of God meant standing outside defensible boundaries. And I know that I am one who wants the safety of doing justice within a justifiable position instead of risking to do the will of God which might break the rules. I am much more comfortable being a rational, logical, defensible feminist/pacifist/radical.

In my ears now is the song of Deborah. It is a song of courage and power. A song of women interpreting the will of God, risking their lives to do the will of God. It is a song of shattered role expectations. It is a song that breaks the rules that justice may be done. It is a song that invites each of us to greater freedom—freedom from the roles put on us by society, freedom from the limitations within. A song of full personhood for us all. It is a song that reminds me that I am sometimes afraid to sing. For it is hard to sing the song of Deborah, especially if I must sing it alone.

THE REV. PRISCILLA LANE DENHAM *is a third generation Baptist minister. She currently works as a chaplain at Allentown State Psychiatric Hospital in Pennsylvania and as a pastoral counselor/family therapist. She is an acting supervisor in the Association for Clinical Pastoral Education. She is expecting her first child.*

My God, My God, Why Have You Forsaken Me?

MARIE M. FORTUNE

*And those who passed by derided him. . . . Those who were crucified with him
also reviled him.*

> *And when the sixth hour had come, there was darkness over the whole land
until the ninth hour. And at the ninth hour Jesus cried with a loud voice, "Eloi,
Eloi, lama sabach-thani?" which means, "My God, my God, why hast thou
forsaken me?" And some of the bystanders hearing it said, "Behold, he is calling
Elijah." And one ran and, filling a sponge full of vinegar, put it on a reed and
gave it to him to drink, saying, "Wait, let us see whether Elijah will come to take
him down." And Jesus uttered a loud cry, and breathed his last. And the curtain
of the temple was torn in two, from top to bottom. And when the centurion, who
stood facing him, saw that he thus breathed his last, he said, "Truly this man was
a son of God!"*

—MARK 15: 29–39, RSV

*Cast your burden on the Lord, and he will sustain you; he will never permit the
righteous to be moved.*

—PSALM 55:22, RSV

*There is therefore now no condemnation for those who are in Christ Jesus. For
the law of the Spirit of life in Christ Jesus has set me free from the law of sin
and death. . . . If the Spirit of him who raised Jesus from the dead dwells in you,
he who raised Christ Jesus from the dead will give life to your mortal bodies also*

65

through his Spirit which dwells in you. . . . We know that in everything God works for good with those who love him, who are called according to his purpose. . . . What then shall we say to this? If God is for us, who is against us? . . . Who shall separate us from the love of Christ? Shall tribulation, or distress, or persecution, or famine, or nakedness, or peril, or sword? . . . For I am sure that neither death, nor life, nor angels, nor principalities, nor things present, nor things to come, nor powers, nor height, nor depth, nor anything else in all creation, will be able to separate us from the love of God in Christ Jesus our Lord.

—ROMANS 8:1–39, RSV

Abandoned by God. Left alone in the midst of terror. Facing unimaginable pain and fear, anticipating his own death as imminent. Hanging from a cross, naked, humiliated and abused by the crowd.

At this moment, Jesus' faith falters. In this moment, he questions God's faithfulness to him. My God, why have you left me here alone? Why have you given me up to this terrifying experience?

It is probably in this single moment that Jesus' humanness is most apparent. And here that we can most readily identify with his experience.

He has been betrayed by his friends, tried and condemned to die, beaten, humiliated, stripped, and nailed to a cross, when finally he cries out to God in despair and perhaps anger: *Why, why have you forsaken me, too?*

Jesus was a victim—a victim of the violence of a system that would not tolerate his teaching any longer. But more than that, he was a victim of personal violence—i.e., physical harm done to his person. It is in the midst of this pain and terror that he cries out to God.

Violence—the overt physical destruction of a human being.

As I have been working on the problems of sexual and domestic violence for the past three years, I have been acutely aware of a paradox: on the one hand a real concern and interest expressed by many in churches, and on the other hand a denial and minimization that places the lowest priority on the problem of violence, especially as it is experienced in the family: "It's no big deal—it doesn't happen that often." As I have pondered this paradox, I have concluded that as a society we have become so desensitized to the effect of overt, personal violence that we inevitably minimize its importance—e.g., Saturday cartoons, advertising which portrays a beaten and bound woman outrage only a few. It is not real to most of us; we see it so often, in so many forms, and usually glamourized, it doesn't *appear* to hurt anymore.

As I have talked with many groups about family violence and have suggested that perhaps nonviolence in the family is the better way, I have been met on many occasions with a "Yes, but . . ." response. "Yes, but the children need discipline." "Yes, but what am I supposed to do when she doesn't have dinner on the table on time or when she nags me?" "What am I supposed to do when he makes me angry?" "Yes, but . . . what other way is there?"

These responses have made it clear to me that *my* assumption that any physical violence between persons in the family is destructive is not shared by many people. So I decided that maybe I needed to back up and consider the question of *why* personal violence is destructive on many levels.

Think about the last time someone struck you or grabbed you and it hurt, or threw something at you—it may have been when you were eight years old or yesterday. How did you feel? Afraid, alone, ashamed? Did you tell anyone? Did you think about what this experience meant in light of your faith? In considering the question why personal violence is so destructive, I looked to contemporary theologians and was disappointed by what I found.

Particularly since the Second World War, theologians have addressed at great length the issues of violence and nonviolence: the theory of a "just" war; the question of whether Hitler should have been assassinated in order to stop his violence; the civil rights movement and the practice of nonviolence as a strategy for change; the debate over whether or not violence can be justified to resist political and economic oppression in the Third World; and now, how to counter the unimaginable violence of nuclear arms. All very serious and pressing questions for us to ponder as Christians.

Yet *nowhere* do I find an attempt to *theologize* about the experience of personal violence in our lives here and now, today. My hunch is that this is because most contemporary American (male) theologians have never been mugged, have not been taught to fear rape as a daily threat, and do not acknowledge the fact that 60 percent of couples will experience physical violence at some point in their relationship and that the family is the most violent institution in the United States. Thus, for them violence is an academic, societal issue for debate, rather than a personal human experience known to many in our society.

The experience of personal violence or the threat of violence is all but ignored by most theologians.

The scriptures, on the other hand, hardly ignored the issue, and it is here that we find some understanding of the experience.

Violence: an overt act or threat of physical harm or destruction. The gun-to-the-back, knife-to-the-throat, fist-to-the-face kind of violence—the slap, the push, the kick, which, contrary to the glamourized TV message, result in serious physical injury *and* overwhelming terror.

The Psalmist knew the experience of personal violence and cries out in the midst of it:

> Give ear to my prayer, O God; and hide not thyself from my supplication! Attend to me, and answer me; I am overcome by my trouble. I am distraught by the noise of the enemy, because of the oppression of the wicked. For they bring trouble upon me, and in anger they cherish enmity against me. My heart is in anguish within me, the terrors of death have fallen upon me. Fear and trembling come upon me, and horror overwhelms me.
>
> —PSALM 55:1, RSV

And when carried out by someone close to us, it is even worse.

> It is not an enemy who taunts me—then I could bear it; it is not an adversary who deals insolently with me—then I could hide from him. But it is you, my equal, my companion, my familiar friend. We used to hold sweet converse together; within God's house we walked in fellowship.
>
> —PSALM 55:12-14, RSV

It is violence which says to the recipient: I am in charge here, and I decide whether you live or die. Victim: overwhelmed, overcome, dispossessed, subdued, overpowered, violated, defiled, denied, dehumanized, humiliated, terrorized, alienated, isolated.

Fear is the result. Fear that demoralizes and diminishes a person. The pain of the broken ribs, the fractured skull, the cuts and bruises last for days. The fear lasts even longer. As Marge Piercy describes the experience of rape: "There is no difference between being raped and going head first through a windshield except that afterwards you are afraid not of cars but half the human race."

And in the midst of the fear and pain, perhaps the most painful of all—the sense of abandonment.

Some Christians would like to believe that "bad" things don't happen to "good" Christians: if you are really being a good Christian, God will protect you from all evil. This kind of teaching from the church serves to set people up. Because then, if they are assaulted, they have to choose: either they weren't really being a good enough Christian *or* they have been lied to and God doesn't really care—God has abandoned them. This seems not a very fair choice to present to a person who is suffering.

One of the most common stories told to me by abused women describes how, in the midst of the woman's abuse, she sought help from family, from friends, clergy, or doctor, all of whom turned away from her, left her alone. Inevitably, she too fears abandonment by God.

Again the Psalmist:

> My God, my God, why hast thou forsaken me?
> Why art thou so far from helping me, from the words of my groaning?
> O my God, I cry by day, but thou dost not answer;
> and by night, but find no rest.
>
> I am poured out like water,
> and all my bones are out of joint;
> my heart is like wax,

it is melted within my breast;
my strength is dried up like a potsherd,
and my tongue cleaves to my jaws.

—PSALM 22:1-2, 14-15, RSV

This kind of experience, which results from an act of violence upon another person, is blasphemous. As every person is a creation of God's own image, whose whole self is sacred and precious, *any* physical assault on a person contradicts the very image of God—and is so destructive to that person as to render her (or him) unable to fulfill *her* responsibility to love God and her neighbor.

The final tragedy is the reality that, even as the victim is so injured and dehumanized, so is the abuser, whose alienation and isolation are as great. *Nobody wins* when physical violence is threatened or carried out. The wounds to the body and the spirit are deep for both. The greatest sin in violence is that both the victim and the abuser are driven away from God, are driven to cry out in their isolation: O God, why have you deserted me?—just as Christ cried out in his victimization on the cross.

The scripture speaks clearly to the experience of violence. The Psalmist speaks out consistently against violence; to the violent, the word is one of judgment and justice. "But thou, O God, wilt cast them down into the lowest pit; men of blood and treachery shall not live out half their days. But I will trust in thee [Ps. 55:23, RSV]."

And to the victim, what word from the scripture? A promise, a reassurance. That God is present to us through Christ even in the midst of the pain of violence. "Cast your burden on the Lord, [who] will sustain you [and who] will never permit the righteous to be moved [Ps. 55:22, RSV]." "For I am sure that neither death, nor life, nor angels, nor principalities, nor things present, nor things to come, nor powers, nor height, nor depth, nor anything else in all creation, will be able to separate us from the love of God in Christ Jesus our Lord [Rom. 8:38-39, RSV]." God is faithful and gives us strength so that we can resist the power and destruction which threaten body and soul.

As I met with a group of mothers, all of whose husbands

had sexually abused their children, we talked about some of their religious concerns. One woman there told me a story which described her experience of God's presence. She said she always thought of God as walking beside her; she would visualize God's footprints alongside hers. When the trouble began with her abusive husband, she lost that sense of God's presence. She felt there was only one set of footprints, and those were hers. But as she reflected on the pain of her experience, she began to see it differently. She realized that the footprints were, in fact, God's. And that her footprints were not visible because, for that time, God was carrying her. She had a very real sense of how God was present in her life. This truth came to Jesus, even as he faced a torturous death, and the fear that God had deserted him. Nevertheless, it was clear to all that he was a child of God, and God was faithful to him.

The message is clear: Violence inflicted upon a person contradicts God's purpose for our lives, especially our lives together in families. "People are not for hitting and abuse." This is a message which runs contrary to much of what we learn in our culture—TV, books, school, family. It is a message which calls for justice and respect in our relationships with each other.

We must remember that Jesus did not die of old age or pneumonia—he was killed, a victim of violence. In his death and resurrection is the hope and promise that we should not suffer the brokenness of spirit and body which he knew, and that we should not inflict the brokenness on others. He lived and died and rose again, that we might have life, and have it abundantly. Praise be to God.

THE REV. MARIE M. FORTUNE *was ordained in the United Church of Christ and served in the parish. She is now the founder and director of the Center for the Prevention of Sexual and Domestic Violence in Seattle, Washington.*

How Can This Be?

MARGIE M. FRANK

So the disciples went and did what Jesus had told them to do: they brought the donkey and the colt, threw their cloaks over them, and Jesus got on. A large crowd of people spread their cloaks on the road while others cut branches from the trees and spread them on the road. The crowds walking in front of Jesus and those walking behind began to shout, "Praise to David's son! God bless him who comes in the name of the Lord! Praise be to God!" When Jesus entered Jerusalem, the whole city was thrown into an uproar. "Who is he?" the people asked. "This is the prophet Jesus, from Nazareth in Galilee," the crowds answered.

— MATTHEW 21:6–11, TEV

The chief priests and the elders persuaded the crowd to ask Pilate to set Barabbas free and have Jesus put to death. But Pilate asked the crowd, "Which one of these two do you want me to set free for you?" "Barabbas!" they answered. "What, then, shall I do with Jesus called the Messiah?" Pilate asked them. "Crucify him!" they all answered. But Pilate asked, "What crime has he committed?" Then they started shouting at the top of their voices: "Crucify him!"

When Pilate saw that it was no use to go on, but that a riot might break out, he took some water, washed his hands in front of the crowd, and said, "I am not responsible for the death of this man! This is your doing!"

— MATTHEW 27:20–24, TEV

Ride on, ride on in majesty!
Hark! all the tribes "Hosanna" cry:
O Savior meek, pursue thy road,
With palms and scattered garments strewed.

Ride on, ride on in majesty!
In lowly pomp ride on to die!
O Christ, thy triumphs now begin
O'er captive death and conquered sin. . . .

Ride on, ride on in majesty!
In lowly pomp ride on to die!
Bow thy meek head to mortal pain!
Then take, O God, thy power, and reign!
—HENRY MILMAN

How can this be? Jesus is given the VIP treatment, the Palestinian equivalent of a ticker-tape parade, is cheered as a hero, with the crowd's asking God's blessing upon him on Sunday—and on Friday, five short days later, Jesus is cursed, beaten, mocked, spat upon, and finally condemned to one of the worst kinds of execution. He is crucified because a crowd now full of hate demands his death.

Surely there's something wrong here! It doesn't seem to make much sense. In fact, if this were a story in a novel, we'd probably question the author's ability to write realistically. Is it possible for the people to change their minds about Jesus that much within less than a week? we ask.

As with nearly all the happenings in the Bible, we wish that we had more details. We wish that we could ask questions and get answers from those who were really there. Better yet, how much we wish that we might have been there ourselves—at least, I'd like to have been part of that crowd cheering Jesus on Palm Sunday, wouldn't you? What an event to tell your grandchildren about!

I don't know about you, but I couldn't possibly have stayed around to witness the crucifixion. But I surely would like to have heard the story of the trial and crucifixion from those who were there.

As things stand now, we just haven't enough facts to be sure why such an unlikely turn of events happened within less than a week.

Many Bible scholars see evidence, as they read the New Testament, that Jesus seems to have been losing popularity with the crowds for some time toward the end of his ministry, for a number of reasons—among these, that he was less and less willing to do miracles and healing as he emphasized his teachings about God more and more.

Even more significant, he was becoming increasingly unpopular with those in authority, those who held the power in the Jewish community—the Pharisees, the scribes, the priests. His public image as a folk hero and savior of the common people threatened their positions.

Those who take this view, that Jesus had gradually been losing popularity, maintain that the Palm Sunday event was a momentary kind of reburst of popularity among those who saw him as a possible leader against the conquering Romans. Apparently, before the week was over, such followers of Jesus decided that just wasn't going to happen. Jesus was never going to lead an army against the Romans. Better to be rid of him and look elsewhere for a new leader.

Other scholars speculate that the Palm Sunday crowd which yelled, "Hosanna in the highest," was not the same as the Good Friday crowd which yelled, "Crucify him!" We are talking about two different groups of people. This seems more likely to me.

We are still left with the very difficult problem of why Jesus, a good man, God's very special son, the person most like God to have ever lived in this world, should have to die in this terrible, painful, humiliating way—a death totally undeserved. How could this have happened? Is there no answer?

There are, of course, several answers which have been given by Christians throughout the centuries, summed up by such phrases as: Jesus died for our sins; Jesus died because God planned it that way; Jesus died to redeem us.

There are other answers which are somewhat less common, but which have also been around for a long time: because Judas was greedy; because Jesus chose to be a martyr; because Jesus was a dreamer. (A realist wouldn't have gotten himself into such a mess!)

I think I see some truth in all of these reasons, and also in another I'd like to talk about right now. The idea which I'd like to discuss is that there is something about us human beings that wants to hurt or destroy the truly good, the truly beautiful, that which most deserves to live. There's something of the vandal in all of us. We can all identify with the once popular song, "You Always Hurt the One You Love."

This seems to be part of our human condition. Perhaps it's jealousy which motivates us to destroy the lovely. Perhaps it's blindness which prevents us from seeing what we are really doing. Perhaps it's childish delight in being a destroyer when we are unable to be a creator.

Whatever the reason, we all have some of this terrible urge to hurt, to destroy, to kill, at times. It seems to me that this is one of the things the Easter story is all about. *We are all sinners!* We *all* do unforgivable things to people, and to animals, frequently when they are totally undeserving of such treatment.

Peter hurt Jesus by denying him. Judas hurt Jesus by betraying him.

And we hurt our husbands, wives, parents, children, and friends!

Who here can say, "That isn't true about me!" Who can honestly say, "I never knowingly hurt anyone I loved"? Unfortunately, I don't believe any one of us can say that.

There seems to be something about the human condition (blame it on the devil, if you wish) which makes us unable to always be fair and good, even to those who deserve it.

But there is a wonderful truth we learn from Easter. We learn that, just as there seems to be something about us which wants to hurt and destroy, there is something about God which wants to create and maintain the good and the beautiful in our world. Ultimately the worthwhile things will survive, just as Jesus did.

This is one of the clear, shining truths we can cling to in this confusing and frightening age in which we live. God would not let Jesus and what he stood for die in 33 A.D. God will not let that happen today, either.

We know it to be true that all of us, even those who mouth the praises of Jesus on Sundays, during the week often become people who try to destroy him—destroy him by failing to live any differently than we would have if he hadn't come into this world; destroy him by showing him no respect, by cursing and swearing and using his and God's name in vain, foul language we would never use to his face; destroy him by ignoring what he

said about cheating and lying and being selfish; destroy him by
ignoring both him and God in every way we can, often so much
so that if it were against the law to be a Christian most of us
would probably never be brought to trial, because there would
not be enough evidence around to convict us of being Christian,
followers of the Christ!

Perhaps one reason the story of what happened to Jesus on
Good Friday continues to move us every time we hear it is
because if we are honest we know, in our hearts, that *we* might
well have been among those who cried, "Crucify him! Crucify
him!" How we live, what we do and fail to do, says this ever so
plainly.

O God, forgive *us,* for we too know not what we do.

> When Jesus came to Golgotha they hanged Him on a tree,
> They drave great nails through hands and feet, and made a
> Calvary;
> They crowned Him with a crown of thorns, red were His
> wounds and deep,
> For those were crude and cruel days, the human flesh was
> cheap.
>
> When Jesus came to Birmingham, they simply passed Him by,
> They never hurt a hair of Him, they only let Him die;
> For men had grown more tender, and they would not give Him
> pain,
> They only just passed down the street, and left Him in the
> rain.
>
> Still Jesus cried, "Forgive them, for they know not what they
> do,"
> And still it rained the winter rain that drenched Him through
> and through;
> The crowds went home and left the streets without a soul to
> see,
> And Jesus crouched against a wall and cried for Calvary.
> —G.A. STUDDERT-KENNEDY

THE REV. MARGIE M. FRANK, *an ordained minister in the
Christian Church (Disciples of Christ), is in a team ministry with her
husband. They have pastored churches in Kentucky, Ohio, Maryland,
Illinois, and West Virginia.*

Can Isaac and Ishmael Be Reconciled?

LAURA GELLER

The Torah portion for Rosh Hashanah deals with two themes. The first is the birth of Isaac. "And God remembered Sarah . . . and Sarah conceived and bore Abraham a son in his old age." The birth of Isaac is quite significant because, as we learned several chapters earlier, it is only through Isaac that God will establish the covenant. Isaac is more than just a child—Isaac is the future, the one through whom there will be a future. As we read this story we remember that God will ask Abraham to sacrifice this son, and so also to sacrifice the future. The second theme is the sacrifice of Ishmael, Abraham's firstborn, whose mother is Hagar, Sarah's handmaid. After Isaac is born, Sarah feels competition between Ishmael and Isaac, so Sarah demands that Abraham throw Hagar and Ishmael out, leaving them to die in the desert. Abraham is devastated—after all, Ishmael is his son—but God tells Abraham to listen to Sarah, to banish Ishmael and his mother. God promises Abraham that they will live and that Ishmael will be the father of a great nation. So Abraham sacrifices Ishmael and sends mother and son out into the wilderness.

Two sons, two sacrifices. Rosh Hashanah is a time of

remembering: "And God remembered Sarah." God remembers
the deeds of our ancestors and of us; we remember the year just
ended. Today we remember Abraham and those two sons, both
standing on the edge of sacrifice. We know that Isaac is the
father of the Jewish people and that Ishmael is the father of the
Arab people. When we read the story of Ishmael's banishment
in the context of our modern reality, it's very depressing. Isaac
and Ishmael can't be in the same house. Even God agrees that
Ishmael must be banished. The Torah portion seems resigned to
a belief that the tension between Isaac and Ishmael is unresolv-
able, even cosmic. Certainly that feeling of depression is a
current one, as we think about the modern descendants of Isaac
and Ishmael. Anyone who reads the newspaper must share the
feeling that the situation between Arabs and Jews is unresolv-
able.

Those of us on campus certainly have that feeling of
depression. A major thrust of Hillel's activity this past year
involved responding to Arab propaganda that by all counts was
anti-Zionist and by most counts anti-Semitic. Arab students
refused to meet with us, so any hope of working out a *modus
vivendi* evaporated. We felt the tragedy of the Torah portion
acted out in our lives; Isaac and Ishmael couldn't stay in the
same house without conflict.

These problems exacerbated a basic tension for us at Hillel:
How can you talk about Israel on a campus like USC, which
seems to be less than hospitable to Zionism. How do we
represent Israel—what kinds of programs, movies, speakers?
Let me give you an example. Last November we had the
opportunity to bring Meir Pa'il to campus. Pa'il was at that time a
member of the Knesset representing the left-wing Sheli party, a
party which disagrees with Begin's policy concerning the occupied territories and advocates a two-state solution to the Israeli–
Palestinian conflict. Some of our students felt we should not
bring him to campus, arguing that because Israel is beleaguered,
all Jews who love Israel should be careful not to supply ammunition to Israel's enemies. In their minds, any public criticism of
Israel is that ammunition. Therefore, they argued, we should
either bring pro-government speakers or speakers who would
talk about "nonpolitical" issues such as *aliyah*. Others of us,

myself included, felt first of all that there are very few nonpolitical issues concerning Israel, and secondly that Hillel has the responsibility to bring all reasonable points of view concerning Israel to the attention of students and faculty on campus.

The question of the right or wisdom of a Jew in the United States to be publicly critical of Israel is an important and very current issue. The dilemma has two horns. On the one hand, Israel is extremely vulnerable, isolated and regularly criticized by her enemies and most of the world. On the other hand, many people feel that the policies of the present government exacerbate that isolation and put stumbling blocks in front of peace. How should a Zionist, a lover of Israel, respond?

I went to Israel this summer to try to understand that question and, hopefully, to find some answers. What I found was very upsetting. Israel is in serious trouble, perhaps more serious than ever before. There is a confusing paradox; on the heels of Israel's greatest success, peace with Egypt, morale seems to be at its lowest point. Inflation approaches 120 percent. To understand what that figure means, consider an example: this summer banks were advertising regular passbook accounts offering 93 percent interest. Many Israelis work two jobs just to keep up with inflation. I met a young American couple, both social workers, who had recently made *aliyah*. Between the two of them, they had three social-work jobs. In American dollars, together they brought home $890 a month, and their expenses, allowing only $25 a month for entertainment of any sort, came to $882. Each month they saved $8.

Everyone is depressed about the economy. The rate of *yerida*, emigration from Israel, is the highest it has ever been. One source says that 1500 Israelis are leaving Israel each month. Most of the Israelis who leave would go back in a minute if there were to be another war. As one Israeli explained to me, "Israel is worth dying for, it's just not worth living in."

A major source of Israeli depression seems to stem from the contradiction raised by the political situation. Israel is a Jewish social democracy of about 3 million Jews, which presently rules over 1.2 million Arabs. The situation is untenable. If it continues, Israel will have to stop being Jewish or stop being democratic. If it is a democracy, the Arabs must be given equal rights, and soon, given the high birth rate among Arabs, Israel will no longer be a Jewish state. If it is to remain Jewish, these Arabs can never be made full citizens, and so it will cease being a democracy. Either option is a perversion of Zionism.

The root of this contradiction is the issue of settlements. Since 1967, under the Labor government, there have been settlements in the occupied territories. The arguments for these settlements were based on security considerations under Labor. The settlement policy was based on two general principles. First, settlement would take place in strategically important areas devoid of Arab inhabitants. Second, when the time came for a peaceful resolution to the conflict, Israel would retain the strategically important areas and return the Arab-populated areas to the relevant sovereign bodies. Now, under Begin's government, an entirely new settlement policy is operative. Begin argues from the perspective of Eretz Yisrael Shlema—greater Israel. For him, all Eretz Yisrael—the land of Israel—is an indivisible unit, including the West Bank and Gaza, and because it belongs to the Jewish people by biblical and historical right, there can be no compromise. From this perspective, the Sinai is different from other areas conquered in 1967 because Sinai was not part of the biblical Eretz Yisrael. For Begin, the settlements serve not only as a means of establishing an Israeli presence in vital areas but also as a means of obliterating the Green Line, the 1949 armistice demarcation line. The crucial change in Israel's policy is that security is no longer the key consideration in regard to settlements.

Many people in Israel question the security argument that is still advanced by the government to justify the settlements. One question asked is how would the outpost settlements fit into the overall defense strategy of Israel in time of war? Remember that immediately after the outbreak of the Yom Kippur war the Israel Defense Force ordered the evacuation of the settlements on the Golan. A related question concerns how the Israel Defense Force would be able to protect the 600-odd settlements in the occupied territories in the event of a surprise attack.

Of even more concern is the question that was echoed by many of the people I spoke with: What are the real costs of the settlements in terms of resources drained from necessary social services and in terms of the growing Arab resentment? As Hirsch Goodman, the military affairs correspondent for the *Jerusalem Post,* reports in *P r e s e n t T e n s e:*

> As the number of Jewish centers within Arab populations increases, so must the size of the military required to protect them. Similarly, as the uniformed personnel in evidence—maintaining the law, enforcing the curfews, carrying out the security checks—grows, so does the resentment of the local population. . . . Beyond these factors is the question of how the problems of maintaining security under present circumstances have affected the military, the police and other Israelis. The protracted occupation has had a negative effect on the morale of Israel's armed forces. Sharp ideological differences are developing among the country's youth. . . . There is increasing unwillingness to serve in typical "occupying" roles, such as enforcing curfews or fighting sixteen-year-old schoolgirls who throw rocks. . . . For the first time in the history of the state, there is a question among many in uniform, in the reserves or about to be inducted as to the desirability of the service they are being called on to undertake. . . .

It's important for us to remember that 80 percent of the Israel Defense Force is made up of reserve units, regular Israeli citizens who are called into active duty for an average of thirty days a year. As a law professor pointed out to me, "These men [reservists] are called on to do the work of an occupying army. That work is not pleasant, and those who do it are affected by it. In fact, it is bound to affect the entire fabric of Israeli society."

Many in Israel are concerned about this issue. I quote from a May editorial in Ha'aretz, a major morning newspaper, four days before six Israelis were killed in Hebron on their way home from evening prayers.

> The situation in the West Bank is deteriorating and it is not excessively imaginative to suggest that recent events in the territories are the beginning of a civil rebellion. [The roots of the deterioration] originate in the situation itself, not in the alertness or lack of alertness of the security forces. The fatal laws of a regime of military occupation, according to which repression produces terror and terror produces greater repression, and so on, are continuing to force the conquerors and the conquered to

act contrary to common sense—or to historical experience, thereby making it even more difficult to find a constructive solution which would provide at least a partial answer to the national aspirations of the conquered and the vital security needs of the state of Israel. . . . The reality which we have not changed—neither by words nor by settlements nor by legal argument—is that in the West Bank and the Gaza Strip one nation is trying to rule over another nation against its will. . . .

Several weeks later the *Jerusalem Post* published an article by Mendel Kohansky, which argued:

We are now experiencing a process of brutalization of our collective lives, a process which started thirteen years ago, but which is now accelerating at an alarming rate. What was unthinkable yesterday is happening today, what we fear now may become routine tomorrow. . . .

The groups of young men who, armed with sticks and stones, invaded an Arab town, a couple of weeks ago, and left the streets strewn with shattered glass, were doubtless sons and grandsons of Jews from eastern Europe who had personally experienced the horrors of pogroms. And if the objects of their retaliatory wrath were this time only cars and homes, one could soon expect human victims—on both sides. Violence follows the iron rule of acceleration.

The underlying cause of violence—on both sides—is the occupation of Arab territories. As long as the conquest is in force, violence will follow violence, with a constant increase in ferocity.

Whatever advantages may accrue to the conqueror from ruling another people are undone by the heavy price the conqueror has to pay in terms of the weakening of the moral fiber of his people—of the soldiers who may have to perform tasks abhorrent to a decent person, of the administrators whom circumstances may force to take so-called "strong measures," of the people as a whole.

The brutalization of our life is followed by a vicious polarization in our society. The verbal violence which leaks out of cabinet meetings has its counterparts among citizens of lesser importance under less august circumstances. . . .

Our politicians are fond of saying that Israel's occupation of the West Bank and Gaza is the most benevolent that ever was. They do not realize that this is a contradiction in terms. There is no benevolent occupation, as there is no benevolent dictatorship, as there is no comfortable jail. Some occupations are more brutal, some are less, and the latter tend to become more brutal in response to resistance. . . .

The situation is intolerable. Many Israelis feel powerless to change it. Abba Eban pointed out in a lecture to the American Jewish Congress that the real danger is the loss of a belief in the solubility of our problems, and the possibility that Israel will lose its sense of its own eternity.

There are some hopeful signs. The Sephardic Chief Rabbi Ovadia Yossef argued recently that Jewish law considers human life more sacred than land, and therefore Israel should evacuate the West Bank rather than risk war. Similarly, he continued, Israel should negotiate with the Palestinians in order to bring about peace. Another hopeful sign is the existence of Peace Now. Peace Now began in March 1978, when 350 reservists sent a public letter to Begin, which said in part:

> We write you out of the deepest concern. A government that will prefer the existence of Israel in borders of the greater Israel to its existence in peace in the context of good neighborly relations will arouse in us grave misgivings. A government that will prefer the establishment of settlements across the "Green Line" to the ending of the historic conflict and to the establishment of a system of normal relations will raise questions about the justice of our cause. A government policy that will lead to continued rule over 1,000,000 Arabs is liable to damage the Jewish democratic character of our state and would make it difficult for us to identify with the basic direction of the State of Israel.

The Peace Now movement has grown rapidly, claiming 250,000 supporters. I spent some time with some leaders of Shalom Acshav (Peace Now), and I left feeling that the movement is at a critical turning point. It is clear what they are against—settlements—but they have not yet agreed upon what they stand for. The difficulty of formulating a platform from a group as diverse as Shalom Acshav is formidable, but necessary if it is to remain an important force in Israel. The leadership is involved now in formulating a new statement about Zionism: What does it mean to be a Zionist, now that Israel is an established country? What kind of Israel will emerge, should emerge, from the current crisis? What is the Zionist vision? The energy generated from this kind of activity is the most positive optimistic force that I experienced in Israel.

Others too are asking these kinds of questions. The secular *kibbutz* movement, for example, recognizing that the *kibbutz* is changing as Israel changes, is beginning to search for ways to explore spiritual roots. Informal exploratory meetings are going on between the *kibbutz* movement and Hebrew Union College. The root of this kind of questioning is very profound—it reaches to the core of Zionism. What kind of Israel do we want to create? Should it be a state like any other state? Are there values that we need to collectively get back in touch with? Is the Israel that exists all that it could be?

This summer raised a lot of questions for me. I left feeling that Israel and Israel's future are of primary importance to me. Even as I struggle here in the diaspora to build a creative Jewish community, I know that I need Israel in order to build that community. I need a Jewish country where Jews are faced with the impossible task of building a society rooted in Jewish values. I need a Jewish country where wonderful novels and poems are written in Hebrew, where Jewish scholarship explores the richness of our tradition. I need Israel to challenge me, to force me to ask myself if my Jewish commitment is authentic. I realized this summer that Israel really is the Isaac of our Torah portion, that Israel is the gift we've waited for, just as Sarah waited and waited for Isaac, that Israel is in a real sense, just like Isaac, the key to Jewish future. And I also realized that Israel stands on the edge, that the knife is raised to sacrifice her, just as Abraham once stood ready to sacrifice Isaac. Who holds the knife? Not only the enemies of Israel, but, more important, those forces within that are pulling Israel apart. And, most important, we seem ready to let the sacrifice continue by standing by. American Jews have an important role to play to see that our future isn't sacrificed.

There are many different ways we can play that role, ensure that future. For some, the way is *aliyah*, immigration. An American sociologist I met, who moved to Israel eleven years ago, argued that Israel needs *aliyah* from the West to insure that

Israel will continue to be a democracy. Most of the immigration now consists of Jews from countries with no history of democracy; Israel needs immigrants who understand democratic institutions and processes, to safeguard democracy.

Involvement begins with visiting Israel. Last year we finally pushed through a junior-year-abroad program in Israel. All undergraduates should try their best to spend a year in Israel; the opportunity that spending time in Israel provides for understanding the country is priceless. Faculty should explore sabbatical opportunities or even vacations. Some people have suggested that just as Israelis have to give one month a year to reserve duty in the Army, perhaps diaspora Jews should be urged to give one or two years of service to Israel, on a *kibbutz*, in a development town, or wherever he/she could make a contribution.

As Theodore Mann, the ex-head of the Conference of Presidents of Major American Jewish Organizations, argued recently, "We are *one* people who have chosen to be citizens of different states." It follows from his definition that we have a responsibility to be involved with each other, for diaspora Jews to be involved in Israel.

If we really are one people, if we really are involved with Israel, then it follows that we can participate in the life of Israel. True involvement, true relationship, includes the privilege of loving, productive criticism. It is our responsibility to support the responsible dissident voices within Israel, the voices that are calling for our support. Criticism can be a healing force if it emerges out of a loving relationship.

Recently, more than fifty influential American Jewish leaders, including three past presidents of the Conference of Presidents of Major American Jewish Organizations, added their names to a public letter drafted by Shalom Acshav, denouncing extremism within the Israeli government. The statement argued: "Extremists in the public and within the government, guided by secular and religious chauvinism, distort Zionism and threaten its realization." There is no question that it is a difficult decision to publicize dissent within the Jewish community, but it is a necessary decision when the Prime Minister of Israel claims that the American Jewish community is 100 percent behind policies that many feel are suicidal. We can criticize the policies of the government of Israel at the same time that we support the state of Israel.

The right to criticize comes from a real relationship, real involvement. Involvement demands that we spend money and time in Israel, that we understand the issues that affect the security and future of Israel. I saw several examples of projects where American Jews can spend time and money in Israel. I'll mention one: Project Renewal, a project where diaspora cities link up with an Israeli slum community in order to respond to its specific needs. Los Angeles' community is called Musrara, a neighborhood in Israel which spawned the Israeli Black Panthers, a militant organization of Jews from Oriental countries, the lower classes of Israeli society called the "second Israel." Musrara needs money to build a community center, to house a health clinic, a day care center, a senior citizens' club. Musrara needs dentists and doctors who can volunteer for several months at a time, students who can spend a summer working with the neighborhood children, social workers, urban planners, concerned friends.

There are many other groups that need our support. The Israeli Civil Liberties defends the academic freedom of Arab students in Israeli universities and students' right to express political opinions. It works with the Bedouins in the Negev to fight government appropriation of Bedouin land to build an airport. It needs our money and support. The fledgling Israeli feminist community needs a lot of help, to build shelters for battered women, to run women's centers in Israeli cities. The New Israel Fund needs money to help small progressive groups within Israel do their work of social change and Arab–Jewish rapprochement.

We are one, just as the United Jewish Appeal campaign argues, and, being one, we can't sit idly by when policies in Israel must be criticized and dissident voices need to be supported. Because our whole future is at stake.

From tomorrow's Torah portion we learn that, while Ishmael is banished, he does not die. And Friday we'll read that Isaac is not sacrificed. But are the brothers ever reconciled? Do the father of our people and the father of the Arab people ever manage to come together? They come together only in tragedy, to bury their father Abraham. God forbid that we must wait for tragedy to bring their descendants together.

RABBI LAURA GELLER *was ordained in 1976 at Hebrew Union College. She serves as director of Hillel at the University of Southern California.*

Both Boxes

GRACIA GRINDAL

*He also told this parable to some who trusted themselves that they were righteous
and despised others: "Two men went up into the temple to pray, one a Pharisee
and the other a tax collector. The Pharisee stood and prayed thus with himself,
'God, I thank thee that I am not like other men, extortioners, unjust, adulterers,
or even like this tax collector. I fast twice a week, I give tithes of all that I get.' But
the tax collector, standing far off, would not even lift up his eyes to heaven, but
beat his breast, saying, 'God be merciful to me a sinner!' I tell you, this man went
down to his house justified rather than the other; for everyone who exalts himself
will be humbled, but he who humbles himself will be exalted."*

*Now they were bringing even infants to him that he might touch them; and
when the disciples saw it, they rebuked them. But Jesus called them to him, saying,
"Let the children come to me, and do not hinder them; for to such belongs the
kingdom of God. Truly, I say to you, whoever does not receive the kingdom of
God like a child shall not enter it."*

—LUKE 18:9–17, RSV

It is recorded that in a certain village, after the Sunday-school
class had spent the hour considering the story of the Pharisee
and the publican, the teacher said, "Now, children, let us bow
our heads and thank Jesus we are not like that nasty Pharisee."

Though we are admonished in everything to give thanks, I
think it fair to say that the teacher missed the point.

The text has been much with me ever since last January,

when I heard a young American tourist in Canterbury Cathedral tell her mother that the place was, to be sure, awful pretty, but really it was of little use these days. Instead of repairing it, the money might well be spent on the poor (words not unfamiliar to a close reader of Scripture). I then watched her mother put what I am fairly sure was an equal amount of money in the "Save Canterbury" box and in the "Help the Needy" box. Since then, I have stood in that moment, watching the scene in memory, freezing in the drafty, damp, cold English cathedral, watching the softly lit Bible stories in the windows, the air thronging with pilgrims of every kind and motive, from Chaucer's clerk to the Wife of Bath, a garlicky and religious crew, scurrilous and wretched, all of us.

That evening at vespers, sitting in the well-worn choir stalls, feeling the wood with my chapped hands, I thought of how concrete and sensual the Christian life is. How full of the ordinary, the flesh.

A group of crass American tourists, Leica cameras swinging at their London Fogs, utterly irreverent. Lord, I thank thee . . .

Easter. A small church in Telemark, Norway. The pews are cold and typically uncomfortable. The hymns drag as only Norwegians can drag them; it is only by sheer dint of effort that I know this is Easter, the mood is more like Good Friday. I freak out on the sunlight dazzling on the baptismal font, where my great-grandfather was baptized, and shut out the altogether trite and silly homily from the minister. The subject, for this day of resurrection, is what a scandal it is that so many Norwegians ski on Easter Sunday, a sin for which I can hardly blame them this morning. Lord, I thank thee . . .

It is Norwegian Independence Day, May 17. I leave my apartment at the University of Oslo, go down to the city center with thousands of Norwegians; the day is brilliant with sunshine and national costumes, flags, the parade of children, the newly green birch, the blue sky, lovely fountains. At my feet a teenager, dressed all in black, is lying in a drunken stupor, a thin line of vomit trailing from his lips. Lord, I thank thee . . .

Later that afternoon, as I am leaving Norway, sitting at the airport, talking in the sunshine by an empty tray in which an abandoned ice cream cone is melting, a friend and I express regret that we have not been together more—but what with children, jobs, and travel, there just hasn't been time. Ah, it would be fine if life weren't so full of trivia, even on sabbaticals. If we could only learn to live better, he says. Lord, I thank thee?

A few days later, in Minneapolis, at the graduation of my brother from college, my sister and I are sitting in the bleachers, supporting the sweaty backs of our great-aunt and -uncle, who find bleacher sitting difficult in their old age. We watch people streaming in the door. We know lots of them. My sister and I watch a former teacher of ours greeting old students. She looks at me with tears in her eyes, saying, "It takes a lot of energy to support a community."

Later that summer my sister tells me that at work one day, during the United Fund campaign, an appeal had come to their office. After the appeal, my sister was just about to express shock that there had been so little support from their office (since in their work they often suggest people go to the United Appeal for funds), when she realized that her colleagues were all angry. They were angry at the crass way the money had been asked for, and all vowed piously that they would not give one red cent as long as they were asked in that way. She affirmed the truth of the observation that one is seldom in the presence of religious talk these days, unless it is from people saying why they will not give money. One has to be religious to say "no" there.

Later that summer, we pack up a U-Haul trailer and drive through heat and traffic, through Chicago and other desolations, with all the worldly goods of my little brother on his way to law school. It is a trail of tears. The car overheats, the air conditioner is on the blink, and my eyes run constantly with hay fever. We arrive late Sunday afternoon with the stuff, and begin the ritual of moving in and cleaning—on the theory that the family that cleans together will never part. I observe through my tears and the Lysol and wet rags that this is a real proof of my love for little brother.

And now that I am back from sabbatical, someone says that it must be good to·be back, in the swing of things, with all the routine, though the committee work and teaching is something of a load one could do well without, especially after the sabbatical, when one can really live. People call and ask me to join this, belong to that, make a speech, teach Sunday school, give money. Someplace I hear an alum remark on how awful it is that Luther is always asking for money. The alum sounds more spiritual than his wardrobe looks.

It really does take energy to support a family, a community. It takes money, too. Our tithes, our time, our life. And we should not be surprised that it does. It takes more than good wishes to put on a party. It is not enough to say we really care about each other and then not write letters home, read each other's papers, listen to each other's lectures, give money to our Lutheran colleges. It is through and by visible means that we show love for each other. Life is trivia, but it is through trivia that we glimpse life's larger meanings. To rise above such trivia would be to leave our bodies, to deny the beautiful, the visible, the human, éven the ugly—a denial I do not choose to make, either as poet or Christian.

The Pharisee is much with us. When I think it a waste of time to enter into the community, I sin against it. The most offensive thing about the Pharisee is that he thinks he is not like others. He is even thankful for that. He may do some nice things, but the worst thing is that he thinks he is pure in heart and he is not. No one is.

If there is anything the Bible does say clearly and loudly, it must be that we are like other people, that we are brothers and sisters, brothers and sisters to smelly, miserable, gaudy tourists in Canterbury, boring preachers in Norway, drunks in Oslo. We are a pretty ragged bunch. Any time we think that we can rise above that, we begin to deny the marvelous mixture of God's blessing to us here on earth. And then we must cry God 'a' mercy, mercy, for we have sinned.

And I can tell you this morning, with a full, glad heart, looking out at all of you, my students, my friends, and boring committee partners, that there is mercy aplenty. God sent his son into the world to take flesh like ours, to become what we are, physical and visible. His life on earth among us redeems the time, this time, our life together; the trivia; the boring meetings; the long, hard days; the squabbles in the dorms, with colleagues; lonely weekends; days when nothing seems to go right. Love calls us to the things of this world.

The lady putting money in both boxes is right. For it is of the Lord's mercies that we are not consumed, because his compassions fail not; they are new every morning, and it is that word we must bring each other as we live in God's beautiful world. It is a word of forgiveness and hope, and I bring it to you this morning. Mercy, mercy—God loves us and blesses us.

GRACIA GRINDAL *is associate professor of English at Luther College in Iowa.*

Dry Bones and Rolled Stones

JAMIE R. GUSTAFSON

The hand of the Lord was upon me, and he brought me out by the Spirit of the Lord, and set me down in the midst of the valley; it was full of bones. And he led me round among them; and behold, there were very many upon the valley; and lo, they were very dry. And he said to me, "Son of man, can these bones live?" And I answered, "O Lord God, thou knowest." Again he said to me, "Prophesy to these bones: Behold, I will cause breath to enter you, and you shall live. And I will lay sinews upon you, and will cause flesh to come upon you, and cover you with skin, and put breath in you, and you shall live; and you shall know that I am the Lord."

So I prophesied as I was commanded; and . . . they lived, and stood upon their feet, an exceedingly great host.

Then he said to me, "Son of man, these bones are the whole house of Israel. Behold, they say, 'Our bones are dried up, and our hope is lost; we are clean cut off.' Therefore prophesy and say to them, Thus says the Lord God: 'Behold, I will open your graves, and raise you from your graves, O my people; . . . then you shall know that I, the Lord, have spoken, and I have done it, says the Lord.'"

—EZEKIEL 37:1–14, RSV

If then you have been raised with Christ, seek the things that are above, where Christ is, seated at the right hand of God. Set your mind on things that are above, not the things that are on earth. . . . Here there cannot be Greek and Jew, circumcised and uncircumcised, barbarian, Scythian, slave, free man, but Christ is all, and in all.

—COLOSSIANS 3:1–11, RSV

Now on the first day of the week, Mary Magdalene came to the tomb early, while it was still dark, and saw that the stone had been taken away from the tomb. So she ran and went to Simon Peter and the other disciple, the one whom Jesus loved, and said to them, "They have taken the Lord out of the tomb, and we do not know where they have laid him." Peter then came out with the other disciple, and they went toward the tomb. . . . and [they] saw and believed; for as yet they did not know the scripture, that he must rise from the dead. Then the disciples went back to their homes.

But Mary stood weeping outside the tomb, and as she wept she stooped to look into the tomb; and she saw two angels in white, sitting where the body of Jesus had lain, one at the head and one at the feet. They said to her, "Woman, why are you weeping?" She said to them, "Because they have taken away my Lord, and I do not know where they have laid him." Saying this, she turned round and saw Jesus standing, but she did not know that it was Jesus. Jesus said to her, "Woman, why are you weeping? Whom do you seek?" Supposing him to be the gardener, she said to him, "Sir, if you have carried him away, tell me where you have laid him, and I will take him away." Jesus said to her, "Mary." She turned and said to him in Hebrew, "Rabboni" (which means Teacher). . . . Mary Magdalene went and said to the disciples, "I have seen the Lord."

—JOHN 20:1–18, RSV

In Greek mythology there is a figure named Sisyphus, a man who was doomed by the god Zeus forever to roll a large stone up a hill in hell. Just before the stone reached the top, it would roll backwards, against every effort of Sisyphus. Forever straining at pushing this mighty stone, Sisyphus would spend eternity never accomplishing his task, entirely without hope.

Do you ever feel that sense of endless, hopeless, grinding effort in your life—that a good portion of your life consists largely in rolling a huge stone uphill, an effort in which you are entirely alone and dare not stop? That stone may have one label or many: filling all the requisites for each rung in the corporate ladder, lest you be left behind; being all things to all people at work or at home, so you'll be loved; trying to do something worthwhile to make up for past sin; struggling for achievement so as to be noticed.

Maybe one or more of these is yours; maybe your stone has a different label on it. The point is, you're rolling it uphill, and every day—every week, every month, every year—it becomes heavier and heavier.

And you'd like to stop rolling it, but that seems a hopeless situation.

Ezekiel knew a hopeless situation. He was a prophet to the exiles, to Israel cut off from its homeland, a people in despair.

Led by God to stand overlooking a valley that must have been an old battlefield, he saw that the valley was full of bones, *dry* bones. Dry bones were exceedingly dead, you might say, for the marrow of them—which meant life to the ancients—was dried up.

For the exiles, their hope of restoration to their homeland was dead—"We are clean cut off!" they cried. And Ezekiel, their prophet, stood at that valley, symbol of the grave of their hopes.

You are probably not an exile, but you may stand at the valley of dry bones, at the grave of your hopes. Perhaps as you gaze upon it you see: the death of someone you love; a move away from home that seemed like an exile; a debilitating illness or handicap; the breakup of your marriage; alienation from your family—or some other death of hope.

The message I would share with you today is: You no longer have to mourn in the valley of dry bones or struggle to roll that stone uphill, for you have a God who knows your condition and has conquered *death,* which makes dry bones of our lives, and *sin,* our alienation from God, our aloneness that keeps us forever fearfully rolling the stone uphill.

Ezekiel was prophet to the exiles, but he was prophet *for* God. And so, as he stood at the grave of their hopes, he listened for God's word.

"Son of man, can these bones live?"

"O Lord God, thou knowest."

He did not say, "This is hopeless, absurd, impossible!" He gave the situation in faith to God. And a second word came: "Prophesy to these bones. . . ."

And he did as he was commanded—prophesied in faith, and the Spirit of the Lord filled those bones, and they lived.

Faith stands at the edge of the absurd, the impossible, and reaches out to God.

Ezekiel took the step that must be the first step for each of us—turning in faith to God.

But what is the ground of our hope for turning in faith to God?

See the dark garden that dawn, when Mary came to the tomb, the cave, with its huge stone that had marked and sealed the death of her hopes—and found the stone *rolled away*.

Peter and John, whom she told, came running, entered the tomb, saw and *believed*. And from that moment on, their lives were changed. Someone has said that the early disciples, the early church, made no attempt to *explain* the resurrection—it explained *them*. They were no longer a huddled lot of frightened people, but a people who moved forward courageously with a message of undying hope. No longer enslaved to their fear, they awaited the outpouring of the Holy Spirit and then moved forward to be the living church.

The God who did the impossible, who defeated death—by no mere resuscitation experience, but by *resurrection*—the God who rolled the stone away for us that first Easter is the God who will raise you from your valley of dry bones, is the God who will redeem you from your endless rolling of your stone uphill.

That's what it means to say God conquered sin and death by raising Jesus Christ in power. God conquered death—both the physical death we all face and the death of our hopes. God conquered sin—the power it had to hold us chained to our past, forever rolling our stones uphill.

Have you been afraid to stop pushing at your stone, fearing that if you did, you'd somehow lose control of all those parts of your life and be crushed?

Because of Easter, you *can* stop pushing at it, but you have to take your hands from it and turn with them outstretched toward God. *That*'s where faith comes in—the faith that *God will not let you be crushed*.

And God, who gave his own son to live and die for you, God who raised Jesus Christ, God who loves you enough to show you that nothing will separate you from that love, God will not let you be crushed when you turn away from your stone to him.

And how are we to live, once we have turned in faith to God?

Blondin, the famous tightrope walker, said to a man one day, "Do you believe I can cross Niagara Falls on a tightrope with a man on my back?"

Enthusiastically the man answered, "Oh, yes!"

Blondin looked searchingly at him and asked, "Will you be that man?"

To *say* we turn in faith is one thing, to *live* it is another. But when you turn to God, accepting the gift he has given you in Jesus Christ and receiving baptism, you are entered upon a new life and helped to live it out.

In the passage from Colossians are the words "put on the new nature." They mean that you actualize what has already happened; you accept what God has done for *you* and in loving obedience enter the new life given you in baptism.

You put to death many things: immorality, covetousness, malice, and others—but not in the old way of trying to bundle them all up and roll them uphill. No longer do you try to make putting them away the *means* to your salvation. Rather, putting them to death is a *consequence* of your relationship with Jesus Christ. Moved from within ("I will put a new heart within you"), joyfully accepting what God has *already done for you,* you will put away malice, slander, and all the others, for you will want more and more to express the love of Christ which dwells in your heart.

Ezekiel prophesied *with faith* at the grave of his people's hopes.

Peter and John saw *and believed* at the tomb where the stone was rolled away.

Will you turn in faith to God—turn from your uphill struggle, turn at the grave of your hopes?

Turn to him, and he will set you free. Your dry bones will live again with his Holy Spirit within them, and you will no longer have to roll your heavy stone, because God, who loves *you,* has already rolled the heaviest stone away.

THE REV. JAMIE R. GUSTAFSON *is pastor of The First Church of Christ, Congregational, in Bedford, Massachusetts. She has served as a preaching instructor at Andover Newton Theological School. Her joys in parish service include preaching, worship, pastoral care, and the dedicated laity and staff with whom she shares her ministry.*

The Impatience of Job
EUGENIA LEE HANCOCK

Has not man a hard service upon earth, and are not his days like the days of a hireling? Like a slave who longs for the shadow, and like a hireling who looks for his wages, so I am allotted months of emptiness, and nights of misery are apportioned to me. When I lie down I say, "When shall I arise?" But the night is long, and I am full of tossing till the dawn. My flesh is clothed with worms and dirt; my skin hardens, then breaks out afresh. My days are swifter than a weaver's shuttle, and come to their end without hope.

Remember that my life is a breath; my eye will never again see good. The eye of him who sees me will behold me no more; while thy eyes are upon me, I shall be gone. As the cloud fades and vanishes, so he who goes down to Sheol does not come up; he returns no more to his house, nor does his place know him any more.

Therefore I will not restrain my mouth; I will speak in the anguish of my spirit; I will complain in the bitterness of my soul.

—JOB 7:1–11, RSV

The words of Job leave us anything but comfortable. They are the words of a man in pain and misery. They are words of a suffering man, a man whose life, as he had known it, was utterly destroyed. His is a story of horror.

Job was not underprivileged, or a person who had two strikes against him because of his race, sex, or economic background. He was a wealthy man, with a good home and wife and kids. Job owned a prosperous family business, servants, and land. He was a good citizen, a moral and blameless man, respected in the community for his fair and honest dealings. He was Godfearing. He took his faith seriously.

Suddenly there was a drastic change. He lost his money; he lost his prestige and family; he lost his friends. Once a man of power, respect, and security, he was reduced to nothing more than scabs and sores. He had lost everything, even his health. Job crashed like the stock market in 1929—just as hard and just as swiftly. He hit bottom.

The story of Job is threatening—even terrifying, if we admit it. His words cry out from the depths of suffering so raw, so real, and so naked it makes us cringe. The story of Job whispers reminders of our own frailty and suggests the possibility that such suffering might be our fate. We feel relieved that Job's situation is not ours, and we count our blessings, or knock on wood.

We don't like to think about his story because we do not want to dwell on the morbid or remind ourselves that such suffering could, in fact, invade our lives. So we shut out all reminders, all hints of such pain. We look for the comforts that might distract or insulate us from those fears.

And yet, Job's story also possesses a frightening quality of familiarity. We all know stories of bizarre misfortune and personal tragedy. Stories that we repeat in hushed tones or gossip about:

> Stories that at once intrigue and repel us.
> And for a moment,
> we stifle a wave of panic, or feel embarrassed, or
> remind ourselves that it is none of our business.
> But we know, too,
> the sting of personal tragedy:
> the death of a loved one;
> or the loss of a job,
> broken dreams, broken loves . . . the horror of cruelty,
> the pain of defeat, or rejection, or illness,
> alienation . . . estranged or confused relationships
> secrets . . .
> hunger
> unfulfilled want

> unfulfilled need
> we all know pain
> we all have suffered
> we all know the experience of suffering:
>   in diverse ways
>   and to different degree.

Even if we have never admitted it to ourselves. Or anyone else.

All over our city there are scenes of suffering that haunt us like bad dreams. It is easier to look away from humanity, almost unrecognizable, lying barefoot in a pool of blood and wine, or in a doorway or under newspaper, than to look into eyes that reflect a tortured soul. It is easier to avoid the pictures of child slaughter and genocide in the newspaper than to confront the irrational dimensions of evil and suffering in this world. Easier to ignore the signs of suffering that suggest anything less than perfect order. It is easier to reject the "suffering" and "alienated" than to feel our own pain or remember our tragedies, of which "they" remind us.

The theologian Simone Weil writes, "Everyone despises the afflicted to some extent, although practically no one is conscious of it." Fear is the root of hatred.

I find myself identifying with Job. I, too, was prosperous. As a seminary student, I was graced with scholarships and financial security, privileged to study at an outstanding seminary. Employed and eager to get on with the business of life. I was shaping my future.

On September 13, 1975, the arthritis that had lain dormant in my body for five years returned with such fierceness that the pain was so intense that I could neither sleep nor function, but only sit up and hold my swollen joints. I had seen my grandmother's body eroded by arthritis and was terrified that her fate could be my own. My personality changed as I grew chronically fatigued and depressed. I did my best to ignore the truth my body was expressing: that I was racked with pain and inflammation to the extent that my joints refused to perform their expected tasks like walking to the grocery or reaching for a plate in the cupboard. I could not admit to myself the depth of my sickness until I crashed so hard that even my survival was in question. Once strong and self-confident, I felt defeated and ashamed. Only weeks earlier, I had been working in a stable, handling horses twelve hours a day. I could no longer walk, but only shuffle. I was bent into a woman thrice my age.

I did not know what I had done to deserve this. My community of peers changed. I began to notice who took one step at a time getting on and off a bus, because I did. I knew the utter frustration of dependency, the rage that swells when one is unable to put on socks, or lift a cup to drink. I know the slow burn of resentment that comes when another withdraws a handshake at the sight of braces, or when eyes study a crippled walk. Now I have seen both sides.

As a victim of rheumatoid arthritis, I now know that suffering is normal. It is not the exception in life, it is the rule. My eyes were opened as never before. Because I suffered, I saw suffering in others I was blind to before.

> We suffer but do not talk about it. But suffering is
> the human condition: we are wounded and scarred,
> broken and bleeding
> hurt and hurting.

It is common practice to look at Job as a paragon of virtue. We are often reminded of the "patience of Job" when we are faced with an especially trying situation that we have no choice but to endure. But to speak of the "patience of Job" is a gross misrepresentation of the book, since it takes into account only the beginning and the ending of the story, ignoring the intermitting thirty-five chapters that comprise the bulk of the book.

In the beginning of the book, we are introduced to a Job who is a pious and mute sufferer, willfully accepting the succession of personal disasters, without question or rage.

This tolerance, however, does not last long. After a seven-day silence, we meet a Job who is anything but the pious and patient sufferer, enduring the ultimate test. Rather, we meet an anguished and angry man who unleashes vehement protests and blasphemous tirades against the injustice of his suffering. It is almost shocking, if not wholly unexpected, to discover such rage against God recorded in the Bible. Job held nothing back. He was even willing to curse God—even in the face of the religious expectation that he would die if he indeed did curse God, because his life was not worth living. It was hell.

Job's friends, hearing of his misfortune, came to comfort him, offering him little sympathy, and some, not so friendly advice. They are shocked by his railings, counseling him to "take it like a man" with a word or tear. They were convinced that the turn of events in Job's life was clearly the will of God and unquestionably demonstrated that Job had committed a grave sin. They are convinced that Job's suffering is punishment from God. His friends spent their energies trying to extract a confession of guilt from the suffering Job, certain that, once he had confessed, Job's former life of prosperity would be restored. They are quick to judge, unswerving in their righteousness, and persistent in their defense of the doctrine of individual retribution, that Old Testament notion that suffering is the result of personal sin. The righteous prosper, and the wicked are punished.

Job's prosperity was viewed as a sign of his favor with God, and his misfortune as a judgment upon his wickedness. The attitude touted by Job's three—and yet a fourth—unfeeling examiners concluded that Job's suffering, his pain and his misery, was punishment for something Job had done. Their task, then, was to find out just what he had done.

The doctrine of individual retribution is still with us today. My mind can never let go of the question, "Why did this happen to me?" I am always looking for an answer and inevitably end up searching my heart and my history for the action responsible for my suffering. I sort through the list of sins I am guilty of committing, looking for a conviction. I assumed that somehow I was responsible for my condition. I was embarrassed and ashamed to admit to others the extent of my illness, afraid that it would reveal some truth about me of which I was unaware. I feared rejection and loss of respect, I feared judgment of incompetence, I feared being broken—obviously broken. What had I done? Why was it I that possessed this personal demon? Surely because of weakness, lack of faith, or the condition of my soul.

Those who will not recognize the suffering in all our lives

tend to hold those who suffer responsible for their condition. "You get what you deserve." "It's their problem and no one else's." "She made her bed, so she can lie in it." In the late nineteenth century, the "gospel of wealth" expressed the widespread belief that poverty reflected poor character. That attitude remains at the heart of our economic and domestic policies today. We continue to blame the poor for their poverty. On the other hand, if the afflicted are not blamed for their condition, their suffering is often romanticized. We are convinced that suffering is somehow good for us—cleansing the soul, bringing us closer to God. We often hear how illness is a special burden, or even a blessing for us to bear, or people dismiss the tragedy of a retarded child as a special trial visited upon the parents by God to strengthen one's character or teach a lesson.

Surely such rationalizations are attempts to cope with enormously difficult situations, but such claims, in fact, imply that God is inflicting the pain and the hurt, the crisis and the tragedy into our lives. Suffering can bring enlightenment, patience, and increased knowledge of God, for God is indeed at the edge of survival. Terrence de Près, in his book *The Survivors*, tries to capture and recreate the spirit and the life that were present in the midst of the concentration camps in Nazi Germany. Although he never actually names it such, it is clearly the presence of God in and among the lives of the suffering that continually provided strength and sustenance for those caught in the web of suffering and evil. Although God is at the edges of survival, it is wrong to create or tolerate senseless suffering for the sake of enlightenment. All these experiences—cleansing the soul, enlightenment, communion with God—all are possible in experiences other than suffering. Besides, there is so much suffering in the world, of which we are a part and which we cannot handle, we need not create our own. However, God is present where there is suffering: God is indeed present in suffering.

And so Jesus concerned his ministry with the suffering of others on all levels—the blind and the mentally ill, the desperate, the searching, the hungry, the outcast, the robber, the prostitute. And Jesus himself suffered. On the cross, Jesus himself suffered deeply. In Jesus' suffering we see the face of God. In the face of Jesus, we see the suffering of humanity. In the face of Jesus, we see the suffering of God.

A friend of mine, with whom I attended seminary, spent a year of his training working with Mother Theresa, a Roman Catholic nun whose ministry is among the discarded and dying in Calcutta, India. One day my friend was making rounds with one of the brothers when they came upon a boy whose flesh was rotting and stank, and whose mouth was filled with maggots. The brother went to the boy, picked him up, held him, and began to clean out his mouth.

Shaken, Bruce asked the brother how he could manage to touch the boy. "There was Christ," he replied. Humanity—we—are inextricably linked and unified as one, one Body. We act out our recognition and acknowledgment of this reality in holy communion. Suffering is universal. Suffering is not your suffering, or my suffering, but *our* suffering.

In his life, Jesus experienced suffering as well as triumph. In the Matthew account of the crucifixion, there is vivid natural imagery that describes the state of the earth at Jesus' moment of death. There is an earthquake; rocks break open; the curtain in the temple was torn open. It was as if the whole creation expressed and experienced the grief of God. God suffered when his son was crucified.

And God suffers when God's children suffer, as parents cry out over a child who is hurt and in pain. God suffers when we do. God suffers because I do, and you do. In the words of Alfred North Whitehead, "God is the fellow sufferer who understands."

The idea that God would inflict senseless and meaningless suffering upon me or you or anyone of us is sadistic and perverse. How, then, could we believe in a God after concentration camps of Auschwitz and Dachau? To ascribe senseless and meaningless suffering to God, to simply interpret pain as God's judgment, is to deny the reality of evil. And to make that mistake is fatal; we lose our lives and we lose our humanity. In the faces of the suffering, we see daily crucifixions.

God knows we deny ourselves the right to suffer. We relativize our situation, telling ourselves it is indulgent to allow ourselves to suffer, that we don't have the time or the right to suffer, that the next person is worse off than we. We're taught to count our blessings, not to share our suffering. But the truth is, we're all suffering; it's the human experience. But if we cannot acknowledge or claim our own suffering, recognize our hurt, admit to our tragedy, then we truly cannot have true compassion for others. Identification is the wellspring of compassion. In you, I see myself. We must acknowledge our fears of those who are different from ourselves, instead of the fear and insecurity (is it catching?) their differences bring. If we face the fact that we are afraid, we may touch the terrifying issue of our own death.

Job is not a stoic hero; in fact, his words of self-defense clearly made his companions uncomfortable. Job is a hero because his incessant self-defense cuts right through the heart of the mythology that links suffering to sin. As Job refused to believe his suffering incriminated him, he frees us from the guilt and pain of judgment. We need not hide our suffering in embarrassed silence, fearful that it will incriminate us. We can join Job in expressing our rage against pointless and unjust suffering in our lives.

Throughout the poem, Job pleads his case to God, refusing to accept blame for his misfortunes, holding fast to the truth that his suffering was senseless and unjust. He did not deny his suffering or mutely resign himself to it, but he recognized it without saying it was deserved. And he would not restrain himself from speaking out—he refused to remain silent.

Job's unrelenting demands for justice express his faith in a God of justice and mercy. The theologian Ernst Bloch comments that Job is pious precisely because he does not believe, which is to say that Job rejects the primitive beliefs in a God lacking compassion, mercy, and feeling. Job is a hero because he does not accept the blame for his condition, he refuses to accept the judgment of his friends. Job finally said, "Enough is enough," that he would rather be dead than endure the quality of life he was subject to. And by taking the risk to curse the darkness, Job teaches us that God can tolerate our rage. In allowing himself to cry out against the injustice of his suffering and the inhumanity of his condition, Job said *no* to the realities that are wrong and evil. Expressing this rage against injustice enabled Job to say *no* to evil he might otherwise have tolerated by accepting the blame. If we deny our suffering, we deny the vision of what could be. For the vision of wholeness, the vision of repair grows out of the recognition and acknowledgment of the brokenness. If we deny the evil, we eliminate the chance for a better world, and hand it over to the devil. Like Job, we must cry out in anguish and anger against the suffering and injustice in our world and in our lives.

If we are the people of God, then we must join God in the struggle against diseases, hunger, oppression—all evils that cause suffering in our world. We must claim our own suffering and address the suffering of others. In the story of the man at the pool recorded in John, that was read this morning, Jesus addressed the man, inquiring of him if he wished to be healed. Jesus offered this man the chance to tell his story (to Jesus), and the man said that he couldn't move fast enough to benefit from the healing waters because he was crowded out; that he had no one to lift him into the pool. And so the man told his story to Jesus, and Jesus knew what to do, for Jesus knew what the man needed.

I believe we are called, therefore, to use our resources and strength and join God in the struggle, and, like Job, have courage to raise our voices and say no to the injustices of this world. If we can claim our suffering to one another, then we will discover that the story is larger than just your story or my story; that it is our story of suffering and that we are free to reject the judgments of others and our own guilt. If we tell our story, then others will know if we need help, and we can know what kind of help others need. And so, like Jesus with the man, we can heal one another.

THE REV. EUGENIA LEE HANCOCK *is assistant minister and minister for Healing and Health Care at Central Presbyterian Church in New York City. She also serves as program associate to Professional Church Leadership of the National Council of Churches in the area of Women in Ministry.*

The Enigmatic God
CARTER HEYWARD

We are told that upon completion of "The Hallelujah Chorus," Handel fell to his knees, beside himself, overwhelmed because he had seen God—and the *beauty*, the *power*, the *majesty* of God were extraordinary.

Elie Wiesel, incarcerated in a concentration camp during World War II, tells of having watched a young boy his own age (about ten) being hanged by the Nazi soldiers. As the boy writhed in agony, refusing to give in to the rope, one of the witnesses asked another, "Where is God?" The response was silence. The boy continued to struggle, and the man asked again, "Where is God?" Still, silence. Finally, as the boy succumbed, the man asked again, "Where is God?" And his fellow prisoner replied, "God is there. Hanging on the gallows." Wiesel speaks of the *utterly helpless* God.

What of this God, this terrible good, this holy terror, this Father, Son, and Holy Spirit Trinity? This Mother Goddess giving us birth and taking us back again into her womb the earth? This God of many faces, to whom have been ascribed many names? *Who is our God?* I ask, believing, to quote one of my students, that "God does not mechanically answer our questions, but rather moves us to ask them." And unless we encounter God honestly—probing, seeking, risking offense—we do not encounter God at all.

In the beginning, long before there was any idea of "God," something stirred. In that cosmic moment pulsating in possibility, God breathed into space, and groaning in passion and pain and hope, gave birth to creation. We cannot remember this easily, for we cannot easily bear to remember the pain and the hope of our own beginning. But it was good.

It was far better than we can imagine. For coming forth from God—in God, with God, by God—(as were all created things), we were shaped by God, in God's own image, formed in the being of God, daughters and sons of God. We are living reflections of and witnesses to God's own possibility. It was very, very good. For being human meant being *with* God. (To be *without* God would be not to be at all.)

James Weldon Johnson suggests that God created us because God was *lonely*. Various "process" theologians suggest that God created us because God needed us to help God continue to become. It may be that God created us simply because it is the nature of God to create, or that God created us because God, having begun to "come to life" Godself, realized that the only way to experience life would be to share it.

And so we were created in God's own being, to move with God, in God, by God, into the passion and the pain and the wonder of creation.

Long after the dawn of creation, a small group of people in the Middle East began to speak to one another of God. Other people believed that there were many gods: gods of rain, of sun, of war, of fertility, vying for supremacy. The people of Israel believed, however, that there is in fact one God, who is the creator of all and who has created us in God's own image.

Furthermore, the people of Israel heard God promise them that God was with them on the earth, empowering them to do what it is in the being of God to do: to LOVE, to reach out to one another and to creation itself, aware of the worth and value of every created person and thing. God showed the people of Israel that God was/is not a far-distant God, spinning holy wheels off high in the sky, but rather passionately involved in creation, history, and human activity.

Long before Jesus, God made Godself known as One immersed in the affairs of being human. Human history was, in fact, sacred history, the story of God's own being moving in creation itself.

The people of Israel wanted to know more about this God in whose being they were bound up. So Moses spoke to God and asked God what he, Moses, was to tell the people God's name was. (For the Israelites, there was much in a name; a name was a revelation of a person's true character.)

And God responded. God did not give a long list of credentials or a speech about power, authority, and might. God did not "spell things out," but responded simply, "I AM WHO I AM" (or, in other translations, "I AM WHAT I AM," or "I WILL BE WHAT I WILL BE").

God could hardly have given a more enigmatic reply, the sort that would be totally unacceptable to most of us, to admissions committees, teachers, or psychiatrists. We would be likely to hear "I am who I am" (in response to "Who are you?") as outrageous, impudent, defiant, disturbed. Certainly evasive. God *was* evasive. Moses could not pin God down. Approaching God in fear and tremor, seeking clarification, we are met with a riddle. *I am who I am.*

What about God is God saying?

Could it be that God is *not* being evasive, but clear, straightforward and to the point? And that the point is that God *is*, in fact, evasive, elusive, not one to be pinned down, boxed into categories and expectations! God will be what God will be:

> God will hang on the gallows.
> God will inspire, fill, overwhelm Handel with power and splendor.
> God will be battered as a wife, a child, a nigger, a faggot.
> God will judge with righteousness, justice, mercy those who batter, burn, sneer, discriminate, or harbor prejudice.
> God will have a mastectomy.
> God will experience the wonder of giving birth.
> God will be handicapped.
> God will run the marathon.
> God will win.
> God will lose.

God will be down and out, suffering, dying.
God will be bursting free, coming to life, for
God will be who God will be.

If this is so, then God is suggesting to the people of Israel
and to us that the very minute we think we "have" God, God will
surprise us. As we search in fire and earthquaking, God will be
in the still, small voice. As we listen in silent meditation, God will
be shouting protests on the street. God is warning us that we had
best not try to find our security in any well-defined concept or
category of what is "Godly"—for the minute we believe we're
into God, God is off again and calling us forth into some
unknown place.

God is saying something prickly to any of us who believe
that our way is God's way—hence the only way. God is alerting
us to the fact that God's own growth and movement will not be
stunted by our low tolerance for ambiguity and change. God will
not be confined to our expectations of who God "ought" to be.

And God surely knows that most of us cannot bear much
God. When God says, "I AM WHO I AM," our characteristic
response is one of utter denial. We do not easily hear what God
is saying. Instead, we opt for the creation of our own idol, one in
which we can believe: a god-idol who, as Sister Corita Kent said,
is "like a big Bayer aspirin: Take a little God, and you'll feel
better."

But, what if:

In seeking to feel better, we are avoiding God's moving us
toward growth?

In seeking God always as light, we are missing God as
darkness?

In avoiding change, we are missing God's plea for us to
move into the wonder of some unknown possibility?

In perceiving God as our Father, we are refusing to be
nurtured at the breast of God our Mother?

In seeing God only in our own colors, shapes, styles, and
ways of life, we are blinded to God's presence in others' colors,
forms, and ways of being?

In looking for God in the magnanimous, that which is great,

we are overlooking God in the most unremarkable places of our own lives?

In running from death, in trying to hold onto life, we are utterly missing the presence and power of God in aging, in letting go, in dying itself, in moving graciously along with God?

In perceiving God always in that which is sacred, holy otherworldly, religious, we are failing to see God in the secular, this world, the office, the home, the classroom, our day-to-day relationships, work and play?

What if, in seeking God always in the Bible, we are missing God in the newspaper?

What if simply to be with God, live with God, know God, love God is enough—in living and in dying?

Might it be that being human is simply *being with God*—and seeking, and finding, God's presence in all reality?

That being alive is both a terror and a wonder, an adventure in living and dying—all with God, in God, in which terror and death do not lose their sting—but are experienced graciously.

The people of Israel had to struggle with this enigma. Their expectations of a Messiah who was to save the nation, beat down the enemies, rout out the wicked, suggests also Israel's needs, and ours, for a God we can count on to bring us light, life, and victory. I AM WHO I AM is hard to bear.

And Jesus Christ did not come to clarify the enigmatic God, to help us put God into an incarnate box that we can carry around and show off as "God." Jesus did not come to reveal God's power, God's might, God's victory. Rather, Jesus came as one created in God, by God, empowered to move with God, into the pain, the passion, and the wonder of creation itself. Jesus accepted the vocation of being truly human, in the image of an enigmatic God.

In Jesus, we are able to discern a person in whose human being God was made manifest, and a God in whose holy Be-ing human life was lived fully. "Christ" is that way of being in which God and humanity, the creator and the created, the infinite and the finite, are experienced and manifest as One way of being.

Jesus Christ lived and died to show us what being human is all about. In Jesus, we see what it means to be a daughter or a son of God, to bear God's name; in Jesus, we perceive that being human, in the image of I AM WHO I AM, means simply that *we are who we are!*

As God's namesake, Jesus was who he was, free of all expectations and categories, defiant of any expectation that would stunt his growth as a person of God.

Jesus lived and died allowing himself, by God's grace, the freedom to be himself, regardless of customs, laws, and expectations that he be some other.

The people who wished him to be a political zealot found him to be a person of prayerful spirituality; those who wanted him to be a pious, sweet man discovered they had on their hands an offensive activist. To those who wanted him to be Messiah, he retorted, "Get thee behind me, Satan." And in the presence of those who wanted him to explain himself, he stood silently. The enigmatic God reflected in enigmatic personhood.

When I probe the depths of Jesus Christ, I realize that as Jesus was who he was, so too am I put here by God to be who I am. Jesus could not be who I am. I cannot be who Jesus was. My vocation as a person of God is not to imitate Jesus—not to try to recreate the being of a person who lived in a different world, in a different time, with different life-experiences and possibilities. My vocation as a person of God is to live with God, in God, for God, in my own time, as graciously as I can.

Our business, our birthrights, and our beings are in God, here, now. As such, with individual interests and persuasions, we are together in One Christ: a way of being in which God's Being and human being are experienced as one.

There are four qualities which, I believe, are ways of being I AM WHO I AM. No one of the four can stand alone. They are overlapping pieces of a whole cloth, the tapestry of creation itself: Wisdom, Passion, Justice, and Prayer.

• **Wisdom.** Wisdom is a virtue close to the heart of God, we are told in scripture. Wisdom is the perception of the wholeness of all that is. The wise person, like God, knows that there is more to life than her/his own little world; that there is more to living than pursuing happiness. The wise person will face reality, ambiguity, and tension. She/he is able to live into, not flee from, matters of life and death.

Moreover, she will do everything she can to deal creatively, realistically, empathetically, with conviction, in her everyday comings and goings. She is no fool. She is, in the words of St. Matthew, "as wise as a serpent, as innocent as a dove," aware that she is, God with her, put in this world, here, now, to participate fully in the affairs of this world—loving this world as God does—and using everything at her disposal to work cleverly, carefully, wisely for the good of the whole.

• **Passion.** As wisdom allows us to perceive the breadth of God and of creation, the wholeness of it all, so passion allows us to discern the depth. To be passionately committed, passionately involved, passionately immersed in God, in life itself, is to be involved and immersed in enigma. To experience one's own dying as the boy hangs on the gallows, to realize one's own shortcomings and capacities for wrongdoings when Nixon resigns, to realize the extent to which living involves dying, and to know that to the extent that we are afraid to die, we are afraid to live! In passion, we find our resources, our energy, our courage, our motivation, a way of being human as Jesus was human. In passion, we are aware that we are infused by the Spirit of God. (This is what birth is all about, what creation is, and what baptism signifies.) We are created as Spirited people—Holy Spirited people.

Immersed in passion, we are aware that the Book of Common Prayer (even the new one!) misses the point when it says, "Christ has died, Christ is risen, Christ will come again." In fact, *Christ is dying, Christ is rising, Christ is here again!* And the wise passionate person will know that Christ has as much to do with the secular arenas of our lives as with the sacred; as much to do with the profane as with the holy; as much to do with the sexual, the political, the social, as with the spiritual. The passionate person who is wise will realize that God is just as present in the kitchen, the classroom, the hospital, the prison, the bed, as in church. The passionate person is one who can cut through to the heart of the matter, whatever the occasion, and discover God.

• **Justice.** Suppose Jesus' friends had advised him to speak only

of God and to stay out of religious and secular politics. Suppose
they had warned him not to offend people. What do you
suppose he'd have said? The Bible as a whole speaks of justice as
"right-relationship" between and among people. Justice presup-
poses community as fundamental to human life with God. In
justice, there is no such thing as a person living simply for
him/herself. I am suspicious of anyone who tells me she or he
has "found the Lord," or been "converted to Christ," or is
"committed to Jesus" if that person is not passionately committed to justice for *all* people—black, yellow, red, white; poor,
rich; straight, gay; sophisticated, simple; well-educated, poorly
educated; sick, healthy; male and female.

Some years ago, yearning for justice, I was saddened and
angered by white governors blocking the doors to schools and
universities to prevent black people from entering. Today,
although the racial crisis in this country is far from resolved,
other issues cry out for justice. And I am fired up by, and
compelled to call to account, state legislators who willingly put
their own reelection, economic interests, and their own insecuri-
ties above clearly and simply affirming that "equality of rights
under law shall not be denied or abridged by the United States
or by any state on account of sex." I do not believe that a person
who is truly aware of his/her birthright and responsibility to be
with God in ongoing creation can sit back silently in this world. I
believe we are compelled and empowered to risk whatever we
must risk to create, with God, a climate in which *all* people can
be who they are. It is a matter of doing justice, of standing up to
be counted, a stand infused by the passion of the Holy Spirit;
informed by wise perception of the wholeness, the breadth, the
interdependence of the issues at hand; and empowered by
prayer.

• **Prayer.** The Gospel that speaks most explicitly about social
activism, Luke, is also the Gospel in which Jesus is most often
portrayed at prayer. Prayer is the opening up of oneself to the
presence and power of God, perceiving what is invisible to the
eye and hearing what is inaudible to the ear.

Without prayer, passion may become restless, manic activity. Without prayer, wisdom is empty and becomes "intellectual-
izing," spinning conceptual wheels to no particular end. (With-

out prayer, for example, theology may talk *about* God, but cannot draw us further *into* God.) Without prayer, justice is doomed to disillusionment, because we are unable to see beyond what the eye can see, and all we see is injustice. This terror may lead us eventually to rage, to futile outcry, to apathy; to feelings of helplessness, violence, or suicide. With prayer, we hear and see that something is happening, stirring, moving, coming forth out of the awful pains and groans of labor and travail. Something is being born again and again wherever there is any justice, any wisdom, any passion. And, in prayer, we know well that this something is God—in us, with us, for us, carrying us along.

In the beginning of all that is coming into being, something is stirring, pulsating with possibility. The Spirit of God is breathing forth. Groaning in painful hope, God is giving us new birth, bringing us into ways of being who we are, empowering us to live our lives. God is drawing us into the terror and the wonder of being human, of finding God in ourselves and in the world, and, in the words of the poet Ntozake Shange, of "loving God fiercely." It is a way of being in which all our laughter is at the heart of God, and all our tears are streams of living water. In the name of God, I AM WHO I AM.

CARTER HEYWARD, *Ph.D., M.Div., is associate professor of Theology at the Episcopal Divinity School in Cambridge, Massachusetts. She is a graduate of Columbia University and Union Theological Seminary, and was ordained an Episcopal priest in 1974. She serves on the Boards of the National Gay Task Force, the Feminist Theological Institute, and the Women's Theological Center in Cambridge.*

This Ministry: God's Mercy . . . Our Hope

ROSEMARY KELLER

I am powerfully drawn to St. Paul through the scripture lesson from the fourth chapter of 2 Corinthians. In these verses, beginning with the words "having this ministry by the mercy of God, we do not lose heart," Paul gives a deeply personal testimony of his ministry in Jesus Christ. The Paul we encounter here is straightforward, honest, vulnerable about his experience as a servant of God among the people. He wore no mask in his relationship with the Corinthians but was a real person whose strength and weakness were revealed as he shared the Gospel with them.

One thing that Paul is doing in his openness with these people is setting the record straight about the integrity of his ministry. He has been wounded by unjust criticism heaped upon him and is justifying the validity of his ministry to his congregation. False leaders had come to Corinth to the congregation Paul had founded. In their exercise of leadership, they deliberately sought to undermine the authority of Paul—and they succeeded.

A spirit of contentiousness developed in the congregation, "a gifted, strongheaded, and unsteady church." Paul wrote this letter filled with love and pain for his people. Both the pain which they had inflicted on themselves and on him, and the unshakable affection which he felt for the people come through in 2 Corinthians.

It is a model of ministry that Paul shares with us today, a ministry of authenticity. His authority for ministry came from no order of clerical office in a constitutionally organized church. There was no distinction in the church at the early date of about 57 A.D., when this letter was written to the Corinthians, between categories of "clergy" and "laity." Paul was part of the *laos*, the whole people of God. His authority came from a call from Jesus Christ to stop persecuting and start serving. Let me read again some of his words from 2 Corinthians 4:

> Therefore, having this ministry by the mercy of God, we do not lose heart. We have renounced disgraceful, underhanded ways; we refuse to practice cunning or to tamper with God's word, but by the open statement of the truth we would commend ourselves to every person's conscience in the sight of God. . . . What we preach is not ourselves, but Jesus Christ as Lord, with ourselves as your servants for Jesus' sake. . . . But we have this treasure in earthen vessels, to show that the transcendent power belongs to God and not to us. We are afflicted in every way, but not crushed; perplexed, but not driven to despair; persecuted, but not forsaken; struck down, but not destroyed; always carrying in the body the death of Jesus, so that the life of Jesus may also be manifested in our bodies.
>
> —2 CORINTHIANS 4:1–10, RSV

I believe that every one of us can identify with the ministry about which Paul speaks here. Because of the grace of God and the hard work of God's servants, we have been brought into a mutual ministry shared by lay and clergy, women and men, today.

The ministry of the whole people of God must not be taken for granted. It has not always been so. It was not until 1870, eighty-six years after American Methodism was organized, that lay*men* were sanctioned as part of the governing body of the church in the General Conference of the Methodist Episcopal Church. Two groups broke away from the Methodist Episcopal

Church during these years, primarily to permit lay representation: the Methodist Protestant Church and the Wesleyan Methodist Church. Similarly, in the United Brethren Church, it was not until 1889, eighty-five years after the founding of that denomination, that laymen were granted legislative authority at General Conference, along with ordained ministers.

Further, we must recognize that the word "layman" was not construed to mean women as well as men when the denominations were founded. The United Brethren Church expanded laity to include laywomen among their delegates four years after laymen were admitted to governing structures, but it took thirty-four years in the Methodist Episcopal Church, until 1906, when women were finally recognized as laity.

Similarly, the ministry of women as ordained clergy has only much more recently been affirmed. The United Brethren Church sanctioned ordination of women in 1889, but when that denomination merged with the Evangelical Church in 1946, the practice of licensing and ordination of women was quietly abandoned. The ordination of women at the 1956 General Conference of the Methodist Church climaxed a movement begun seventy-six years before, when women first sought to be ordained. The movement for ordination of women in the Methodist Church took four years longer to be successful than the movement for women's voting rights in secular society.

It has taken a long time to recover the vision of the ministry of all Christians. Throughout this history, however, there have been women and men who took courageous stands within the mainstream of the church on behalf of an authentic ministry shared by the whole people of God.

Over 125 years ago, in 1853, Luther Lee preached at the ordination service of Antoinette Brown in the First Congregational Church of South Butler, New York. Antoinette Brown was the first woman ever to be ordained in the United States.

Basing his sermon on the text from Galatians 3:28, "There is neither Jew nor Greek, there is neither slave nor free, . . . for you are all one in Christ Jesus," Lee concluded that "in the church, of which Christ is the only head . . . there is no distinction of persons as under the law, males are not preferred before females, for ye are all one, in respect to dignity and privileges

under the Gospel dispensation." Certainly Luther Lee's un-
equivocal statement, and his witness as a man at the first
ordination of a woman, was the strongest affirmation that the
ministry of all Christians is not just a lay cause, or just a woman's
cause, but a human cause which is rooted in the Gospel of Jesus
Christ.

Phoebe Palmer has witnessed to the authentic ministry of
Jesus Christ to me. She was one of the great lay evangelists of
Methodism in the late nineteenth century, who preached
throughout the world. In her Tuesday Afternoon Holiness
Meetings, held in her home in New York City, she drew together
a most diverse group of white and black Christians, ranging in
status from bishops to domestic servants, to share their witnesses
for Jesus Christ. She led one revival in the Methodist church in
Evanston, at which Frances E. Willard received entire sanctifica-
tion. The revival was supposed to run for four days, but it
continued for four weeks because the Spirit was at work among
the people.

In 1872, Phoebe Palmer wrote a book entitled *The Promise of
the Father*, which remains one of the strongest statements ever
written for the ministry of all Christians. Urging ministers to
recognize the gifts of ministry of their Christian sisters, she
quoted from the vision of the prophet Joel recorded in the
Pentecost story in Acts 2:

> And in the last days it shall be, God declares,
> that I will pour out my Spirit upon all flesh,
> and your sons and your daughters shall prophesy,
> and your young men shall see visions,
> and your old men shall dream dreams;
> yea, and on my menservants and my maidservants in those
> days
> I will pour out my Spirit; and they shall prophesy.
> —ACTS 2:17–18, RSV

Phoebe Palmer did not succeed in shaking the foundations
of her denomination in 1872 to admit women in the preaching
ministry of the church. But she recognized that such a victory
could not even be her goal, stating in her book:

We did not set out to write a popular book. . . . We have concluded, though, at the risk of not publishing a popular work, to stand
up with truth. In this holy fear, and in his name, it is our purpose
to exhibit, in this volume, his faithfulness in pouring out his Spirit
on his daughters and handmaidens . . . Not Wesley, not Fletcher,
not Finney, not Mahan, not Upham, but the BIBLE is the standard,
the grandwork, the platform, the creed. . . .

The church in many places is a sort of potter's field, where the
gifts of woman, as so many strangers, are buried. How long, O
Lord, how long before we shall roll away the stone that we may see
a resurrection?

To recover the story of Luther Lee, Phoebe Palmer, and
hundreds, thousands of others, so many of whom are still
unidentified in this larger vision of the ministry of all Christians,
is to recognize that much of their experience followed that
described for us by Paul in 2 Corinthians 4:1–10. First, they
endeavored to preach an open statement of the truth, as plainly
and directly as they were able. They sought to renounce
underhanded ways of tampering with the Gospel which would
water down the message to a bland, appealing popular word.
Further, they recognized that they were way out of step with the
times—that the "gods" of this world who advocated ministry as
the function of one office, one sex, or one race had blinded the
minds of large segments of the people who miss the focus of the
Gospel, the light of the glory of Jesus Christ. Moreover, those
who strove to recover the ministry of authenticity lived out of
the basic commitment to preach not themselves but Jesus Christ
as Lord. Many of these people were literally struck down,
ostracized, persecuted. They were only able to press the Gospel
that all persons be included in ministry because they had
incorporated Paul's dictum into their lives: their strength and
hope came not from popular acceptance, approval, or advance-
ment, but from Christ's power working within them to discern
the heart of the Gospel and to apply it vigorously without
qualification.

If there is one call and one ministry, then clergy and laity
need to rethink the roles that have commonly been assigned
them. Paul's words in 2 Corinthians 4:5, "What we preach is not

ourselves, but Jesus Christ as Lord, with ourselves as your servants for Jesus' sake," are the words of liberation from traditional role models. Clergy have normally been seen as authoritarian leaders. Because of their position, training, and status, clergypersons have the first word, if not the last. The so-called success of the church has been vested almost entirely in ordained ministers.

What this amounts to in practice is that the people take their signals from the clergy, adjusting as best they can to the style, the theology, and concerns of the pastor—and repeating the process with every new appointment. Laity are "second-class Christians," cast in the role of unpaid assistants to the clergy.

What would it mean for clergy and laity to live out of the belief: We are servants unto each other for Jesus' sake? I think it would mean that pastors can be ministered unto, can experience the power of the Good News from their congregations, as well as share it with them. It would mean that a higher level of biblical and theological education would become a priority within the congregation, as the whole people of God seek together to discern their ministry and determine what the mission of their church should be. Mutual ministry will mean, further, that the personal gifts of the Spirit and the professional expertise of the members will be taken more seriously in determining what the outreach of the church to society should be and what human resources are available to do the needed work.

When clergy and laity engage in ministry together, the whole people of God bear responsibility for decision-making. The process may be more painful, with differences of opinion more widely recognized. This is a less efficient means of administration, because all the ends cannot be tied up so neatly when power is spread more widely. It will be a "calculated inefficiency," however, as Letty Russell puts it in her book, *The Future of Partnership*, because laity and clergy have decided that shared authority is necessary for mutual ministry.

The many clergy and laity who have entered into ministry together know that it has some perils as well as great possibilities. But the ministry of Jesus Christ has been given to all of us by the gracious mercy of God. I believe it is our hope for liberation from traditional roles assigned to clergy and laity, men and women, and for the fuller work of ministry to which we are all called.

DR. ROSEMARY SKINNER KELLER *is associate professor of Religion and American Culture at Garrett-Evangelical Theological Seminary. She is co-editor with Rosemary Radford Ruether of* Women and Religion in America: Vol. I, The 19th Century *(Harper & Row, 1981) and with Hilah Thomas of* Women in New Worlds: Historical Perspectives on the Wesleyan Tradition *(Abingdon, 1981).*

Realism and Hope

MARY D. KLAAREN

*For everything its season, and for every activity under heaven its time: a time to
be born and a time to die; a time to plant and a time to uproot; a time to kill and a
time to heal; a time to pull down and a time to build up; a time to weep and a time
to laugh; a time for mourning and a time for dancing; a time to scatter stones
and a time to gather them; a time to embrace and a time to refrain from
embracing; a time to seek and a time to lose; a time to keep and a time to throw
away; a time to tear and a time to mend; a time for silence and a time for speech;
a time to love and a time to hate; a time for war and a time for peace.*
—ECCLESIASTES 3:1–8, NEB

You probably know what is going to happen Wednesday night.
At the stroke of midnight, people will jump up and down and
hug each other and shout, "Happy New Year!" You might watch
all this on TV, or witness it at a party—or perhaps you will
choose to celebrate the New Year by going to bed early. But I
daresay that all of us—however we usher in the New Year—
want it to be a good year. We want that for our world, and we
want that for ourselves.

Some of us even make resolutions, because we want to make
sure that the year ahead be an improvement on the year just
passed. I don't make resolutions anymore because I can never
keep them, but if I made one this year, it probably would have

something to do with my sewing scissors. You see, about twenty years ago my mother gave me a pair of sewing scissors, a finely crafted pair of left-handed ones, and every time I used them, they cut beautifully. Unfortunately, they don't make scissors of that quality anymore—and, even more unfortunately, my scissors are lost. It's been several weeks, and I have just about given up hope of finding them. But should they reappear, I would be tempted to make a resolution. I would resolve that every time I used those scissors, I would put them back into my sewing box immediately—and no one else in our family would ever borrow them. And if I could do that, then, whenever I wanted those scissors, they would be there!

I suppose many of us want to control our lives like that. We want to believe that if we do things just the right way, then life will get progressively better. "If I love my children enough, they will grow up to be happy and secure." "If I get into a good college, I will have an array of golden opportunities at my fingertips." "If I work hard enough, the business will succeed." There is some truth in that; there are causes and effects we all know about. If you eat lots of candy, and never brush your teeth, you probably won't have many teeth left by the time you are an adult! The passage I just read from Ecclesiastes focuses on a truth which is deeper than causes and effects. The writer of Ecclesiastes calls our attention to the ebb and flow of life. "A time to be born and a time to die; . . . a time to weep and a time to laugh; . . . a time to seek and a time to lose."

People in our time find it hard to accept the ebb and flow of life. We prefer to see life as a logical progression of events. In fact, if we were given the chance to rewrite Ecclesiastes so that it would show this logical progression, we might write: There is a time to be born, then a time to learn, then a time to build, a time to embrace what has been built, a time to laugh, a time for love, and a time for peace.

The writer of Ecclesiastes did not put it that way, because our living does not proceed in that way. Life is not a series of experiences carefully built one upon the other so that the painful and unpleasant ones are slowly weeded out. To be sure, life is filled with moments of wonder and glory—times to laugh, dance, and embrace—but that is only one side of it. There is another side—times to weep and mourn and refrain from embracing.

There is an example of this two-sidedness of life right here in our congregation. Just three weeks ago we experienced the wonder and joy and power of God's presence, as we received twenty-two new members into our fellowship. But did you know that in the month ahead the deacons will drop thirty other people from the membership of this church—thirty people who at one time came forward to join our fellowship, but people with whom we now have no contact at all? "A time to pull down and a time to build up; . . . a time to seek and a time to lose."

The wisdom of Ecclesiastes reminds us that the most fundamental aspects of our living really cannot be managed or controlled. There are wonderful moments of joy—but not always, and they do not last forever, because times of joy are punctuated by times of undeniable pain and deep sorrow. There are times to withdraw from life in quiet and solitude and perhaps sometimes in fear—but not always, and they do not last forever, because there will also be times to reach out and embrace one another and the challenge of life itself.

Just how do we respond to this two-sidedness in our lives? Well, some of us make resolutions and try to master the situation. "If I always put my scissors away and hide the sewing box, then those scissors will never be lost again." Or, "If we make contact with every church member at least once every year, then we will never again lose contact with so many members." We force ourselves to be optimistic. We think we can find out exactly what is necessary to master life, and we resolve to do it.

It is tempting to place our ultimate trust in some achievement of our own, but more often than not, that just does not work. How many New Year's resolutions have you been able to keep?

Others of us respond to the two-sidedness of life not with forced optimism but by abandoning hope almost altogether. "There is nothing I can do," we say. "I am a victim of circumstance." Well, if you have really been lonely lately, or unable to find a job, or feeling that you just never will be able to get your act together, then you know what that hopelessness is like. No one is exempt from it. The wisdom of Ecclesiastes acknowledges that, and our own experience proves it. Yet somehow, even in the midst of despair, it seems that there is a glimmer of hope in each of us, waiting to be kindled.

I was told about a young mother with three small children who worked very long hours every day, earning barely enough to keep her apartment warm and food on the table. Yet every day she bought a lottery ticket, which seemed like such an obvious waste of her hard-earned money. When asked why she gambled with money which was so precious, she replied, "I know it seems unwise to you, but I buy a lottery ticket every day because one dollar is really not much to pay for twenty-four hours of hope."

Hope—we all need it to go on living. But hope must not be confused with a kind of forced optimism. True hope is solid and lasting, far more lasting than what comes from buying lottery tickets. Solid hope is grounded in the knowledge that God participates in the ebb and flow of our lives. God, the Creator from whom our life has come, is not only the giver of life but the sustainer of life. We cannot master the year ahead, but neither do we need to despair about it. God will sustain us, no matter what.

God does not sustain in the abstract. God enters the ebb and flow of our living. God is present to us, wherever we are, and in whatever conditions we find ourselves. God knows about the two-sidedness of everyday living. The road to Bethlehem was hard traveling for pregnant Mary, and when she got there, there was no room at the inn. But the baby was born! God came to you and me through the birth of his son. That is what Christmas was all about!

We can face the new year with hope, solid hope, hope grounded in the knowledge that, in the ebb and flow of the year ahead, God will be there, to inspire us and guide us, to rejoice with us and sustain us. For our times are in God's hands.

THE REV. MARY DECKER KLAAREN *is associate minister of South Congregational Church in Middletown, Connecticut. She is a graduate of Yale Divinity School and was ordained in the United Church of Christ. She is married and the mother of three children.*

In Celebration of Heroes and Nobodies

MARY McGEE

Welcome to a celebration of heroes and nobodies. Yes! Heroes and nobodies. After all, it's November. Remember November: All Souls' Day; the month of those poor souls and that often forgotten feast of All Saints. Remember those heroes: John the Baptist, Babe Ruth, Jane Addams, Emily Dickinson, Albert Einstein, Joan of Arc, John F. Kennedy, Charles Lindbergh, St. Teresa, Martin Luther King, St. Christopher, Madame Curie, John Wayne, Florence Nightingale, Joe Namath, St. Hippolytus, Etheria. Who is your hero?

Remember the nobodies: The lost souls, the unknown soldiers, the nameless ancestors, the Charlie Browns, the silent leaders, the unsung heroes.

But how do you remember nobodies?

Will anyone remember you?

We're all nobodies in this slap-bang world of standardized tests, stereotyped personalities, and gross generalities.

Do you even have a hero?

We always seem to be singing laud and praise of somebody! How often do you compliment others?

Ah, yes: November! Remember? The month of compliments and thanksgiving. We give thanks for friends, lovers, food, heroes, education, luck, blessings, good business, peace. We busy ourselves preparing meals, invitations, prayers, gifts, letters, liturgies, to share with others.

But how often do you give thanks for yourself? Yes, you, the nobody sitting there in the pew next to the other nobody, that person you worship with, that nobody without a name. Remember, you are created in God's image. Give thanks for that! Give thanks for yourself for a change. Your personality within yourself is unique among people. Your uniqueness is God's concept of you, it is God's image of you, it is God's love for you!—and God's love is an individual, personal love. If you devalue yourself, you devalue God and God's love for you. God doesn't expect you to be perfect. But God hopes you will appreciate and take care of that most precious gift he has given you—the gift of yourself.

In today's first reading for this thirty-first Sunday of the year, the Book of Wisdom says:

> But you have mercy on all, because you can do all things;
>   and you overlook the sins of men that they may repent.
> For you love all things that are
>   and loathe nothing that you have made;
>   for what you hated, you would not have fashioned.
> And how could a thing remain, unless you willed it;
>   or be preserved, had it not been called forth by you?
> But you spare all things, because they
>   are yours, O Lord and lover of souls,
>   for your imperishable spirit is in all things!
> Therefore you rebuke offenders little by little,
>   warn them, and remind them of the sins they are committing,
>   that they may abandon their wickedness and believe in you,
>   O Lord!
>   —WISDOM 11:23—12:2, NAB

This is the reading from Wisdom. This reading *is* wisdom and speaks quite to our theme of heroes and nobodies. Too often we think of ourselves as nobodies. We forget that God made us and would not make something that was without worth, beauty, or meaning. Reflecting on this reading we find we are infinitely more wealthy than we ever thought possible. For we are beyond price. Each one of us is unique and therefore irreplaceable. And so we must recognize the uniqueness that is each one of us. For a minute, be your own hero. Think about it. Think about the great person you are. Think about the person *you* feel *you* are. Yes! That part of your person that you think no one knows, recognizes, or appreciates but yourself. Respect yourself for what you are in yourself. Doing this, you will be able to grow in appreciation and respect for the person sitting next to you, the nobody without a name. For you begin to realize that the individual mystery which each of us is, is part of the plan. Yes, even Zacchaeus, whom you will meet in the Gospel today, is part of the plan. Remember Zacchaeus, the tax collector? Remember how we always stereotype him as the greedy old tax collector? Remember how we thought Jesus would ignore him and pass him by? Well, the surprise is on us when Jesus reaches out to this nobody and makes him a hero in our eyes. The Lord honours Zacchaeus by going to his house for dinner.

How do we understand this?

We must remember that there is good in everyone, even the worst of sinners. We must remember that the actuality of living itself is the goodness. We need to recognize that bit of hero which is in each of us. Be your own kind of hero.

See these nobodies sitting here behind me. [At this time the five people, dressed all alike in white albs and with clown-white faces, who have up till this time been sitting behind me on the altar steps, frozen in a pose, move into position to pantomime the Gospel as I narrate it.] Frozen. Listless. Almost indistinguishable from one another. Well, the secret is, there is somebody behind those masks—a person that is more than a face. But you would never really know it from looking. They could have fooled you. But believe it! Each one of them is unique. Each one has something to give. Just like all of us. And today these nobodies are going to come alive and be the heroes. For what they have to give, they are giving to you as they share with us the good news of today's Gospel from Luke (yes, remember Luke, he's one of those heroes). So listen and watch today's good news as the bad guy tax collector becomes his own kind of good guy hero and learns to take pride in himself and his profession.

Upon reaching Jericho, Jesus decided to pass through the city.

In this city there was a man named Zacchaeus. As a crowd gathered in expectation of Jesus' arrival, some in the crowd, seeing Zacchaeus, called out, "Come here a minute, Zacchaeus. So you're the chief tax collector. Quite a wealthy man, I suppose. So why are *you* running after this man Jesus, Zacchaeus? You're not poor, or sick, or hungry. You're no concern of his. You're just a filthy rich tax collector. A loner. A nobody."

Well, Zacchaeus could not resist his curiosity and went after Jesus and the crowd, trying to see what Jesus was like. But, being of small stature, he could not see over the crowd.

So Zacchaeus ran on in front of the crowd and climbed a sycamore tree which was along Jesus' route, so that he could see this man Jesus.

When Jesus came to the spot where the tree stood, he looked up and said, "Zacchaeus, hurry down. I mean to stay at your house today."

Zacchaeus quickly descended and welcomed Jesus with delight. When this was observed, everyone began to murmur, "He is going to a sinner's house as a guest!"

Zacchaeus stood his ground and said to the Lord, "I give half my belongings to the poor, Lord. If I have defrauded anyone in the least, I pay him back fourfold."

Jesus said to him, "Today salvation has come to this house, for this is what it means to be a son of Abraham. The Son of Man has come to search out and save what was lost."

THIS IS THE GOOD NEWS OF THE LORD.

The good news today is that the Son of Man came to seek and to find that which was lost. What was lost was the pride and recognition of the self. Jesus restored this to humankind by accepting each individual as unique. So often we lose sight of ourselves. And so today we have come together to celebrate that part of ourselves we had lost, yet are now beginning to recognize. But before we can fully celebrate ourselves, let us pray to the Lord for the strength to be ourselves.

MARY McGEE, *a Roman Catholic, is a Th.D. candidate in History of Religions at Harvard University. Her specialization is the study and implementation of interreligious dialogue (esp. Christian with non-Christian), comparative ritual, the indigenization of liturgy and liturgical arts, and women's ritual roles in the World Religions.*

The Ephesians Vision: Universal Justice

VIRGINIA RAMEY MOLLENKOTT

Samuel Taylor Coleridge once referred to the Book of Ephesians as the most divine composition known to humanity. Although I would find it hard to choose a single favorite among the books of the Bible, I have always valued the Book of Ephesians for the mature inclusiveness of its vision. Worshipfully and prayerfully, I'd like to quote part of the third chapter of this excellent epistle. I'll be quoting from the Revised Standard Version; but in case you'd like to compare my text with that of your own Bible, you will notice that I have made a few changes in the direction of a more inclusive language. By that I mean a language which pointedly recognizes the presence of women as well as men in its audience. I also mean a language that frees us from thinking of God as limited by human sexuality—for God transcends sex, just as God transcends every other human limitation. I assure you that no change involves tampering with the substance or meaning of the scripture text. Here, then, is Ephesians 3:3–10 and 14–19 (RSV):

> The mystery was made known to me by revelation, as I have written briefly. When you read this you can perceive my insight

into the mystery of Christ, which was not made known to the children of humanity in other generations as it has now been revealed to Christ's holy apostles and prophets by the Spirit; that is, how the gentiles are fellow heirs, members of the same body, and partakers of the same promise in Christ Jesus through the Gospel.

Of this Gospel I was made a minister according to the gift of God's grace which was given me by the working of God's power. To me, though I am the very least of all the saints, this grace was given, to preach to the gentiles the unsearchable riches of Christ, and to make all people see what is the plan of the mystery hidden for ages in God who created all things; that through the church the manifold wisdom of God might now be made known to the principalities and powers in the heavenly places. . . .

For this reason I bow my knees before the Parent from whom every family in heaven and on earth is named, that according to the riches of God's glory God may grant you to be strengthened with might through the Spirit in the inner person, and that Christ may dwell in your hearts through faith; that you, being rooted and grounded in love, may have power to comprehend with all the saints what is the breadth and length and height and depth, and to know the love of Christ which surpasses knowledge, that you may be filled with all the fullness of God.

In this passage we are presented with a marvelous paradox: If we are sufficiently rooted and grounded in love, we will be empowered to know something that *cannot be known*—namely, the love of Christ that surpasses knowledge. How can we know that which cannot be known? The answer to that question is best found by close attention to the biblical text, and in particular to the interesting chain of thoughts by which the author arrives at the paradox. He begins verse 14 by reminding us that the God to whom he bows his knees is the Parent from whom every family in heaven and on earth is named—a reminder of the oneness and unity of the whole human family because of our common origin. From this reminder he moves to a reminder that God's strength is given to us through the presence of the Holy Spirit in our deepest inner being and through the indwelling of the Christ-nature within us. So the passage moves from asserting our *external* oneness through the original creation to our *internal* oneness through redemption and the new creation.

Having provided these two sweeping reminders of human solidarity in Christ Jesus, the firstborn of the New Humanity, the passage then promises that if we are rooted and grounded in love (the natural result of the awareness of our oneness with all other members of God's creation), then and only then will we have the power to comprehend the infinite dimensions of the love that surpasses knowledge. In other words, this kind of knowing cannot be possessed like an object; it can only be experienced. And the experience brings fullness. Sensing and acting upon our solidarity with all the rest of God's creation, we become "filled with all the fullness of God"—a staggering statement if ever there was one. What an identity: "filled with all the fullness of God"!

Everything else in the Book of Ephesians is centered around the theme of the epistle, which is announced boldly in the first chapter: that the mystery of God's will as a plan for the fullness of time is to unite all things in Christ, including things in heaven and things on earth (verses 9–10). That theme is developed in our passage by stressing that the pagan gentile converts have, in Christ, been made into one person with the Jewish converts.

In order to grasp the significance of the Ephesians theme for the way we live our lives here in the twentieth century, we need to remind ourselves that the sharpest point of controversy in the early church was the controversy over whether converts from paganism, the gentiles, should be forced to become Judaized by being circumcised and following all the Jewish customs and ceremonies. As recorded in the fifteenth chapter of Acts, the resolution of this controversy occurred at an apostolic council meeting in Jerusalem. At the time it was decided that since both the Jewish and gentile converts had received salvation the same way, through the grace of the Lord Jesus, the gentile converts should not be made to feel like second-class citizens by being forced to obey ethnic laws foreign to their own background. Thus the New Testament provides details about how genuine Christian love wipes out hierarchy and breaks down social barriers. The history of Christian missions would be full of justice, love, and mutual honor had this example of the primitive church been followed instead of ignored. The making of

Jew and gentile into one person in Christ Jesus was intended to be the paradigm of further unifying. Christ's control would gradually extend outward in infinite love until it washed away all the barriers human beings have erected against each other, including economic barriers, political barriers, and sexual barriers.

For a conscientious first-century Christian with Jewish roots, brought up in careful observance of the law and then converted to faith in Christ Jesus, it must have seemed nothing less than scandalous to allow gentiles to achieve full acceptance in the church without the observance of Jewish purity rituals. In order for us to grasp the shocking nature of breaking down the distinction between Jew and gentile in the early church, I think a contemporary parallel is necessary. The nearest parallel today would be, I think, the sense of scandal many conscientious Christians feel at the thought of allowing first-class citizenship to Christians who have discovered in themselves a homosexual orientation. The Jewish converts to Christianity could cite passage after passage in their Bible, the Old Testament, to prove that people who did not observe Jewish laws and rituals could not possibly be the children of the promise. We learn from Acts 15 that their perfectly honest scruples were overcome only through repeated reminders that every Christian gets salvation the same way, through faith in Christ Jesus; and through the apostolic accounts of how the Holy Spirit was working among the gentile converts.

I believe that the contemporary rejection of homosexual Christians can be overcome in the same way. Instead of requiring that gay people try to earn their salvation by giving up responsible expression of their sexuality, thus laying upon people burdens too heavy for them to bear, the Christian church needs to remind itself that every Christian gets salvation the same way, through the grace of the Lord Jesus. And the church needs to pay attention to the remarkable work the Holy Spirit has been doing through homosexual Christians. I make this point not simply because of my concern for social justice, but because I think that only a contemporary example can make us grasp the impact of the passage which is our text: "The gentiles are fellow heirs, members of the same body, and partakers of the promise in Christ Jesus through the Gospel." For many conscientious Jewish Christians, that statement was mind-blowing. It was as mind-blowing as if Ephesians had been written today and had addressed heterosexual Christians with this message: "Homosexual Christians are fellow heirs, members of the same body, and partakers of the promise in Christ Jesus through the Gospel"! In other words, the passage is intended to make us realize that the intention of God is nothing less than the breaking down of the toughest, highest barriers we can think of.

When Jesus was asked how human beings could identify their neighbors, he told a story to his Jewish audience about a good Samaritan. Instead of supplying a hero from Judaism, or at least from a group the Jews could feel sympathy with, Jesus chose to honor a member of the despised Samaritans, with whom most Jews had no dealings whatsoever. By forcing a group of people to think favorably concerning a person of outcast status, Jesus was illustrating the same principle that the Ephesians author is driving at by saying that, in Christ, gentile and Jewish converts have been transformed into one person, partakers of the same promise. It is only by grasping and acting upon this principle of oneness in Christ, the New Humanity, that we can be rooted and grounded in love and thus be filled with all the fullness of God.

The famous psychologist R. D. Laing has written an interesting essay called "Us and Them." In it he points out that "each person is the other to the others," so that "We are They to Them as They are They to Us." He suggests that if the human race is going to survive for very much longer, it is going to be necessary for each of us to expand our definition of Us until it includes all the people we have been classifying as Them. Otherwise, in destroying Them we are going to destroy all of Us as well. Even "on the basis of the crassest self-interest," he reasons, it is necessary for human beings in the nuclear age to realize that "We and They must be transcended in the totality of the human race." Thus we see a secular humanist urging, simply on the basis of self-interest, a human solidarity that the Bible has been proposing to us for many centuries.

Let us make no mistake, though. Being rooted and grounded in love—that is, recognizing human solidarity by creation and redemption—begins a process which will demand of us a death to our old natures, a turning away from our terrific selfishness. In 1971 the President of Tanzania wrote the following words in *Maryknoll Magazine*: "So the world is not one; its people are more divided now, and also more conscious of their divisions, than they have ever been before. They are divided between those who are satisfied and those who are hungry; they are divided between those with power and those without power; they are divided between those who dominate and those who are dominated, between those who exploit and those who are exploited. And it is the minority which is well fed and the minority which has secured control of the world's wealth and over their fellow men." And he went on to mention the fact that this well-fed minority has white skin and has adopted the Christian religion. No wonder so many people of the Third World identify Christian churches with imperialism, racism, sexism, and brutal exploitation!

Perhaps an illustration will help us comprehend the enormous injustice which divides the family of humankind here in the twentieth century. Let's imagine that the whole human race alive today—over 3 billion people—is a village of just 1000 persons. In that village of 1000, only 164 persons could be classified as living a moderately comfortable life. The other 836 persons are living lives of desperation and degradation. They are poor, diseased, economically oppressed, sexually oppressed, and politically oppressed. Yet the passage we are considering tonight asks us to remember that every family in heaven and earth is named after the divine Parent, and that in Christ Jesus those whom we have regarded as *They* are brought into complete and utter identification with Us, since we all become one body, one person, "partakers of the promise in Christ Jesus."

What would we do if we ourselves were not among the 164 persons who are living moderately comfortable lives in the global village of 1000 people? I think we would try with everything in us to overcome the barriers and achieve a more equitable distribution of resources. But if we obey the insight of Ephesians 3 and of many other New Testament passages that tell us that the human race is a single organism because of creation and redemption, then we are forced to recognize that in the eyes of God, who is love, we really are one with the 836 others who are living under conditions of grinding poverty and oppression!

We have admitted that if we were members of the oppressed group in the global village, we would try our best to achieve a more equitable distribution of resources. But the Bible tells us that we *are* in fact united to those people: the gentiles, the others, the outcasts, those whom we think of as *Them*, including the poor. "The gentiles are fellow heirs, members of the same body, and partakers of the promise in Christ Jesus through the Gospel."

Some people may be thinking, "That means we Christians only have to be concerned for those oppressed persons who are confessing members of the Christian religion." But I remind you that, according to the Ephesians author, it is the will of God to "unite all things in [Christ, the New Humanity], things in heaven and things on earth." Since the goal is the total uniting of the entire creation, being rooted and grounded in Christ's love means seeing *every* human being as in Christ, identified with Christ, a member of the New Creation.

It is important to notice that the Ephesians author speaks of uniting all *things* in heaven and earth under the authority of Christ. All *things* would include not only all human creatures, but the whole animal world, the whole vegetable and mineral world, and all the societal structures such as national governments, business, religious, and military hierarchies, and even multinational corporations. Although my early religious training emphasized the importance of decency only in interpersonal relationships, I have come to see that the Bible requires of me a political responsibility that goes far beyond the private sphere of life. This has been particularly difficult for me to grasp because as an American woman I was brought up to believe that my role in life should be primarily in the private sphere, centered in human relationships. I should not seek leadership in church or society, but should play a quietly supportive role under the authority of male leadership. Only during the last decade have I learned that the New Testament teaches equality through the *mutual* submission of male and female in the home, church, and society. Between my female socialization and the concept that salvation is a private relationship to Christ that has nothing to do with social justice and political responsibility, I have a great deal of inertia to overcome.

For instance, I had always assumed that when Jesus said to Pilate, "My kingdom is not of this world," he meant that the Kingdom of God is a purely spiritual matter, having nothing to do with the unjust social structures of this world. I therefore found it easy to believe what I was taught, that Christian churches properly have no business getting involved in politics and social reform. Preaching the "simple Gospel" was all that Christian churches should do—and of course the simple Gospel was defined as a private contract between the individual and God, a contract completely divorced from issues of justice. Although of course Christians should give coffee and sand-wiches to hungry alcoholics once they had sat through a sermon in a rescue mission, Christians had no business trying to correct unfair laws and unjust economic policies. Such evils would only become worse and worse until the catastrophic reentry of God into human history through the Second Coming of Christ. What was the point of working for peace and social justice when war and injustice were inevitable?

But I have come to see that Jesus was not telling Pilate that his kingdom was otherworldly in the sense that it was unrelated to the inequities and injustices of a fallen universe. Rather, Jesus was telling Pilate that his kingdom had nothing to do with national egotism, with the racial, religious, ethnic, economic, and sexist ego-interests that pit human beings against each other. Jesus was saying, "I am the King of the Jews, all right, but not in the narrow, worldly way *you* would define as being King of the Jews. Not in the sense of King of the *Jews* as a nation pitted against the Roman nation and oppressed by the Roman nation. My kingdom is not of this world because it is a kingdom where *there is no oppression at all*—no dominance, no enforced submis-sion, no inequity, no division, no walls of hostility. My kingdom is not of this world because it is a kingdom in which all the others, all the outcasts, all the poverty-stricken, all the people considered to be secondary become fellow heirs, members of the same body, and partakers of the promise."

It is because all things are to be brought into subjection to

Christ that the Ephesians author urges us to fight against "the principalities, against the powers, against the world rulers of this present darkness, against the spiritual hosts of wickedness in the heavenly places" (6:12). We read earlier that it is God's will that "through the church the manifold wisdom of God might now be made known to the principalities and powers" (3:10). These principalities and powers include the American military machine, the Houses of Congress, and the huge corporations whose selfish interests control so much international policy. In other words, this passage tells us that it is the urgent job of Christian churches to let our contemporary principalities and powers know about the fact that God views the whole family of humankind as a single entity, that injustices done to any segment of humanity are injustices against the person of Christ and the body of the New Humanity, and therefore are felt as injustices against us all.

When Christian churches and individual church members remain silent in the face of this world's enormous inequities, we place ourselves in heresy. When we assume that whatever our government does to other nations must be all right because it is Us against Them, we are guilty of national egotism, which is a form of idolatry. When we forget that everyone else in the world is equally precious to God as we are to ourselves, we are guilty of personal egotism, which is also idolatry. When in our homes we still assume that the male's career is necessarily primary while the female's is secondary and supportive, we deny mutual servanthood and desensitize our children to the oneness and universality of Christ's body. When we see anyone else as secondary to ourselves because of poverty or skin color or belief or for any other reason, we deny what the New Testament insists upon, that all of us are members of the same body and partakers of the same promise.

The promise is as infinite as the breadth and height and length and depth of the love of Christ. But we can limit the effects of the promise *for ourselves* through a failure of perception. If I perceive my oneness with the whole human family, I will struggle against unjust principalities and powers on behalf of the other members of Christ's body. But if I refuse to struggle against egocentric world powers in myself and in society, I deny my own membership in that body and cut myself off from the enjoyment of knowing the love of Christ that surpasses knowledge. And if the structures of the organized Christian churches refuse to work actively to establish justice in this world, then they are refusing to cooperate with the plan of God, which is *through the church* to make known the oneness of God's human family to the principalities and powers. Many of America's churches have become tools of the status quo, part of the injustice of American society, providing rationalizations for the rich instead of decent opportunities for the poor. Such church structures are among the principalities and powers that the Christian must war *against*, since they exclude from their leadership those persons who are poor, nonwhite, female, or otherwise second-class. Any failure to "do justice" is a failure to perceive the infinite dimensions of God's promise. And that failure of perception deprives us of our heritage, which is to be "filled with all the fullness of God." What we give is what we get. We are Them. They are Us.

What, exactly, is the promise of which all humanity is intended to partake? The promise is nothing less than God's covenant, God's pledge, which goes all the way back to God's covenant with Abraham that, because of his faith, through his descendants all the nations of the world should be blessed (Genesis 18:19, etc.). In a very strong passage in the fourth chapter of Romans, the apostle Paul warned that those who attempted to limit God's intention by making people obey Old Testament laws in addition to placing their faith in Christ Jesus were in fact breaking their own covenant with God and refusing to live by the promise. The implication for us today is that if we ourselves are to enjoy being partakers of the promise, we must recognize the infinitely inclusive dimensions of that promise, and we must act accordingly.

Many biblical scholars have noticed a close connection between Colossians and Ephesians. But some have worried that there is a discrepancy or contradiction in the way terms are defined in the two epistles. For instance, the Greek word translated *economy* or *plan* is used in Colossians 1:25 to mean a task or stewardship assigned to a human being, whereas in Ephesians 3:9 the same word is used to mean God's purpose for the consummation of world history. But there is no real contradiction. The point of Ephesians is that, by acting upon human oneness within God and because of God's Spirit within us, we are "filled with all the fullness of God." Therefore what we human beings do in striving against injustice is actually the divine plan working itself out through our human stewardship.

Scholars have worried that the word *mystery*, which to Paul means a "revealed secret," is defined in Colossians as "Christ in you, the hope of glory," but is defined in Ephesians as uniting all things in Christ and specifically as reconciling the Jews with the gentiles. But here again, there is no discrepancy. Whereas Colossians stresses the *personal aspect* of the mystery, that the Christ is in each of us, Ephesians stresses the *political effects* and ultimately the cosmic effects of dying to egocentricity and living in the new nature. Similarly with the definition of God's economy or plan: whereas Colossians stresses the personal aspect of God's assigning a task to a human steward, Ephesians stresses the cosmic results of God's cooperation with human agents.

A similar thing happens with the word translated as *fullness*. In Colossians 1:19 the word fullness is applied to God's dwelling in the Christ, but in Ephesians the word fullness is applied to the church as the body of Christ, which Christ dwells in and God fills. Here again, there is no contradiction. Ephesians simply expands to the full political and cosmic dimensions the same principle that Colossians introduces on a more personal, relational level. It is because of the personal relationship within the Trinity, the filling of the Second Person by the First Person, that the Second Person has the power to redeem the whole creation from personal and structural egocentricity, which is sin.

A choice continually lies before us, both as individual persons and as a corporate body. The choice is this: Are we willing to let our perceptions be cleansed so that we can recognize our oneness with the whole family of humankind? Will we accept the responsibility of that vision? Are we willing to wrestle with principalities and powers so that God's plan of universal justice may be furthered in our lifetime? Only in this way can we hope to "know the love of Christ which surpasses knowledge, that [we] may be filled with all the fullness of God." Only in this way can we fully believe and enjoy the fact that we are "partakers of the promise."

VIRGINIA RAMEY MOLLENKOTT, Ph.D., *is an evangelical feminist, author, lecturer, and professor of English at William Paterson College. She is a member of the interreligious Task Force of Women of Faith in the '80s, and serves on the 12-member N.C.C.C. committee to prepare an inclusive-language lectionary.*

Job: The Confessions of a Suffering Person

CHRISTINE NELSON

Job began speaking again. If only my life could once again be as it was when God watched over me. God was always with me then and gave me light as I walked through the darkness. Those were the days when I was prosperous, and the friendship of God protected my home. Almighty God was with me then, and I was surrounded by all my children. My cows and goats gave plenty of milk, and my olive trees grew in the rockiest soil. Whenever the city elders met and I took my place among them, young men stepped aside as soon as they saw me, and old men stood up to show me respect. The leaders of the people would stop talking; even the most important men kept silent. Everyone who saw me or heard of me had good things to say about what I had done. When the poor cried out, I helped them; I gave help to orphans who had nowhere to turn. Men who were in deepest misery praised me, and I helped widows find security. I have always acted justly and fairly. I was eyes for the blind, and feet for the lame. I was like a father to the poor and took the side of strangers in trouble. I destroyed the power of cruel men and rescued their victims. I always expected to live a long life and to die at home in comfort. . . .

But men younger than I am make fun of me now! Their fathers have always been so worthless that I wouldn't let them help my dogs guard sheep. . . . Now I am about to die; there is no relief for my suffering. At night my bones all ache; the pain that gnaws me never stops. God seizes me by my collar and twists my clothes out of shape. He throws me down in the mud; I am no better than dirt. I call to you, O God, but you never answer; and when I pray, you pay no attention. You are treating me cruelly; you persecute me with all your power. You let the wind blow me away; you toss me about in a raging storm. I know you are taking me off to my death, to the fate in store for everyone. Why do you attack a ruined man, one who can do nothing but beg for pity? Didn't I weep with people in trouble and feel sorry for those in need? I hoped for happiness and light, but trouble and darkness came instead. I am torn apart by worry and pain; I have had day after day of suffering.

—JOB 29:1–18; 30:1, 16–27, TEV

His name was Bill. He was a friend of mine. His father died when he was young. His stepfather rejected him. Now his mother was dying. He felt all alone in the world. Bill was preparing for the ministry because he cared about people. But Bill didn't feel people cared about him. Bill began to contemplate suicide.

I and others tried to support him. We listened, we comforted, we reasoned with him, we tried to get his mind on other things, we tried to get him involved in activities. Sometimes we just sat with him without saying a word, because we saw how much he was suffering. His response to us was: "You could be with me twenty-four hours a day. But if I wanted to kill myself I would find a way."

Bill was suffering. He asked the question, "Why me? What have I done to deserve this?" Bill knew we could not answer this question. Bill knew the answer could come only from God.

Bill is a modern-day Job. I meet Job again and again in your faces, in my face: "Why me?" Or, as the children's song goes, "Nobody likes me, everybody hates me. I think I'll go out in the garden and eat worms."

The match-up is our pain versus our faith. Where is God in the midst of our suffering? How you and I respond to our suffering makes or breaks our faith. For in our suffering we ask: Is our faith able to make sense out of our pain?

I believe faith in God can carry us through our suffering. *God is with us.* Faith can be known only by living it. Faith in God gives us the courage to struggle with our pain. Growth in faith is a consequence of us gutting it out with God. This is the comfort we of the church have to offer our world. This is the good news we are called to share with those who are suffering. This is the life-giving task God has given to us: to heal the brokenhearted. *God is with us.*

"Why me, God?" Our first response is: *Am I being punished for my sins?* Job's friends told Job to examine himself; there must be some unconfessed sin in his life. We play that game too. A young couple's baby died from "sudden infant death syndrome." The parents were hysterical, blaming themselves, the doctor, and God. The truth is, no one was responsible. *Suffering comes to us all, regardless of how good we are.* Faith calls us to have realistic expectations about our world. Faith calls us to accept suffering as part of life—like the sun and the rain. "God grant us the serenity to accept the things we cannot change, the courage to change the things we can, and the wisdom to know the difference."

A second response is to *feel sorry for ourselves.* "Poor, poor pitiful me," says the pop song by Linda Ronstadt. Joni Eareckson became a paraplegic after a swimming accident in her late teenage years. As her pain challenged her faith, she realized this: "I had to get past myself before I could see handicaps come at us in all shapes and sizes: broken homes, broken hearts, anxieties, doubts, loneliness. And the confines of your soul may seem as limiting as a wheelchair." We all have our sufferings, our pain, our limitations. We can bury ourselves in pessimism and pity. Faith calls us to seek God's help in accepting our limitations.

A third response is to view suffering as *God teaching us a lesson for our own good.* This view of God really upsets me. It's like saying a good parent is one who burns a child's fingers on the stove in order to teach the child never to touch it again. Our loving God doesn't strike us with cancer in order to show us the value of suffering or to teach us patience. *God is with us, yes.* God is with us, sustaining us through the suffering; God does not cause the suffering. God is with us in the midst of our pain, comforting us, guiding us, encouraging us, assuring us of God's love. The value comes in having God as our sustaining life force, not in learning the virtues of suffering.

This is the message Job receives: *God is with us.* God is with us in the best of times and in the worst of times. For we humans are made for communion with God. When Job's well-ordered world fell apart, Job lost his sense of assurance of God's presence in his life. Job discovered his life made no sense without the presence of God. We need to make that same discovery. *God is with us.*

This is the comfort the church has to offer those who are suffering. This is the assurance we are called to give to one another. *God is with us.*

As we studied Job, one of the questions I asked our *Through the Bible* classes was: "If you had been Job's friend, what would you have said to him?"

After some thought, most responded they would *listen* to Job, listen to Job's pain. This is the most vital thing one person can do for another—to take another person's pain seriously, to accept that person as they are. It is the suffering ones who must struggle with their questions and strain to understand themselves in the darkness of their pain. It is our task to symbolically make known the presence of God in the midst of people's pain by *being present with them.* Ecclesiastes 4:9–10, TEV, says: "Two are better off than one, because together they can work more effectively. If one of them falls down, the other can help him up. But if someone is alone and falls, it's just too bad, because there is no one to help him." *God is with us*, present in our presence.

A Phil Donahue TV program featured a group called "survivalists," who prepare hideaways in the mountains to which they can escape in case of the collapse of civilization. It was interesting that many members of the TV studio audience were furiously angry at these people who thought they could run away. We know we need the presence of one another in times of suffering.

One of the most difficult aspects of suffering is to *let the pain go.* We all have painful relationships in our lives—people whom we love deeply but who have hurt us deeply. Those people who, when we see them, we cross over to the other side of the street. Those people whom we find it difficult to say a kind word about.

One of my deepest pains is to see this happen in a church. Here is where we should be able to live together even while holding differing opinions. Here is where we should be able to struggle together through our sufferings. Here is where our faith in God should lead us to live out "love thy neighbor as thyself."

I'm not speaking about being gushy or painting on a plastic smile, or even of giving in to the other out of an "attempt to be Christian."

Faithful Christians will have differing opinions, will have conflicts, will hurt one another. Faith is struggling through our pain together. We will not always like one another's opinions or behavior. But we are called to care for the person, to call the person a child of God.

Let the suffering go. Release old heartaches, old grudges. The pains of the past are the greatest deterrent to blessings in the future. No one else can deliver you from the prison cell of your pain.

Some of the greatest men and women of our times have been saddled with disabilities and adversities but have overcome them with the help of God.

Lock someone in a prison cell, and you have a John Bunyan.

Raise someone in abject poverty, and you have an Abe Lincoln.

Afflict someone with asthma as a child, and you have a Theodore Roosevelt.

At birth, deny a child the ability to see, hear, and speak, and you have Helen Keller.

Label someone a religious fanatic and you have one of the greatest theologians ever, Jonathan Edwards.

If you and I can *let go of our pain* and move forward to embrace what is yet to come, we will find the Lord will bless the latter parts of our lives even more than the first parts, just like Job's. *God is with us.* Let us let go of our pain.

THE REV. CHRISTINE NELSON *is minister of St. Peter's UCC in Punxsutawney, Pennsylvania. She is a corporate member of the United Church Board for Homeland Ministries.*

The Wounded Healer

SALLY PALMER

*And when the hour came, he sat at table, and the apostles with him. And he said
to them, "I have earnestly desired to eat this passover with you before I suffer; for
I tell you I shall not eat it until it is fulfilled in the kingdom of God." And he took
a cup, and when he had given thanks he said, "Take this and divide it among
yourselves; for I tell you that from now on I shall not drink of the fruit of the vine
until the kingdom of God comes." And he took bread, and when he had given
thanks he broke it and gave it to them, saying, "This is my body which is given for
you. Do this in remembrance of me." And likewise the cup after supper, saying,
"This cup which is poured out for you is the new covenant in my blood. But
behold the hand of him who betrays me is with me on the table. For the Son of man
goes as it has been determined; but woe to that man by whom he is betrayed!" And
they began to question one another, which of them it was that would do this.*

*A dispute also arose among them, which of them was to be regarded as the
greatest. And he said to them, "The kings of the gentiles exercise lordship over
them; and those in authority over them are called benefactors. But not so with
you; rather let the greatest among you become as the youngest, and the leader as
one who serves. For which is the greater, one who sits at table, or one who serves?
Is it not the one who sits at table? But I am among you as one who serves."*

—LUKE 22:14–27, RSV

What do you do when you feel discouraged, when you feel hurt
by the wounds of this world? Some people try to hide. They curl
up under a blanket and hope that everyone who is bothering
them will simply go away. Some people get angry. In their hurt,

149

they lash out at others and maybe even plot their revenge. But some people, when they feel discouraged, look long and hard at the cross. They find in it a sense of strength, a way to go back into the very world in which they were hurt, and try again. These are the *wounded healers*. And that's what this sermon is all about.

You see, we do our best to follow Christ—to look long and hard at the cross and to shape our lives by him who suffered on it. And what we must always remember is that the Christian faith never promised us a "rose garden," but it does promise us *strength to face the real conditions of life* and *love, which we are commanded to share with others*.

You see, we *worship* not a building, nor a congregation, but a Savior, who took upon himself the sins of the world. It was his suffering that healed us. And, by facing our own suffering, no matter what the cause, and reaching back out with his love, we too can become *wounded healers*. . . . Hear again from the Gospel of Luke:

> And when the hour came, . . . he said to them, "I have earnestly desired to eat this passover with you before I suffer. . . ." And he took bread, and when he had given thanks he broke it and gave it to them, saying, "This is my body which is given for you. Do this in remembrance of me." And likewise the cup after supper, saying, "This cup which is poured out for you is the new covenant in my blood."
>
> —LUKE 22:14–20, RSV

Hear also what follows Luke's record of the Last Supper. The disciples, instead of understanding what he was saying—instead of understanding that *he offered himself* for our wounds—were arguing amongst themselves about who was greatest. What a tribute to Christ's Last Supper! But sometimes we make the same mistake. We're so anxious to be something ourselves that we forget who Christ is. Hear again his answer: "Let the greatest among you become as the youngest, and the leader as *one who serves*. For which is the greater, one who sits at table, or one who serves? . . . I am among you as one who serves [Luke 22:24–27, RSV]."

You see, the presence of Christ always astonishes us. It always provokes us to look back at ourselves with humility. We think we have all the answers. Then we discover that we serve a God who doesn't need our answers but our willing obedience.

You see, Christ was hurt. He suffered more than any of us ever will. But, his response was to care for those who hurt him: "Father, forgive them, for they know not what they do." "Woman, behold your son." "I do not pray for these only, but also for those who believe in me through their word, that they may all be one." "This is my body, which is given for you."

You see, it was the wounds of Christ that healed us. And if we are to follow him, we must become *wounded healers*. That is, we must never wish suffering upon ourselves, just as God never wishes it for us. But when we do suffer—by sin, by sickness, by circumstance—we must respond by reaching back. We must continue to care. We must become *wounded healers*.

I think we all know what this means. But let me offer two examples. The first is a person who suffered but never reached out in the midst of her pain. Perhaps you've heard the story of this woman. She was a hypochondriac who had back troubles, arthritis, and frequent insomnia. After a life where she complained all the time about how *she* felt, this miserable woman passed on to her Maker. This hypochondriac asked for one simple inscription on her tombstone. It was this: "I told you so!"

Then there is the true example of a woman who was diagnosed a victim of multiple sclerosis. She and her husband decided to make the best home possible for their young children. They moved to a town where it was easier for him to work and help care for the family. Then he came down with lung cancer. Now that he has passed on to his Maker, this woman has gone to work at her husband's job. She doesn't complain about her difficult lot in life. She just cares for others with all her strength. And, she's probably one of the best counselors the State of Colorado has ever had.

You see, we all suffer, but *it's what we do with our suffering* that makes all the difference in the world. We can wallow in self-pity. We can try to hide. We can be angry. Or *we can look long and hard at the cross*. Hear these affirmations of our faith. They're from the Heidelberg Catechism:

QUESTION 1: What is the only comfort in life and in death?

ANSWER: That I, with body and soul, both in life and in death, am not my own, but belong to my faithful Savior Jesus Christ.

QUESTION 2: How many things are necessary for thee to know that thou in this comfort may live and die happily?

ANSWER: Three things: First, the greatness of my sin and misery. Second, how I am redeemed from all my sins and misery. Third, how I am to be thankful to God for such redemption.

You see, faith constantly reminds us who we are. We can try to exist with the illusion of self-sufficiency, with the narrow assurance that *we've* got all the answers. Or we can understand that we need others, yet we continue to hurt them and they continue to hurt us. Yes, we are wounded people, but we have the *promise of God* that makes us whole once more. Yes, we are wounded people, but we have faith, we have hope, we have love. And, *we always have the choice—to become bitter with the scars of living, or to become wounded healers.*

Hear again Christ's words:

Blessed are the meek, for they shall inherit the earth.
Blessed are those who hunger and thirst for righteousness, for they shall be satisfied.
Blessed are the merciful, for they shall obtain mercy. . . .
Blessed are the peacemakers, for they shall be called sons of God.

—MATTHEW 5:5–9, RSV

And, on this special day, as you return to face the headaches and the heartaches of your own situation: *Blessed are you, who make your pain a source of healing for others!*

THE REV. DR. SALLY LENTZ PALMER *has served UCC churches for 7 years and taught religion courses in seminary and in college. Her publications include:* The Gift of Life *(Westminster, 1980),* The Missouri Plan for Evangelism *(Missouri Conference, UCC, 1979), and "A Theology from Ministry" (The Iliff Review, Fall 1977).*

Created in Her Image
BEATRICE PASTERNAK

[Sermon at the Mother Thunder Mission—Episcopal worship using non-sexist liturgy]

Last Saturday evening Martha Blacklock offered me the opportunity to preach here tonight. She even gave me twenty minutes to think it over. And I had to say "yes" because preaching is a temptation I have not yet learned to resist, and because after that twenty minutes had elapsed I realized that I was already thinking about how I would start and what I would say. But all of that went out the window the next morning, and I have to begin with my own immediate awareness of the problems of being a feminist Episcopalian.

As the lay reader at the early service last Sunday morning, I was leading the prayers in the first part, making no changes from the prescribed Rite I—except that I do say in the Prayers of the People "give thanks for all *people*," and again when leading the Confession I say "judge of all *people*." Well, as we approached the table at the Offertory, the celebrant said, "I want to show you something," and opened the service book to the Confession and pointed to "men." He let me know that changing the word in the Intercessions was okay, but it was "confusing" to change it when the congregation was involved in saying the prayer as well. I just smiled and continued to help him prepare the elements. But I wondered during the rest of the service how I would respond if he brought it up again afterwards. After all, he is my rector—and I might have had to deal with some reality!

I hope none of you here will be disappointed to know that I did not decide to make an ethical stand and fold my alb and sink off into the sunrise. No, I hoped that I could have said, "I understand, but I hope you will understand that I have difficulty leading prayers for the men present and not including myself and the other women." But I would not have trudged off, because I believe I have a place in that community and no one there will ever hear what I have to say, my witness to this movement or any other, if I leave in a huff. And that's a lousy decision, and a very hard one. And maybe that makes me not a revolutionary but a conservative. And maybe if the early Christians had felt that way we wouldn't be here tonight. But it is how I faced the possibility of such a decision, and how I would answer it still tonight. However, I hope that, like Alice when the caterpillar asked her, "Who are you?" I might reply, "I know who I was when I got up this morning, but I think I must have changed several times since then"!

Last spring I wrote and presented a homily when the Reverend Bea Blair celebrated for the first time a nonsexist liturgy she and I developed in our parish. As it happened, the service fell on the Wednesday night of the torrential rainstorm during the transit strike, and the only people present were Bea and I, the rector, another man on the staff, and the Altar Guild lady. We felt we owed her a service, since she'd come out on so terrible a night, so we did it. And for the first time there was in our parish a liturgy where "God the Father" was *not* present, but where everyone there *was* included in God's love and presence. We try to celebrate that liturgy whenever Bea celebrates at our midweek evening service. And copies of the homily are available to help the congregation better understand and relate to the language and imagery. We hope they take one home and consider the thoughts I tried to share with them.

Yes, we need to do that service more often. And I haven't yet had the nerve or the faith to ask another priest on the staff to use the service when I am the lay reader. Perhaps I will move closer to that, now that I've realized it. After all, if as a part of what I claim to be my lay ministry, I don't try to lead the ordained men in my parish, I'm not living up to what I profess to be doing. And if I don't, it has to be because I am not willing to take the risk implicit in making such a request.

In my written and spoken vocabulary, risks/opportunities are used with an unspoken "slash" between, almost as one word, because to me they are "indivisible under God." And, I think this concept pertains to us here tonight and to the premise of Mother Thunder, because we take a risk every time we use an opportunity to tell people that some of us feel disenfranchised in their form of worship—that we feel excluded by the masculine imagery of God and all those who surrounded "him" and were important in the history of the Old Testament and the writing of the New. But I think we, as lay and ordained people, have to take that risk, or we'll forever be using a borrowed church, saying our prayers, and going back to the male world the rest of the time, and conforming to those precepts and subjugating our feelings in order to fulfill our contract or obligation in that society. And we are the only ones who can bring about any change in that outlook for our own future.

You know, we strive to eliminate the masculine image of God or the Risen Christ, and yet to do that without a written text means being able to do what I call "mental acrobatics," so that I keep in mind where a sentence is going and consider as I speak it whether I'm going to need a pronoun and whether I can finesse it or rework the whole thing before I am too far along and committed to saying something that will offend me most of all! And sometimes I can't stop the flow and the negative imagery happens, and I have to accept it and keep trying to make my point with the hope that the very act of trying to include all people in my speaking and thinking will be transmitted to those who hear me and have some input on them. And even that is better than if we *didn't* talk to one another. And sometime, that other person *will* hear me!

I would like to share with you two moments in my life this summer. The first happened one morning when I discovered as I got off the bus that I was about to walk the two blocks to my office with a doctor who also had an office in the same medical center, on the same floor as ours. We talked about vacations, and he said he hadn't had one yet—that God hadn't looked at his checkbook lately. I said that she hadn't looked at mine, either. He sort of sputtered, and said he'd heard that people said such things, but no one had ever said that to him before. I said that I simply felt that if *I* am created in God's image, then God must be both male and female. In a nonthreatening and nonaggressive way, I felt I had been honest with myself and another person.

The second moment happened one Sunday when I worshiped at St. Mark's-in-the-Bowery. They have a loose Rite III service which they have devised, and in the final hymn ("I Am the Bread of Life") were the words ". . . and she who eats of this bread, She shall live forever, She shall live forever." Now I had not had anything to do with planning that service, so this hit me like a ton of bricks. It was everything I had been trying to tell people about. It was what my homily had tried to convey to my parish. It made me know that I—and we—am doing something important and valid. Because suddenly *I* was in that hymn. She—me—shall eat of this bread and live forever!

For several months I have been working with four other women hoping to start publishing an interfaith women's journal. One of those people is Jewish, and from her I have been reminded that we are not alone in trying to open up the liturgy; the Jewish women have been at it for a while, too, and have made some great strides. Consider that their struggle is in opposition to 3741 more years of male imagery than we've had! The risks they are taking are just as real—and the opportunities just as great—as our own. After all, it has to be threatening to many men to have us only recently move from the home to the office in leadership roles, and now we want to share their traditional roles in the temple and church as well! We're struggling to get in, and they're struggling to stay in. And the reality is that God expects us to find a way to work it out. She loves us—all of us!

The first time I heard someone say in public that God might be given female imagery was in Bea Blair's sermon one Sunday last spring in our parish. A few of us knew her plan, and I participated by administering the chalice, to be present on such a historic occasion—and because with others in the chancel I was prepared to form a "flying wedge" to protect her and get her out if the congregation turned on her. But, except for a few rustling feet and shiftings of bodies, we came through all right. Bea used both male and female imagery of God in her sermon, and took the opportunity and the risk of standing in the pulpit and giving us another point of view in telling the Good News.

The first Christians—women and men—risked acceptance of Jesus as the Risen Christ and went out to preach that Good News. But—and let's be clear about this—they did so on the basis of 3741 years of Mosaic law and history based on the male imagery of God, and the social mores of their time. We need to understand that all of that formed the basis for their perception of "the son" of "God the Father" become incarnate and "made man" and crucified and dead and buried and a risen "Lord" on Easter Day. There simply was no other way to express what they felt was happening in their lives. And it has been transmitted to us primarily by male scribes and explained by male theologians and philosophers. (At least, they are the ones who got published!) What we, here, 1980 years later, are proposing is that those perceptions can and must be changed to be more inclusive. To affirm our personhood in the sight of God. That the God who represented a father figure to the Jews, who gave us the Law, the Torah, the Decalogue, the structure of first Jewish and later Christian life, is indeed the God of Abraham, Isaac, and Jacob—and also the God of Sarah, Rebecca, Leah, and Rachel. The God of *all* our ancestors!

In a sense we, gathered together in this place, experimenting with this worship service, experimenting with how it feels to have a liturgy that speaks to us, have kinship with those first Christians trying to live with the enormity of the Risen Christ. They had to find a way to make that work for them by changing some of their lifelong Jewish understandings and by adding to their perceptions and possibilities. And that is our mission as well.

If the Holy Spirit is alive in this place among us, then she is alive in our home parishes as well. And I believe we must find validity in those places as well as in this place.

This feminist or nonsexist or open liturgy cannot be "ours" only. If we do that we will defeat our purpose—just as the first Christians could not keep their knowledge of Christ to themselves but were instructed to spread the Word, the Good News, throughout the world. We have to witness that there can be an inclusive, loving, open liturgy. And I submit that we have to share that with other women—and men—of faith. This is not "ours" any more than we can exclude others from the possibility of the sacraments or knowledge of the Spirit in their lives. I believe this movement will perish if we take that attitude. I think we need those men of faith who hear us and want to work with us to witness the Good News in language to which we can all relate.

This community needs to be nurtured and supported so that it will grow too large for this place, by adding to the numbers of women and men who come here to share this kind of worship service and take it away with them. I hope we do not isolate ourselves from one another. Jesus came into the world to save each of us—and we cannot call ourselves Christians if we now seek to separate out as women, calling upon the personhood/selfhood we have discovered, and have in effect "his," "hers" and "ours." "Ours" is the only way—it is God's way, it is the Way of the Cross, and we are the ones, women and men, who can put forth new, all-inclusive language and imagery and make everyone welcome in the sharing of the sacraments and acclamation of the Risen Christ, the Good News, the Word of God!

BEATRICE PASTERNAK *is of Jewish heritage and was baptized a Christian while in college. She is a New York City medical secretary, editor, and writer, and has studied at The National Institute for Lay Training at General Theological Seminary and the Institute of Theology at the (Episcopal) Cathedral of St. John the Divine. She is licensed as a Lay Reader and to administer the Chalice in the Episcopal Diocese of New York, and is a parishioner at the Church of the Heavenly Rest.*

Chafing Dish, Apron Strings
GAIL S. RANSOM

*Now as they went on their way, he entered a village; and a woman named
Martha received him into her house. And she had a sister called Mary, who sat at
the Lord's feet and listened to his teaching. But Martha was distracted with much
serving; and she went to him and said, "Lord, do you not care that my sister has
left me to serve alone? Tell her then to help me." But the Lord answered her,
"Martha, Martha, you are anxious and troubled about many things; one thing is
needful. Mary has chosen the good portion, which shall not be taken away from
her."*

LUKE 10:38–42, RSV

My heart goes out to Martha. She and I are sisters, cut from the
same fabric.
Anxious to serve.
Anxious about many things.
Attempting to show hospitality and warmth through what we do
rather than who we are.

We, like Martha, have tried to remain obedient to the teachings
of our culture.
We know how to behave at social gatherings.
We know how to get good grades.
I can offer a cup of coffee, pour it without spilling.
I can say "no" politely.

We treat elders with deference.
We mediate affection with gifts.
We cook too much food for our dinner guests—slaving away over a hot stove for hours in an attempt to offer proper hospitality.

Martha, who hid from her company behind a chafing dish, is our sister.

Martha and I have much company.
Perhaps you.
Are you anxious about many things?
Attempting to dish out according to cultural requirements?
Serving systems which promise great favors for your obedience —high-paying jobs, social status, a sense of belonging?

We Marthas can easily fool ourselves into thinking that we are serving society, progress, the common good—or, yes, even ourselves—through our frantic, fractured, distracted efforts.

Like Martha, we open our interiors to potential friends, lovers, and leaders, and then slip away to prepare some elaborate concoction to offer in our stead—as if our very presence was not gift enough.

We would leave our guests unattended while we prepare our surrogates, even pulling away braver brothers and sisters in the name of service.
Service to self doubt.
Service to our fears of intimacy.
Service to our fears of being met, found out, transformed—of learning a new ethic which might alter our allegiances and therefore, our lives.

No, better to stay in the kitchen than meet and commune with a friend.

Better to stay in the kitchen, where we know how to prepare the potatoes and dish out the company lines, than meet One who would ask great things of us, One who would open our hearts to the love, pain, suffering, and glory of bearing God's presence into our broken world.

No, better to stay in the kitchen.

Better to pile up the packages, the cookie jars, the coffee mugs, the rock and roll, the TV set, the shopping malls, the Hallmark cards, the birthday gifts, the three-piece suits, the six-course meals—than face each other as merely human, fully present, ready to be touched, changed, moved by the presence of another, by the presence of an incarnate God.

But Mary did it. What a brave woman she was! Perhaps she knew her need so intensely that she could not do otherwise, only listen and learn, listen and learn, listen and learn as a parched sojourner thirsty for the Way.

Mary is also our sister. For we too are parched sojourners, thirsty for the Way. We too are hungry for the truth. The sustenance we prepare in our offices and kitchens will never satisfy. That which we fuss over and offer as surrogate will never be enough. And we know it.

We are called to be like Mary. We are called to leave the many things which distract us and take the position of student at the feet of a teacher. Listen and learn. Listen and learn. Listen and learn.

Only "one thing is needful," says he. And "Mary has chosen the good portion, which shall not be taken away from her."

We are called to do likewise, to leave our kitchens and chafing dishes, to unwrap our apron strings and sit at the feet of Jesus, God-with-us, to listen and learn, listen and learn.

For, of all things about which we are anxious, only one thing is needed. And that portion can never be taken away.

GAIL RANSOM *lives in Houston, Texas, where she continues to explore the relationship of art to theology, spirituality to creativity, and Mary to Martha through writing, music composition, workshops, and concerts. She prepared for her arts ministry at the Yale Institute of Sacred Music and is a graduate of Yale Divinity School. She previously served as director of Religious Education and the Arts at The First Parish in Lincoln, Lincoln, Massachusetts.*

Three Women from Moab

CAROLE A. RAYBURN

Paul defines faith, in Hebrews 11:1, RSV, as "the assurance of things hoped for, the conviction of things not seen." How well this describes some women in Moab in times long ago. No one knows for sure whether their story took place in pre- or post-exilic times. In the days when the Judges ruled, there was a famine in Bethlehem–Judah. A man and a woman went to Moab, a fertile land, to save themselves from starving in Bethlehem. The choice of leaving their beloved family and friends and their homeland was made only after much painful deliberation. In Moab, the true God was not worshiped. They, as the chosen people of God, would not be given any special consideration in this strange land. Out of their desperation, though, they chose to cast their future with this ancestral home of Moab, the son of Lot.

After the family had lived in Moab for some time, the husband, Elimelech, died, leaving behind his wife, Naomi, and his two sons, Mahlon and Chilion. No doubt the grieving widow was grateful to the Lord for the emotional and physical support of her two sons. The sons thought about marrying and starting their own families, though they were perhaps hesitant about choosing Moabitish women. While the law of the Israelites did not expressly forbid marriage between them and those of the tribes of Ammon or Moab (as it did forbid unions with Canaanites), it did not encourage such matings. In fact, in later times, such as Nehemiah's period, the special law of Deuteronomy 23:3–6 would be interpreted as forbidding Moabite–Israelite marriages and as excluding the resulting children from the congregation of Israel. Mahlon and Chilion, though, were of marriageable age and desirous of finding wives, whether or not they were in a foreign environment. Two Moabitish women, Ruth and Orpah, married the sons. The family lived and worshiped together for ten years. The two young women, though of a different religion, observed the Israelite mother and her sons—their husbands— worship God. Perhaps they participated at times in this worship, out of respect for their new families. Then tragedy struck once more, this time a double blow: both sons died. We are not told how they died, whether through natural causes, disease, wartime, or criminal assault.

What is significant is that, in times so harsh on women, three women were left alone to provide for themselves. In the societies of that day, women were at best thought to be creatures who needed protection. If women were not taken care of by generous men, many thought, they would perish. The one situation worse than simply being a woman then was being a widow—a "used" or nonvirginal woman and one apt to be without financial means besides. And a childless widow—one without sons, especially— would be considered almost worthless. Thus, the two younger women, probably in their late twenties when widowed, had little to commend them in the eyes of the world and to prospective husbands: they had neither children nor dowry.

The plight of Naomi was even more tragic. She had left Bethlehem–Judah as a wife and a mother of sons. This accorded to her the highest status that a woman could have in the culture of those times: raising children to God's glory in the House of Israel. Now, when she might have been enjoying watching her grandchildren grow, she had lost all that she held precious. Or nearly all, since she still had her undaunted faith in God. Deeply saddened by losing her loved ones, she nonetheless did not forsake her Creator. This woman of God had suffered the pains of leaving her homeland, her kin and friends, to go to a strange land. Why, oh why, had she lost so much that mattered to her?

God had allowed a great tragedy to befall her, and she continued to ponder why. Holding steadfastly onto her faith in her Redeemer, she did not allow even this terrible circumstance to shake her faith in the one true God, Creator of all and provider for the widowed, the homeless, the helpless and weary.

While she still held onto the possibility that God could still do wonderful things for even her, she focused upon the immediate reality of her pitiful predicament. Naomi was to say to her friends, upon her return to Bethlehem, "Do not call me Naomi [which means "pleasant," "delightful"], call me Mara [which means "bitter"], for . . . the Lord has brought me back empty. Why call me Naomi, when the Lord has afflicted me, and the Almighty has brought calamity upon me?" This response is found in Ruth 1:20 (RSV).

Naomi was facing the same internal struggle in her suffering as Job would face. In her mind, the fault was not with her God but somehow—though she did not understand how—with her. Though deeply grieved by her losses, she did not testify against God. In an almost quiet acceptance of her fate, she did not cry out bitterly against the God of the universe, but she acknowledged that God had dealt harshly with her. In declaring herself to be "bitter," she appears to be indicating that she was suffering severe pain and experiencing soul-rending grief. But she did not hurl rancorous or resentful accusations toward God nor clamor in self-righteous indignation or self-pity. She was, though, ashamed before her friends and kin to return empty of husband and children.

God had special plans for restoring to Naomi a good and an abundant life. Of her it could have been said, as in Luke 17:19 (RSV), "Rise and go your way; your faith has made you well," and as in Ephesians 6:16, RSV, "Above all, [take] the shield of faith, with which you can quench all the flaming darts of the evil one." She conquered through her faith in God, overcoming all that Satan might have dealt to her. She withstood the test and, through the faith that God gave to her, she endured all.

But the book of Ruth is more than a story of one woman. It is the tale of three women at the most crucial time of their lives. They are alone, except for God and God's ever-abiding love and concern for them.

Do you believe that there is something predictive in the names that people are given? Or at least self-fulfilling in prophetic accuracy in the meanings of names? "Ruth" is not a Hebrew name, but rather it is a Moabitish word that some think is connected with the verb *ra'ah*, literally, "shepherding a flock" and denoting "to associate with," connoting "friend" or "friendship." "Orpah," however, meant "neck" or "stubbornness." Perhaps, then, their naming was another instance of the kind of prophecy concerning persons' lives that was evident with the naming of the twelve sons of Jacob.

When Naomi heard that the famine had ended in Bethlehem, she was determined to return there. She packed her belongings and paused pensively before beginning the long journey home.

Naomi had grown to love her two daughters-in-law over the years that they shared together. They had been a family. Yet now Naomi was to return to her land, which would be as strange a country to the young women as Moab had once been to Naomi. She would not wish to subject them to adapting to a new and perhaps uninviting environment, to leaving behind other family and friends in their native Moab. Naomi had observed the two women over the past ten years, noticing how they had adopted the ways and beliefs of the Israelites to themselves, not only externally but internally—a matter of the heart.

Stopping in her journey, she said lovingly to Ruth and Orpah, "Go, return each of you to her mother's house. May the Lord deal kindly with you, as you have dealt with the dead and with me." Sensing the deep loss of their mates that only a widow can fully understand, she expressed her motherly prayer that God would grant them second husbands.

It was a touching and deeply moving moment. The younger women wept when Naomi kissed them and released them from any obligation of following her to Judah. Still, out of love and duty to their mother-in-law, Ruth and Orpah wanted to go with her. Deciding as a last recourse to confront them with the cold, hard realities of life, Naomi entreated them to be sensible: she had no more sons in her womb for them to marry, and she had no husband with whom to produce future sons.

Orpah cared for her mother-in-law, and she had been a

good and loving wife to Chilion. She had had many opportunities to observe the Israelites and how they lived and worshiped, and to learn who their God was. Her knowledge of God was from the perspective of distanced intellectualism and not heartfelt religious conviction that this was the one true God before all other gods. Orpah's god was the god of Moab—Chemosh. Accompanying Naomi to the border of Moab, Orpah thought of how sad she would be if she left behind all that she had ever known, if she forfeited remarriage to care for her mother-in-law, and if she were to be an outcast in a land uninviting to Moabites. She reasoned that Naomi's God had not protected her from the tragic losses of her husband and sons. Even Naomi herself had admitted that her God had dealt bitterly with her, Orpah thought. Besides, how was she, a mere woman in a cruel and unjust world where the unmarried or widowed woman might be sexually and brutally assaulted at any time, to help another woman who was alone? Orpah rationalized that Naomi was devout and had inner strengths; she would make it somehow. What *she* needed to do most in life, Orpah thought, was to create a new beginning for herself among her own people.

In this decision, Orpah failed life's most crucial test, letting eternity slip through her fingers like a gossamer butterfly. She missed the mark on at least two counts of faith. Both of these concerned her relationship with Naomi and, through Naomi, Orpah's relationship with God. In the words of James 2:14–17, RSV: "What does it profit . . . if a man says he has faith but has not works? Can his faith save him? If a brother or sister is ill-clad and in lack of daily food, and one of you says to them, 'Go in peace, be warmed and filled,' without giving them the things needed for the body, what does it profit? So faith by itself, if it has no works, is dead." Thus, what good did it do for Orpah to express, even tearfully, how much she was concerned about Naomi and to say how much she loved her, unless she put this love into practice? Here was Naomi, a woman alone in a fearful environment, and Orpah would think primarily of her own loss and of her chances to improve her lot. True, Orpah might have taken care of Naomi on her own terms, remaining in Moab and returning to her heathen god. Naomi, however, would never have forsaken the true God. Orpah lacked the faith that God could provide for her and for Naomi in Bethlehem. While Orpah had the example of the faith of Naomi in coming to a foreign land, she concentrated upon the losses of her mother-in-law instead.

Nor did Orpah envision that three women alone could be used to the glory of God, in some wonderful way. She lacked the faith of which Christ spoke in Luke 12:24, when he said to the crowd, "Consider the ravens: they neither sow nor reap, they have neither storehouse nor barn, and yet God feeds them. Of how much more value are you than the birds!" How sad that Orpah, so close to the kingdom of God, went back to her people and to her heathen gods, lost forever to condemnation.

Ruth was a different kind of woman. No amount of logical reasoning or gentle persuasion was going to convince her to leave Naomi, the Godfearing woman whom she had learned to love and respect over the years. In her own quiet, steadfast way, Ruth held onto her mother-in-law. The Bible says, "Ruth clave unto her"—she held onto her and refused to be separated from her. This conversion was fervently real and of proportions of the wrestling of Jacob with the angel at Peniel in Genesis 32:22–31. Ruth, as did Jacob centuries before, fought firmly to acquire the blessings of God in being one of God's children. Neither Ruth nor Jacob would take "no" for an answer from God, even if it meant a fight to the death.

To the repeated entreaties of Naomi for Ruth to leave her, Ruth responded in resoluteness. To Naomi, a woman with powerful faith in the worthy and true God, Ruth would cling tightly. Ruth would not return to Moab after she had brought Naomi to Bethlehem. She would dissolve all ties to Moab. Although she still had some emotional ties to her country, to her people, and to Orpah, she made a decision based on faith and intellect: She would claim as her own the God of Israel. She passed the test of Naomi, showing her firm resolution to stay with Naomi and her God. In this decision, Ruth reflected real love. She demonstrated concern for the welfare of another, deep respect and devotion, loyalty and affection for a loved one, and intimacy of a relationship based on more than emotionality.

Bound to her mother-in-law by a common lifestyle and what was coming to be a common faith, Ruth was a kindred spirit to

Naomi, though not genetically related to her. The future looked rather dark and bleak to Ruth, who was husbandless, childless, and poverty-stricken besides. As a woman alone, she would encounter societal rejection, possible sexual aggression, financial impoverishment, and years of loneliness. Even had she been a Jewess, she could not have taken advantage of marrying the next living brother to her deceased husband in order to raise children to his name, in levirate fashion, because her brother-in-law had died also. Willing to become a wanderer or a beggar if necessary to stay with Naomi, she would go anywhere that Naomi chose to go.

Ruth knew of the Israelites only through Naomi and her family. For the first time, she learned from Naomi's intimations that women from Moab could not marry Israelite men unless they acknowledged the God of Israel. Ruth had entered into marriage with Mahlon without having a covenant relationship with his God. In his haste to marry Ruth, Mahlon had not been honest with her about the customs of Israel. However, Ruth had long ago begun to accept God, sacrificing all that even a Semite of her time could have given up: home, family, native beliefs, rights of protection of one's homeland, and even of burial with her people. She gave up all that she had known for a poor widow who had admitted that she had nothing to offer Ruth. Nothing, that is, but the only really important gifts in life—her love and her God. Decisively, Ruth says in the Book of Ruth 1:16, "Your people shall be my people and your God my God," renouncing forever the god of Moab and embracing the God of Israel.

In verse 1:17, Ruth says that she will even die and be buried in the same place in which Naomi is laid to rest. Burial places in Palestine in those days allowed for the bones of family members to be placed together in a common repository in a family tomb, in a pit cut out of a rock. Not even death would separate these two women. Ruth's words of loving concern were soothing and reassuring to the older woman, who had lost so much to death. In Ruth's oath, "May the Lord do so to me and more also if even death parts me from you," she spoke the name of Yahweh, and thus unceremoniously indicated that she had joined the people whose God is Yahweh. Naomi could not turn away such love, knowing that it was of God.

Ruth truly followed the advice of Jesus to the rich young ruler in Matthew 19:21, RSV, "If you would be perfect, go, sell what you possess and give to the poor, and you will have treasure in heaven; and come, follow me." Ruth gave up all that she had and all that she might ever have in remaining in Moab, in order to cast her lot with God and with God's people. She did not neglect the needs of others on this earth in finding her own way to God. Note well, beloved, she took care of her sister in the Lord first, and *then* she followed her Lord herself. Desirous of storing up her treasures not on earth (as Naomi suggested at first that Ruth do), she aimed to store up her riches in heaven instead. Her heart, as Jesus was to teach centuries later, would always be where her riches were (Matthew 6:19–21).

Her choice involved all of the elements of a true choice for God:

1. The surrender of a false belief: She renounced the Moabite god, Chemosh.

2. The choice involved sacrifice: To her, it was worth anything she had to endure to be with one who represented God to her, as did Naomi, and to find God.

3. God grants us help in making a right choice: God implanted within Ruth's heart a growing conviction that life was incomplete and destitute without the abiding presence of the Lord.

4. A decision is forced, and the test comes in which there must be a forsaking of one thing and the firm adoption of another: Ruth had to chose between a life in Moab with a false god or a life in Bethlehem with the God of Israel.

5. The right decision has great rewards: In being willing to forsake her life in Moab and even on this earth, if necessary, she found her life anew in a loving, merciful God who gave her not only marriage to a wealthy, kind kinsman of Naomi, as well as a share in the man's bountiful fields where she had once been a mere gleaner, but also the priceless and precious share in the ancestry of our Lord Jesus Christ, whose grandmother Ruth was.

In establishing a covenant relationship with God, Ruth also found the true solution to the broken unity of shared faith which she and Mahlon had experienced. Her deep love of what she had witnessed in Mahlon finally attained spiritual unity so that the memory might bring together that which was out of harmony in the past. In our lives with our loved ones, we experience the best of everything when we share the same deep religious convictions with them. She now had this too in her new life with Boaz. Bringing joy to Naomi in her old age, Ruth was blessed of women by God in a most special way. Through her strong faith in God, she could have said what Paul was to say centuries later in 2 Timothy 4:7–8, RSV, "I have fought the good fight, I have finished the race, I have kept the faith. Henceforth there is laid up for me the crown of rightousness, which the Lord, the righteous judge, will award to me on that day, and not only to me, but also to all who have loved his appearing."

Beloved, is that reward going to include me? Is it going to include you? Let us make our covenant relationship with God now, from an ever deepening desire for God to fill our lives with the Lord's will for us, wherever that may take us. We must be willing to "die" with Christ to "live" with God. Once each of us has gone down into the watery grave with Christ in baptism, we must continually die to the old person, forsaking all other gods—resentment, greed, selfish interests, self-righteousness, even pious self-criticism—to claim the true God of Israel. We must *daily* struggle with decisions and with self, refusing to let go of God. We must be willing to fight, even to the death, for God's eternal blessings, entreating our Maker not to ever leave us. Further, we must cling to each other as members of the family of God, forsaking pettiness, critical tendencies, and jealousies to be together with one another as we seek God in prayer—as Ruth clung to Naomi in her search for God. In this way we will truly be God's own, and God will be ours for all time and eternity. For this is love, which is real and forever!

CAROLE A. RAYBURN, Ph.D., M.Div., *is a clinical psychologist and seminary graduate. She had hoped to work in the ministry as much as women in her church are allowed to do this. Currently, she is getting back to her private practice of clinical psychology, until a clearer way is made known to her to also do pastoral work.*

Last at the Cross
NANETTE M. ROBERTS

When I was asked to speak today on women's issues from a biblically based standpoint, the phrase "last at the cross" popped into my head. But very little in the world is ever totally spontaneous, and obviously a series of occurrences led up to my wanting to talk about the people—especially the women—who remained with Jesus as he died. Their loyalty and bravery are obvious, and are clearly meant to contrast with the actions of Judas, the disciple who betrayed Christ, and with those of Peter, the disciple who denied him.

Yet Peter, despite his denial, is one of the great saints of the church, celebrated as the founder of the line of priests who made Christianity possible. Joseph of Arimathea, who procured the body for burial, is remembered in story and song. But the women at the cross are easily overlooked. Indeed, only a few weeks ago I read an otherwise wonderful sermon, a sermon so good that it was published as part of a distinguished sermon series, in which the writer declared that Jesus had died all alone, because all of his disciples had left him. Yesterday morning a speaker at a church meeting declared that when Jesus died, "only eleven men" were left in the world to do his work. "And," he then added, "a handful of others." Clearly, these statements reflect a common failing, a tendency to see only the people whom one thinks are important in a scene or an event, and to forget or overlook the others. But there were others to carry on Jesus' work; some of them were women, and some of those women were with him at the cross.

Modern anthropologists and historians are only just beginning to note and to correct a common practice of the past, which has been to look at a society or at an event in history in terms of what *men* do, and then to describe that society through what they learn from or about the men, totally overlooking the fact that there is another half to that society, a female half. Margaret Mead once said that men's activities in a society, whether they be to wage war or catch butterflies, are always considered the most important work in the society. But women are equally members of a society, and without recording their actions we do not have the whole picture. Failing to see women is a common practice. Because of that kind of mental bias or shortsightedness, it is easy to look back at biblical Christianity and see there only the actions of the important people, the men.

Now, obviously men's actions *have* been of decisive importance in Christianity, since for most of our two-thousand-year history men have held the power, written the theology, and ruled the churches. But in this day, when scholars, individuals, and many churches (including, thank God, our own) are trying to redress that imbalance, it is important to look once more at those *women* who were among the last at the cross.

Make no mistake, the Gospel tells us clearly that they were there. Mark, which is probably the earliest of the Gospels, speaks *only* of women as being there, and includes among them Mary, Jesus' mother; Mary Magdalene; and a woman named Salome, who, Mark says, "had followed Jesus in Galilee and ministered to him." He says in addition that there were "also many other women who came up with him to Jerusalem." Matthew, probably the second of the Gospels in time of composition, also speaks *only* of women, and he says that "many women" were there. Luke and John, however, say that there were *both* women and men. Certainly these accounts should remind us that there were many women, some named, some nameless, who followed Jesus throughout his ministry, ministering to him. Since the word *disciple* means simply "follower" or "student," these women were in every sense of the word among Jesus' original disciples. And there is no question of their fidelity, for the Gospels tell us that they were either the last or among the last at the cross.

Two days later, it was women alone who came to the tomb to anoint the body, and discovered the empty tomb. Their presence at the tomb is of course understandable, for ministering to the dead and preparing a body for burial have in many societies been tasks specifically assigned to women. A former student of mine once told me that in the part of Sicily from which he came, one of the few paying jobs open to older women was that of being a hired mourner at a funeral. And anthropologists have noted that in many societies women not only bring us into the world, but they also nurse us and prepare our bodies as we leave this world.

I hope that you don't see that as morbid. To me, there is a nice feeling of completion there, a sense of the centrality of women to the most basic human experiences, to those moments when people most need ritual and comfort and care. And these biblical women—Mary, Mary Magdalene, Salome, and the others—also performed these central tasks, being last at the cross and first at the tomb, ministering to the body of Christ.

Now, two thousand years later, the phrase "the body of Christ" has taken on a larger meaning. It's like the phrase "the body politic," and refers at least on one level to the sense of shared beliefs that make us a religious community, and to the covenant that binds us together. But it is important to remember that before there was a community called the Body of Christ there was a literal, flesh-and-blood body of Christ, to which women ministered. Yet somehow, as we have preached Christianity, we have let these women and their story be overlooked.

Throughout recorded history, women have tended to be *invisible* members of the Body of Christ, just as they and their experience have tended to be invisible in secular history. As you know, I work with family issues, and I remember studying the work of Philippe Ariès, the famous historian of the family. Ariès believes that *childhood* as a concept did not really exist before the eighteenth century; he declares, for example, that the men of the middle ages had no sense of such a passage in human life.

He is, of course, unaware that when he says *men* (and thinks he means *humankind*), he is really saying *males*, for can anyone doubt that childhood existed for women, who spent their lives (and often lost their lives) with and for children? Indeed, as one historian has said, the history of women is written on the forgotten tombstones of a country's churches. But in history, and in a great measure in our churches, women have tended to be invisible. Oh, we've filled the pews—today we are even a majority there—but we do not fill nor have we ever filled the seats of power. As the great French writer Simone de Beauvoir commented, *men* make religions, *women* worship. This surely has been true of Christianity. How did it happen? And, even more important, what can we do about it?

As to how it happened, it's not hard to find in the record the systematic exclusion of women from a central place in Christianity. Elaine Pagels, in her book called *The Gnostic Gospels*, studies the Gnostic Christians and points out how important women seem to have been in this sect, which arose almost immediately after Jesus' death. But Gnosticism was soon declared a heresy, as you know. The apostle Paul often speaks as though women were important in the development of the faith, but very quickly he too is circumscribing or even prohibiting their input as anything but worshipers—not movers and shapers of the church. Yet modern feminist scholars have found inscriptions on first- and second-century tombstones which refer to women as "leader of the synagogue," and there are in the Roman catacombs murals which show a woman celebrating the Eucharist. But such activity on the part of women was too new, too revolutionary. Slowly the customary practice of male dominance in Semitic, Roman, and Greek society became the customary practice of Christianity as well.

By the fourth century A.D. it had become Christian dogma that Jesus' nature was exactly the same as that of the Father God, and the ease with which Christianity referred to God as *he* or *him* was doubly reinforced, leading to a frequently held misconception that seems to imply that the essential thing about Jesus was his *maleness*, not his *humanity*. These ideas easily reinforced traditional concepts of male superiority and female inferiority.

Throughout the writings of the early church, we find a comfortable conviction of the centrality of men to religion and life, and the peculiar "otherness" of women.

Some in the early Christian tradition ranted and raved against women. My favorite among all the ranters and ravers is Tertullian, who said to women, "Sisters . . . do you not know that you are Eve? The sentence of God on your sex lives on. *You* are the takers from the forbidden tree. *You* are the first breakers of the divine law. *You* are the Devil's gateway. . . . How easily *you* destroyed man, the image of God. Because of the death which *you* brought upon us, even the Son of God had to die." Man was the image of God; woman, whatever she was, wasn't in that image. St. Augustine, wondering why God had made women in the first place, decided that it was so that more virgins would be born, and even St. Thomas, much later in the history of Christianity, says that although all people should love their parents, they should love their fathers the most, for the "father is the principle of our birth in a more excellent way than the mother." And surely some of the father's excellence derives from his good fortune in having been made male, in the image of God.

This incredible literal use of the concept of the male image of God has its humorous aspects, but some of them were deadly. In the late Middle Ages, Europe went on a witch hunt, and two fifteenth-century priests wrote a book to help interrogators identify witches. They pointed out that the basis of witchcraft was the Devil, who ensnared the witch through "carnal" or fleshly lust. Now, as everyone who was anyone knew, women were more prone to carnal lust than men; therefore it was logical that most witches would be women. And, to nobody's surprise, they were. In addition, the two men reflected that, since when God became flesh he took on the shape of a man, the male shape was forever after particularly protected against the temptations of the Devil. I suppose that this could be seen as funny, but its humor fades when we remember that the result of this attack on women because they were born in the wrong image was the death of at least 300,000 women in Europe and America, over several centuries, death after brainwashing, public humiliation, and often terrible torture.

The slow movement away from second-class citizenship that women have made in relatively recent times is probably well known to you all. Protestantism has opened doors, but slowly and often unwillingly, to the fuller participation of women in the church. Still, the effects of centuries of discrimination and exclusion will take a long time to eradicate. We must work on the legacy of these practices, which tend to make us doubt women's abilities if not their devotion, and to be unwilling to see women fully in the role of pastor in the pulpit, or leader of the church.

The history and the present situation of women in the Christian church causes many of us pain. Last week I attended a conference at which one of the speakers was Sister M. Theresa Kane, the courageous nun who, some of you may remember, reminded Pope John Paul during his visit to the United States in 1979 of the important issue of the ordination of women. A Catholic woman there, her voice shaking with suppressed tears, told how she loved her church and her religion, and said that she could be nothing else but a Catholic, but that she could not set foot inside a Catholic church, nor could she let her daughters go, because of the humiliation she feels women suffer there every time they listen to the language and know what the church's view of women is.

Well, many Protestant women and Jewish women feel the same pain. We feel it when we hear God, who is certainly spirit or force or love or wisdom or all of those things and much more than any words can tell, referred to only as *he* or *him*, so that the divine is squeezed into a concept of exclusive maleness; many women feel the same pain when they try to sing the words of many of our hymns, or when they hear our Christian community referred to as a *brotherhood*, our faith described as the *faith of our fathers*, or are told at Christmas that all *Christian men* should rejoice. Many of us have left the church because of this pain, or have become lukewarm members of the Body of Christ.

And yet many of us have stayed, choosing to be, like those biblical women, among the last at the cross. Perhaps we have done so because we have perceived that there was a hidden message in Christianity, a treasure hidden there, waiting to be preached. For certainly, as modern scholars are increasingly pointing out, Jesus' attitudes toward women were extraordinary for his time. Indeed, many have observed that Jesus was what we today would call a feminist. And perhaps it is because of that treasure that those women remained faithful at the cross.

Think of it: In a society which would not accept the testimony of a woman in a court of law, he sent women out as witnesses, to announce not only his resurrection but also to announce that he was the Messiah. The woman at the well was the first person to whom he revealed who he was, and on the basis of her witness, many came to believe in him. In a world in which a menstruating or bleeding woman defiled anyone or anything she touched, Jesus responded with healing compassion to the bleeding woman in the crowd who touched his garment. In a world where women were forbidden to study the holy teachings, Jesus affirmed the need and right of Mary, Lazarus' sister, to do just that, and told her complaining sister Martha, "Mary has chosen the good portion, which shall not be taken away from her." And in doing so he affirmed women's right to be full and equal members with men in the Body of Christ.

Those who wish to address women's issues from a biblical perspective would do well to reexamine these women of the Bible, these women who ministered to Jesus, traveled with him, and were among the last at the cross. And certainly we Protestants, who are generally rather uncomfortable with Mary the mother of Jesus because of our attitudes toward Catholicism, would do well to reexamine what we know of Mary. For far too long she has been presented to us as the epitome of all that is passive and subordinate, the willing martyr, the unthinking vessel used by God. But I think we need to know more about this extraordinary woman who mothered so extraordinary a son. After all, there had to be some reason why God picked her!

Many of us today are influenced by what is called "liberation theology," a theology which asserts that we find God in the struggle of the oppressed for liberation, and in the struggle for justice and mercy in a world full of injustice and pain. So we should remember that when Jesus described his mission, he used words from the prophet Isaiah which proclaim just such a theology. Let me paraphrase them for you. Jesus said, "The spirit of the Lord is upon me. For I have come to preach the good news to the poor; to heal the brokenhearted; to preach release to the captives and the recovery of sight to the blind; to set at liberty those who are oppressed; to preach the acceptable year of the Lord." The acceptable year of the Lord of which he spoke may well have been the jubilee year, the year in which, by Jewish law, the land was to be left fallow, all debts were to be forgiven, and those who had gone into bondage because of their debts were to be set free. That would be good news to the poor indeed! If that is what Jesus was talking about, what an upsetting of the status quo that would have been! He was preaching a theology of liberation.

But when we see that he had such an idea, should we not wonder at the part played in his development by his mother? For if you remember, Mary greeted the news that she would be the mother of the Messiah not with a passive acceptance, but with the joyful pronouncement: "My soul magnifies the Lord, and my spirit rejoices in God my Savior . . . he has shown strength with his arm, he has scattered the proud in the imagination of their hearts. He has put down the mighty from their thrones, and exalted those of low degree; he has filled the hungry with good things, and the rich he has sent empty away." A woman who saw God's work in that way was, I would submit, a mother fit to raise a child who would go forth to preach the liberating theology of the Good News. And she, as we might expect, went with Jesus in many of his travels, and was among those who stayed faithful, at the cross and beyond.

What I would like to leave with you this morning is a heightened sense of the fact that the women of the Bible need to be seen with new eyes, eyes that see both their *presence* and their *importance*, eyes that are aware that, in a world where they could not be rabbis or judges or doctors or community leaders, women still heard Jesus' message, became his disciples, caused others to be his followers, and acted upon his teachings. At the same time, they also ministered to this extraordinary man in ways typical of women of their time—they cared for him in his travels, they stayed with him through his suffering, and, when he was dead, they went to anoint the body in which Christ had lived.

We, who are now part of that body, who ritually break bread in its memory, can do no other than affirm these women as Jesus' disciples. Let us acknowledge that we have tended to make them invisible, and resolve to correct that injustice. Let us determine to hear the voices of today's women equally with those of men, and to make full use of their gifts. And let us resolve never again to forget that just as Christ's flesh-and-blood body did not die alone or unloved, so in the Body of Christ, of which we are *all* a part, women, like men, are still there, at the cross, willing and able to do Christ's work of justice, liberation, and love. May it be so.

NANETTE M. ROBERTS, *a native of Minnesota, studied in France on a Fulbright Scholarship. She received her doctorate from New York University, where she held a Woodrow Wilson Dissertation Fellowship in Women's Studies. Presently at the United Church Board for Homeland Ministries, she is Secretary for Family Life and Women's Issues and General Secretary-elect of the Division of Higher Education.*

Woman as Oppressed; Woman as Liberated in the Scriptures

ROSEMARY RADFORD RUETHER

Hannah also prayed and said, "My heart exults in the Lord; my strength is exalted in the Lord. My mouth derides my enemies, because I rejoice in thy salvation.

"There is none holy like the Lord, there is none besides thee; there is no rock like our God. Talk no more so very proudly, let not arrogance come from your mouth; for the Lord is a God of knowledge, and by him actions are weighed. The bows of the mighty are broken, but the feeble gird on strength. Those who were full have hired themselves out for bread, but those who were hungry have ceased to hunger. The barren has borne seven, but she who has many children is forlorn. The Lord kills and brings to life; he brings down to Sheol and raises up. The Lord makes poor and makes rich; he brings low, he also exalts. He raises up the poor from the dust; he lifts the needy from the ash heap, to make them sit with princes and inherit a seat of honor. For the pillars of the earth are the Lord's, and on them he has set the world.

"He will guard the feet of his faithful ones; but the wicked shall be cut off in darkness; for not by might shall a man prevail. The adversaries of the Lord shall be broken to pieces; against them he will thunder in heaven. The Lord will judge the ends of the earth; he will give strength to his king, and exalt the power of his anointed."

—1 SAMUEL 2:1–10, RSV

181

1 Samuel 2:1–10 is the canticle of Hannah rejoicing in God's redemption of her from the curse of barrenness and her thanksgiving for her son, through whom she will be exalted.

The text reveals the ambiguity of women's position in the biblical tradition. On the one hand, the story of Hannah gives graphic illustration of women's oppressed condition in Hebrew society. As a wife, Hannah has only one justification for her existence—to bear a son and male heir for her husband. Lacking that honor, she is accounted worthless. It is not simply that she is childless. If she had only girl children, she would still be accounted unfortunate. Only male children can redeem woman's existence. The idea that she might have a girl rather than a boy is, in fact, not even considered in the text. It is simply understood that only a male is desirable. What effect this must have had on women through the ages—that they are born and grow up knowing that their existence is a disappointment to their mothers and fathers, that their mothers are "dishonored" through their birth!

The story of Hannah, leading up to the canticle, also gives us further insight into the low esteem in which women were held. Hannah is praying for a son, her person filled with emotion. Yet the priest who sees her assumes that she is drunk! Would a man praying in an emotional way be assumed drunk? One wonders. It seems that the initial assumption of the priest is that a woman's emotions are base and lacking seriousness. It is only when she explains the source of her emotion—the one emotion (desire for a son) that would be respected by a Hebrew male—that he takes her seriously and gives her his blessing.

Finally the story shows the way women in patriarchal societies internalize their own oppression. This is shown not only by Hannah, who cannot regard herself as an acceptable person until she has borne a male heir. It is also shown most poignantly in the behavior of the second wife, Peninnah, who is the mother of many children and uses this status to deride Hannah. The need of women to justify themselves through motherhood thus divides women from each other, shaming the barren woman and giving the fertile woman a tool for pride and contempt for the other.

We can also see in this situation the conflict in which women are set in polygamous societies. Hannah, although childless, we can assume to be her husband's favorite wife. Yet her childlessness throws her favor in jeopardy, even though her husband tries to assure her of his love. Peninnah, on the other hand, feels herself in a second-rate status in this respect and is trying to use her fecundity to oust Hannah and put herself in the position of the favorite wife. Women have often been seen in patriarchal societies as competitive with each other, as not liking each other. Seldom is it recognized that this competition is built into the structural dependency of women in the system.

Finally God chooses to cure Hannah of her curse and "open her womb." We might note that in the Hebrew version of such divine activity, there is no embarrassment toward the sexual act itself. God does not give Hannah a child through a "virgin birth," but by acting within the natural sexual intercourse of Hannah and Elkanah.

Now Hannah hymns her thanksgiving as one who has been redeemed and exalted by God. The emphasis in her canticle changes somewhat. First Hannah's exaltation is seen as an example of God breaking the power of the mighty and giving strength to the feeble. Those who have been full go begging, while those who have been hungry are filled. Does this mean that God is a God of justice who comes to vindicate those who have been oppressed and to put down the mighty? Who is the mighty one who has been brought low by Hannah's redemption from barrenness? Is this merely a domestic triumph, Hannah's vindication against Peninnah? Do we have here only a continuation of the patriarchal competition between women? Or is the reference supposed to be more prophetic, a symbol of Israel as the oppressed people who will be vindicated by God, while the mighty ones of the world will be brought low? The text seems to move in this direction, making Hannah, the oppressed woman, a symbol of the oppressed people, the oppressed nation, in a world of mighty empires.

But the possibility that Hannah's redemption from barrenness is a symbol of God's redemption of the oppressed and the defeat of the oppressors is not carried through. The following stanzas move in the direction of seeing this event simply as an example of the arbitrary sovereignty of God. God can do whatever he wills. He raises up and he puts down; he kills and he brings to life. The Lord makes poor and he makes rich. Hannah's story is in danger of simply being an example of unexpected change of fortune and God's sovereignty over all changes of fortune. The question of the moral status of good or bad fortune becomes unclear. God is said to be responsible for barrenness and poverty as well as fecundity and wealth. He gives and withholds these gifts as he wills.

But then the text reverts back again to the struggle between God's elect, God's faithful ones, and the wicked. Hannah's redemption again is put in the context of a vindication by God of the righteous over against the wicked, the adversaries of God. But it is not clear on what grounds they are God's adversaries. Is it merely because they are Israel's national enemies? The canticle ends with a vision of God's anointed, the messianic king, established on the throne of Israel, through whom God will reign to the ends of the earth.

The message of Hannah's canticle thus remains ambiguous. It falls between a moral vision of God's righteousness as vindicator of the unjustly oppressed and simply God's arbitrary power as sovereign over changing human fortunes. Also its vision of the victory of the righteous Israel against the wicked lies between a moral vision of redemption and simply a nationalistic triumph over one's foes, with Yahweh as Israel's national war God who will defeat her enemies and make her a great power in the world.

It would not be outside the limits of our topic to compare Hannah's canticle to that of Mary in the New Testament "Magnificat" (Luke 1:47–55). Mary's hymn of thanksgiving for her forthcoming child is modeled on that of Hannah. Yet several of the ambiguities which we found in the earlier text have now been clarified. For Luke, Mary's childbearing makes her an agent of God in human redemption. Through her, God's messianic work will enter history. Moreover, the focus is no longer on curing her from barrenness. Her childbearing is completely gratuitous. She does not need to justify herself through having a child.

Luke makes the crux of God's messianic action in history the vindication of the oppressed and the bringing low of the mighty.

There is no longer any doubt about the moral character of this drama. The oppressors have not been put in this position by God, but rather express thereby their sinful arrogance. God acts to bring them low and to exalt the lowly in order to create a new situation in history, where there will be no more poor and rich, no more oppressors and oppressed. God does not simply reverse fortunes, putting some in the position of oppressors and throwing others into oppression. The end of the messianic drama is no longer a national triumph in which the former slave becomes a slavemaster and the slavemaster a slave. Rather there is a new situation, where there is no longer slave or slavemaster. This is the radical clarification of the meaning of God's messianic action in history that has been disclosed through the prophetic mission of Jesus, and is clearly seen in Luke's reworking of the canticle.

Mary as woman is seen by Luke as a symbol of Israel, but specifically as a symbol of the poor and oppressed of history. As a woman of a nation held in no esteem in the world, she represents the poor who will be filled with good things, those of low degree who will be exalted in the messianic transformation of history. Moreover, the ability of women to cooperate with God and to make a decisive contribution to God's redeeming work in history is no longer confined to childbearing. As a virgin, Mary is not expected to justify herself through childbearing. Instead, the focus of her action can be shifted to another plane. It is not just her motherhood that is her redeeming work, but rather her act of faith, her assent to God. It is this act of personal faith, this ability to hear God's word, that makes her the "co-redeemer" with God. Without Mary's willing cooperation, God could not have acted in history!

Women are no longer redeemed by childbearing in the Gospels, but by faith. This advance is lost in the later New Testament; e.g., 1 Timothy 2:15, which reverts back to the traditional patriarchal standpoint. This also means that scripture is not of one piece, but contains a mixture of good and bad ideas. Prophetic vision is the critical norm, not only for society and religion, but for scripture as well. When the woman in the crowd raises her voice to give the traditional praise of Jesus' mother, "Blessed is the womb that bore you and the paps that gave you suck," Jesus rebukes her by saying, "Nay, rather, blessed is she who hears the word of God and keeps it" (Luke 11:27–28, RSV). This is not a put-down of woman. It means that woman is now raised from the level of biological instrument to that of person, whose dignity lies in her personal freedom. Nor, for Luke, is it a put-down of Mary. Mary, for Luke, is the exemplar of those who hear the word of God and keep it. It is for this reason that she makes possible God's messianic entrance into history.

For Luke and the Gospels generally, it is not surprising that it is precisely a woman who is the one who hears the word, whereas the mighty, the scholars and priests, do not hear it, refuse to hear it. This indeed is the heart of Jesus' message, that the Christ has come to seek and save the lowly and despised ones of history. It is they particularly who will hear and understand him, whereas the religious and social elites will not be able to hear his radical message that "the first shall be last and the last first," and "those who would be first in the Kingdom must become last and servant of all" (e.g., Matthew 20:26–27).

Mary's canticle thus clarifies the message of Hannah's canticle and carries us to a new level of understanding of God's messianic work in history. Salvation is not just reversal of fortunes, but is the ending of all unjust fortunes. This happens only when we seek out and identify with those who have been oppressed and despised in this present world.

DR. ROSEMARY RADFORD RUETHER *is a Roman Catholic feminist theologian. She holds the Georgia Harkness Chair of Applied Theology at Garrett Evangelical Theological Seminary.*

Sometimes There's God, So Quickly

SHARON BLESSUM SAWATZKY

O Lord, our Lord, how majestic is thy name in all the earth!

Thou whose glory above the heavens is chanted by the mouth of babes and infants, thou hast founded a bulwark because of thy foes, to still the enemy and the avenger.

When I look at thy heavens, the work of thy fingers, the moon and the stars which thou hast established; what is man that thou art mindful of him, and the son of man that thou dost care for him?

Yet thou hast made him little less than God, and dost crown him with glory and honor. Thou hast given him dominion over the works of thy hands; thou hast put all things under his feet, all sheep and oxen, and also the beasts of the field, the birds of the air, and the fish of the sea, whatever passes along the paths of the sea.

O Lord, our Lord, how majestic is thy name in all the earth!

—Psalm 8, rsv

There is a beautiful moment in the play *A Streetcar Named Desire* by Tennessee Williams. A person named Blanche is trying to hold her life together. Her world is falling apart. She is looking for some solid ground to stand on, some center for her life. She desperately needs to be loved. Unfortunately, she is one of those

187

people who talk all the time, and the way she talks all the time repels the very thing she wants most, which is for someone to love her.

Blanche meets a man named Mitch, who also has a social problem. He is much overweight and, as he explains to her, he perspires profusely. He is a very lonely person and much in need of love also. They get to the point where Blanche is able to share with him one of the tragic moments in her life. She tells him the terrible story, and when she is finished, Mitch takes her in his arms. He says, "You need somebody, and I need somebody too. Could it be you and me, Blanche?"

She stares at him in disbelief. Eyes filling with tears, she reaches for him and says this lovely line, "Sometimes there's God, so quickly." The scene closes.

It is an amazing thing that suddenly, in the midst of this distressful life, a person is graced by God. Occasionally, when you are not expecting it, something is awakened within you and you must connect to the God-presence in this world. It may happen in relationship, as with Blanche and Mitch. Or it may happen in nature, as with the Psalmist.

Agnes Sanford tells about her first sudden awareness of God. She says:

> I was in a bad mood; my children were sick, the house was a mess, and I climbed thunderously into the car to fetch my friend and helper, Elizabeth. As I drove through the frosty late winter countryside, all of a sudden everything changed. And yet it was the same. I saw the pale earth-shine of the early moon in the sky and I was part of the moon and knew the feeling of moonness. I was part of the pinpoints of winter wheat pushing through melting snow. I was part of the peach tree whose twigs were beginning to glow with uprising sap. I could feel the sap pushing its way into life. The pulse of God and his world was in my pulse. . . .

Sometimes there's God, so quickly. . . .

We have a little house in the wooded hills of Pennsylvania. One Friday night, tired and hungry, we turned down the little gravel road in the dusk. Suddenly in front of us were a doe and her two fawns—sweet, swift, soft-eyed animals, which stood to the side of the road, watching us watching them. Two more appeared, and then another. We were speechless, as if entering an enchanted forest. It was more than us and the deer; it was God, so quickly. . . .

One of our first nights up there, Jamie wanted me to come see something. You know how it is—you're reading or talking or working, and a child always wants your attention when you'd rather not be bothered. But he was insistent—as he always is—and so he persuaded me to come out to the porch. It was incredible. The crickets and katydids were playing in concert louder than I'd ever heard. It was like standing in the middle of an orchestra pit. The sounds resonated inside us, and we were at one with that universe. God—so quickly.

Since that concert has become evening ritual to us, I bought a little book by Winston Abbott about cricket song. He writes:

> The days drift downward
>   as the floating leaves
>   are gone
> And we know, both you and I,
>   that each contains its precious moments—
>   moments when our spirits are free
>   as free as they may ever be.
> Yet each moment is speeding toward eternity.
> It is getting late, so very late, and we have
>   yet to listen to the song of the cricket.

The Psalmist may not have mentioned cricket concert, but he too seemed to experience the sudden wonder of God in the world: "When I look at thy heavens, the work of thy fingers, the moon and the stars which thou hast established . . ."

Sometimes there's God, so quickly.

Maybe you're thinking that you haven't really seen the glory of God lately. Maybe you've seen less majesty and more misery. Yet, think with wonderment on the signs around you:

- the healing process when someone recovers from illness,
- the thoughtful listening of a caring friend,
- the minuscule life in action under a microscope,
- the surprising resilience when life is shattered,
- the growing of garden from seed to harvest,

- the growing of child in body and mind,
- the embracing hope of Begin and Sadat;
- I've even heard that the rising sun speaks of God's wonder.

The lump that rises in your throat when you hear a song you love; the affection that rises in your heart when you see an old friend—these moments move us to life's depths, which we call God.

Sometimes there are things in our lives that cloud the majesty of God. That doesn't mean the stars have stopped shining; only we have to work harder to be in their light. The simple, splendid order of God designs its way throughout the universe, and the wonder of it may grab you at any second.

We are an immeasurable speck in the immense galaxies. Yet we are part of a divine creativity.

Our troubles come when we lose perspective. There are two basic problems that arise. The first is that we may glorify ourselves and think that we are at the top of the order of creation. (Of course, you and I don't do that, but we know people who do.) Albert Schweitzer had something to say about that:

When we consider the immensity of the universe, we must confess that we are insignificant. The world began, as it were, yesterday. It may end tomorrow. Life has existed in the universe for a brief second. And certainly man's life can hardly be considered the goal of the universe. Its margin of existence is always precarious. Study of the geological periods shows that. So does the battle against disease. When one has seen whole populations annihilated by sleeping sickness, as I have, one ceases to imagine that human life is nature's goal.

The second problem, the other side of the coin, is when we think we are at the bottom of the order of creation. There is a rabbinic saying that the worst thing the evil impulse can do to you is to make you forget you are a child of the King.

To sense the awesome presence of God in this world is to gain insight into who we are, where we belong, to find our place in the scheme of things.

Like the Psalmist, if we behold any of the majesty or the mystery of the divine at all, we must then be moved to consider that this is God's world, not ours, that we are, in fact, responsible to carry out the divine artistry at work. In the magnificent masterpiece of the universe, we are to be paintbrushes creating a more beautiful scene. But our work must be in harmony with the design of the Creator. We get in trouble and out of perspective if we go off on our own color scheme. Or if we think our brushstrokes aren't important!

There is an artistry at work in the cosmos, creating colorful systems of love and truth. You and I are such an insignificant part of it—yet we are one with the artist.

Once there was a man who was lonely and shy and pushed all the awful feelings deeper inside as he filled himself with food. Across the room was a woman who was sad and really had no one to talk to. They did not look up.

Once there was a boy who lay on his back and counted the stars. When he was twelve, he knew the sky by heart. He wears thick glasses now and studies mathematics. How he leans over his paper and figures out the stars. Now his little girl looks up at the sky. She wishes he would too.

There could be God, so quickly.

SHARON BLESSUM SAWATZKY *is a writer, educator, gardener, bread-baker, needlepointer, dreamer, and poet. She lives with Henry, David, Jamie, and affectionate pets in Chatham, New Jersey.*

The Movement of Suffering

DONNA SCHAPER

My God, my God, why hast thou forsaken me? Why art thou so far from helping me, from the words of my groaning? O my God, I cry by day, but thou dost not answer; and by night, but find no rest. . . . A company of evildoers encircle me; they have pierced my hands and feet; . . . they divide my garments among them, and for my raiment they cast lots. But thou, O Lord, be not far off! O thou my help, hasten to my aid! . . . You who fear the Lord, praise him! . . . For he has not despised or abhorred the affliction of the afflicted; and he has not hid his face from him, but has heard, when he cried to him.

—PSALM 22:1–2, 16, 18–19, 23–24, RSV

Therefore, . . . consider Jesus, the apostle and high priest of our confession. He was faithful to him who appointed him, just as Moses also was faithful in God's house. . . . Now Moses was faithful in all God's house as a servant, to testify to the things that were to be spoken later, but Christ was faithful over God's house as a son. And we are his house if we hold fast our confidence and pride in our hope.

—HEBREWS 3:1–2, 5–6, RSV

So they took Jesus, and he went out, bearing his own cross, to the place called the place of a skull, which is called in Hebrew Golgotha. There they crucified him. . . .

When the soldiers had crucified Jesus they took his garments and made four parts, one for each soldier. But his tunic was without seam, woven from top to bottom; so they said to one another, "Let us not tear it, but cast lots for it to see whose it shall be." . . .

So the soldiers did this; but standing by the cross of Jesus were his mother, and his mother's sister, Mary the wife of Clopas, and Mary Magdalene. When Jesus saw his mother, and the disciple whom he loved standing near, he said to his mother, "Woman, behold your son!" Then he said to the disciple, "Behold your mother!" And from that hour the disciple took her to his own home.

After this Jesus, knowing that all was now finished, said (to fulfill the scripture), "I thirst." A bowl full of vinegar stood there; so they put a sponge full of the vinegar on hyssop and held it to his mouth. When Jesus had received the vinegar, he said, "It is finished"; and he bowed his head and gave up his spirit.
—JOHN 19:17–30, RSV

Three-part sermons have a traditional form. They move from the difficulty to the bridge to the solution, from the problem to the conflict to the promise, from the sin to the repentance to the salvation. This three-part sermon will not be like that. This will have the movement of suffering: from avoidance to recognition, then to brokenness, and then to trust and acceptance. If you hear vaguely Elizabeth Kubler Ross's stages of grief, you will be on the right track; but if you hear her stages neatly in some sort of textbook order, you will be on the wrong track. The movement carries us through three verbs: "to see," "to feel," "to trust." And so to the first part, about seeing.

The temptation of Good Friday is to talk about someone else's pain. Of women who are assaulted on faraway city streets while the public watches and does nothing to help. Of blacks in South Africa, who arm themselves for a freedom war even though they haven't asked our permission, even though we would tell them not to bother if they would just ask our advice. Of children who are abused by their parents. And equal rights amendments that may not pass even though we travel to Washington every week on the strength of our American Express cards and our best nostalgia for the old days in front of the White House. These pains are real, and to some filtered extent they are ours.

The crime of Good Friday is that it will not permit such borrowing of pain. Good Friday assaults us with our own, and, look to other arenas as we may, it will always drive us back to our own. It is a dangerously honest day, one that seeks to spend capital and will not settle for increased debt.

Good Friday strolls onto the small stage of our lives and always appears too large. We borrow pain for the sake of restoring proportion, not just because we can tolerate others' difficulty better than we can our own. We borrow the pain because somehow that's where our innocence tells us it really is. To whatever extent we really hurt, we always know that the globe has tales that will compete with our own. The hungry in China have made us eat our vegetables for a long time. But to the guilt of a century of senseless anonymous crosses, Good Friday adds the tale of a cross with a name on it. Jesus' cross. My cross. Your cross. In the hit parade of oppressions, somehow we know that our Western variety is not number one. And even on the courts of pain, we hate to lose a competition.

But even if our pain is not the largest in the world, it is still there. It doesn't matter how special we think we are as white Americans, as Yale people, as a chosen minority surrounded by a hostile and hurting world. The cross is a rough slab of reality stewing in its own exaggeration, breaking through our categories of paradox, irony, and grayness, reminding us of death. It polarizes the lovely ambiguity in which we choose to rest. It comes as a criminal to us: unwanted, terrifying, boundary-trespassing. It steals our comfort from us. We are no longer at ease in our own spiritual neighborhood. It makes a mockery of safety, of our sense that we own what we carry around.

The cross reminds us that the issue is us and what we have become. It repeats our cocktail party conversation about how the bottom of our Western value system has fallen out and isn't it an awful shame the way people act: no moral fiber, no sense of purpose, nothing like the good old days of cultural integration.

The cross reminds us that disaster is a possibility from which no one is immune.

It tells us that the old consolations of religion, class, art, and race have lost their blessing.

It reminds us that we are not judged by the ease with which we identify with centers of power but by the ease with which we identify with the poor and captive.

It reminds us that we can be as easily corrupted as anyone else.

It shines a bright light on the empty space within us, which we thought we had guarded so well.

It reminds us that, spiritually, we are like a stone, hard and cold inside.

That there is sometimes no song in our hearts.

It tells us the true story of our boredom.

Why we drink so much.

Why we go shopping when we are depressed.

Why we turn our eyes away when talking to someone.

Why we explain ourselves so much.

How we are really, despite the comforts of love and work, alone.

The issue here at the beginning is whether or not we can recognize our life in the symbol of the cross or whether we must borrow life through which to see it. The issue here is avoidance.

I remember when the word "pain" first came out. It was a year or two ago when it actually entered the vocabulary of those who drink coffee from filters and pride themselves on their transcendence of American culture. I remember that I found it embarrassing as a cult word. "My pain," "your pain," "their pain." I remember saying, *"What pain?"* There are no nails in our hands, no thirst on our lips, no mountain entryways I frequent. How exaggerated, how overly dramatic. How overdone!

Perhaps you feel that way today. My images may not work for you. Perhaps you have not been attacked by Good Friday, by the cross that was someone else's cross a long, long time ago. Perhaps you find the Psalmist's anguish overly dramatic. Perhaps we have no sense of forsakenness.

Pain, I'm sure, is nothing to covet. And only at great risk of paternalism and self-aggrandizement do we borrow it. If we're looking for excitement and drama, we had better look elsewhere. John Berryman, the poet, whored after pain all his life. He thought it would improve his poetry. He was jealous of the Dostoevskis of the world, those who had lived with totalitarianism and really know. God, was he jealous! But his quippy conclusion, "Pain is good for an artist as long as it doesn't kill him"—that missed the point entirely.

"Good for" is not a category that pain can tolerate. Pain is not a means to the end of self-improvement. Pain like the pain of the cross obliterates the self. And its poetry is the poetry that is released only after the self is released. The release of the self is the message of the cross. But first we must be willing to look at, to see the high price we pay for hanging on.

This part is much simpler. If the first was a searching with you for the symbol of the cross in our lives, this part is about a finding. If the first part was about seeing, this part is about feeling. If the first part was to establish the tension, this is the part about the tearing, the brokenness. About ways to hang on a cross. If the first part gave you space, this part will crowd you. James Baldwin in a book called *The Uses of the Blues* reminds us that you can't know anything about life and expect you can get through it clean. The most monstrous people are those who think they are going to. If you can live with the full knowledge that you are going to die, if you can live with the reality of death, you can live. If you can't do it, if you spend your entire life in flight from death, you are also in flight from life.

More simply put, if God chose a cross for his own son, what can we imagine that he has in store for us? Oh, I forgot. We are really in control of our lives. We can go out and look for pain if we want to or avoid it if we want to. We might look for it because it serves one of our life goals. Our poetry, for example. Or our self-actualization. Or our goal of being a more passionate, turbulent person, one like our Lord, acquainted with grief.

But now I remember. Good Friday. The thief in the night. The one we didn't want to see. We are not in control. God is not in control either. God abandons the world this day as on no other. And even when he returns, he brings no manacles, no strings on which to hang us. The only certainty is that we will die. The rest involves us in the terror of choice.

The advocacy of vulnerability is therefore ridiculous. We are vulnerable. There is no need to try to become more so. What little control we have is in the area of whether we feel that or not. "When he cries out to you today, do not harden your heart against him." And should you be able to accomplish a hardening of your heart, be warned about the breaking of hard things. Know about shattering. The advocacy of vulnerability is ridiculous. The stones cry out with their reminder that we are responsible for the decisions we make: that in love, the thing we need the most, we are most vulnerable; that the world wants more from us than we'll ever be able to give it; that there are things we cannot control, no matter how we manipulate the buttons; that we will die with some love unshared, some work undone, and some life unlived. The advocacy of vulnerability is ridiculous. All that we can do is recognize it—and know some rage at its necessity.

So what is there left to say? That the ordeal by fire is necessary? That it is desirable? That we grow by suffering? That pain is unavoidable in human life? That we are vulnerable whether we choose it or not? That we should know some pride at how well we are moving through the stages of grief?

Not one of these is the message of the cross. The cross communicates all of these, but it says one thing more.

The cross permits Jesus to say: I will not despise my humanity. I will love it. I will love it through and beyond the pain. While it was hatred of humanity that killed me, that hatred is not the final word. By loving his own humanity, he loved ours too. Leaning on the power and promise of God Almighty, Jesus gave up his self. "Into thy hands I commend my spirit." There was no other way to conquer death. There is no other way for us either. And so to all our gospels of self-fulfillment, Good Friday presents a threat. It shows that on the day when every person's hand is raised against God, God could take it. That we could not escape his love that easily. That there is a love that will not let us go, no matter how we squirm in avoidance and hang on to anger. No matter what our level of self-defense, there is a love that will not let us go, no matter what the pain we bear or how broken we find ourselves.

So the advocacy of the day is not an advocacy of seeing pain. Or an advocacy of feeling vulnerability. Good Friday comes to steal ourselves from us. It exposes our false ownership. The advocacy of the day is trust. To lean on the promises and the power of God. To get ready for the Sundays that follow Fridays, when our self is returned to us, but only after we have been willing to let it go. Jesus commended his spirit to God's hands, only to have it returned in the form of a gift. We too are so called: to look at the genuine lifelong oppression of owning and defending our selves, to look pain square in the eye and love it to death, to be broken for the sake of a humanity which is our own. It's life at the point of maximum danger.

Where, actually, it's always lived. But today we see it. And we feel it. And we are given the power to trust even the abandonment of our selves to the purposes and power of God's almighty hands.

DONNA SCHAPER *is pastor of First Congregational Church in Amherst, Massachusetts.*

Frontiers
YVONNE V. SCHAUDT

Wisdom has built her house, she has set up her seven pillars. She has slaughtered her beasts, she has mixed her wine, she has also set her table. She has sent out her maids to call from the highest places in the town, "Whoever is simple, let him turn in here!" To him who is without sense she says, "Come, eat of my bread and drink of the wine I have mixed. Leave simpleness, and live, and walk in the way of insight."

—PROVERBS 9:1–6, RSV

And one of the scribes came up and heard them disputing with one another, and . . . asked him, "Which commandment is the first of all?" Jesus answered, "The first is, 'Hear, O Israel: The Lord our God, the Lord is one; and you shall love the Lord your God with all your heart, and with all your soul, and with all your mind, and with all your strength.' The second is this, 'You shall love your neighbor as yourself.' There is no other commandment greater than these." And the scribe said to him, "You are right, Teacher; you have truly said that he is one, and there is no other but he; and to love him with all the heart, and with all the understanding, and with all the strength, and to love one's neighbor as oneself, is much more than all whole burnt offerings and sacrifices." And when Jesus saw that he answered wisely, he said to him, "You are not far from the kingdom of God." And after that no one dared to ask him any question.

—MARK 12:28–34, RSV

Late one August night, almost as if out of a dream, I found myself drawn inside a still-forming circle of pickup trucks on the

Navajo reservation in Arizona. We were returning to Canyon de
Chelley when Alice, a Navajo medicine woman traveling with us,
pointed to the cluster of fires set back off the highway. It was a
Squaw Dance.

The sweet-smoked fragrance of burning piñon trees mingled with the freshness that soft rain brings to sage and other
weeds peculiar to that area. And although clouds covered the
stars, their presence was reflected in the twinkling flames that
warmed this inner circle of humanity. I nestled quietly into the
weeds and the soft earth to observe—I thought. And perhaps I
did—though I do not know for how long, or at what point I
joined them. Playful voices, in a tongue I could only know with
the heart, filled the night and my imagination with song.

Yet every now and then, and almost like an intruder, a drop
of rain would nudge my cheek, gently reminding me of my
separateness. I was the intruder, from another time and from
another world; from that foreign culture which broke in upon a
homeland and claimed it—"the Frontier." Obviously, what it
was to the Indians around the first century A.D. and what it was
for our ancestors are two very different realities. Even so, as the
songs and smoke from the fires rose into the night, I could not
help sitting still in wonder at the richness of humanity yet to be
explored.

Human beings seem prone toward exploring, whether it be
in a laboratory, on an excavation site, or through a telescope.
Until recently, many worlds of fascination have remained hidden in a veil of mystery by the limits of our knowledge. One
small wonder, however, unfolding before our very eyes is our
own planet earth.

Leaving footprints in the fine gray dust of the moon's
surface, the Apollo 15 astronauts were privileged to see the most
spectacular sight ever revealed to humankind: the rising of
earth on the crater-scarred moon. In the presence of that
memory, David Scott recalls, "I steal a moment and glance
straight up into the black sky, where the crystalline sphere of
earth—all blue and white, sea and clouds—gleams in the abyss
of space. In that cold and boundless emptiness, our planet
provides the only glow of color." A colleague, Michael Collins,
added that the pictures of earth do not do it justice. It glistens

with a brilliance unreproducible in a photograph. "Out of your spacecraft window you see earth shining like a great beacon; you're attracted to it mightily."

Reflecting upon these two descriptions and that summer night in Arizona, I am reminded of the words of T. S. Eliot: "We shall not cease from exploration / And the end of all our exploring / Will be to arrive where we started / And know the place for the first time." ("Little Gidding," Part V.) For if, in the tree of creation, this small blossom called earth is unfolding before us, does it not bring our spacefaring ventures a bit more down to earth? In this context, may I mention three very interesting things which seem to be happening in relation to our travels?

First, we have begun exploring the heavens only to rediscover the earth. For the first time we are truly comprehending the earth as a biological unity. We are realizing not only its biological wholeness, but its uniqueness. If, for example, we take the well-known fact that each one of us on earth has our own unique fingerprint, would not the earth likewise hold its own unique fingerprint of life in the universe? If so, does this not imply that the earth and all its inhabitants are one-of-a-kind works of art amid the whole of the universe?

Or consider the terrain. If we have yet to see a rerun of the same sunset, I wonder if there could possibly be an exact duplicate of the Grand Canyon, the Everglades, the Himalayas, or the Amazon jungle? Perhaps there are worlds of similarity, but in all probability there is only one earth in all of creation. So it seems that in our extraterrestial explorations we have arrived where we started and know this garden of earth for the first time.

Yet we have discovered even more. For in the dawning awareness of the unique nature of the earth, we have also begun to rediscover the unique nature of ourselves as human beings. The Psalmist long ago expressed the wonder of human creation in terms of birth: "Thou didst form my inward parts, thou didst knit me together in my mother's womb. I praise thee, for thou art fearful and wonderful. Wonderful are thy works! Thou knowest me right well; my frame was not hidden from thee, when I was being made in secret, intricately wrought in the depths of the earth [Ps. 139:13–15, RSV]." Today we still marvel at the mystery of birth and the intricacy with which we have been knit together—yet we marvel in an added dimension. Again, if our earthly and solar patterns of uniqueness hold true, then we too are a one-of-a-kind human form in all of creation. How colorfully rich, then, do our racial and cultural distinctions become.

Third, along with rediscovering the earth and ourselves, we have begun to realize the special nature of our existence and the responsibility this implies. This morning's New Testament lesson includes reference to the Sh'ma: "Hear, O Israel, the Lord our God is one Lord." In Hebraic tradition, this affirmation of God's unity calls the people of Israel to attention. It compels them to actively listen individually and to then respond communally to the injustices that exist. This watchword of faith, particularly when combined with the New Testament command to "love thy neighbor as thyself," presents us with a significant challenge—and exciting possibilities. It compels us to eat of wisdom's bread and to drink her wine of understanding. It urges us to marvel at creation and the richness that we as human beings bring to each other in our unity and diversity. And it calls us to actively listen and respond to the words of one who, two thousand years ago, prepared the way for the Frontier of Love.

Before our spacefaring ventures, it was much easier to stand with the ancients in wonder, looking up to the heavens for fuller understanding—up to the heavens, where all the answers to the mysterious rhythm of the universe seemed to sparkle amid the stars. But now I wonder. As we travel together on this crystalline vessel called earth, I wonder if the eyes of heaven do not look to us for illumination.

May we build our fires to reflect them, and celebrate together the frontier that is here among us through Jesus Christ our Lord.

THE REV. YVONNE V. SCHAUDT *is assistant minister at King's Chapel in Boston. She is a graduate of Andover Newton Theological School and is a World Council Scholar.*

Suffering
DIANE TENNIS

They are all makers of idols; they are nothing and the works they prize are useless. Their servants see nothing, they understand nothing, and so they will be put to shame. Who ever fashioned a god or cast an image without hope of gain? Watch how its devotees will be put to shame, how its sculptors will blush. Let them all come together, let them appear in court. They will be both terrified and ashamed.

The blacksmith works on it over the fire and beats it into shape with a hammer. He works on it with his strong arm till he is hungry and tired; drinking no water, he is exhausted. The wood carver takes his measurements, outlines the image with chalk, carves it with chisels, following the outline with dividers. He shapes it to human proportions, and gives it a human face, for it to live in a temple. He cut down a cedar, or else took a cypress or an oak which he selected from the trees in the forest, or maybe he planted a cedar and the rain made it grow. For the common man it is so much fuel; he uses it to warm himself; he also burns it to bake his bread. But this fellow makes a god of it and worships it; he makes an idol of it and bows down before it. Half of it he burns in the fire, on the live embers he roasts meat, eats it and is replete. He warms himself too. "Ah!" says he "I am warm; I have a fire here!" With the rest he makes his god, his idol; he bows down before it and worships it and prays to it. "Save me," he says "because you are my god."

They know nothing, understand nothing. Their eyes are shut to all seeing, their heart to all reason. . . .

Thus says Yahweh, your redeemer, he who formed you in the womb: I, myself, Yahweh, made all things, I alone spread out the heavens . . . who says of Jerusalem, "Let her be inhabited," and of the towns of Judah, "Let them be rebuilt," and I will raise their ruins once more.

ISAIAH 44:9–19, 24–26, JB

203

Suffering is not a compound sentence. How many times have you heard this one? "I know it hurts, friend, but you'll get over it." Uh-uh. No, she doesn't know about your hurt. No, she doesn't know you'll get over it. And the clincher as to how you know she doesn't know is that she hurried on to the "but": "*But* you'll get over it"—right in the same sentence with your hurt. And suffering is not a compound sentence. Suffering stands alone. Let us not hurry on to God's new thing. Pause over the pain of captivities.

We are forever looking for explanations. Why? is the recurring human question. We search for origins, causes, reasons, and roots. When we can't find an answer, we invent one. Even the anguished, outraged cry is: "Why?! My God, why?"

There are traps in explaining things. One is to approve of suffering. "Why do we kill people in electric chairs?" "Because they have killed people." "Oh, well then, that's okay." Once we blame folks for creating their own suffering, then suffering is okay. Blaming victims gets to be a habit. So we can look at the poor and say, "What did you do so wrong to get yourself to be so poor?" "He hurts, but he brought it on himself" won't do. Suffering is not a compound sentence.

Another trap is to think we can change anything. Explain. Fix it. Fixing things is very popular. That's why the pharmaceutical companies are doing so well. You have a headache? Fix it! Don't suffer. When people shoot drugs, it's called a fix. Which fits nicely with our "fix it" mentality. I came across the name of a Prussian chaplain popular in the 1880s. Fifty years before *Mein Kampf*, this man advocated the exile and death of Jews. I went to my professor and told him of this discovery and that the documents didn't tell me much more. Could he please tell me why the chaplain held that opinion? My professor said patiently, "If I knew the answer to that, I would know the answer to the German question." (That's what the Holocaust is called in history books: the German *question*.)

Explain it. Or change it, or both. There just aren't explanations and fixes that cover suffering. Suffering is not a compound sentence.

Captivity is a particular kind of suffering. Oppression is a special description. There's so little power to do anything about it. There's so much opportunity to feel worthless. Children are captives of powerful adults. Battered children don't like themselves. After awhile grownups don't have to hurt them. They'll hurt themselves. The sheer habit of pain has taught them that's what they deserve. For a time, oppressors don't have to distribute punishment to any slave class. They'll do it to themselves. Indian women herded other women onto funeral pyres. Now, women with low self-esteem herd each other into offices of preachers and psychiatrists.

Sometimes preachers and psychiatrists feed self-esteem. Sometimes those counselors blame the patient, make her feel worse, and encourage her to stay in oppressive situations that caused the problem. Evangelical women have described in a recent publication one of many cases of a mother who was encouraged by Bible-quoting counselors to stay with her husband through a variety of sadistic punishments to her and her child. Advice is something there's a lot of. The Jews in captivity have their counselors, too. Some say, "Stay in your place. Better fed than dead." Others say, "You are God's people. Oppression is never the last word for God's people. You are getting out of this." When? How? How to get on in an oppressive place? How to get out of an oppressive situation? Or both?

The scripture lesson has two clues as to what *won't* work. One is idol worship, and the other is tyranny. Isaiah 44 makes fun of the Babylonians for exhausting themselves creating gods out of leftover wood. Then they'd get more tired, because they had to carry those gods around. Here's a pitiful image of people burdened down with the baggage of invented, leftover gods. Now, the Babylonians are on top for the moment. That makes them and their gods look pretty good. After all, what has our God done for us lately? Maybe changing gods and getting on top is a better deal. But then Isaiah 49 says some pretty scary things about the consequences of playing tyrant. ". . . the captives will be snatched away . . . oppressors will eat their own flesh." Gosh, things are tough, folks, but we are not eating on each other. Idol worship and tyranny aren't any better than captivity. Like drugs, they are temporary fixes. And they bring with them their own particular kinds of suffering.

Think about the sheer load of carrying idols. Things are big idols in this country—carved gods or other expensive art, cars, machines, land, furniture. When you get enough things, then you have to insure them, lock them up, hire somebody to take care of them, replace them, clean them, add to them, protect them. It's tough to be rich! Americans are really into it, though. We don't feel rich. We just want security. The world's luxuries become our necessities. I don't believe tanks in the streets will bring in a dictatorship here; a guaranteed annuity might. We idolize security that much. Guaranteed annuity? Nothing is for sure. Not even annuities. That's what happens when we make idols. We forget.

Think about the life of the tyrant. If you hold somebody captive, you'd better have a bodyguard. You had better have weapons. Don't sleep soundly. If you hold a whole race of people captive, don't sleep at all. You'll be distracted from living, just keeping slaves. If they don't get you, some other tyrant will.

You might just as well stick to God, who doesn't have to be carried around like extra baggage. God does not reward loyalty by eliminating suffering, either. In fact, there are particular kinds of suffering predictable for God's people. Martin Luther King knew that so well. But he stuck with God anyway. At least there is meaning in that kind of misery. Christians share the load of meaningless misery. Just stuff. Still the scriptures give no reason. The scriptures say only: God is in it with us. God hates oppression. God resents suffering. You have company in the capricious and purpose in the pain.

The discerning Christian understands that: Suffering is not a compound sentence. Suffering is real. Oppression is intolerable. Do not be trapped by explanations. The discerning Christian knows that faithfulness will cost something; faithlessness will cost something else. Pick one. Christians opt for the costs of faithfulness. Just because, with our God, we hate oppression. We resent suffering. We will accept only the unavoidable risks of faith and be outraged at all the rest, all the time.

THE REV. DR. DIANE TENNIS *is a denominational staff member in the Office of Professional Development of the Presbyterian Church in the United States. Much of her work is with church-employed women and she has been active in women's issues since graduating from Union Theological Seminary, N.Y. in 1958.*

Mary's Christmas Announces Freedom to Captives

MARGARET ELLEN TRAXLER

Women in jail or prison incarnate Mary, the mother of Jesus. It seems that no other group of women so duplicates the waiting and pondering of Mary.

Of all the mysteries of the Blessed Virgin Mary—the glorious, joyful, and sorrowful—it is the joyful and sorrowful which are found reflected in the lives of imprisoned women.

At Christmastime, however, it is the pondering in one's heart and the waiting of Mary that have Gospel implications for prisoners. Several times daily the prison routine includes a head count to see if all the "numbers" are accounted for. Mary and Joseph went to Bethlehem, the City of David, because Caesar's head count was decreed. Today, standing in line for prison head count, Mary ponders about "my possible parole or pardon . . . my case review . . . my children alone on the streets, and who will keep the little ones from the stove . . . my mistakes, for which sorrow can neither heal nor shorten the gestation period for my aborted mothering and nurturing . . . my children—can they forgive or understand their mother?"

The word went out from Caesar Augustus, and the lines of Mary and Joseph's lives were redrawn with new designs and sudden plans. There were adjustments, a journey, and a lonely homelessness.

To Mary in prison, another Caesar speaks the command in the voice of the bailiff, the judge, the warden, the guard, and all those who speak from legal heights and change the destinies of ordinary people.

Women in jail have not been convicted of any crime. They are too poor to pay bail, and so they must wait for their "presentation" in court. Here the new Herods, the new Pilates, oftentimes well-meaning, explain that "we have a law, and that law says . . ." This observance is so well kept that very often even life is protected with death penalties. Mary must listen quietly, or she will be handcuffed to a chair for the judge and jury to see while they ponder over her guilt or innocence. Whatever the decision, she must say, "Thy will be done."

The mysteries in Mary's life baffled her as she waited for the unknown, and they continue to baffle Mary in prisons today. She prays in her cell for her children, because every woman in prison has, on the average, two children "out there." A law is written in a mother's heart and from this she cannot escape. She cries out daily, nightly, "They have no wine."

"My children have no clothes . . . my children have no one to see that they get to school . . . no one to see that they get breakfast and wear overshoes to school . . . no one to see that Susie's teacher is reminded about the possible epileptic seizure . . . no one to be tender to them as they are put six in the bed at night."

An unfeeling guard says, "Why didn't you think of that before you stole the check?" They have no wine, and they forget the Gospel story where Jesus made all things right. Theirs is a cry of darkness.

The Blessed Virgin Mary was torn and troubled in the flight into Egypt. It was a journey of pain without a known destination with a comforting welcome and warm blankets at the end. Mary knows also today that same bewildering journey, in a rattling bus to the court, where she is locked in a room called the "bullpen." There are no benches there, and she waits, sometimes all day, for her minute, two minutes in court. At night the bus returns her to jail in her continuing flight into that most frightening future. Finally there is the final trip from jail to prison, where she is given a green trash bag to carry her possessions (a snapshot of her children, a comb, a partially used bar of soap, the buckle that fell off her shoe).

There is a holiness in poverty but not in the destitution which women in prison know. A child calls, "Mama, when are you coming home?" The children think she's in the TB san, the hospital, or taking care of Grandma. "Darling," she answers, "I'm coming home as soon as I can. Promise you'll be good." She cries out in prayer lest she lose custody of her children. "Mother is a sinner," she weeps to herself. There is probably no resident father to claim custody, but the "system" is filled with welfare bureaucrats with lofty ideas on what is a mother and what substitutes for a mother's heart. She is in prison, and that is the case against her.

Her incarceration is her purification. Upon her release, she gets ready for her reintroduction to the welfare machine. Her children represent her utmost need, and these she holds up one by one in the temple of the welfare office pool, where desks are lined up, around which she must play musical chairs. This game is played for the greater part of a day, until it's her turn to talk to her welfare caseworker. Society slaughters the innocents in new and unfeeling ways, but no future is so bleak that there is no hope. Just as Mary hurried into the hill country to wait on Cousin Elizabeth, there is given a sign of comfort administered by women to women. Men, for all their goodness, are married only to power, their status, and to them women have no rights except those granted by men. This explains the powerlessness of women: Men hold the keys but refuse to share, not realizing that only in sharing can both men and women enjoy tender and abiding love for one another.

Mary and Elizabeth understand this. In the dayrooms of the prisons, Mary shares her yarn with Elizabeth, who is knitting a cap for her child; Mary goes to comfort Elaine, who is ill in her cell; Mary goes to solitary, where Nora is serving twenty-nine days for "creating a scene" in the dayroom. Women comfort women. It is Mary helping Elizabeth.

And at Christmastime it is a season for pondering on Mary's joyful and sorrowful mysteries as they are lived out anew by today's women who are among the poorest and the most abandoned.

Hope resides in the smallest signs, and in prison a woman's heart will find hope. A star in the sky points toward a stable. There is some straw, and she's the first to hear the cry of the baby.

MARGARET ELLEN TRAXLER *has been a School Sister of Notre Dame for 37 years. She founded the National Coalition of American Nuns, co-founded the Interreligious Task Force on Soviet Jewry and presently is the director of the Institute of Women Today. The latter is an organization sponsored by 10 national Catholic, Protestant and Jewish women's organizations in search of the religious and historical roots of women's liberation.*

My Prayer "Grows Up" as I Grow Older

DIANA TREBBI

The words "what was spoken to you" bring my prayer life to mind. Although I felt this would be difficult to talk about, I nevertheless felt I wanted to share with you some of my experience in this realm. Besides, I thought it would be a good thing to do on this evening before the first Sunday of the Advent season, to speak out loudly against our culture out there, which daily blares out its one-note message, heralding the arrival of Christmas: Buy, buy, buy!!

The way I pray—that is, relate to God—reflects how I'm feeling at the moment, and is a part of how I'm relating to other people around me. There are times when I speak to God in monologue-like fashion. When I'm feeling threatened, weak, and helpless and that there is a lot wrong with me, I make the mistake, not of speaking from weakness, because that's all I can do at the moment, but of assuming that the other, whether it be God or my family, friends, or student companions, cannot understand, cannot care about me, and are unable to help me in my current distress. Yet I am impelled to express my discomfort, fear, and anxiety, but in a manner which excludes any authentic relation to another, and the personal growth and strength this always brings.

What I've just described, it seems to me, is acting like a child who is still unable to fathom the rich potential which another person always represents. When I pray in this manner, I don't leave myself room to realize who God is, to whom it is I am speaking, and so the psychic horizon is filled with the sound and images of my own miseries, concerns, and strivings. What I want to express becomes primary, and, as it were, God gets lost here because all I'm doing is "looking out for Number One" in the spiritual realm. When I communicate in this mode, I am excluding the possibility of getting in touch with the healing power in other people, and in God.

At other times, I am aware of my own uniqueness, my needs, desires, and dreams as expressed by me, Diana Trebbi. In interchange with others, these needs are satisfied, the desires fulfilled, the dreams heard and encouraged. The other person becomes a vehicle for me to improve my own self-image. I am an adolescent again, in that I understand that the world, nature, and other persons have an independent life and existence of their own, but I use that notion exclusively for my own benefit. In the beginnings of true dialogue with others, I dimly perceive that the effect of a dialogue is to change both participants—not just one side. But the gain of the other seems secondary, because I place priority on my own benefit. What is important is that I don't see God just as some distant, mythic, archetypal figure in the distant heavens, nor is God merely a projection of my own needs and fears (as Freud seems to say). God, like other people, is at the same time a part of myself and outside myself, except that I'm relating to God pretty much in line with our present culture of narcissism. I am still benefiting at the expense of the other.

We know that the dialogue has been proposed as the ideal notion for human relationships because it implies equality for both participants. It is paradoxical in Christian prayer experience, that this is both true and not true. God allows my selfishness, fear, lack of faith and trust to limit my perception of who God is. What is unique to the Christian religion is the dynamic, ongoing revelation of the meaning of God for each devotee. We're not meant to be just friends or buddies or whatever the ethic of the '60s was having us teach in Christian Doctrine classes. Rather, we're meant to be like God. There is a sense in which God is completely other, unknowable, mysterious, and, above all, hidden; and the awareness of this dimension of God strikes terror and anguish in my heart. These feelings, along with long meditation on Jesus' words in the scriptures, have kept me striving to interiorize this God, who at times does seem to be completely an "other." Here is where Jesus' sayings are of great importance for my spiritual life, because in uttering them he is revealing what God meant to him, and what it is possible for us to find in our relationship to God: "You must call no one on earth your Father—you have only one father, and he is in heaven [Matt. 23:8–12, JB]."

The word "mother" would fit in here just as well. Insights from psychology tell us that it is of the utmost importance that we free ourselves from the undue influences, in adult life, of what our parents mean for us, think of us—realizing, of course, that we can never free ourselves from the mark of our genetic lineage.

In these words, Jesus is offering us a very large measure of personal freedom. I believe this kind of freedom can be achieved by anyone who sets her/his heart on it. It is a pretty arduous path, at times boring and frustrating, but in this struggle there is given a dynamism which keeps it vital for me. I have been practicing the prayer of silence for about seven years now, and can say that in some ways it has given me a greater sense of personal freedom than I ever experienced before. There has been little help or encouragement, because the culture disconfirms this kind of "useless" activity, and because it is so difficult to talk about. Several years ago I reread *The Cloud of Unknowing*, a little book on prayer by an unknown person in fourteenth-century England, who for this period of time has been my ongoing spiritual guide. It is teaching me that praying is relating with utmost concentration, and it involves suppressing any thought of what God is like and, as it were, having nothing remain in the conscious mind save a naked intent stretching out toward God. There is merely the effort to sustain one's attention on God in the depths of one's being. One result of this practice, I've noted, is an increased capacity to grasp other persons as they stand before me in situations of daily life. All of sacred history tells me that this work of changing our perceptions of God also changes our notion of who we are.

Scholars tell us that the Judaeo–Christian religion has done more than any other to elevate the individual person. Isaiah, in Chapter 8, writes that when God spoke to him, the experience was so overwhelming that it changed the prophet's perception of himself—now he was a man "of unclean lips." And Mary, after her encounter with the divine, could rejoice in who she was: "God who is mighty has done great things in me, blessed is God [Luke 1:49, JB]." The saints confirm for us that the quality of our personal relation to God makes all the difference. St. Thérèse of Lisieux tells us: ". . . the more I am united with God, the more I am able to love all my sisters."

I have spent twenty years as a woman religious, and during that period of my life I prayed and continue to pray in all three manners just described, but there is no question in my mind as to which is the best. The third manner of prayer has been confirmed for me in many ways. I've come to it in the middle of great personal changes experienced over the past twenty years. Several events radically changed my consciousness. The first was the Second Vatican Council, which had the effect of profoundly changing the active religious orders so that the old monastic forms of life were for the most part excised. The other things which happened were a deep involvement with a feminist consciousness-raising group of Catholic lay and religious women who continue to actively work to improve the position of women and men in our church—including ordination to priesthood for all who desire it. I became aware that I was living my everyday life in a religious patriarchal structure, and now it began to make less and less sense to me. At the same time, I was undergoing a long and arduous psychoanalysis, which helped me to free myself from a dependent relation to my parents and move toward greater autonomy. These events proved to place too much stress on the old monastic fabric, which up to this point had been the warp and woof of my life.

Now I'm continuing my journey without the titles of "sister" and "mother," which for so long were the designations of personhood and work in the religious life. I believe that now I am called to stand with other women who are striving to regain their sense of being blessed—a sense of their dignity and worth, which God means us to have in the act of creating us, but which society up to now has largely denied to women and other minorities.

I remain convinced that this is a time of history when each woman counts in the struggle for recognition of who she is. It is necessary to carry on this struggle in our everyday lives and in our own respective congregations, because all Western religions are inherently patriarchal and have demonstrated a vested interest in remaining so for some time to come. The antiphone I've quoted reminds us that God will deliver, if in faith we sustain that vital relation with God in our private lives. In these liturgies we are beginning to create something positive as women of faith—we are creating our own public space. This is very important, and in all this, I believe, God is working with us.

Religion, more than any other social system, provides the symbols for alternative meanings to life. If Christianity has a future, I believe it lies in achieving the following:

- a new definition of female-male relationships, and its implications for individual identities as sexual beings;
- the ramifications of this for family life, and the connotations of what it means to be mother and father;
- a new equitability between women and men so that it will influence religious theory.

Advent is usually characterized as a time of waiting, as the holy ones down the centuries waited for the Messiah to come. If my prayer life has taught me anything, it is that God never waits. The revelations we seek are always there; we must learn how to find them. Our liberation as women of faith rests on our ability to grasp our own unique relation to God and in understanding who we are. What God speaks to each, if faithfully heard, will be a source of fulfillment for women, men, and children; and a source of present and future rejoicing.

DIANA TREBBI's *characteristic mode of prayer developed through several radical changes of consciousness, leading to a form of enlightenment. Christian enlightenment for Diana has meant greater clarity in perceiving the contradictions in human history, and more energy in reconciling them.*

You Are Not My God, Jehovah

PEGGY WAY

We know that in everything God works for good with those who love him, who are called according to his purpose. For those whom he foreknew he also predestined to be conformed to the image of his Son, in order that he might be the firstborn among many brethren. And those whom he predestined he also called; and those whom he called he also justified; and those whom he justified he also glorified.

What then shall we say to this? If God is for us, who is against us? He who did not spare his own Son but gave him up for us all, will he not also give us all things with him? Who shall bring any charge against God's elect: It is God who justifies; who is to condemn? Is it Christ Jesus, who died, yes, who was raised from the dead, who is at the right hand of God, who indeed intercedes for us? Who shall separate us from the love of Christ? Shall tribulation, or distress, or persecution, or famine, or nakedness, or peril, or sword? As it is written, "For thy sake we are being killed all the day long; we are regarded as sheep to be slaughtered." No, in all these things we are more than conquerors through him who loved us. For I am sure that neither death, nor life, nor angels, nor principalities, nor things present, nor things to come, nor powers, nor height, nor depth, nor anything else in all creation, will be able to separate us from the love of God in Christ Jesus our Lord.

—ROMANS 8:28–39, RSV

The Affirmation of the morning progresses through four simple sentences:

> YOU ARE NOT MY GOD, JEHOVAH!!!
> I WILL SPEAK WITH MY BROTHERS.
> I WILL AFFIRM MY SISTERS.
> I WILL CRY UNTO MY GOD: LET US FREE ONE ANOTHER. AMEN.

YOU ARE NOT MY GOD, JEHOVAH!

I will not *bow down* before a god who has men pray: "I thank the Lord that thou hast not created me a woman. . . ."

I will not *worship* a god who only trusts his priesthood and his power and his prophecy to men. . . .

I will not *serve* a god for whom woman *was* unclean for twice as long when she bore a girl child . . . or a god for whom a woman's mission *is* to listen and a man's mission to speak.

YOU ARE NOT MY GOD, JEHOVAH! Let us look into these things. . . .

> The human spirit is to be a soaring one . . . which stands on the abyss but yet affirms . . . which is so deeply rooted it is free . . . which chooses to what or Whom its bondage is to be. . . .
>
> I WILL NOT HAVE MY SPIRIT AND MY NATURE SO IDENTIFIED I CANNOT SOAR! I WILL NOT LIVE WITH A FIXED NATURE ANYMORE. . . . You are not my god, Jehovah, who will recognize me only by my sexual function. My brothers are measured by other standards than their sexuality, and their moral value is not limited to procreative roles. . . . I will not have a god who will not have me WHOLE.
>
> I am a body . . . and a mind. I am a womb . . . and a soul.
>
> I am a wife . . . and a spirit. I am a mother . . . and a person.

WHAT AM I TO DO WITH A GOD WHO ONLY KNOWS OF WOMEN AS HARLOTS OR VIRGINS? AS TEMPTERS OR CLOISTERED? AS PLAYGIRLS OR NONPERSONS TO BE PLACED UPON RELIGIOUS PEDESTALS?

I do not know which is the greater insult to my creation:
to be forever a daughter of Eve whom men fear through
their sin-obsession; or to be forever pedestaled, protected
from the storms and stresses and creativities and responsibilities of human development which produce persons
and adults. . . .

WHAT DO I DO WITH A GOD WHO DOESN'T SEEM TO UNDER-
STAND OR VALUE MY BEING OR BECOMING, MY CREATION
AND MY CREATIVITY?

JEHOVAH, YOU ARE SO ONTOLOGICALLY MASCULINE with all of the
worst cultural features of what it is to be man—prideful and
vengeful, image-protecting and loving war, jealous and insecure,
omnipotent, and in so many hidden ways afraid of women. YOU
WILL NOT EVEN LET ME SERVE YOU AT YOUR ALTARS—AND THERE
MUST BE MALE MEDIARIES TO A MALE GOD.

O Father McKenzie, you give it all away: God is, of course,
masculine, but not in the sense of sexual distinction. IN
WHAT SENSE, THEN? Jehovah, I do not understand your
bondage to a sexual role and its pervasiveness throughout
your history. . . .

YOU ARE NOT MY GOD, JEHOVAH!

The Affirmation
                    of the morning
progresses through four
                              simple sentences:

YOU ARE NOT MY GOD, JEHOVAH!
I WILL SPEAK WITH MY BROTHERS.
I WILL AFFIRM MY SISTERS.
I WILL CRY UNTO MY GOD: LET US FREE ONE ANOTHER.

I WILL SPEAK WITH MY BROTHERS—and I will call you brother
even though you will not call me sister . . .
          . . . for we must love one another or die . . . for we must
          be partners in the Created Order over which the human
          persons, man and woman, were given dominion.

I will speak with my brothers. . . .

> I will go into your secret places and your sanctuaries
> where you hide from partnership. Where the prophets
> gather, and the priests . . . where the kings govern and
> the pure minds teach . . . where the courts define and the
> generals fight. . . . I will go into your secret places and
> discover there your hidden mysteries.

> AND WHAT I WILL FIND IS THE VALIDATION OF THE PETER
> PRINCIPLE!!!!!

> And I will say to my brothers: What is it in your secret
> places that I am incompetent to do? I truly do not
> understand. I look around me at your world, I am a
> stranger and afraid in a world I never made, where I
> cannot breathe your air; nor save our sons from your
> wars; nor protect our daughters from your person-
> empty-principles; nor with my black brothers and sisters
> enter your institutions; where I cannot govern my coun-
> try or community, nor even minister among my sisters.

> I do not need to claim that I could do a better job. But do
> you sense no need for me—for my resources, competence,
> and creativity? For I too was created with the image of
> God within me.

I will speak with my brothers—and I will call you brother even
though you will not call me sister, for we must do the tasks
together rather than argue about preordained sex roles. Do you
not feel your bondage too? To bear it all? To have to be that
which may not be your nature either? How is a creative world to
be born out of fixed natures? The tasks can be neither defined
nor implemented, because the partnership cannot yet even be
conceptualized! BUT I WILL CALL YOU BROTHER EVEN THOUGH YOU
CALL ME NOT SISTER and meet me face to face and look upon me
as a resource WITH—and not FOR—you.

> I will say to my brothers that when the baby's diaper is
> dirty the task is that it must be changed—and not to
> argue over whether *the hands* should be with or without
> hair. And when our children cry out to us for change, we

must *reach out our hands* together. And when there is crisis we must *both* be knowledgeable and open and strong. And when the world shudders we must neither of us have a role-retreat where we pretend that to be human is to celebrate our fixity.

For it is a time for person-recognition and for touching through the roles that bind us to the wrong gods—a time of definition which we *all* must do, and of repossessing, building, and creating that which may be old *and* new, a time for standing there on the abyss together and affirming and acting on what we must be and do.

JUST HOW WELL DO YOU SEE THE WOMAN NEXT TO YOU?
I WILL SPEAK WITH MY BROTHERS—and I will call you brother even though you will not call me sister.

The *Affirmation*
of the morning
progresses through four
simple sentences:

YOU ARE NOT MY GOD JEHOVAH!
I WILL SPEAK WITH MY BROTHERS.
I WILL AFFIRM MY SISTERS.
I WILL CRY UNTO MY GOD: LET US FREE ONE ANOTHER.

I WILL AFFIRM MY SISTERS and they will affirm me . . . and WE will become a we learning to trust ourselves and one another . . . and we will BE our emerging natures, which are human, and can soar, choosing our direction, our responsibility, and our bondage.

We will affirm one another, and call into being our images of wholeness and our realities of creativity. . . . We will support one another when we are told we are physically, intellectually, morally, and spiritually inferior. . . . We will learn from one another that this is not true—that to be a woman is beautiful in many more ways than we have been led to define it. . . .

And we will affirm our uniqueness among ourselves and will give support to one another . . .

to the woman who is not married by twenty-two and experiences what it means to be a cultural disaster . . .

to the woman who is widowed and her sources of enrichment all dry up, for she may not be a self in her own right . . .

to the woman, young or old, who is a freak because she seeks out learning, lets her spirit soar, does battle with the structures which impede her, and cries alone at being called that dreadful epithet: She's masculine . . .

to the political radical who has chosen a course of pursuing change, and to the mother in the home who has chosen to remain there . . .

to the woman who retreats and lives out her dry days uncertain even of why she fears life so. . . .

AND WE WILL AFFIRM OUR UNIQUENESSES AMONG OURSELVES AND WILL GIVE SUPPORT TO ONE ANOTHER, and we will learn how not to stereotype, and how to listen, and define, and feel, and act. . . .

And we will strive to understand our creation and our history:

—CREATED in the image of God which is in the human person, and not the sexual role, with the nature, dignity, and common mission to continue the creative processes;

—SAVED by an incarnation whose importance is not its masculinity but its ongoing Presence, Reality, and Revolutionary character;

—FREED to participate in history neither as slave nor master, but as co-creator of the persons and the churches, the governments and the universities, the affirmations and the judgments;

—RESPONSIBLE to feel all that it does mean to be human, and to learn how best our children can be human.

AND AS WE ARE BECOMING, WE MAY FREE OUR BROTHERS, TOO.

I will affirm my sisters . . . and they me. We are too beautiful in our creation to be wasted . . . and too responsible not to stand up.

> The Affirmation
> of the morning
> progresses through four
> simple sentences:

YOU ARE NOT MY GOD JEHOVAH!
I WILL SPEAK WITH MY BROTHERS.
I WILL AFFIRM MY SISTERS.
I WILL CRY UNTO MY GOD: LET US FREE ONE ANOTHER!

I WILL CRY UNTO MY GOD: LET US FREE ONE ANOTHER!

My God: surely you do not choose to be ontologically masculine, burdened with cultural forms and sexual stereotypes. Let me create you with the men, Almighty God! Let my experiences be as real as theirs, my formulations as acceptable, my accountabilities to you as deep.
I will cry unto my God: let us free one another.

My God: surely you do not choose to limit those who serve you to fixed natures and to restrict the forms of the response. If that had been so, cultures would have killed you long ago!
I will cry unto my God: let us free one another.

My God: surely you do not try to hide your presence so that it cannot be discerned . . . or can only be discerned by an elite . . . or can only be discerned correctly by a masculine interpreter. . . .
I will cry unto my God: let us free one another.

My God: surely you do not limit an accountability for your creation to the men. I WANT TO BE JUDGED TOO! And surely you do not give them special protection from discerning all their narrowness of view. . . .

My God, My God! What have they done to you? Coopted you to their own ends so you find a corruption of yourself facing another corruption of yourself in battle. Made you scapegoat for all our deaths and dying. Killed you at our desire, and set up Ph.D. requirements to speak of you. Clouded you in rhetorical facticity and changed you always to meet the fashion.

I WILL CRY UNTO MY GOD: LET US FREE ONE ANOTHER.

I have a brother. And his name is Paul. And we both serve you, although we each have problems in expressing what you mean to us, and are, and have been, evermore will be.

ALL THINGS COME FROM GOD. My brother Paul is honest to confess to you, even when he has just finished limiting me. And I too am created in your image.

And with my brother Paul, I claim my right to serve my god, define the God-reality, affirm the God-presence.

FOR I AM SURE THAT NEITHER DEATH, NOR LIFE, NOR ANGELS, NOR PRINCIPALITIES, NOR THINGS PRESENT, NOR THINGS TO COME, NOR POWERS, NOR HEIGHT, NOR DEPTH . . . nor abyss of the present, nor masculine structures and definitions of me, nor limits of the church itself which is absurdly called she, NOR ANYTHING ELSE IN ALL CREATION WILL BE ABLE TO SEPARATE ME FROM THE LOVE OF GOD IN CHRIST JESUS OUR LORD.

—WHOM I would *serve* as a full human being
—*in whose name* I would speak prophetic words
—*in whose ongoing Creation* I would govern with the kings
—*in whose Presence* I would be a priest;

in whom
there is neither Jew nor Greek,
slave nor free,
male nor female.

THE AFFIRMATION OF THE MORNING:
YOU ARE NOT MY GOD, JEHOVAH.
I WILL SPEAK WITH MY BROTHERS.
I WILL AFFIRM MY SISTERS.
I WILL CRY UNTO MY GOD: LET US FREE ONE ANOTHER.
AMEN.

THE REV. DR. PEGGY WAY *is a theologian whose primary commitments are to the communities of the church.*

Today Is All We Have

TERRY WERTH

Here we are. A group of Christian women. We have everything in common. We have nothing in common. We are different ages, different backgrounds, different vocations, different interests. Yet we are all women who are about to share the same dinner, in the same place, and will answer to the call of being "Christian" and being "human." And I suspect that we have at least one more thing in common—we all procrastinate.

Procrastination—I hate that word; just hearing it wells up oceans of guilt inside of me. It conjures up visions of my cupboard doors, which I have been meaning to wash off for who-knows-how-long; or the neatly stacked pile of mending, which I can now ignore in good conscience because they are all winter clothes; or the letter I know my grandmother is eager to receive, but I'll wait till something *really* interesting happens— like a meteor lands in our back yard.

I once read on a Salada tea bag (you know you have a really high-class speaker when she quotes from Salada tea bags) that if we were all to confess our sins to one another we would have to laugh for lack of originality. Life has taught me that this is true, and I suspect that procrastination is one of the most common, most annoying sins that we have in common.

My big defense against accepting responsibility for the procrastination in my life is one tacky little phrase—often mumbled under duress—"I work best under pressure." But it is

227

absolutely true. Honestly. So I don't procrastinate like all of you; I simply wait for my hour of greatest potential—which is usually an hour before the deadline.

The real tragedy of procrastination is that it is so nonproductive, so wasteful, like living your life in neutral gear, not going backwards or forwards, just not going anywhere. Procrastination has been called the art of keeping up with yesterday. We become masters of the might-have-been and could-be, when we really need to be masters of the here and now. How can we fulfill our true potential as Christians and as women, if we indulge ourselves in noble thoughts but no noble actions; if we go through life as a spectator rather than a participant; if we put off the good we can do, waiting for a better opportunity, but never seize the opportunity?

I suspect that the reason most of us procrastinate is that we are waiting for something to come along that is worthy of our whole effort, our total commitment. We have, somewhere along the way, decided that the piddling demands of daily living are not worth investing or immersing our energies. What we fail to recognize is that, in order to be more than just undead, in order to be alive, really alive with the Spirit, we need to live each day.

In an article by Bishop Hogan entitled "Who Is This New Woman Among Us?" he considers what Mary, the mother of God, may have to say to us as Christian women with the new demands of this day, because she had to be "new" in her own time.

What was Mary really like as a human being? When you sift through the legendary image projected by the profusion of literature, art, and music created in her honor, it is difficult to discover her true nature. And scanty references to Mary in the Gospels need to be understood in light of the history and culture of those times. Much of what we can glean about her is more conjecture than established fact. However, a few significant insights stand out clearly.

First of all, she was not a procrastinator like Jonah—who, when he was called by God, asked to be excused for the moment. Mary was a woman of strong faith, who took her God very seriously. She had come to know him in a totally new way. No woman before or since has been selected to be the mother of

God. Her deeply intimate, personal knowledge of her God, in faith, gave her the courage to say "Yes" to this unique new calling.

Another important insight for today's people is the quality of Mary's relationships with those she loved. We can only imagine the kind of awareness she had of the child she carried and the kind of prayer that grew out of her tender concern for him. Her response to the elderly Elizabeth, which took her on a difficult journey for anyone, especially for one pregnant, certainly shows her total commitment.

Perhaps the strongest witness that Mary shows us is her attitude regarding Jesus' death. It is her faith, her total commitment to God and his son, that enabled her to stand at the cross when the other disciples, except one, had fled. And when no offense or no reproach was left to her silent standing there before the silent gaze of everyone who could see.

Surely we find in her life many signs that this woman was equal to the task of her life—that her stature is equal to the task of any age. Her faith, her concern for others, her strength of purpose, her tremendous compassion, her total commitment to Jesus and his people, whom she made her own, were a new kind of greatness in her own times.

Is not our daily life worth our total commitment?

Total commitment (TC) is getting the bills paid on time, instead of putting it off because it is a dull, colorless task.

TC is getting the kitchen floor mopped when it needs it, or leaving it unmopped when your child needs you.

TC is a not-my-will-but-thine attitude toward every day. And the reason TC is so important is that every day is all we have; all we can be sure of is today. TC is what Jesus Christ was all about.

Jesus is not "sort of" the son of God. He is not the Lord of Mediocrity. He did not make a modest sacrifice. He is the living, dying, and resurrected example of TC, and each moment wasted is one less opportunity we have to live out our TC to our Lord.

In my recipe box, intermingled with the recipes, are some of my favorite quotations. One of my favorites is a prayer you can find on a loaf of Monks bread:

This is the beginning of a new day. God has given me this day to use as I will. I can waste it or use it for Good. What I do today is important because I am exchanging a day of my life for it. When tomorrow comes, this day will be gone forever, leaving in its place, something I have traded for it. I want it to be gain, not loss; good not evil; success not failure; in order that I shall not regret the price I have paid for it.

God is calling us each day to renew the world—not by a blood-and-thunder revolution, but by a revolution in the hearts of people, and starting with each one of us. He calls us to renew the world over a cup of coffee, at the supper table, at the voting place, in a letter to the editor, in the office, at school, in a note to a friend, in a batch of cupcakes, in a pair of mended jeans; we are called to renew the world the way God, through Christ, intended it. These are merely puttering, petty, mundane things —unless they are done with all your strength and soul and heart and mind, unless they are done out of TC for God in Christ.

We may have come this far without TC. We may have come this far bogged down with procrastination, but like good athletes, totally committed to the race when they have already spent themselves, we can get a second wind, we can give it all we've got from here on. We can decide to eliminate the word "procrastination" from our vocabulary and, more important, from our daily living. And like the Blessed Mother, we can use our strong faith, the quality of our relationships, and our total commitment to Christ, to be fully alive and eager to witness as followers of Jesus

TERRY SCHREIBER WERTH *has published two photographic/ poetry collections,* Poems for a Pregnant Lady *and* Coming Another. *She serves on the Liturgy Committee of St. John the Evangelist Roman Catholic Church. She is also a member of Rochester Poets and is literary arts chairman of Northwest Arts Council. Mrs. Werth graduated from Elmhurst College and lives in Spencerport, New York with her husband and two children.*

Also by Caroline Stafford
THE HOUSE BY EXMOOR
MOIRA

The Teville Obsession

CAROLINE STAFFORD

S

SIMON AND SCHUSTER · NEW YORK

Published by Simon and Schuster
A Division of Gulf & Western Corporation
Simon & Schuster Building
Rockefeller Center
1230 Avenue of the Americas
New York, New York 10020

Designed by Eve Metz
Manufactured in the United States of America

1 2 3 4 5 6 7 8 9 10

Library of Congress Cataloging in Publication Data
Stafford, Caroline.
The Teville obsession.

I.   Title.
PZ4.S7779Te [PS3569.T165]   813'.5'4   78-1429
ISBN 0-671-24032-3

For Julie
and
for David
each in their own way godparents to Rhosllyn

THERE WAS NO WARNING when I was summoned to the library by my cousin, Edward Tilmer, that he wished to discuss my future. For his mother had been dead nearly three months, and nothing had been said in all that time. It was true that I had served as her companion, but she was bedridden and wandering in her mind, in need of constant care. I never suspected that the Tilmers now planned for me to take the aging housekeeper's place!

Edward's brief announcement stunned me.

Removed from school at fourteen, forced to earn my keep over the past seven years by making myself useful to Edward's wife Jessica, I had helped in the nursery, mended and sewed for the family, and finally attended old Mrs. Tilmer. At least such occupations could not be considered humiliating. But a *housekeeper*—!

"No," I cried angrily. "No, I shall do nothing of the kind! I am a Somers, and not a common servant for you or anyone else!"

"Well-trained house servants are not to be sneered at, my dear Melanie," he said smoothly, relaxed and at ease behind his mahogany desk. "You must consider yourself fortunate to have a home at all! Not a penny to your name, and no family but ourselves."

"Yes," I broke in rudely, "yes, I know, I might have found

myself a charge on the parish, and I cannot say I wouldn't have preferred it!" Whenever I rebelled against their demands I was always told to be grateful and reminded that destitute orphans were generally sent to the workhouse. It was an empty threat, for the Tilmers were eager to stand well with their neighbors. But I often found myself wondering if it would be such a frightening alternative after all. At least one was prepared there to earn one's livelihood! What could I do, besides amuse old ladies and set a very fine, neat seam? "I didn't receive a *farthing* for my duties with Mother Tilmer, and yet I served her long and well. I shall advertise for a place as companion—at least strangers will recognize the difference between charity and exploitation!"

"And how shall you find a recommendation? I cannot in truth recommend a young woman of your uncertain temper and ungrateful manners to anyone of *my* acquaintance. You are penniless, Melanie—we feed you, clothe you, care for you in every way—and you have no choice at all about your future. So long as there is a need for you here, there is a place for you here."

"Precisely—for as long as I am useful to you, I shall *never* have a future! Hand-me-down clothes, a cheerless room, menial tasks, and an occasional reminder that I am fortunate to be here with my cousins. Do you suppose I am so humble that I shall be content with such a meager life?"

"Beggars are not choosers, Melanie. Cultivate a more gentle nature, and you will discover that your lot is not as intolerable as you think."

"I hate you, Edward Tilmer!" I cried, beside myself with fury at his calm face, long and heavy and unfeeling. "I hate you both—" Unable to endure another moment in his presence, I turned and ran.

Flinging open the library door in my mad rush to escape, I nearly collided with Johnston, the butler. Brushing past him with my head down to hide the impotent tears filling my eyes, I was not so fortunate in the second encounter. The tall dark stranger waiting in the hall by the stairs caught me

and steadied me almost before I had realized that he was directly in my path. Mumbling an apology, I broke free of his hands and went up the stairs as quickly as I could, acutely aware of the spectacle I had made of myself, yet goaded into fresh anger by my undignified exit from the library.

Dinner was sent to me on a tray that night. My cousins apparently wanted no repetition of embarrassing scenes at their dinner table.

Had they really expected to prevail without a struggle, simply because I was alone and dependent on them? I had come to Tilmer Hall as a child of nine, bereft of my parents and my home at one blow. Edward Tilmer was my father's second cousin on his mother's side and therefore not in line to inherit either Somers Court or its revenues—they went to another distant cousin, and Edward merely got an orphan with a respectable fortune in his wardship. I don't know what became of my fortune over the years betwixt nine and fourteen—Edward told me that my investments had been poor and what money there was had been spent on my upbringing. In my worse moods I suspected him of having embezzled it, for the only other trustee was an older man, a friend of my father's. Since being pitched into a stone wall on the hunting field, Mr. Molyneux had not been himself for nearly eight years, and could not have accounted for any of my cousin's transactions or questioned any of his decisions. Only my pride and self-respect stood in the way of Edward's latest scheme.

Thelma, the dour upstairs maid, was oddly enough the only friend I had in this house. When she came to collect my tray she paused to gossip.

"The mistress is in a rare taking this night," she said, automatically setting the room to rights as she talked. "Angry with you for your quarrel with the master, and angrier still that a visitor was a witness to it."

I felt the hot blood in my cheeks. "I hadn't heard the knocker," I admitted.

9

"Yes, Miss, no doubt of that! A lord, mind you, and come to see that Irish mare of the master's." She shook out the folds of the dull blue draperies, trying to give them a grace they had long since lacked.

"The chestnut? Is he selling her?" A beautiful hunter but not up to my cousin Jessica's weight this year.

"So Joel has told me. Squire Towle it was who spoke of her to his lordship, and he has come to have a look. Seems he has a fine stallion he wants to match with her."

"Who is he?" For no one had bothered to inform me that a guest was expected.

"It's Lord Teville," she replied briefly, and suddenly fell silent.

"Not a familiar name," I said after a moment. "I've not heard of him." Mrs. Tilmer had enjoyed discussing titled London society with me as I read to her from the newspapers.

"No, Miss, and a lady like *you* wouldn't of," she replied primly.

"Why? Is there something wrong with him?"

"No, Miss, it's not my place to repeat scandal of my betters. But I heard the mistress telling her maid that she never thought she'd sit at table with such a man!" She picked up the tray and turned toward the door. "He is on his way to London and will stop only the one night."

"Then I shall not have to face him again," I replied thankfully.

But the next morning a deep and soft blanket of snow covered the grounds of Tilmer Hall and clogged the roads to London. The great white flakes drifted out of heavy gray skies and gave no sign of slackening by midday.

Tired of my self-imposed confinement in my room, I laced my boots and caught up my cloak, eager for a walk even in the snow. I tried to slip out of the house unseen, but as my luck would have it, I met Cousin Jessica halfway down the stairs.

"Where are you going?" she demanded coldly, eyeing my cloak as if it displeased her. It was one of her castoffs.

"For a walk."

"See that you don't track snow all over the hall when you come in—that man is still here, you know." She pursed her lips, her round face puckered with ill-humor. "Such a disgrace last night—I shall never forgive you! Ungrateful—"

I stayed to hear no more, but ran lightly down the steps and out into the soft, silent world of the shrubbery beyond the rose gardens. Here the wind was less fierce. I walked for a quarter of an hour, aimless and withdrawn into myself, debating the endless circle of questions about what I must do. Matters had gone beyond repair now, and a time for decision had come. But what decision? Where on God's earth could I go, with no means to advertise, much less the price of the cheapest coach fare to carry me anywhere? To whom could I turn? In our quiet corner of Buckinghamshire, there was no one who would take my side in any quarrel with my cousins. The vicar was an old, gentle soul lost in his passion for incunabula. The squire was a bluff, hearty man who knew horses and every fox in three counties—scarcely the sort to involve himself in my affairs even if his wife would permit it. My cousins had seen to it that I had made no friends to whom I might confide my circumstances.

I paced the shrubbery, leaving a bare track to mark my passage, and then swung off toward the home wood, fighting the snow and wind as if they were my adversary, not the tall, snow-mantled stone house at my back. I was in no mood to meet anyone, much less Lord Teville again. He was coming through the trees to my left and had no doubt seen my bottle-green cloak long before I had noticed him. I continued on my way, still hoping to escape, but he lifted a hand in greeting, and I had no choice but to wait for him. He came striding through the drifts, snow flecking his heavy cloak and touching his thick dark hair. As he caught up with me I had the impression that he too had been walking off a mood, for his gray eyes were not as friendly as his smile.

Taking advantage of the opportunity to apologize for my rude behavior the day before, I said at once, "I'm Melanie

11

Somers. I must thank you—for helping me keep my feet—and beg pardon—for my bad temper. It was a poor reception on your arrival at the Hall."

"I should beg pardon for interrupting a private discussion," he said lightly. "Are you also a visitor, Miss Somers, or related to the family?"

"I'm an orphan," I said, trying to maintain a light tone in my turn, and not eager to acknowledge my connection to the Tilmers.

"So am I, as it happens. Then you live here?"

"Yes. I live here."

He had turned to walk beside me, but the tone of my voice made him glance down at my expression, half-hidden beneath the unbecoming hood.

"I see. You weren't at dinner last evening."

"No," I replied, still acutely aware of my disgrace. "I really oughtn't to be talking to you now." Trying to throw off my depression, I summoned a smile to turn the words into a jest. But he seemed to read another meaning into them.

"Well, you can't very well avoid me completely. Until this clears—at least until the snow stops falling—I'm afraid I'm a guest, welcome or not. I have just walked out to the main road, and there's no hope of getting through."

"You are traveling to London?" I asked. How easy for a man to come and go as he pleased.

"Yes, for my sins. Business, not pleasure."

We came out of the wood on the east front, and I looked up at the tall, smoking chimneys. Again he glanced at my face, and then asked quietly, "Do you really hate it so much?"

Taken unawares, I turned quickly.

"It's written in your face. And echoes in every word." His voice was impersonal.

"Yes, I hate it," I said tightly, unable to stop myself as the long-pent-up feelings spilled over. "If I had any choice—any *honorable alternative*—to living here, I would leave immediately—now, if I had to walk through drifts high as my head!" It was improper to make such a confession to a stranger, a guest in my cousins' house, but I was beyond

caring as I fought for self-control against the rebellious spirit that overwhelmed me.

"Any honorable alternative?" he repeated slowly, as if the words had touched a responsive chord in him. I scarcely heard him, merely nodding in answer, involved in myself and the emotions that had swept away the last shreds of common sense. "May I ask why?"

Before I quite knew how, I had told him the whole story, briefly and crisply, as if I were speaking of someone else. Standing there, his hair white with snow, he stared down into my face, a frown between his eyes.

"How old are you?" he asked abruptly when I had finished.

"Twenty-one," I answered. "What does it matter? Twenty-two in March."

"You are of age, then?"

"Yes. But it doesn't signify, I told you—there is nothing left to inherit."

"What of your other cousin, the one who inherited the estate and lands?"

"I have never met him. He showed no interest in me at nine, why should he now?"

"Why, indeed?" He absently flicked off the snow at the edge of my hood, sending a small cascade of soft white flakes drifting between us. It was gently done, but I sensed the power in those long, slender fingers and involuntarily stepped back. "Did I frighten you?" he asked quickly, his attention returning to me. For an instant there was a flash of anger in the somber eyes, gone so swiftly that I was not certain that I had read it correctly.

"No," I said, and yet he had, in some indefinable way. I could almost feel the suppressed violence in this man. "I . . . was startled."

"How gracefully phrased!" he said caustically. My bewilderment must have shown in my face, for he looked searchingly at me. "Have the Tilmers told you nothing about me?" he asked in some surprise.

"I didn't even know your name until last night," I replied truthfully. "Or that you were coming to Tilmer Hall."

"I am not . . . a sought-after guest," he said after a moment. "People call me the Devil Baron. God knows, they have good cause. What's more, I ride and drive as if the Furies themselves were at my heels. I can drink any man I know under the table. I've gambled wildly, and rarely lose—the devil's own luck, they say. And I live the life of a recluse ten months out of the twelve, because I can't bear my own company and yet am more comfortable alone. My house is on the Welsh borders, and tradition says it was built in seven nights by Merlin himself. Both the house and I are haunted. You have every reason to be frightened of me."

But I saw the bitter pride in his eyes as he finished, as if he forced himself to speak the truth as a penance.

I suddenly wondered if his wife had died. Unbearable loss might account for his torment and his reckless behavior. "Were . . . are you married?" I asked as gently as possible.

He laughed harshly. "Married? Who would wed with the devil?" He turned away, and we walked in silence for a time. "I have one virtue," he went on suddenly in a quieter voice. "I know myself. And I know better than to ask any woman to share a life such as mine."

"Perhaps you judge yourself too severely," I said, choosing the words carefully. "Perhaps you see yourself as worse than you really are."

"No," he said softly, bitterly. "No, I am not too severe with myself. So long as I can accept the truth, I'll remain sane." He glanced across at me. "Are you chilled? You have been out in this weather for a very long while."

"I'm accustomed to the cold."

"Do you often have guests at Tilmer Hall?"

"Occasionally. I rarely saw them while Mrs. Tilmer was alive. She was restless when visitors called, forgetting that she was no longer responsible for them and fretting about menus or airing the guest chambers or whatever came to mind. Though her room was on the east, away from the drive and the stables, she always sensed that someone was expected."

"And so you soothed her and read to her and kept her quiet?"

"Yes."

"And none of the young men lured you from your duty?"

I laughed. "There were young men only for Susan or Mary or Jane. With three marriageable daughters, none of the young men could be spared for *me*."

"Have Susan, Mary, and Jane married happily?"

"It would appear so. There are only the boys now, and both away at school."

"Which leaves you free to become the housekeeper."

"No!" I said vehemently. "No, I shall not!"

"I hope you may find a solution for your problem, Melanie Somers," he said bleakly. "Not everyone does." And then he took my arm and led me toward the side door of the house.

Lord Teville stayed two days longer, until the roads were passable. He bought the Irish mare and arranged to have her sent to his home as soon as the weather permitted. I saw little of him. My meals continued to be sent upstairs, and I was not asked to join my cousins and their guest in the drawing room after dinner. But we met twice more on my walks and were silent company most of the time, tramping the beech woods and out across the stubbled fields beyond. It was a natural silence, both lost in our own thoughts and yet sharing an unspoken need of a fellow human being even in our isolation.

I often watched the tall, moody figure striding beside me through the deep snow, seeking some further clue to his character. He said nothing more about himself and asked no questions of me. Yet I could sense the tension in him, barely suppressed, and something else that eluded me. Neither of us referred to the wild confidences during the storm. I had tried to persuade Thelma to tell me what she knew of him and got only a grim shake of the head in reply. But there must have been scandal—even Lord Teville himself had intimated as much. Once I caught the younger maids whispering about him in the morning room and judged from their chilled expressions that the subject was a forbidden one. Their guilty start as I entered confirmed this suspicion, but it was not possible to question them. I was between-stairs in their eyes,

neither servant nor family. And I would never have confessed my curiosity to my cousin Jessica. Still, I was drawn to him, and told myself that wildness was often magnified by rumor into profligacy.

It was with regret that I watched Lord Teville drive away. Standing by an upstairs window, I saw the carriage pull out from the terraced steps before the door and gather speed as it swung into the circle leading to the drive. As it swept around the far end of the loop, I saw Lord Teville touch his hat in a silent farewell, almost a salute, as if he knew that I was there, somewhere, among the blank and unfriendly windows of the house.

The brief pleasure of his company vanished in the struggle that lay before me. For two weeks I held out against the pressures of my cousins. Confined to my room, my only ally the maid Thelma, I endured the harangues and lectures and threats that poured over me with a silence that was my only defense. Sometimes I wondered why I was not sent packing for my stubbornness, and again considered the possibility that I had been cheated of my inheritance. For no other reason would Edward Tilmer have stood for my unrelenting refusal to learn the housekeeper's duties.

In the end, I was spared by a message from their youngest daughter that her first confinement had begun. My cousins left in haste to be with her, and I was forgotten in the hurry. For three long weeks I enjoyed the luxury of their absence, walking the silent passages and sitting in the silent rooms, never feeling at home or even welcome in any of them, but nevertheless grateful for the respite I had been granted.

My cousins returned near the end of the fourth week, still in high spirits from celebrating the advent of a grandson, and I faded quietly into the background. But soon after the neighbors had been informed of their good fortune and the news had lost its excitement, I was summoned to the library once more.

Steeling myself for a renewal of our struggle, I was surprised to find Edward and Jessica sitting before the blazing hearth, a letter in his hands and a look of consternation on

her face. Entering after my knock, I stood waiting for them to speak.

"What do you know about this Lord Teville?" Edward began.

"More to the point," Jessica put in suddenly, "*more to the point*, what were you about while he was here? A man of his reputation!"

"I scarcely saw him—you know that," I said, mystified. "What does it matter?"

"He has written to say that he wishes to call on you next week if we have no objections. What is this all about?"

"I don't know," I said, as stunned as they. "Surely he must have told you—" I broke off, remembering that he had shown some concern for my future. Had he heard of a position that might be available for me? Or discovered something about my cousin's wardship? I felt a surge of hope.

"Told us what?" Edward demanded.

"Why—told you what his business with me must be," I finished lamely. My cousins must not guess how much could depend upon that proposed visit or they would never allow it.

"He does not. I've half a mind to tell him he isn't welcome here!" Edward said petulantly. "He ought to have stated his business."

I was frightened suddenly. How could I convince them without betraying myself? Desperate, I kept my face unconcerned, and replied with a semblance of calm indifference, "Whatever you prefer. I really don't care," and turned to go.

"Well, quite frankly, I'm curious," Jessica said then. "Tell him Melanie may receive him on Wednesday next. We'll discover the truth then from him."

My hand trembled on the knob, but Edward was agreeing with her. I left, shutting the door quietly behind me. They were still discussing the subject as I hurried upstairs. Yes, he must have heard something about Edward's management of my affairs! I thought happily. It could make all the difference in the world! If there was even a *little* money left I would be free!

And so until he came I allowed myself to dream pleasantly

of my escape from Tilmer Hall, my cousins, and all the un-happiness of my years here.

Lord Telville arrived late on that March afternoon, and to my relief, asked Johnston, the butler, for me.

Johnston, torn between disapproval and curiosity, escorted me to the drawing room, where Lord Teville was waiting. "Miss Somers, my lord," he announced as he opened the door, then lingered to watch my reception.

I walked into the room to find my visitor standing by the hearth. His expression was somber as he greeted me, and I feared that his news had changed for the worse between the letter and his arrival.

"Won't you be seated, my lord?" I asked, attempting to appear at my ease in spite of the disappointment that threatened to stifle me.

As he looked about the dark, overfull room, rosewood sofas and cluttered, paisley-draped tables in the fashion that was becoming popular, a flicker of distaste crossed his face. "Is it too cold for you in the garden?" he asked brusquely. "I can't breathe in here."

"I'll send Johnston for my cloak," I said. "Meanwhile would you care for refreshments, my lord? You have had a long drive."

"Nothing, thank you."

The butler soon brought my cloak, ending the curious, strained silence between us, and with something like relief Lord Teville took my arm and led me outside toward the shrubbery.

There he was more at ease and said at once, "I'm sorry. I find that house as depressing as you must. Are they still after you to become the housekeeper, or is that settled now? Past history?"

"Very much present history," I said quietly. There was the painful memory of my outburst at our first meeting to remind me to watch my unruly tongue.

"Well, I daresay we can put a stop to that soon enough."

He turned to me abruptly. "Miss Somers, you told me that any honorable alternative was preferable to remaining here. Did you mean what you said?"

"Yes. I still mean it," I replied with resolution. "I am willing to go *anywhere,* do *anything* to escape this place, so long as my principles are not violated. I would not be here now if there had been anywhere else I might go."

He took a deep breath, his gray eyes holding mine. "Then would you consider a marriage of convenience an honorable alternative?"

Caught completely by surprise, I could only stare at him in wordless confusion, wondering if I had heard aright.

"Yes," he said swiftly, "yes, I know it's a shock for you, and I must beg your pardon for such an unceremonious proposal. But you see, this is difficult for me as well. I had never expected to marry—"

"You are asking me to marry you, my lord?" I asked, finding my tongue at last.

"Do you find the idea so distasteful? Tell me so, and I shall not press further."

"But, my lord—"

"My name is Mark. Mark Trecourt."

"We have not known one another—"

He turned away toward the tall leafless crown of the home wood beyond the shrubbery. "Does it matter? I know we are comfortable together, and that you are frightfully unhappy here. I don't ask for your affection—I never shall—but perhaps this one good deed will weigh a little, and if you can stand my company, perhaps you can help me endure the empty years ahead." He turned back, his face twisted in a grimace of pain. "I told you I never planned to marry. My cousin Noel will be my heir. I would never bring children into this world with my heritage. The marriage settlement will be generous, and if you ever fear me—or are repelled by my presence—you will be free to go and do whatever you like. This will be put in writing, Melanie, for your protection. I am not as mad as they claim, my dear, but damned

near it. Will you accept such a risk? Or does Tilmer Hall seem a haven by comparison?"

I was trying desperately to take in all that he was saying to me, to weigh the words carefully, confused and shaken though I was. "I had not dreamed— My lord, I do not wish to exchange my cousin's charity for yours!"

"It isn't charity I offer you, merely a bargain. And my name is Mark."

"Are you certain, my—Mark? Is this what you really *want?* Or are you pitying me because I poured out my anger and frustration in a fit of unthinkable bad manners?"

"I've given it careful consideration, Melanie," he said, guiding me toward the path to the home wood. "It's an answer for *both* of us. Yes, certainly anyone with an ounce of compassion must sympathize with your intolerable situation. But I asked you to marry me because we are at ease together. You can't imagine what that means to me! In all fairness, you should have an opportunity to marry for love and happiness. I can't give you these, either of them. But there is independence—financial and personal independence—instead. Whether you remain with your cousins or venture out into the world on your own, you haven't a bright prospect for happiness anyway. At least as my wife, your problem will be resolved."

The temptation, the truth of what he said, flooded through me. A voice urged me to accept, to be free once and for all of the Tilmers and everything they represented. Yet another voice urged caution. Although my cousins had treated me monstrously, they were familiar to me. This man was a *stranger.*

"Why do people whisper about you and call you the Devil Baron?" I asked, halting to face him.

His eyes followed a flight of rooks as he said, "The Norman title, de Téville, was anglicized to Teville, which to a Welshman is only a breath away from 'devil.' I suppose it fitted those early barons, arrogant and land-hungry invaders that they were. The name has been revived for me—I've got a

damnable temper and there have been . . . scandals of one sort or another. My tenants don't like me, the villagers are suspicious of me, and even my own servants tread warily. They would like nothing better than to see my uncle take my place as lord of Rhosllyn. God knows where it will all end—" He broke off and gestured wryly. "Small wonder they call me devil. Shall I give you time to consider, Melanie? The last thing I want is to rush you into a decision you may regret."

I compared the tall, broad-shouldered figure before me, the dark hair and shadowed gray eyes, the straight nose and grim mouth, with the three plain men my cousins had married. Theirs had not been love matches either, merely the best offers. Was I so wrong in accepting *this* man? He had title, fortune, a pleasing appearance, but most of all had so far shown a consideration for me that was painfully touching in my empty life. And in spite of his frank appraisal of himself, I thought possibly loneliness or disappointment in love had caused his strange moodiness. Turning from him to the tall chimneys of Tilmer Hall, I thought about my future.

If I remained here I would eventually have no alternative but to accept the housekeeper's duties. My cousins would wear me down in the end, for there was nowhere else to go. Instead I was offered marriage, a house of my own, a husband who might in time come to terms with his haunted wildness and find happiness once more—

As if he had followed my thoughts, he said gently, "You may face a long life in another sort of bondage, tied to a husband who is locked away in the attics, raving mad—or worse."

I raised my eyes quickly to his, but there was no hint of wry jest in them. A chill swept over me. In a moment of clarity I saw how fortunate I was at Tilmer Hall compared to many women who must make their own way in a rough world. Yet I *hated* my enforced drudgery here—I was as desperate to escape as any half-starved, cruelly abused London

waif. How many other chances would come my way? What should I do?

Then, for some inexplicable reason, his bleak prediction challenged me. He could set me free from Tilmer Hall— might I not in turn help him find hope? Or at the very least, peace of mind. Summoning a smile, I said formally, "I shall be honored to accept your offer of marriage."

For the first time I saw him smile in return, a transforming, warming smile that touched his eyes and gave them a depth that shook me for an instant. He lifted my hand and bent to brush the fingers lightly with his lips. "You have made me very happy," he said with equal formality, before giving me his arm to return to the house.

Our strange bargain was sealed, and in that instant I unwittingly became the stalking horse for a murderer.

There was consternation in the library when we broke the news to my cousins. They were as shocked as I had been, but not as speechless.

"We are in mourning for my mother-in-law," Jessica said primly. "The marriage could not take place before the year is out, if then."

"A quiet wedding with only the family present is acceptable," Mark replied evenly. "Mrs. Tilmer was not a near relative of Melanie's, after all." He drew an envelope from his pocket. "In any event, I have brought a special license."

"But that's unthinkable—hole-and-corner!"

"Scarcely that. You yourself point out that the family is in mourning. Of course with your presence at the ceremony, there can be no suggestion of stealth," he replied firmly. "I am sure you would not wish it otherwise."

The hint in his stern voice gave Jessica pause. She thought of her daughters and their dull but well-to-do husbands. A peeress might become an asset to Susan's growing family of girls or stand godmother to one of Mary's boys. I could see the calculations cross her face as she weighed the loss of a housekeeper against the possible benefits.

Edward began to speak unctuously of my lack of dowry, but Mark brushed his words aside. "My solicitors have drawn up the necessary papers. Melanie will be well provided for, I assure you. In her own right."

There was a sudden gleam of greediness in my cousin's face. "Do you feel it wise to burden a young woman with financial matters? A trustee, perhaps—"

"No," Mark said shortly. "No trustees. My man of business is sufficient for her needs. I prefer it so."

Edward had the grace to flush.

Without a direct reference to his reputation, which both Edward and his wife seemed strangely reluctant to make to his face, there could be no insurmountable obstacle put in Mark's way. In another fifteen minutes the forthcoming marriage was arranged, and Johnston was sent for champagne to toast our happiness. As my cousins lifted their glasses to me I felt a last flicker of doubt race through me, and then Mark smiled again and I was reassured.

But several days after Mark's departure for London, Edward Tilmer tried again to persuade me to put my financial affairs in his hands. I refused point blank, and when he continued to badger me, was goaded into telling him my suspicions about the disappearance of my own fortune.

We had a flaming quarrel then, ending in a bitter mutual denunciation.

"Proud, aren't you, you little fool! Do you *know* what sort of man Telville is? Has he told you the *truth* about himself?"

"Enough. It doesn't matter to me. Anything is preferable to becoming your servant!"

"Is it? Think again, my dear Melanie. When your rash marriage comes to grief, you'll *crawl* back to Tilmer Hall, grateful for a place with us and eager to become even a scullery maid, if we'll have you!"

"Never! Do you hear? Nothing could *ever* bring me back to Tilmer Hall again!"

"Never? We shall see! You'll discover soon enough that you have leaped from the saucepan to the fire," he said

furiously, and then Johnston entered to announce luncheon and I escaped to my room. Flushed and breathless with anger, I could not have swallowed a bite of food.

Within two weeks I became Lady Teville and a wealthy woman in my own right. The full terms of the settlement were privately arranged, and Edward could learn nothing about them. But before the world at large my cousins put a very good face on the matter. Mark was not the sort of man to cross openly and they were unusually wary of his displeasure. For all their avid curiosity to know how I had managed to attract Mark on such short acquaintance, they never asked a direct question, though Jessica often tried to pry by hinting at his reputation.

"Of course he is scandalously   you know. Violent, even. Are you certain . . ."

"Quite certain," I replied, continuing to sort through my meager possessions.

"Well, a man doesn't acquire such a name without good reason!" She looked at me across the neat piles as if on the point of saying more, but after a moment added only, "I will say he has never been known to chase women, though every *other* sin is laid at his door. A taint in the blood, I've heard."

"I'm not concerned. Many young men settle down after marriage." But Mark was twenty-nine, nearly. If only Mrs. Tilmer were alive and I could ask her about the Trecourts! I turned away to hide my uneasy face from Jessica's probing eyes. It was too late to turn back now.

The private ceremony was so swiftly over that I scarcely had time to feel anything except dazed. My replies were in a voice far calmer than I had imagined possible, and then Mark's deeper tones echoed them before his lips coolly touched mine in the traditional kiss. My ivory satin gown whispered over the stone flags of the lovely old church, and with Mark's hand beneath my elbow we stepped out into the pale April sunlight.

Immediately afterward we planned to leave for the Welsh borders, pleading the distance to excuse ourselves from anything more elaborate than a small reception. The neighborhood, curious and rather reserved, came to wish us well. They would never have guessed that I was the ugly duckling becoming a swan. Jessica's careful acting presented a picture of a very dear daughter happily married and leaving behind loving foster parents.

As we settled ourselves in the carriage and the door closed upon us, I sat back wearily. "Thank God, that's over," I said, and shut my eyes as the wheels rattled down the loop of the drive. I had no desire for a last look at Tilmer Hall.

Mark touched my hand briefly. "It was well done. You can be comfortable now." He stretched his long legs and tossed his hat to the seat opposite. "Warm enough?"

"Yes, thank you," I replied, my feet against the wrapped hot stone and my hands nestled in a sable muff he had brought me from London. While I had been preparing for my wedding and the departure from Tilmer Hall he had returned to London to shop for me. His excellent taste had pleased me and surprised my cousins. There were no hand-me-downs in the trunks lashed to the back of the well-sprung carriage.

"I'm sorry your family could not be here for the wedding," I added as we drove out of the wrought-iron gates and turned north. "I hope no one is ill?"

He smiled ruefully. "No, they are quite well. They didn't come because they didn't know there was to be a wedding. I sent an express to Rhosllyn only this morning."

"They didn't *know*—but surely they would have wished to come!" I felt a chill of apprehension.

"Possibly. My uncle would have felt it his duty, certainly. I didn't want them to come." Suddenly his voice was cold. "I would not permit their doubts to spoil this day for you. We are safely married now—it won't matter what they say or do!"

WE DROVE INTO BANBURY in a blinding downpour. Mark directed the coachman to the inn in Parsons Street and turned to me.

"Contrary to what we told your cousins, I thought you might indeed prefer a leisurely journey to Rhosllyn. You will wish time to grow used to me, after all. And the servants will have an opportunity to prepare for you. The house has been a bachelor establishment for nearly eight years, in spite of Cecily's endless efforts to inject a feminine note!"

"Who is Cecily?" I asked.

"My cousin—my uncle Rhys's daughter," he said briefly, and leaned forward to open the door as the carriage came to a halt.

I was grateful for Mark's thoughtfulness, though I strongly suspected he had his own motives for the delay. He had been pleasant and considerate during our brief meetings at Tilmer Hall, and I knew no real reason to regret my decision, but the enormity of what I had done struck me as we drove through the countryside, and I was suddenly quite shy. I had never looked beyond the wedding or imagined my arrival at Rhosllyn. Escape from my cousins had occupied my thoughts to the exclusion of any other consideration. Now I was shocked, a little frightened even, by my readiness to marry a total stranger. What would Mark's family and friends think of me

if they knew? Indeed, what had his solicitor thought as he drew up that agreement granting me a generous settlement and my personal independence at the same time? I had finally found the courage to speak of this to Mark, but his reply was terse and unconcerned. "My family won't know. As for Briggs, he was acquainted with your father, I believe. Besides, he hopes you'll be the making of me." And so I had questioned no more, silently resolving to deserve such confidence.

Although the inn was crowded, a private sitting room had been prepared for us, and I was pleased to find a warm fire waiting in my bedchamber as well. A red-cheeked girl named Nell appeared with hot water and helped me change from my traveling costume to a gown of watered silk in a shade of deep rose. Then she suggested rearranging my hair in a more flattering style. Afterward I stood before the glass staring back at my reflection, bewildered by what I saw. Was the pretty, dark-haired girl really me? Had the lovely clothes made such a difference? Never having owned anything half so becoming—indeed, anything becoming at all!—I was unprepared for the startling change in my appearance.

Nell smiled at me in the glass, breaking the spell, and I turned away to pick up a woolen shawl in the same warm color, before going downstairs to the sitting room. Mark joined me almost at once.

"Have they made you comfortable?" he asked, crossing to the decanters on a small table by the window.

"Quite comfortable, thank you," I replied, smiling.

He began to pour a glass and stopped to turn to me. "You do take sherry?"

"If you please."

He filled the glasses and brought one to me, then withdrew a slim velvet case from his pocket and dropped it in my lap. "These will go well with your gown, I think," he said matter-of-factly and went to stand by the hearth, one strong, well-shaped hand resting lightly on the mantel.

Surprised, I opened the case and found a slender necklace

of blue sapphires set in white gold, tear-shaped buds in a delicately wrought chain of leaves. It was exquisite and I stared speechlessly at it.

"My mother's," Mark said briefly. "My solicitor had the Teville collection cleaned for me."

His mother's jewels. Somehow the sapphire necklace in my hand made the marriage seem more real than that short service in St. Mary's Church had done. "Mark—I hadn't thought—it's lovely!"

He smiled faintly as he took the necklace from me and fastened it about my throat. The links felt cool against my bare skin and I suppressed a sudden shiver. Had the heirloom brought with it a sense of foreboding? But as I caught sight of myself in the glass during dinner, the warm flash of blue in the candlelight dispelled any lingering disquiet I might have felt.

It was still raining heavily the next morning and my memory of Banbury is one of damp stone and hurrying, drenched figures passing along the shop fronts. But Worcester was full of sunshine, the cathedral catching the afternoon gold in its glass and refracting its beauty across the nave floor as we entered.

It was pleasant to wander about in the cool quietness. Our footsteps echoed in the stone vaulting and our voices rang hollowly among the pillars. Mark took me to see King John's tomb, but I lingered at the chantry of the boy Prince Arthur, the elder brother of Henry VIII and first husband of Catherine of Aragon. He had died at sixteen at Ludlow, the border home of the Princes of Wales, and was buried here in a tomb whose lacy beauty had not dimmed with the years.

Afterward we strolled along the river and over the bridge to see the cathedral at its best, the west front holding the warmth of the sun in its stone. "I like this town," Mark said absently. "It is vigorous and yet peaceful—the past is here and yet isn't overwhelming." He gestured around us. "The last battle of the Civil War was fought here, and Charles II

had to flee for his life. Two hundred years ago, and no sign of it left. In Rhosllyn we dwell on nearly a thousand years as if they were yesterday."

"What happened so long ago?" I asked, not really wishing to hear and spoil the beauty before me.

"The Welsh ruled the valley. They had taken it back from the Saxons. And then the Normans came and took it from both."

Relieved, I smiled. "Scarcely a matter to lie awake over!" I said lightly, watching the townspeople bustling about their affairs.

He seemed to become aware of me suddenly. "No. Of course not," Mark replied firmly, but without the usual ring of conviction in his voice. Yet why should the past disturb him so? We turned back the way we had come in silence.

There was only one incident to mar our journey, and that occurred at the inn in Worcester. A drunken man tried to force his way into our private sitting room in the mistaken belief that it was his. Mark stood by the table, his napkin clenched in his hand, while the waiter explained nervously that Lord Teville had indeed reserved this chamber.

"Teville, is it?" the red-faced gentleman said, turning to stare owlishly at Mark as the waiter scurried away to find Dawson, the innkeeper. "Oh, yes, I've heard of you," he went on, a sneer in his voice. "You're the one who—"

He got no further. Mark's chair spun away as he launched himself at the intruder. I choked back a cry of alarm as he hit him, hard. The man reeled from the force of the blow and crashed against the far wall of the passage. Without another sound he slipped to the floor and lay there.

Dawson came running up. "Get that sodden fool out of here," Mark ordered curtly, and slammed the door shut in the innkeeper's face.

He stood for a moment, back to the door, his mouth grimly set and his gray eyes nearly black with rage as he fought to bring himself under control. Too frightened to move, I

thought he had forgotten my presence until he said with an effort, "I'm sorry." Picking up his napkin and the overturned chair, he took his place at the dinner table again. "I won't have you needlessly hurt. Forget it if you can."

Still shocked by the sudden explosion of anger, I said shakily, "Yes, of course," and hadn't the courage to ask what the man was about to say.

Ludlow, our last halt before reaching Mark's home, was lost in mist as we drove up to the Feathers Inn. The lovely black-and-white façade shimmered like an insubstantial ghost, but the candlelight in its windows gave forth a bright welcome. Mark ducked his head as we passed through the low-beamed entrance and spoke to the graying man who came from behind the desk to greet us.

In two days I had grown accustomed to the courteous attention given to Lord Teville and his wife, but here I sensed a strange undertone of reticence in the man's pleasant voice. And then an older woman in neat black hurried from the parlor to take me upstairs, her smiling welcome barely covering her uncertainty as she recognized Mark.

"Such a day we have had!" she said nervously as we went down the passage, making room for a harassed governess with her numerous noisy charges. "Beautiful it was until nearly three, and then in comes the mist, and rain by morning of a certainty." She clucked her tongue as she opened the chamber door and stepped aside for me to enter. "The sheets will be damp too, for these mists find their way right through the walls. But never doubt, my lady, that Betty will be up to warm them properly before you retire."

I thanked her, and she hesitated in the doorway after a last sharp glance to make certain that all was in order—the fire burning briskly on the hearth, hot water before it, and clean towels by the oak washstand, the draperies drawn neatly and the pale gold coverlet smoothed across the bed—to add, tentatively, "May I wish you happiness, my lady?"

"How very kind of you!" I replied. "Thank you."

She appeared to be on the verge of saying something more, thought better of it, curtsied, and hurried out, gently closing the door behind her.

The next morning a watery sun woke me, and after breakfast Mark and I walked about the town, built on rising ground partly encircled by two rivers. He pointed out the places of interest—the castle, the half-timbered buildings of Tudor times, the attractive inns, the quite large fifteenth-century church of St. Laurence, where a white cat chased a butterfly in the shadow of the doorway. And then we went down Broad Street, through the medieval gate, curving down toward the old stone Ludford Bridge over the Teme.

I expected Mark to turn back the way we had come, but he continued across the bridge, mounted some steps, and then took a rough track high above the river. Once again I had the odd feeling that he himself had no wish to hurry on to Rhosllyn. Suddenly, on the other side, Ludlow Castle rose on its craggy cliff, its fortress strength apparent here as it had not been in the town.

"The Welsh came this way," Mark said. "Impressive, isn't it?"

"I didn't realize it was so large!"

"No, the town hides it, of course. Here is history for you, Melanie. Edward IV, Richard III, the little Princes who died in the Tower of London, even young Prince Arthur and his Spanish bride—all of them saw that castle just as you see it now. A Norman began it in 1085, and not until the Tudors came to the throne did it know real peace. I often come here and wonder about those Norman forebears who wanted to carve a small kingdom for themselves along the Marches. It really was a kingdom. William granted them complete independence so long as they didn't meddle with him or stir up the country in their own battles with each other." He smiled suddenly. "These Normans were the worst of the lot, and the Conqueror knew it. That's why he sent them here to hold back the Welsh while he settled himself in England. A Trecourt was one of Roger de Montgomery's knights and in

thirty years' time had earned a title—murdering, betraying, and taking advantage of every opportunity that came his way. I've been to Téville, you know. It's a tiny fishing village on the Norman coast, no bigger today than it was in 1066, God knows. Not much of a beginning, but enough for a determined man."

I stared across at the castle, seeing it and its grasping, violent builders through Mark's words. He brought them vividly to life and I was curious to know more. But Mark had finished with the past.

"It's time I told you about Rhosllyn," he said, leaning against the gnarled trunk of an ancient tree. "You ought to know."

"Yes, I'd like that," I replied, glad he had broached the subject himself. I had tried to think of a way of doing so during our walk.

"Understand this: whatever I may have done in the past, you have nothing to fear from me. I'll see to that! So don't listen to their gossip. God knows, they'll be quick to tell you the worst if you'll let them. And don't be surprised if they are slow to accept you. That will change as they come to know you better. Above all, their attitude toward me mustn't affect your chance for happiness."

"Who are 'they'?"

He took a deep breath. "My uncle, Rhys Trecourt, and Noel and his sister Cecily, my cousins. They're presently living in the Dower House. Aunt Letitia, Rhys's wife, died five years ago. I've another aunt, Margaret, who lives in Chester and never sees anyone—she's bedridden with rheumatism. Noel is a year younger than I am and Cecily is your age or perhaps a year older. You'll find them friendly enough, I think." He moved to toss pebbles down the hillside toward the river below. "My father died eight months before I was born—pneumonia after a sailing accident off Anglesey. My mother ruined her health nursing him and then died of complications following childbirth. For a month or more my uncle had thought Rhosllyn was his. It must have been an

indescribable shock when he learned there was to be a post-humous heir." Mark began to pace restlessly. "To do him credit, Rhys treated me as his own son—a sickly scrap of humanity who had superseded him, who clung to life with a tenacity that could have been nothing short of maddening—and yet he refused to let the nurses and my aunt make an invalid of me. You see, from birth I was lord of Rhosllyn, and Aunt Letitia tried to coddle me. Rhys always took my part and insisted that I be treated like any other boy. God help me, I don't know why I hate him as I do—it must be the perverse streak of madness in me. Possibly that's also why I'll do anything to prevent him from stepping into my shoes. At any rate, it's clear that the villagers and tenants prefer him to me. After all, he is half Welsh and understands them as I never could. My grandfather's first marriage was to a Pembrokeshire heiress as faultlessly Norman as the Tre-courts, but after her death he chose a girl from Aberystwyth, who was much loved at Rhosllyn and in the village."

He straightened abruptly. "Do what you like with the house. Cecily will tell you it is sacred as it stands. Don't believe her. I won't care if you wish to redecorate the whole of it—in fact, I'd as soon have it changed beyond all recognition!"

"If you dislike it so much," I asked, wondering at his savage tone, "why do you live there?"

"There is nowhere else I can go and shut myself away," he replied, taking my arm. "We still have several hours before us. Let's not dwell on Rhosllyn for the whole of it." And so we took the lane leading to Dinham Bridge, entering the town almost under the castle ramparts.

After an excellent luncheon at the Feathers we embarked on the final leg of our journey. As Mark handed me into the carriage I felt a stirring of nervous anticipation, and twice during the drive found my hands tightly clenched in my lap. Mark pointed out the sights of interest along the road—Stokesay Castle set in its lovely dell, then a tall half-timbered farmhouse framed against the hills beyond, and later two

magpies quarreling furiously in the trees by the wayside. But as we drew nearer the border and Rhosllyn he fell silent as if he, too, dreaded the moment of arrival.

The carriage slowed its pace for a village street and I knew at once from the tenseness in Mark's posture that the journey was over. I turned quickly toward the window and looked out upon a farm, and then beyond it and set in tall trees, I saw the plain gray facade of the church. The yew-shaded churchyard sloped down toward the river, dotted with moss and timeworn markers. The street was lined with houses of gray-green stone or neat half-timbering, most of them edged with borders of flowers and sometimes gardens along the front walk. The village appeared to be prosperous and self-respecting, but I saw no sign of Rhosllyn itself. Perhaps I had mistaken Mark's reaction? And then I knew that I had not. For in the door of the rambling smithy stood a great bear of a man, his dark hair streaked with white and nearly hiding his face altogether. But nothing hid the bare hatred in his dark eyes as he recognized the approaching horses. With a gesture of contempt he turned away to his forge as if to shut out the sight of us.

Just beyond the smithy the road angled toward the stream and the humped bridge beside the tidy stone mill. Ducks swam in the broad waters of the pond beside their own images, unconcerned by our noisy passage above them. And then we were clear of the village. Across the valley was the green pastured ridge of England and on the other side the broken blue hills that were Wales. Sheep and cattle moved in the wake of thin-legged offspring, and a first hint of color marked the orchards. On a slope facing Wales, its back to the domestic checkerboard of England, stood the manor of Rhosllyn.

I could barely see it in the trees, a tall stone house of gracious proportions, windows glinting in the paling light, smoke rising from the taller chimneys. A cloud of rooks were settling into the trees of the park, their noisy chatter faintly reaching us. We turned in at ornate iron gates and passed

the gatehouse cottage half hidden in a mass of rhododendron. The drive curved to the right and then forked, the shorter branch ending almost at once at the Dower House, of mellow golden stone. It was small and graceful, scarcely a hundred years old, the portico flanked by slender columns and surmounted by a balconied window. Gardens fanned out on either side, already a riot of early color. Altogether charming, I thought, as it passed out of sight.

The drive swung through the trees, angled across the slope, and came out suddenly at the main house. Compared to the Dower House, Rhosllyn was grander by far, and yet its gray-green stone seemed bleak and unwelcoming in the fading light. The approach was severe—no gardens to soften the lines or add color to the geometrical perfection of the front. Trimmed yews flanked the great carved door and the knocker was a heavy, medieval iron ring. Both door and knocker appeared to have come from an earlier building.

The carriage drew up, and without waiting for the coachman or the groom, Mark leaped out and unfolded the steps for me. His fingers were taut as he handed me down. I smiled fleetingly into his set face and with a serenity I was far from feeling, approached the opening door.

The portly, graying butler greeted his master and welcomed me to Rhosllyn, bowing formally as I crossed the threshold. Reminding myself that I was mistress here and must go on as I began, I stepped into the tiled hall and waited for the introduction to the assembled staff.

It was mercifully brief, Williams—the butler—indicating each servant by name and duty as I acknowledged the presentations: Mrs. Powell, the spare, dark-haired housekeeper, perhaps fortyish; Mrs. Davies, the plump and rosy-cheeked cook, whose thin mouth belied her cheerful face; Bronwyn, the slender, blue-eyed girl who would become my maid. And so on down the house staff to the staring scullery maid, who blushed furiously when her turn came.

"Thank you," I said to the line of expressionless faces. "I'm sure we shall deal very well together." But in my heart

I wondered. I could sense the coldness behind the respectful facade, and it was clear from their swift, measuring glances that they were seeking to discover more than what sort of mistress I would be.

"Tea will be set out in the drawing room, my lady," Williams was saying as he signaled the dismissal of the staff. "Mrs. Powell will show you the way to your rooms."

Giving Mark a faint smile, I followed Mrs. Powell up the wide stairs, their graceful curve arching above the hall and over the heads of the butler and the dispersing servants. The house had been renovated in the Regency style, elegance and good taste unobtrusively present everywhere and undiminished by the years. After the clutter and darkness of Tilmer Hall, with its massive furnishings and heavy colors, the airy lightness of the old-fashioned, classical decor was somehow refreshing.

Mrs. Powell led me to the second floor and an end suite of rooms overlooking the gardens and the quilt of pasture and hedged fields rolling up the ridge. My sitting room was lemon yellow with curtains of antique gold, while the bedchamber was a delicate blue trimmed in deeper shades ranging from the jasper ware of brocade draperies to the midnight background of the rose-and-cream Turkey carpet. Two chairs by the hearth were of the winged style and upholstered in a floral print of medium blue, port wine, and old gold, matching the bed hangings. The luxury and comfort took my breath away. For all that the simplicity was a generation old, the woods were meticulously polished and the fabrics appeared to be new. Except for faint recollections of my childhood home, I had never enjoyed such beautiful surroundings.

Remembering Mrs. Powell, hovering watchfully at my side, I repressed my cry of delight at the sight before me and told her that I found my rooms very satisfactory. I could not shame Mark by admitting the truth about my past circumstances.

She visibly relaxed at my words, her folded hands dropping down to her sides. "Yes, my lady, and we had so little time—

I'm glad you are pleased!" Had she expected me to complain and set about making changes right away? Or had I accepted her arrangements too readily?

"Indeed I am," I replied, removing my hat and secretly glad of the quiet elegance of my traveling dress. How appalling it would have been to arrive at Rhosllyn in my reach-me-down and much-mended wardrobe! I felt a rush of gratitude for Mark's thoughtfulness in remedying the lack.

After washing my hands and patting my hair into place I followed the waiting housekeeper downstairs once more. The drawing room was still empty, and I decided to explore a bit while waiting for Mark. After admiring the dark portraits along the stair wall and the lovely old tapestry above the tall Tudor chairs in the hall, I turned down a passage that met it at right angles.

Mark was standing near the far end, his hand resting on the knob of a closed door. Expecting him to glance up at once, I continued on my way, then hesitated and finally stopped altogether. Absorbed in his own thoughts he had neither seen nor heard my approach. I tried to read his expression, but it was lost in the shadows of the passage. The set of his shoulders was tense, almost braced, as if he dreaded crossing the threshold and yet was drawn there against his will. The silence lengthened. Oddly reluctant to disturb him and uncertain how to withdraw gracefully, I quietly let myself into the nearest door.

Clearly the music room, I saw at once. The piano stood by tall windows facing the terrace and the formal gardens laid out beyond. A lute hung above the mantel and there was a small harp on the square, carved table nearby. I was tempted to pluck its strings and then remembered Mark, just outside. Crossing the thick rose-and-green carpet, I was starting to glance through the neat stack of music on the shelves when I heard voices from the hall. I hurried back to the drawing room.

It was a long room, pale lime with white plasterwork, draperies in hunter's green trimmed in gold, with gold again in the carpet and on the chairs. The ceiling was in the Adam

style, beautifully worked, and fine paintings hung between the tall windows and above the gilt tables on either side of the white mantel. Mark was waiting for me and there was an older man who rose as I entered and came to take my hand.

"My dear Melanie!" he said cordially, not waiting upon Mark's formal introduction. "How happy I am to welcome you to Rhosllyn and to our family." He led me forward to the tea table, adding, "I am Rhys Trecourt, as you have guessed, I'm sure. Noel and Cecily are sorry to have missed your arrival, but they are in Shrewsbury today for a friend's betrothal dinner." He turned to include Mark in the conversation. "Did you have a comfortable journey?"

"Very," Mark said briefly and took the cup I poured for him.

"And your rooms, Melanie, do they meet with your approval? We had so little time at our disposal—"

"They are very pleasant indeed," I said warmly as he took his cup.

"Cecily will be happy to hear it. She and Mrs. Powell have been busy making this bachelor haven habitable once more. We had begun to think that Mark would never settle down, so you can well imagine our pleasure when we received his letter." He turned to speak to Mark again, giving me an opportunity to observe him more closely.

Nearly as tall as Mark, dark eyes and dark hair, wings of gray at the temples—an attractive, sophisticated man in his early fifties. As he quietly talked I had the odd feeling that his effusive welcome was not characteristic of the man, that perhaps he had been trying to cover the awkward absence of Mark's family from our wedding. After all, it must have been a deep disappointment to him to have been purposely left out. And in the split second of entering the room, I had caught a fleeting expression of relief crossing his face as he saw me for the first time. Almost as if he had feared Mark's ability to choose a wife suitable to Rhosllyn and the Trecourts. Drinking my tea and watching the two men, I sensed the vulnerable warmth on one side and the scarcely concealed

antagonism on the other—a curious relationship for two people who stood almost as father and son to one another.

A pleasant half hour was spent in conversation, and then Rhys Trecourt set down his cup and took his leave.

"I simply wished to say hello. That's done. You'll want to enjoy your first evening at home without well-meaning family underfoot." He smiled at my protests. "No—I was young once! And time enough to know you better, of course. We are merely across the park."

Mark walked with him to the door and returned almost at once, an expression of acute dislike on his face. "I'm sorry!" he said abruptly.

"For what?"

"For putting you through the gantlet so soon." He sighed and sat down in the chair opposite to mine. Weariness or stress had etched lines about his mouth. "We shall have our dinner in the library and to hell with ceremony. I have no desire to shout to you down the length of that cavernous dining room while Williams stares over our heads as if he were deaf."

"Yes, I think that would be much pleasanter. And I'm glad your uncle came to tea! I'm happy to meet your family at last."

He rose quickly. "Don't, Melanie—don't judge any of us by appearance. We are none of us what we seem to be." His back was to me as he bent to place another log on the fire. "I hope to God I've done the right thing for you!"

Frightened suddenly by his intensity, I stared down at this stranger I had married. Mark had seemed so confident at Ludlow. Why was he filled with doubts now? "You have spared me a very dreadful future," I said with difficulty.

"I hope that will be enough," he said somberly and changed the subject.

I was restless my first night at Rhosllyn, tossing uneasily in my bed long after the house was silent and the fire had died down to a red-gold glow. Perhaps the excitement of arrival and my new surroundings had left me too taut for sleep, or

it might have been the strange room and bed. Jessica Tilmer had always declared that travel upset her nerves.

And so I lay in the darkness and tried to compose my thoughts, only to find them roving from one subject to another. Mark's uncle had given every indication of liking me, and the servants had treated me civilly. A proper beginning, surely. Still, Mark's edginess had been apparent throughout the evening, and I had been on the point of believing he now regretted his hasty marriage. Yet as he had handed me my night candle I had caught the expression in his eyes, and it was preoccupied, as if he had dreaded his homecoming for his own reasons. It was difficult to believe that, surrounded as he was by a gracious home, a loving family, and every comfort, Mark could know unhappiness here.

The French clock on the mantel chimed two as I drifted into exhausted sleep, and then almost at once I was jerked out of my dreams by a chilling cry that shattered the stillness. Startled, I sprang from my bed and raced to the window, flinging aside the draperies and peering out into the night, for the sound had surely come from outside. Something was floating through the air just below the eaves, an indiscernible outline, vanishing into blackness even as I opened the casement to see what it was or where it had come from.

Dismayed, I blinked at the empty night below, where the far corner of the house was starkly outlined against the sky, and at the empty darkness of the gray stone walls above. The apparition was gone.

What had I seen? A figment of my dreams, still before my sleep-drugged brain as I had leaned out the open casement, and then swept away by the cool night air? Clutching the windowsill with both hands, I looked carefully for any movement above or below and found none. It must have been a night bird fluttering after moths. Then what had I heard? An owl screeching in the park, or its prey crying out in distress? Chilled by the thought, I quickly drew back into my room, closing the window and pulling the heavy draperies into place. Now I was thoroughly awake again.

A light knock at my sitting room door spun me around sharply, my heart beating fast in alarm.

"Melanie?" Mark called softly. "Melanie, are you awake?"

"Yes," I called, catching up my silk wrapper and walking through to the door. "What is it? What has happened?"

"Will you let me in?" he asked. "Or come with me to the library?"

I opened the door at the urgency in his voice. "What is wrong?" I asked for the second time, for he wore a dressing gown over his clothes.

"Nothing," he replied, but his face was white and drawn. "Please, just talk to me—say anything that comes to mind, but please talk to me!"

"Have you also had a nightmare?" In my concern for him I forgot my flowing hair and lack of petticoats.

His lips quirked. "Yes—a nightmare."

I walked out into the passage and he took my arm, leading me down to the library, the flickering candle throwing our dancing shadows in stark relief against the stairwell wall.

"Do you often have bad dreams?" I asked, trying to talk as he wished me to, yet finding my tired mind empty of conversation at this hour.

"No—yes," he said distractedly, opening the door.

"Why don't you make up the fire while I pour a brandy for you," I suggested gently, taking the candle from his hand and lighting the tapers above the hearth. "Do you know"— gesturing about the well-filled shelves of the book-lined room —"I have never understood why libraries are stocked with books no one reads. And yet there is something comfortable about the smell of good leather bindings and the orderly rows marching in neat ranks from wall to wall. The chairs are always more comfortable here, too, restful and inviting."

He had knelt to start the fire, and I rattled on, saying whatever came to my mind until the blaze caught and he rose to face me.

"Here." I gave him the brandy I had poured out for him and he finished it in one swallow, handing the empty glass

back to me as if it had contained medicine. As I talked he walked restlessly about the room, his mind neither on my words nor on his path. I found myself wondering what dreadful dreams could disturb him so, but dared not ask. Sitting quietly in one of the comfortable chairs, I found words to use, a constant flow in a pleasant conversational tone, as if he were a visitor to tea and rather shy, putting him at ease by never demanding an answer, though always ready to receive one.

After a time he grew calmer or too exhausted to pace any longer. I watched him without seeming to, my mind scarcely following my own words. It was the sound of my voice that soothed him, nothing more—I might have declined Latin nouns or recited the peerage for all he knew.

At last he sank into a leather chair by the hearth and buried his face in his hands as if to wipe away the lingering images before his eyes. "I'm sorry to have ruined your sleep," he said finally. "It was thoughtless of me to drag you so soon into my private hell." He looked across at me, tired, haggard, drained of emotion, but at peace with himself once more.

"You rescued me from mine," I replied. "I can do no less for you."

Mark smiled wryly. "I wish it were possible. Go to bed, Melanie. I'll sit here until the fire dies down."

I rose and went slowly to the door, reluctant to leave him there alone. Then a sudden memory of the Tilmer nursery came back to me, the boys waking in the night and afterward demanding something to eat. Surely grown men were not so different. At least it would be worth trying. "Do you suppose," I asked, "that Mrs. Davies would be furious if we raided her larder? I should very much like another of those glazed tarts we had for dinner."

He showed immediate interest. "Yes, they were quite good. Can you find your way to the kitchen?"

"No. I don't even know how to begin," I said, laughing ruefully.

He rose and took the nightstick from the mantel. "I'll show you." With the stealth of intruders, we went through

the service door in the rear of the hall and down the passage to the dark regions beyond. The candle spurted and nearly went out from some errant draft, and then we were in the great whitewashed kitchen. An older part of the house, it was strongly built and high-ceilinged, a huge open hearth covering nearly the whole of one wall. A quite modern range stood near the bake ovens, a long trestle table crossed the center of the room, and arrays of shining pots and black iron pans too large for the great storage cupboards hung overhead. It was a kitchen designed for a large household, a large staff, and the multitudes of guests generally to be found at popular countryseats before and after the London Season. Someone had done extensive renovations to bring in the latest kitchen equipment, but the cool blocks of stone and the flagged floor had not been altered in the process. I found it quite attractive—pots of herbs along the wide windowsills beneath starched curtains of sea blue that matched the painted chairs and trim, copperware and pewter glinting from the broad mantel and oak dressers, cut flowers in a Staffordshire pitcher on the servants' tea table. Mrs. Davies clearly took pride in her surroundings as well as in her cooking.

"The servants' hall is in through there," Mark said, indicating a door to his left, "and that's the butler's pantry, the larder is over there, and the passage to the wine cellar, and so on."

I looked doubtfully at the tidy room. "It has been cleaned for the night—"

"Nonsense! You find the plates and utensils while I see what's in here."

He disappeared while I took out heavy blue plates and cups and set them on the polished surface of the tea table. As I hunted for silverware and carving knives, he returned with a loaded tray. Bread, cold meats, half a pie, two of the little glazed tarts, cakes, a crock of butter and another of cream, half a chicken, and assorted pots of jellies and jams and conserves that filled the crevices between the larger dishes. Mark grinned at me.

"As well be hanged for a wolf as a lamb," he said, a glint of

mischief in his gray eyes. "Do you know, I have never raided my own kitchen before? God knows what Mrs. Davies will say."

"She may give notice," I warned, making room for his booty on the table as he handed me the platters.

"God forbid. Here, I'll fetch some wine if I can locate Williams' keys. For all I know, he sleeps with them." He was gone for a time and finally returned with a bottle of Bordeaux, still dusty.

Like children on holiday, we found ourselves ravenously hungry, smothering laughter as the cork nearly broke off in the bottle and starting guiltily when a fork fell to the floor with a seemingly thunderous clatter. Mark carved the meats with a generous hand, making himself an enormous sandwich, while I was content with a selection of tidbits, including the tarts. The wine was superb and tasted as well in the thick cups as in crystal goblets. For the first time I saw my husband completely unshadowed by his torment, a charming, handsome man, a delightful companion, an enthusiastic conspirator. His dark hair tousled, his white shirt open at the throat beneath the crimson dressing gown, his eyes dancing with mischief, he was as different as night and day from the haggard, driven man in the library, or even the moody, bitter guest at Tilmer Hall.

For a fleeting instant I toyed with the thought of madness, for Mark himself had spoken of it more than once. But surely he had not meant it literally. What terrible experience, then, could have scarred him so? For if he were not mad, he was certainly ridden by his private devil to the point of madness. I couldn't begin to guess what was wrong, and it was clear that he had no intention of telling me.

But for nearly half an hour we sat in the kitchen in happy oblivion of the rest of the world. Food tasted better that night than it had for many years, seasoned with laughter and nonsense and companionship. And then we cleared away, making up silly tales to explain the disappearance of what we had eaten. When all was as it should be once more, Mark

blew out the candles and led the way upstairs, shielding the nightstick in his hand. He wished me goodnight at my door, and I tumbled into bed, suddenly quite sleepy and unreasonably happy—I *belonged* to Rhosllyn now. The sharing of that impromptu meal had made me a part of it in a way that the servants' welcome and Rhys Trecourt's effusiveness had not.

As my eyes closed I even spared a thought of gratitude for the dream that had awakened me. Otherwise, I told myself contentedly, I might have slept through Mark's summons and never have known how right I had been to leave Tilmer Hall behind and take such an impulsive step.

And in my wretched ignorance I truly believed that all would be well, that I could soothe away all of Mark's troubles as easily as I had soothed away the nightmare, never guessing that I now faced alone all that was evil at Rhosllyn.

Mark was tired but cheerful at breakfast the next morning. Nothing was said about the events of the night, and I was happy to have it so.

Mrs. Powell was waiting in the hall as we left the breakfast room. She stepped forward and said, "If you care to inspect the house, my lady? I am at your disposal now or later."

Mark grimaced. "I have a meeting with the rector. Something to do with the church roof. Will you mind?"

"No, of course not!" I replied swiftly, for I had no desire to become a burden. And no doubt Mrs. Powell would prefer it if Mark was not impatiently following us on our tour. "I shall have a busy morning as well."

"I'll be here for luncheon," he replied, swinging off up the stairs.

I smiled at the housekeeper. "Where shall we begin?"

"In the kitchens, my lady. This way, if you please," she answered without any change of expression.

We inspected the storerooms, the cellars, the laundry, buttery, servants' hall, the kitchen—indeed, every nook and cranny—before turning to the house proper. Rhosllyn was quite large, the central portion set off by two wings to form an abbreviated H. Every room was spotless, the furniture well polished, the draperies well shaken, the table tops well dusted, and even the carpets well beaten. Clearly, the stan-

dards of Rhosllyn were high, for all that Mark had lived here alone for so many years. I began to wonder how much influence Cecily had with the staff, or if what I saw merely reflected Mrs. Powell's pride in her task. It was almost as if the housekeeper took pleasure in flaunting her competence, defying me to find fault or to challenge her position.

With one exception, we entered every room—the morning room in cream and old rose, the dining room with its exquisite paneling from an older period and draperies of crimson and gold, and so on, floor by floor. The guest chambers, the ballroom overlooking the rose garden and the terrace, the sewing room, the servants' quarters, the linen cupboards and clothes presses, even the attics.

Mark's room, next to mine, but on the front of the house while mine faced the rear, was almost spartan in its simplicity, masculine but impersonal. The colors were silver and blue, the furniture of walnut and oak, darkened by time into a rich ebony. There were no paintings on the walls save for two small portraits above the carved mantel, none of the oddments collected through a lifetime and left about on tabletops or shelves, none of the clutter of books or hunting boots or family trophies that usually make a well-lived-in room. Only the silver-backed brushes beneath the shaving mirror, a single calf-bound volume on the night table by the bed, and a crystal decanter with matching glasses on a smaller table near the hearth.

This might have been an infrequently used guest chamber rather than the master bedroom, almost as if Mark were prepared to leave at any moment, never to return. And yet this room had been his since he outgrew the nursery more than twenty years ago. All at once I felt uncomfortable in this puzzling emptiness.

For want of something to say I gestured toward the small portraits. "Who are they?"

"The late Lord and Lady Teville, my lady," Mrs. Powell said briefly.

Mark's parents. I walked forward, feeling an intruder, and

looked more closely at them. Two faces, young and smiling, bearing a clear resemblance to Mark, stared back at me. Dark hair, gray eyes in the father, blue in the mother, a handsome couple and as yet untouched by tragedy. Turning away, I said, "Such a shame, to die so young."

"Aye. And—like others—through no fault of their own," she replied, striving to keep an undercurrent of bitterness from her voice and failing. She stood aside to let me pass before her out of the bedchamber, her face expressionless.

We continued our rounds and eventually came to one securely locked door for which Mrs. Powell did not have a key. It was on the ground floor, just beyond the music room. She let me rattle the latch before confessing that we could not get in.

"This was Miss Margaret's—Lady Spencer's—room, though she never comes to Rhosllyn now, being bedridden these fifteen years," Mrs. Powell added, looking at me quickly from hooded eyes.

"Mark tells me she lives in Chester now," I replied, glad not to have to ask who Miss Margaret was.

"Aye. She was the late Lord Teville's older sister, and a room was prepared for her here when the stairs bothered her rheumatism."

"Why is it locked?" And was it here that I had found Mark last evening, lost in thought, his hand on the knob?

"I couldn't say, my lady." Her eyes dropped from mine.

I shrugged. "Perhaps she has stored some of her possessions in there and keeps the keys herself."

"I couldn't say, my lady." Yet I sensed that she was not being entirely truthful. Was she somehow testing me?

Then we were going through the closets where the china and crystal were stored, and my mind was occupied by other thoughts, with only a fleeting wonder for how the locked room was aired and cleaned over the years.

And so we spent the morning, leaving me with a confused jumble of impressions, a tangled knowledge of the house plan, and a determination not to interfere with the superb

running of the household. I had learned at Tilmer Hall that a good servant expects independence as well as knowledgeable supervision. Mrs. Powell would work harder on her own than under my thumb.

"I hope you will continue to manage as efficiently for me as you have for Lord Teville," I said as she began to unclasp the keys at her waist.

There was a smug expression in her eyes as I finished, as if in some strange way she was gloating over my decision. "I shall come to you for instruction every Monday morning," she said punctiliously as she refastened the ring. "If you will find that convenient, my lady."

"An excellent idea." I nodded in dismissal and walked on to the morning room, glad of a brief respite before luncheon.

I had had barely five minutes to myself before Williams was standing in the doorway, saying, "Mr. Noel and Miss Cecily, my lady."

I rose quickly as Mark's cousins came into the morning room. For an instant we three stared, curious to examine one another in the light of what each had heard. I read surprise on Noel's face, a swiftly hidden antipathy on Cecily's.

He was a younger version of his father, dark and handsome and on the way to the same sophistication in the years to come. Cecily was quite fair, with blue eyes and a well-chiseled nose. While I might term myself pretty, Cecily bordered on the beautiful. She wore her smart black velvet riding habit with an air of elegance that comes of breeding and assurance, and her composure was that of a girl long accustomed to moving in the best circles. While my background compared favorably with hers, I was under the handicap of eight years of quasi servitude at Tilmer Hall and lacked the confidence to match my social standing. Because I knew this at first glance—and what's more, knew that Cecily was equally well aware of her superiority, though not why—I was suddenly shy.

"Good morning," I said, going forward to greet them. "I'm Melanie!"

Noel took my extended hand and bowed formally. "We're happy to welcome you to the family. I'm sorry we couldn't be here last evening," he said. The words faintly echoed his father's but without the false note of effusive cordiality. Noel was polite but distant. "Have we called at an inconvenient time?"

"No, certainly not. Mrs. Powell has spent the morning showing me over the house." Turning to Cecily, I added, "I have you to thank for preparing for our coming. My rooms are lovely."

She spoke for the first time, in a low contralto. "I'm glad you found them to your liking." There was no warmth in her voice.

"Very much so." I gestured to chairs, and as they settled themselves with familiarity in the rose brocade and gilt pair across from me, reminded myself that Rhosllyn had been their home too until Mark had come of age. "Mark has a meeting with the rector this morning, but he has promised to return for luncheon. Won't you join us?"

"Thank you, no, we have promised to ride over to Wood-ham House this noon," Cecily replied, glancing swiftly toward her brother as if for support. Apparently she had no desire to prolong this call.

"Do you ride?" Noel asked, smoothly changing the subject.

"Not as well as I should like," I admitted. Only on rare occasions had I been permitted the use of the Tilmer stables.

"Mark has an excellent selection of mounts," Noel said. "You will find yourself improving rapidly." He smiled then, and I knew that his charm was so much a part of him that he was unaware how devastating it was.

"I hope I won't disgrace him instead," I replied, smiling in my turn. As we talked I could sense that both Noel and Cecily had come here prepared to dislike me. Because Mark had married without his family's blessing? No, it seemed to be more deep-rooted than that. Perhaps in Cecily's case it might be jealousy, but I couldn't fathom Noel's reasons. Whatever they were, his good manners cloaked them completely. And

yet I was increasingly aware that, unlike his sister's, his feelings were not personal, were not directed toward me but rather toward what I represented. Mark had said something about wanting Noel to be his heir. Could it be that his cousin resented our marriage because he feared a child would replace him?

Cecily had little to say, courteous enough when she did speak, yet with a reserve, as if she were here against her will. Noel inquired about my life in Buckinghamshire, and we talked about familiar villages and walks in the Chilterns. His eyes were appraising now, as if he were somehow revising his original opinion of me. And then Cecily glanced at the ornate gold watch pinned to her habit and reminded her brother that they were due at Woodham in half an hour. We rose and I walked with them to the door. Cecily repeated her father's invitation to visit the Dower House, and Noel suggested that we ride together one afternoon. And then they were gone, and I felt that I had borne myself well enough in this first stilted meeting.

It didn't occur to me until much later that neither Mark's family nor the staff had wished me happy in my marriage as they welcomed me to Rhosllyn.

Mark returned for luncheon shortly after twelve. When I told him that his cousins had called, he stopped drawing off his riding gloves and said abruptly, "What did Noel have to say to you?"

"Very little. He did ask me to ride with them one afternoon. Mark, I haven't had an opportunity to ride in a very long while. Will you take me out first? I don't like to ask—"

"Why in God's name should you hesitate to ask me anything?" he said, frowning. "Of course I shall. There's a habit in your trunks, I think, and that Irish mare should be ideal for you." He smiled all at once. "Your cousin Edward would be chagrined to think of you riding her!"

I laughed outright. "The best reason to do well!" He excused himself to wash before the meal, and I stood waiting by the windows, looking out at the gardeners working among the

early roses. After lunch I shall cut flowers for the house, I thought. It was the one omission I had noted in the perfection, but then Mark was a man and not likely to miss their pleasing touch.

He returned just as Williams announced that luncheon was served, and we walked into the dining room together. Mark took his place at the head of the table and I sat at the foot. Between us stretched the polished mahogany expanse, broken only by the elaborate silver and crystal epergne in the center, its arms swirling out on either side to hold three slender tapers each. From the linked initials and the date on an engraved silver scroll in its center, I gathered that it had been a wedding gift to Mark's parents.

After talking over and around it for half the meal, Mark turned to Williams and said testily, "Move the damned thing somewhere else!"

With some difficulty Williams removed the epergne to the sideboard, rearranging the candelabra there to more satisfying angles. As he left the room to bring in the next course, Mark nodded.

"Much better. Did Mrs. Powell show you over the house?"

"Every cupboard and closet. Mark, she is a superb housekeeper. I consider myself fortunate!"

He frowned. "Yes, I suppose she is. Aunt Letitia trained her, of course. A very retiring, modest woman, my aunt, but a formidable opponent of dust and carelessness." He was about to add more when Williams returned with the next course, a platter of cold roast chicken and fresh asparagus, tender yellow stalks garnished with hollandaise.

"Mark, do you possibly have the key to your Aunt Margaret's room on the ground floor?" I asked, all at once remembering. "I daresay it, at least, could use a turning out."

He was suddenly quite still. "Who told you to ask me for the key? Mrs. Powell?"

"No one," I replied. "The door was locked, you see, and Mrs. Powell had no key for it. Heaven only knows when it was cleaned last."

"The room is left as it is for my aunt's use," he said carefully.

"We shall be very sure to disturb nothing—"

"No. I don't want it cleaned. Leave it, Melanie!" There was cold command in his tone that could not be ignored. He changed the subject, and only then did Williams step forward to refill the wine glasses.

Mark excused himself after luncheon, in the grip of one of his moods. Unlike the night before, he had no desire for my company. Restless, I wandered out to inspect the gardens. The roses were fully budded in the shelter of the hedge that bordered the beds, and a few had opened into perfectly shaped cups of color ranging from pure white to deep gold and dark red. An old man, kneeling in the neatly clipped grass of the path, touched his cap as I approached and got stiffly to his feet.

"Good afternoon," I said, and gestured toward the nearest blossoms. "It appears to be a good year for roses."

"Yes, my lady, it is that." His accent was more pronounced than that of the house servants but with the same musical rhythm to it.

"What is your name?"

"Bryn, my lady, and I've been gardener here for fifty-seven years, man and boy," he replied proudly. "Would you care to look about, my lady?"

He was a knowledgeable old man, pleased to have an interest shown in his beloved plants, pointing each variety out by name, and sometimes by its Latin designation as well. There were beds of spring bulbs, of shrubs in geometrical plantings well sheltered for winter pleasure, of woodland groups at the edge of the park, of old favorites such as columbine and foxglove and marigold, with spicy lilies and pinks and night-scented stock set where the breezes could waft their fragrance toward the windows, and finally, shaded by a specimen maple, a small rockery centered by a great fallen monolith, the plants unfamiliar to me.

"What are these?" I asked, and Bryn said with the insular

pride of a native, "From foreign parts, my lady, sent to Mrs. Rhys before she moved to the Dower House and all."

I recognized a few from a small book of sketches made in the Swiss Alps by old Mrs. Tilmer on her wedding journey to Florence, delicately beautiful yet surprisingly sturdy wild flowers. "They are very attractive against the gray of that stone," I said as we walked on. "And they appear to thrive here."

"Mrs. Rhys had a way with plants, she did that," he replied.

"Yes, my wife was an ardent gardener," a voice said behind us, and we turned to find Rhys Trecourt striding toward us. "It was one of her greatest pleasures." He spoke of his late wife with great affection. "And you couldn't have a better guide than Bryn here. He knows every living thing under his care, from grossest weed to rarest plant."

Bryn smiled, and touching his cap, stepped back to take his leave. I thanked him and promised to visit the gardens frequently. Then Rhys Trecourt turned to me and said that he had hoped to find me here.

"I'm on my morning rounds, afternoon though it is. Would you care to accompany me?" He smiled and raised one eyebrow quizzically. "That is, if you are interested in such things as stables and dairy and barn."

I laughed. "Of course I am! They are part of Rhosllyn too. Noel and Cecily called this morning," I added as we cut across the lawns toward the home farm.

"Good! I had to attend that confounded meeting at the rectory or I'd have come with them. Where's Mark?"

"Indoors—the library, I think," I said, looking away. "Gardens don't tempt men away from their duties." Why did I feel a sudden need to excuse him?

We talked pleasantly as we took the footpath beyond the dovecote and came out at the stile over the pasture fence. Rhys helped me over it and we could see the mares and foals in the shade of trees along a small stream. "Mark is interested in horses, as you know of course, but I confine myself to the more mundane aspects of farming. Ah—see the black mare,

there to the left? Three of her foals have gone on to win at Newmarket. Beware the brambles here, you'll catch your skirt." We crossed the opposite stile and came out at the barnyard. He led the way to a stone building near the house.

"My pride," he said, opening the door and gesturing about us at the spotless whitewashed stone floors and walls. "One of the old estate cottages, now the dairy. Mark very kindly allows me to put my theories to the test with the Rhosllyn herds. Healthy cows and healthy milkmaids, clean milking facilities and clean byres. That's the secret of our success, though many of our neighbors call it wasteful and a few term it wizardry. Still, it is a fact that our production has tripled and our quality is matchless."

My cousin Edward had had similar notions, though Squire Towle thought him mad. "You are interested in scientific methods, then?" I asked as he closed the door behind us.

"Very much so. Science has already shown what it can do in agriculture—witness Coke's work in Norfolk," he said, enthusiasm filling his voice and shining in his eyes. "I correspond with a number of men who share a like interest and we exchange ideas. I'm afraid I have no talent for uncovering scientific marvels, but I *do* seem to have a knack for putting them into practice once the concept is shown to me." He laughed. "A pair of hands, not an inventive mind—but someone has to do the ordinary work, I suppose."

"Do you have a laboratory?" I asked as we crossed to the barn.

"Good heavens, no! I haven't the patience required. But tell me that milk is contaminated by unclean conditions and I'll build a showplace dairy to test the point and prove it. Or a better treatment for diseased animals, a new way to pump water, a more effective method of harvesting—" Stopping abruptly, he shook his head. "I won't drone on when you are too well-mannered to cry 'Enough!'"

"On the contrary," I said truthfully, "I find it interesting."

He glanced at me rather quickly as if to judge my sincerity, then went on to say, as we continued on our tour, "Noel is

the inventive one in the family—or could be. Oh, nothing so ordinary as farming methods, I'm afraid," he added with a laugh, seeing my look of surprise. "He has never put his talent to practical use. Still, he did some interesting experiments with steam while at Oxford, and has followed the work of this man Daguerre in Paris. Sometimes he can even be persuaded to design a spectacle for one of Cecily's parties." And then one of the undergrooms brought out a promising two-year-old for our inspection.

It was nearly four when we climbed the last stile, and he was apologetic for mud on the hem of my blue silk. I had not been dressed for walking beyond the gardens. We parted by the terrace steps, and I hurried indoors to change, ringing for Bronwyn to help me.

I was not accustomed to a personal maid, but it was expected that I have one, and Bronwyn was cheerful, if reserved. I pointed out the mud on my skirt as she took the blue silk from me, and explained that I had been to the home farm with Mr. Rhys.

"Yes, my lady, and he's a great one for the dairy," she said warmly. "My sister works there now, and a clean apron she's expected to wear each day, and her hair neatly bound, her hands washed in brown soap. The *cows* scrubbed as well! And she having such pretty hands, to be reddened so! But the milk and cream taste that good they none of them mind now." Her open admiration of Rhys's achievement was quite a contrast to the indifference with which she had spoken only this morning of Mark's concern for his tenants' housing.

As I dried my face she lifted the flowered dress over my head and settled it into place. "And don't be worrying about the blue silk, it will come clean as ever, I'll see to it myself."

"Thank you, Bronwyn," I said as she began to brush my hair. Remembering a gold chain amongst the cases Mark had given to me, I found it and clasped it around my throat. It completed my toilet nicely.

Mark was waiting for me as I came into the drawing room. He appeared to be in better spirits, and I begged pardon for

being late as he rang for Williams. "I have explored the gardens, and your uncle has shown me the home farm," I went on.

"I'm glad you enjoyed your afternoon," he said, and added, "You will be lonely here, Melanie. I can only hope it won't matter to you."

"I haven't had time to feel lonely," I said as Williams entered.

"I'll take you riding tomorrow morning," Mark replied, taking the chair across from mine. "It may provide another interest for you."

At ten o'clock, true to his word, Mark sent for me and we walked around to the stables. The Irish mare, Deirdre, was being led about the cobbled courtyard by a young groom, who touched his cap as we approached, then called to someone within the tack room.

He came out into the sunlight, a tall, heavyset man of Mark's age perhaps, his thick dark hair and dark eyes reminding me of someone, though his rough-cast features were unfamiliar. He touched his cap to Mark, but with an air of insolence that was not quite open.

"Llewellyn Morgan, the head groom," Mark said to me, and then to the man, "Have you had the edge taken off the mare?"

"Aye, my lord," he replied. "She's docile enough this morning." His eyes slid toward me in a look of cold hostility as Mark turned to run a hand over the chestnut's silky shoulder. Surprised, I moved away.

"I'll take the black gelding, then." Mark gestured toward the stables. "Is the gray inside?"

"No, my lord. Will you be wanting him brought up now?"

"Later, perhaps, since Lady Teville hasn't seen him." He led me to the waiting mare and gave me a boost into the saddle. I settled the folds of my crimson habit about my boots as Mark mounted the handsome gelding that Morgan brought out, and the groom at the mare's head handed me my whip before stepping aside. I reminded myself that any nervous-

ness would immediately communicate itself to my horse, and concentrated on managing her out of the courtyard. I didn't wish to disgrace myself before the watching grooms.

The mare behaved beautifully, and I soon took pleasure in the ride, able to talk to Mark without my attention wandering to the reins, the stirrups, and my balance. He smiled and said, "You aren't afraid now, are you? Good! You have light hands, and that's half of riding. She has spirit, this one, but she's well-mannered too. I think you can take her out on your own, providing of course that a groom goes with you."

I was pleased with his praise and felt quite comfortable. Besides, my earlier training was slowly coming back to me. "Are we in England or Wales?"

"We are in Wales—the gate there is on the border, nearly enough. That's why the land was so difficult to defend, you see. No natural barriers to mark the boundaries. And when you have seen the barren hills of North Wales, you'll understand why this fine grazing land was worth dying for. Welsh wool was their cash crop—even in the worst of the fighting the wool would find a way to market." His eyes swept the blue hills to our left. "Merlin is said to have come down from there to build a house on the site of Rhosllyn for an eighth-century prince of Wales. Later the Llewellyns stayed here in the thirteenth century while warring with Henry III, wooing the Trecourts to stand with them against the king. And Owen Glendower visited Rhosllyn as a friend and then an enemy, burning it to the ground before retreating into Wales. It is all in the family archives, and a part of village tradition as well. We don't forget, on the borders."

"I begin to understand why Offa built his Dyke to protect his Saxons from marauders!" I said, laughing.

"The Dyke is behind us—Rhosllyn was beyond the pale in those days." He turned to me. "You shouldn't ride too far the first time. We should go back now."

We made a wide and circling loop, coming to Rhosllyn by way of the park. I felt I knew the way, for the hills at my back and the grazing cattle and sheep ahead left me in no

doubt of my bearings. It had been a pleasant outing, and I liked the mare.

"Shall we try her paces?" I asked, and touched her flanks with my heel. She responded instantly with long, smooth strides that covered the ground. I felt the wind in my hair, singing in my ears, and laughed from sheer delight. Mark was behind me, keeping his distance in order not to startle her into a mad run. I kept my balance easily, leaning forward to help her as she moved, her mane whipping back into my face.

As we crossed the road I saw three people, two gentlemen and a lady, driving in a smartly sprung carriage behind a pair of bays. Neighbors, I thought, and expected to see them wave to Mark or perhaps stop to greet us. But there was not even a polite nod as we passed by. Surprised, I brought my attention back to the mare.

The sound of our hooves drowned out the noise in the stable yard until we had clattered to a halt. Breathless and laughing still, I drew rein and turned to Mark, only to wheel around again. For in the stable a horse was kicking furiously, heels crashing into the heavy wood of the stalls while the grooms shouted angrily. Mark sprang from his saddle, reached up to lift me down, and then raced for the stable, leaving the reins of both mounts in my hands.

Following to see what had caused the commotion, I heard him swear and then shout to Morgan.

The man's voice reached me as he stepped to the door. "—the gray, and he has caught his cheek strap on the hook there. We can't get near enough to touch him, he'll kill himself or one of us."

"He's a valuable animal and you know it! Get the hell out of my way, you fool!" Two grooms backed out in face of Mark's wrath, and I tossed the reins to one of them before slipping into the wide doorway.

A magnificent stallion, a ghostly dappled gray and white, fought wildly against the strap that held him, wide-eyed and foaming, his heels viciously thrashing out at anything within

reach. Morgan stood just beyond Mark, his face blank but his eyes blazing with excitement and hatred as he waited to see what his master would do.

Mark was furious, his eyes ranging over the animal to check for damage before going closer, his lips set in a grim line. Clearly, this was the gray he had mentioned earlier, the pride of his breeding line in spite of its fiery temper. He had been brought in especially for me to see and had somehow been allowed to harm himself. I held my breath as Mark moved slowly toward the stallion, then stepped swiftly to one side as the heavy quarters bunched and the heels flailed. The stallion squealed in impotent rage, jerking at the strap with all the weight of his shoulders. But the stout leather refused to give. Mark tried again, and a hoof grazed his thigh, leaving a long smudge of dirt on his riding breeches. Mark swore and massaged his leg while Morgan simply stood there, silent and watchful.

I was frightened suddenly, for I knew Mark well enough by this time to realize that he would not allow the horse to be injured by endlessly battering himself against the stall. There was already a trickle of blood near one eye where the hook had scratched rather deeply. He tried to move in on the other side, but the gray swung around and Mark was caught between the heavy hindquarters and the stout wooden post. Gasping for breath, he flung himself to the floor just before an iron shoe drove into the wood where his hand had rested. I smothered a cry as Mark rolled out of danger, and ran past the unmoving Morgan to Mark's side. There was straw and dust in his hair and a grim set to his face. Except for a scrape over his cheekbone he was unhurt though winded.

"That horse is far too excited, you can't come near him!" I said, kneeling beside him. Mark got to his feet, stretched down a hand to me and shook his head.

"Go into the house," he said curtly. "You shouldn't be here."

"Please, listen to me," I begged him. "The grooms haven't done anything and neither have you. Let me try? Please?"

60

He turned to me in astonishment. "What can you possibly do? Don't you realize he could crush your skull with one blow? Melanie, do as I tell you, go into the house!"

"No, listen to me. I won't go near him, I promise. Just send them away. Mark, it is worth trying, he'll do himself or you an injury if you force your way in. The grooms have gotten him half-mad already and you are risking your life! Please—"

With the swift decision so characteristic of him, Mark nodded curtly to Morgan, who reluctantly turned away and walked outside, motioning to a groom to clear the doorway. Mark then placed me out of reach in the next stall and said, "Don't move from here, whatever you do. In five minutes I'll do it my way. You'll leave then. Is that clear?"

I nodded quickly, and he edged past the stallion. With one last look at me, he was gone through the door and out of sight, though not out of hearing. I waited for the count of fifty and then began to speak to the enraged animal in a soft voice, soothing and easing his anger, much as I had soothed Mark himself after his nightmare. Careful not to move, in no way trying to come near him, I spoke whatever came to mind, keeping my voice low-pitched and unchanging.

The stallion quivered, his ears pricked forward to catch the only sound breaking the silence. He was still stirring restlessly, jerking his head, ready to lash out with his hooves at whatever moved behind him. But the sudden quiet intrigued him after the shouting, and his restriction bothered him less with no one about to prod him. I would not have dared to go near him even now, but I hoped I could soothe him into tractability before Mark approached him again.

He snorted, nodding his head in short upward jerks as he strained to listen. And then, quite by accident, and because he no longer wrenched and pulled at the cheek strap, a sideways movement of his head brought him free.

I was more frightened then than I had been before, for as he realized that he was no longer held taut, he backed out of the hateful stall and into the wider space of the passage near where I stood. I could have reached out my hand and touched

his glossy hide. But he made no move in my direction except for the twitching ears, and stood almost quietly where he was. And that is how Mark found us when he entered shortly afterward.

The gray let Mark approach and lay a hand on his nose. Then his fingers slid around to the halter. I watched them walk down the passage to another stall before slipping outside.

Morgan was standing there, his eyebrows rising, as I walked into the sunlight. "He's free, then?"

"Yes," I said, and saw the flash of intense disappointment deep in his eyes. He had expected quite another ending—but why should he wish to see the gray hurt? Quite suddenly I knew that it was Mark who he hoped would be caught by those thrashing ironshod hooves. And by interfering, I suspected I had made an enemy. I shivered in the warm sun and turned away.

Mark came out then and spoke to Morgan, obviously giving him a tongue-lashing for allowing so valuable an animal to endanger himself. As my hand touched the door to the back stairs I saw the groom say something to his master, a short, angry remark. Mark lost his temper and replied. I remembered the drunken man in Worcester and stood transfixed. The groom spoke again, looking up to meet his eyes. Mark turned white beneath his tan, and I thought for a breathless instant that he would strike the man with his riding whip, for his fingers clenched about the handle with sudden force. Instead, with an effort that was visible, he leashed his fury, turned on his heel, and walked away, leaving Morgan standing there alone in the stable yard.

Shaken, I went inside and up to my room, passing Mrs. Powell on the stairs by the landing window. Had she been watching the scene below? I thought I glimpsed animosity in her face before she turned away. It was then that I knew where I had seen Llewellyn Morgan before; he resembled the housekeeper closely enough to be her brother, though he was some ten years her junior. The similarity lay more in

the coloring and in the vindictive expression of the eyes than in any facial structure, but I had no doubt of the relationship. Not unusual in itself, but what did surprise me was the fact that brother and sister continued to work here despite an apparent antagonism toward the family. Or toward Mark? I was puzzled and uncertain, but I could ask no one about it.

Rhys Trecourt brought Cecily and Noel to tea the next afternoon. Mark was a stiffly formal host, but no one else seemed to mind. Cecily spoke to him in the casual way of cousins and I noticed that he unbent to her. That Noel disliked Mark was clear enough, though for his father's sake he tried to hide the fact. Instead, he talked to me, and was pleased to hear that I had been riding.

"You seem to have a way with horses," Rhys Trecourt said. "Morgan was stunned when you walked up to that stallion by yourself. Do you know he has half-killed two men? But his bloodlines are without doubt the finest we have, so Mark puts up with his tantrums—yes, and rides him, too, when he has the mood upon him."

Forgetting to deny any credit for disentangling the stallion, I said in shocked surprise, "He rides him? Surely not!"

"Oh, yes!" He turned to stare across toward Mark. "A fine horseman!"

"My father shares the credit for that," Noel said, as if he could not bear to hear Mark praised by his father. "He was sickly until he was twelve and was sent away to school. In fact, my mother wept for days, certain he wouldn't survive the first month. Instead, he came home completely cured." There was bitterness in his voice.

"Well, hardly that, but he was on his way to good health. I felt the risk was worth it, Melanie. I didn't care to watch so high-spirited a lad confined to his room and a tutor when he ought to be living a normal life. So I made the decision, and it was the right one."

"What was wrong with him as a child?"

"He nearly died at birth. It was a difficult time for both of

them, and his mother lived only a short while afterward. We nearly lost him again at four when he contracted a severe case of typhoid fever. He was never strong after that, and I'm afraid my poor wife was overly protective. It was natural enough—she had cared for him since he arrived in this world. He might have been her own child. Noel wasn't born for another seven months."

I thought that that explained much. Noel was their first-born, and yet he had been second to Mark in everything, even to his own parents perhaps. It was a daunting way to grow up, forever in the shadow of someone else, and a cousin at that. Yet it was to his parents' credit that they had given the orphaned child a place in their home and in their hearts. So unlike the way the Tilmers had treated me, even though Mark, by his very existence, had prevented his uncle from inheriting Rhosllyn. Perhaps in time Noel would come to see it that way.

But I doubted that Cecily's feelings would change with time or anything else. As Mark came to refill her cup he smiled down at me, and I caught the flare of bitter envy in her lovely eyes. They dropped to the ruby brooch I wore at my throat to pin the lace of my blue gown and recognized it at once as a Teville heirloom. Her lips tightened. She couldn't know, of course, the relationship that existed between Mark and me; possibly it wouldn't matter if she did. She was my enemy, simply because I had married him.

IN THE DAYS THAT FOLLOWED I quickly settled into a pattern of life at Rhosllyn. And I became increasingly aware of the watchful, unfriendly atmosphere that met us everywhere. On my frequent rides I got to know many of the tenants. There was always the same strange reserve about them that I had felt in the servants, a reserve one did not expect to find in people who have served and worked for a family over several generations. Yet Mark was a just and capable landlord, and the estate was prosperous. Whatever was wrong at Rhosllyn, the undercurrent of tension and ill feeling began to erode the happiness I had known in the first few days.

Since the incident with the stallion I had tried to avoid Morgan. He appeared to have some sort of grudge against Mark and this had somehow grown to include me. Though he gave me proper respect, there was no doubt that he disliked me. And I often saw Morgan and his sister talking together in low voices.

One morning as I passed them on my way across the stable courtyard I heard Morgan say quite clearly, "An eye for an eye, a tooth for a tooth—a life for a life." Startled, I glanced across at him, and found him staring balefully at me. Then his eyes dropped, hiding the expression in them. Mrs. Powell, alarmed, touched her brother's arm, and they moved away. Had I been meant to overhear? It almost seemed that I had. But why?

In the end I was forced, reluctantly, to accept what Mark had told me in Ludlow: the Welsh had neither forgotten nor forgiven their conquest by his English forebears. Mark's wild youth had served only to alienate these people further. And I was English too.

Mark was often moody and sometimes slept ill. I could see the dark shadows beneath his eyes, the tired lines about his mouth as he came in to breakfast. He drove himself relentlessly in his duties about the estate, acting as his own steward as well as overseeing the breeding of his horses. Sometimes I would hear him riding through the park on the stallion, setting a breakneck pace that suited both man and horse. Yet his manner toward me was invariably courteous, and he was usually a pleasant companion at meals and in the evenings. Often I would sit with him in the library as he worked on the estate accounts, occupying myself with a book from the shelves or with some embroidery.

Still, I soon realized that a part of Mark's life was closed off from me, just as Aunt Margaret's room was closed off from the rest of Rhosllyn. That locked door seemed to symbolize the moodiness that shut me out as effectively as any key. Ours was a marriage of convenience; there was no reason for Mark to give me his full confidence. But I treasured the closeness we shared in the kitchen that first night and had hoped it might set a pattern for the future. Instead, he avoided me whenever his depression got the better of him, shutting himself away somewhere until it had passed. Only when his nightmares were unbearable did he come to me—and never mentioned it afterward.

One warm evening as I strolled in the garden with Rhys Trecourt I tried to put my uneasiness into words. "Was it Mark's illness as a child that makes him—irritable at times?"

"His bad temper, do you mean?" Rhys asked, completely misunderstanding me. "He has always had one—his maternal grandfather was famous for *his*. I must say Mark has worked miracles keeping it under control these last few years. I'm proud of him!"

Recalling what had happened in Worcester, and how close Mark had come to striking Morgan, I said, tentatively, "It appears to be quite violent—"

Rhys stopped, his face clouded with unhappy memory. "My dear, that's all long ago, I assure you. Yes, I know, you've probably heard about the ostler at the Feathers in Ludlow. It's true Mark horsewhipped him when he refused to put to a team because of the icy roads. The innkeeper wouldn't allow him near the place for years, though the ostler wasn't crippled for life, as we'd feared at first. Mark was only seventeen then. The bully he rode down late one night on the road to Reading is another matter. The man foolishly tried to waylay him. It's also true Mark nearly killed a jockey whose carelessness maimed one of his finest racers at a Newmarket meet. But the man deserved what he got. You can't altogether blame Mark's *temper* for those incidents!"

I listened, appalled. "I hadn't known . . ."

"And whatever my sister Margaret may say—" He broke off and smiled confidently. "Put it out of your mind! There's *nothing* to worry about. It's all in the past."

But I found myself wondering all the same.

As I felt more confident of my ability to manage Deirdre, I often took her out with only a groom to accompany me. Once I rode with Morgan. There was no one else available or I should have declined his escort. The man's open hostility made me apprehensive. But he was silent and kept his distance, so I soon relaxed and began to enjoy the lovely day.

We had been out for perhaps three quarters of an hour, exploring a stretch of the Welsh side of the valley, when he lifted his hand to point to the hillside ahead.

"There's a fine sight, my lady, from yon ledge," he said diffidently. "His lordship goes there often. Have you seen it?"

The ledge, actually an outcropping of rock, was quite near. And its height and position would indeed offer a commanding view toward Rhosllyn. "No, I haven't. How do we get there?" I asked, interested.

He led the way, skirting a copse of trees as we climbed, and soon we came out into a tangle of undergrowth that led to the jutting ledge. Across from us the sun dappled the green of the English meadows and flashed in the trees as the leaves fluttered in a light breeze. Only the chimneys of Rhosllyn were visible, but the gardens of the Dower House offered a bright splash of color at the corner of the park.

"Would you care to dismount and have a closer look?" Morgan asked. His face was in shadow as he waited for my answer.

It was tempting. The undergrowth was dense but only boot high, and there was no possibility of falling from the rocks, though I didn't care to ride too near the edge on the high-bred Deirdre.

"I'd ought to check that girth," he added as I hesitated. "She's breathing a mite hard from that climb."

"Yes, thank you," I said, and slid to the ground before he could dismount to help me. Tossing the reins to him, I moved briskly through the high grass.

Suddenly I tripped on a bramble and pitched forward, nearly falling on my face. In the same instant something whirred and jerked beneath my feet, then clashed together with a snap that broke the silence like a pistol shot. I cried out in fright, unable to move. And then, heart pounding, I looked down and saw the jagged jaws of a man-trap just beyond the toe of my soft leather riding boot. If I hadn't stumbled, it would have closed on my foot, crushing the bone in my ankle and crippling me for life. Instead, it had caught my trailing skirts, holding me fast.

Morgan was pulling in the dancing horses, and it was a moment or two before he could leave them and come to my aid. I could only stare down at the monstrous contraption and tremble with delayed shock as I realized how near a thing it had been.

And then the groom was at my side, forcing open the steel jaws, and I brushed away tears of fright that had filled my eyes.

"These vicious things—they ought to be destroyed!" I said weakly. "I could have been seriously injured—the next person may not be as fortunate."

"His lordship doesn't allow them," Morgan said shortly. " 'Tis an old rusty one long since forgotten. Now, my lady, you are free. But for a tear in your hem, there's no harm done."

"It might have been Deirdre," I said, still shivering with the horror of it. "Send someone out here to remove it. Today!"

"Aye, my lady, I'll see to it myself," he promised grimly.

I turned back to the mare and he cupped his hand for my foot. As he boosted me into the saddle I realized that his face was flushed with barely suppressed emotion. We rode the rest of the way home in an uncomfortable silence.

It was not until I had returned to my bedchamber and could think calmly that I remembered two things. The trap had been set and it was well oiled. Morgan had had no problem with rusty hinges as he pried them wide enough to release my hem. Why had he lied to me about it being old and long lost in the high grass? Surely he hadn't known it was there!

I was making too much of an unfortunate accident simply because the groom disturbed me. Nevertheless I could not bring myself to ride out with Morgan again.

Several times Mark found his dreams so unbearable that he sought my company in the night. We made no further forays to the kitchen but sat instead in the library or walked on the terrace in the clear night air. Although I slept soundly, his light knock at the door brought me wide awake as if a small part of me lay listening for it to come. I would talk about the events of the day or any other subject that came to mind until he was calm enough to sleep once more. He never referred to these occasions afterward, but I could tell that they served to ease the torment that he endured so silently. What caused it Mark alone knew. I doubted if his family or the servants

were even aware of his sleeplessness, for no one spoke of it to me. And there was no way I could probe beyond the curtain of absolute silence he maintained.

Occasionally Rhys Trecourt or Noel would come for tea or join us after dinner, but it was not often that Cecily accompanied them. She and Noel rode with me from time to time, and I soon came to know both of them better. Noel had begun to thaw toward me, and I was glad that we were fast becoming friends, but Cecily's cool politeness still cloaked an implacable jealousy. I sometimes wondered uncomfortably what violent passions ran beneath that remote façade.

It was not until my third week at Rhosllyn that I became aware that not one of the neighboring landowners—and I had learned from Cecily's conversation that there were several families close by and others well within riding distance—had come to call. At first I attributed this to consideration on their part, allowing me time to settle before I must entertain visitors. But by the end of that week I had seen no one except the rector, who came without his wife, and no one had left a card. I tried to tell myself that there was no cause for concern, but I knew that something must be very wrong. In county society there is no greater pleasure than visiting—the least excuse is seized upon for a call or even a party. And a bride at Rhosllyn, especially Mark's wife, should have been the center of much attention and social activity. Yet other than the Trecourts, I had seen no one except the unfriendly occupants of the carriage the day I had first ridden the Irish mare.

Cecily and Noel were obviously a part of local society, for they spoke of their activities casually, taking them for granted. And I inadvertently learned that they themselves often entertained, though Mark and I were not invited.

One Sunday afternoon I walked down the drive to call at the Dower House, as I had been so often urged to do. But the sound of voices laughing and talking warned me that the Trecourts had visitors. I cut through the rhododendrons, intending to spend fifteen minutes or so in the park, by which

time I supposed their callers would have gone. I hadn't meant to spy, but the footpath led near enough to the lawns behind the house to allow me a distant view of the small terrace. To my surprise, I saw the tea table set out there, with another table just beyond for various delicacies. Guests stood about talking, one older woman in a large brimmed hat strolling with Rhys Trecourt, and younger couples were enjoying a leisurely game of croquet. A garden party, perhaps twenty people in all, and in no way an impromptu gathering. I backed into the shadow of the trees, afraid to be discovered here, yet drawn by natural curiosity to stare at the scene before me. Cecily, laughing up into the face of a tall, fair young man, was exquisite in a gown of lime trimmed with white daisies. Noel, frowning over his next shot, was outlined against the massive arch of wisteria leading to the rose beds beyond the lawns. There was applause as he sent his ball through first one hoop and then the next as it ricocheted off an opponent's ball. I heard him call a derisive challenge to his lovely partner as he stepped aside.

A pleasant Sunday afternoon, this, a successful party that would be spoken of with enjoyment throughout the week by all who attended. But not for Mark or me. For some reason we were set apart, and I suddenly recalled him saying, "I hope you won't find it too lonely here." Now I knew what he had meant. There would be no callers at Rhosllyn, no laughing couples playing croquet on the smooth lawns and beautifully dressed women strolling through the gardens, no small dinner parties or anniversary balls. We would not visit other houses, because no one would visit us. We were outcasts, Mark and I.

Careful to keep out of sight, I slipped away and returned to the house, grateful that I had told no one where I was going, glad that my blunder had been private and not the subject of amused gossip in the servants' hall. And all I could think of, climbing the stairs to my room, was the fact that Rhys Trecourt and his family were accepted by the neighborhood, that whatever Mark had done to deserve ostracism had

not affected them. But because I was his wife I must share his circumstances, and be careful never to let him or anyone else believe that I noticed or minded.

After that I made it a point not to arrive at the Dower House without warning.

And so riding became one of my chief pleasures—with Mark whenever possible, or with Cecily and her brother, occasionally alone with an undergroom to accompany me. I learned to know the surrounding countryside, to ride the byways and crooked lanes that led from village to village, to skirt the estates that marched by our boundaries, and to follow the rough tracks that led to the top of the ridge or to the borders of the blue hills. It was lovely country, quiet and serene, with only birdsong, the lowing of cattle, or the distant music of a cow bell breaking the silence. On several occasions I was fortunate to hear men working in the fields passing the time with singing, as only the Welsh can. Their voices, fine and untrained save by chapel singing, had a natural beauty that touched the heart. Ballads, hymns, Welsh songs in the incomprehensible but liquid language that took on a new softness in music—whatever they chose had a harmony of its own, full and rich and ringing. I would sometimes sit and listen before riding on my way.

The Trecourts sang well too—perhaps from their own Welsh heritage—and Cecily played the piano with great skill. Mark did not care to go to the Dower House, but they could sometimes be persuaded to use the music room at Rhosllyn. I always enjoyed it, and possibly Mark did also. Noel had a delightful way with a ballad and a wide repertoire to choose from. His father was best at the older songs, and as I watched Cecily play for them or accompany herself, the candlelight gilding her hair and etching her lovely profile, I wondered how anyone could fail to respond to such a charming scene. She sang for Mark, and I would sometimes watch his face for signs of feeling, but there were none. Did Cecily realize it too, or was she still hopeful one day of stirring his interest?

Occasionally Noel would sing "The Gypsy Maid," a bitter-

sweet love song about a man whose true love had run away with a gypsy band and left him heartbroken, unable to discover what had become of her. It never failed to irritate Mark, and I was certain that it was purposely done. Nothing was ever said between them, but the tension was always there, in the air. Like Morgan, Noel seemed to take perverse pleasure in probing for a weakness in Mark, or touching a raw wound. Something lay between the three of them—that was becoming clear enough—but no one else appeared to notice except Rhys. I often saw him watching his son and his nephew, a fixed smile hiding the pain in his eyes.

And then I met a third man with a grudge against my husband. It appeared to be quite by accident. On a rainy afternoon the clouds cleared away briefly and I decided to ride, having been shut in by bad weather for several days. Mark was away, the ground was soggy and laced with puddles, and I had no desire to do more than exercise myself and the mare. I had not been back to the village since our arrival, and I thought that direction would offer the driest road for a good run. Though Morgan summoned an undergroom, I saw no need for anyone to accompany me for such a short distance. So I set out alone on Deirdre, mindful of the need to hurry before the rain began again.

I rode across the mill bridge, past the smithy and the inn and the small house that served as a chapel for the Baptists in the village, along a stretch of half-timbered cottages, and on beyond the stone church to the farm gates on the far side. I halted briefly to watch the swollen stream, brown and leaf-strewn from the storms, then turned back toward Rhosllyn. It was tempting to cut across country, but I knew better and kept to the main road. It was just as well, for the mare cast a shoe not ten yards beyond the church walk. Annoyed, I dismounted and checked her hoof just as the first drops of rain spattered down. Remembering the smithy, I led her down the deserted street to it, prepared to shelter there, for I hesitated to go alone into the inn.

The forge was closed, and I looped the mare's reins over

the handle of the door before going to the house beside it. The rain was coming down in earnest, darkening the flags where I stood. No one answered my second knock and I was ready to try a third time when the door finally opened. The smith, bearded and formidable in the brightness of the fire behind him, stood there unspeaking.

"I'm Lady Teville," I said. "My mare has cast her shoe. Could you replace it for me, please?"

He looked out at the mare, head down in the rain, and back to me. "I do no work for the lord of Rhosllyn," he said.

"Yes, I'm aware of that," I replied, for there was a small forge at the home farm. "But I'm sure it doesn't matter." I ended with a smile, expecting him to step out and attend to the mare.

"I do no work for the lord of Rhosllyn," he repeated, and made to shut the door.

Thinking that he was angry because the estate did not usually require his services, I said quickly, "You will be well paid, regardless."

He stopped then, and his expression all at once reminded me that he had turned his back on the Rhosllyn carriage when we had driven through the village that very first afternoon.

"Have they not told you that Owen Evans would stand by while Rhosllyn burned to the ground, aye, and its master with it, and never lift so much as a finger for its salvation?" he asked coldly. "Have they not told you that my Gwenneth has not come home to me yet, and you can walk or crawl home in the rain for all I care? When that devil tells me what became of my daughter I will shoe his wife's mare for a farthing—and not before!"

I stood there, too stunned by his outburst to speak or even to think clearly. "Your daughter—I don't understand—" I stammered finally.

"Aye," he said derisively, "he'll not have told you, the bloody fool, but when you want to know the *truth,* come to Owen Evans. Until then, leave me be!" The door slammed

in my face, the bolt driven home with almost ferocious force.

In the silence that followed I tried to collect my wits and withdraw with some semblance of dignity, but it was a full minute before I could turn on my heel and walk away. Gathering my reins, I swung up into the wet saddle from the mounting block in the yard and turned my back upon the smithy, never looking around to see if Owen Evans watched from his window. Guiding the mare carefully, I rode slowly along the bend of the village street and across the humped bridge over the millpond, ignoring the rain that was falling now in sheets. Angrily I told myself that I might have been home long before this if I had not bothered to stop at the smithy. But such bravado did nothing to dispel my distress or protect my habit from the wet.

Who was Gwenneth Evans? And what had she to do with Mark and Rhosllyn? The smith's daughter who had not come home—that was all I knew. But Evans was certain that Mark knew more. Did he? No one had spoken of her in my presence. Could she have been in love with Mark and run away at the news of his marriage? Somehow I didn't believe it. There was old, brooding grief in the smith's coldness. Whatever had become of the girl was in the past.

The mare turned in at the gates, and one of the children in the cottage, nose pressed against the streaming glass of the front window, waved as I passed. The trees of the drive sheltered me then, and the mare quickened her pace, sensing home and a dry stall.

Morgan splashed out to take Deirdre, touching his cap as he held her for me to dismount. "She has cast a shoe," I said shortly.

Perhaps I was in the mood to blame others for my own wretchedness, but it seemed that he dropped his eyes quickly as if to hide a swift gleam of triumph. Surely, even to annoy Mark or me, he would not have purposely sent the mare out in the rain with a loose shoe!

Of course not, I told myself briskly. Owen Evans had upset me more than I cared to admit, that was all. And what was

he to Llewellyn Morgan, that they might have combined to humiliate me in the village? I was imagining things. Yet there had also been the unexplained incident of the man-trap.

I nodded curtly and walked to the rear door without another word. Mark really ought to be told, I decided uneasily, for I was more than a little frightened of Morgan. But what could I say? What proof was there to connect the groom with either the man-trap or the cast shoe? Only a line of scripture quoted in my hearing, and the look in his eyes as he and his sister watched me. But Mark would be furiously angry; this time he might not succeed in keeping a tight rein on the violence that lay just below the surface of his explosive temper. And it would be all my fault. I might even be mistaken. No, somehow I must try to deal with this myself.

Drops of rainwater marked my passage over the flagged entry and up the stairs to my room. Feeling chilled now that I was no longer exercising, I rang for Bronwyn and asked for hot water to be brought for a bath. She took away the lovely, splattered habit and promised to have it cleaned and pressed for the next day. Jennie, a freckled and shy underhousemaid, came back with her, carrying the heavy cans of water, and so it was not until I was in the tub that Bronwyn asked where I had chosen to take Deirdre today.

"I rode through the village," I said evasively. "It's quite pretty."

"Aye, we like to think it is, my lady. Prettier than Woodham or Stretton Barrow."

"Were you born here?" I was beginning to feel warm again at last.

"Yes, my lady. In the white-and-black cottage two above the church. My father was sexton, though my mother is chapel folk."

"You must know everyone living there."

"And on the farms as well, so I do. Most go to chapel like us." She smiled shyly. "I've been walking out with the miller's son this spring."

"Then it must be a serious courtship," I said, smiling in turn.

"Yes, my lady. He's that thoughtful, and ambitious as well. My mother says he is a good man—but most of the people here are nice."

"Except the smith." I couldn't resist the opportunity to discover what was wrong at Rhosllyn—or with Mark and me. "Why is he so irascible?"

She closed up at once. "I couldn't say, my lady. I'll be heating your towel now if you are ready to step out."

It was as if a door had shut in my face, and I could only pretend I hadn't noticed. Instead, we debated a choice of gowns and ignored the smith's ghost in the space between us. Bronwyn knew the answer to my question and more. Was it because I was Mark's wife that she wouldn't speak?

I went downstairs and found Mark ahead of me, tired and hungry from his long day of rounds among the tenants. He smiled as I entered the library and said, "That shade of dark green is very becoming to you."

Inordinately pleased, I swept a mock curtsey and replied, "The credit is yours. In truth, Mark, I have been very happy with your selections."

"I'm glad. If there is anything you lack, tell me." He looked up and nodded as Williams entered to announce dinner.

As I took my seat at the table I shivered suddenly in the draft from the dining room door, then realized that the front door had opened and Noel was tossing his hat and cloak over a chair in the hall. Mark swore and in resignation asked Williams to set another place.

Noel came in and glanced at the buffet after greeting us. "Shrewsbury cakes. Mrs. Davies knows my weakness—our cook never bakes them half as well." As I gestured to Williams to pass him the platter, Noel turned to Mark. "My father sent me to tell you that the Llewellyn roof is leaking again. Like a sieve, he says—Llewellyn, not my father."

"Damn the man," Mark said wrathfully. "I was there not two hours ago and he had no complaint to make. Not to me."

"I thought he had withheld part of his rent money for the roof last quarter," Noel replied, taking another of the cakes.

"So he did. Which explains why he went to your father, like as not." He waved Williams away and rose. "Forgive me, Melanie. I'm not hungry anyway, and I want to take a look at that roof. Llewellyn is a thorn in the flesh. He'll skimp on work and charge full price if he can, and I'm tired of his games. I'd have him out if I could, but his people have farmed that land since before the Conquest, if not before the Flood. Well, his son is a throwback to the grandfather and a good man. One day, God willing, he will step into his father's shoes, and that will be the end of it." He nodded to Noel and was gone.

I shook my head. "He's tired, he shouldn't go out again. Couldn't the problem have waited until tomorrow?"

Noel shrugged and took the chair at the head of the table which Mark had just vacated. "Possibly."

Incensed, I waited until Williams had withdrawn before I said, "He works as hard as two men, and he really doesn't need to lift a finger. Yet in spite of all he does for his people— decent housing, fair rents, willingness to help in any trouble —they don't appear to appreciate one thing, much less Mark himself! It isn't fair."

Noel looked at me thoughtfully. "He isn't one of them. He's English and Anglican and a peer of the realm. His fore-bears came as conquerors, and the people haven't forgotten that this land was theirs once."

"Nonsense!" I said sharply. "That was eight hundred years ago. It has nothing to say to the present." Or did it? "Besides, you have the same blood as his, and his people accept you."

"Not quite the same. My grandmother was Welsh and quite popular. Because of her we belong." His eyes met mine squarely. "Tell me, if you will, why you married Mark Trecourt."

I stared at him in surprise. What could I say? That I was in love? Even a censored version of the truth would be awkward. I took another serving of sole Florentine, which I didn't want, but it gave me an excuse to remain silent a few seconds longer.

"Because he has qualities I care about," I said finally.

He laughed harshly. "*Mark?* You haven't known him long, have you? My cousin wasn't fit company for decent people! Until he decided to marry you. He may *pretend* to change for your sake, but I can tell you it won't last. He is what he is, and not even your goodness can work miracles." He rose and swung angrily about the room. "I haven't the right to speak against a man in his own house, but someone ought to open your eyes. My father will never criticize Mark, no matter what he does. Cecily has doted on him since we were children together—or else she is the sort to want what she can't have. No one knows what goes on in my lovely sister's head, least of all me. If only my mother were alive—she could advise you."

"Advise me about what? Noel, why do . . . people . . . dislike Mark so? What is wrong at Rhosllyn? If you are concerned for me, tell me the answers."

He stopped by the table, fingering the ornate handle of a knife, aligning it with the edge of the polished mahogany top. "Melanie," he began earnestly, and at that moment the door opened to admit his father.

Rhys came into the dining room and looked from one to the other of us. "Have I interrupted something?"

"No. We were . . . discussing a point of history," Noel said. "It wasn't anything important."

His father nodded. "I am sorry to drag Mark out on a night like this," Rhys said to me. "But with luck he'll catch Llewellyn at his little game and stop it once and for all."

"Have you had your dinner?" I asked, preparing to summon Williams.

"Yes, thank you, my dear. What's this I hear about Deirdre casting a shoe? I saw you ride in during that downpour and thought something was wrong."

"A nuisance, that's all," I replied with forced lightness. "No harm done."

"Unless you take a chill!" he replied. "I wouldn't care for that."

I smiled. "Not very likely."

"Well, you must take care, all the same. If Mark doesn't return in time for dessert, Cecily wants you to come to the Dower House with us. I don't think it would do you any harm, not in the carriage."

I doubted if *Cecily* cared whether I was lonely; it was more the sort of thing Rhys himself would think of. "How kind," I said, "but I really ought to be here when Mark returns. He has had a tiring day."

"As you like, my dear! I understand. I must be on my way. Noel, will you be coming with me?"

Noel hesitated and then nodded, almost as if he had had time to regret his impulse to speak to me. They made their farewells and were gone, leaving the dining room to the silence of Williams' presence and the patter of raindrops against the window as the wind shifted.

Mark returned at ten-thirty, letting himself in. I had left orders for Williams to serve a tray in the library when I rang. Mark came into the room with his cloak still about his shoulders, the wool black with wet. Without a word to me, he crossed to the decanters and poured himself a stiff brandy. As he drank it down I could see his face, white and drawn and haunted. Reluctant to speak first, I rose and took his cloak, spreading it over the back of a chair to dry. He scarcely noticed what I did, taking a second brandy and standing before the fire, one hand gripping the mantel, the knuckles white. As he stared down into the flames he took a deep shuddering breath, as if he were reliving horror.

I wondered if Noel would judge his cousin so quickly if he could see him as I did, tormented and ridden by his private devils.

Mark straightened at last. "What time is it? Have you dined?" he asked, striving desperately for a semblance of normalcy.

"Yes, some time ago. Would you like a tray, here by the fire?" I replied quietly.

"Not now. I can't eat." He sat down in the chair opposite

to mine and rested his head wearily against the back. "God, I'm tired," he said softly. His eyes closed, the lashes dark against his cheek.

I sat in silence for a long while, letting him rest. In repose his face was attractive, almost handsome, the sort of face that would command attention wherever he went—well-structured, intelligent, interesting. There was no indication of the tumult that went on behind the closed lids, unless it was in a slight tightness about the lips. Strength and character about the line of the jaw, determination in the firm chin—a man to note and remember.

Why did I marry him? Noel's question returned to my mind, and I considered it. To escape from Tilmer Hall, certainly. That had been uppermost in my thoughts. But in addition to that I found something in this man to trust. In spite of the hints of scandal and wild temper, and the bewildering dislike I met with here, in spite of Mark's evident distress, I found myself trusting him still.

But who was Gwenneth, and what had become of her? I wished I could ask Mark and so put it out of my mind. Yet he had never offered to take me into his confidence, and I could not intrude.

Without moving he said, "It is growing worse."

"The leak in the Llewellyns' roof?" I asked blankly.

"No. My . . . nightmares. I have them more frequently, and now, tonight, riding through the park—I must have fallen asleep for a moment. God knows, I'm tired enough to be asleep on my feet anyway. And it happened then." He was silent for a time and then added, "If it weren't for you—and my uncle—I'd have put a pistol to my head and an end to my existence, such as it is."

"Mark, no—!"

He looked across at me then, his eyes full of pain. "I am slowly going mad. Do you know what that is like? Not only madness, but the *fear* of it never leaves you—always there lying in wait to strike at one's peace. Like some great black beast hovering in the darkness of the mind, ready to spring

without warning. You don't know *when* it will happen, only that it *will* happen, and there is no escape, no turning back."

I sat appalled, hearing the wretchedness in his deep voice and unable to answer it or to offer any comfort. I had never known anyone who was mad, couldn't begin to know the signs, the symptoms that marked its progress.

"Have you spoken to a physician—" I began, but he shook his head violently.

"*There is no cure.* I know that for myself, better than any doctor. My grandfather—my mother's father—died raving. Even my mother was . . . strange. As a boy I tried to tell myself that it was the shock of my father's death that had turned her mind, nothing more. Certainly not inherited madness. I learned the truth the hard way. Through her the strain has been passed on to me, and the signs are unmistakable. I can't shut my eyes to them, Melanie. It is simply a matter of time."

"What—what are the symptoms?" I asked huskily.

"Ungovernable temper. Violence. And lapses of memory."

A cold wind swept through my heart. "But if you could talk with someone—Rhys, the rector, even to me—"

Mark's eyes scanned my face intently, as if he sought for something there—reassurance or understanding? Then, reluctantly, he shook his head. "I dare not risk losing you. Not yet."

There was finality in his voice. The subject was closed. He got to his feet and said heavily, "I'll light the candles."

But I knew for a certainty that neither of us would sleep at all.

SPRING PASSED INTO SUMMER, the days slipping by in sunlight but haunted by shadow. Though Mark had spoken of madness on the day at Tilmer Hall when he had proposed to me, I hadn't believed he meant it quite literally, that it was a burden he carried with him every day. But I had seen his temper and the violence that sprang from it. Painful though it was, I had no choice but to accept the truth of what he had told me.

More than ever my spirits swung on the weathervane of his moodiness and nightmares. Sometimes when the tension became intolerable he would come to me and pace the floor while I talked about anything that came into my head. Or he would simply sit, worn out, in the chair across from mine and let the soothing silence of companionship flow through him. At other times he would race the wind on the gray stallion or shut himself away from everyone. I found myself wondering if that locked room, Aunt Margaret's bedchamber, was in reality his prison. After all, Mrs. Powell had let me rattle the knob before confessing that she had no key, and Williams had listened intently when I had innocently asked Mark if it might be cleaned. They knew, and had cruelly made me guess, that it could be more than it seemed. I couldn't prevent a ripple of dread every time I passed that secretive door.

It would have helped if there had been someone I could talk to. Several times I considered going to Rhys, but I was afraid Mark might find out and feel I had somehow betrayed him. Besides, Rhys's determined cheerfulness even in the face of Mark's rudeness led me to believe he closed his eyes to the unpleasant truth. Once he had told me the worst of Mark's temper was all in the past, and again, on a day at the barn when he and I had witnessed an explosion of fury that left Mark white and the elder Llewellyn shaking, he had defended his nephew. "The man's a disgrace, after all, and as deceitful and lazy as God makes them. Fences *must* be mended, and gates kept closed, my dear, and Mark was right to take him to task for his stupid carelessness."

"I thought," I said as Mark strode off and left me to follow with his uncle, "that Mark would—that slamming him against the cottage wall would kill him." I took a deep breath to stop the quiver in my voice as we crossed the stile from the home farm. "It—it frightens me."

"And all for the sake of a herd of cattle free to wander the countryside? Yes, I know, my dear," he replied gently, "it seems unnecessarily harsh to a woman. But a man like Llewellyn doesn't understand anything else. Sense must be battered into his head somehow."

"Would you have done it that way? Or Noel?" I demanded.

He turned to face me, a wry smile in his eyes. "Ten years ago I might have—the fool would tempt a saint to violence. And Letitia would have scolded me just as you do now." The smile deepened. "She would have told you *all* the tales of my salad days, come to that, and you two could cluck your tongues over them."

I laughed shakily. "She must have been a delightful person."

"That's better! Indeed, she was very dear to—to all of us," he replied quietly, and changed the subject.

And so I consoled myself with the fact that Mark had never turned on me, that I could soothe his turbulent nature, standing between him and the worst of his ordeal.

But there was nothing that could stand between me and

the threat I faced with Morgan. If I had not been more frightened of rousing Mark's wild temper, I would have spoken to him. With no proof to offer, only unsupported conclusions drawn from intuition and circumstance, I was treading dangerous ground. Morgan could laugh and call me hysterical, overwrought. He might even take savage pleasure in telling Mark that his wife, too, was unstable. Was I only imagining the implacable hatred I saw in the groom's eyes whenever they met mine?

And so we rode together often, Mark and I, covering miles of ground, sometimes taking a packed luncheon in his saddlebags, wandering into churches or along dusty lanes, climbing the blue hills and finding the valleys and mountains of Wales beyond, following a stream along banks strewn with wild flowers—whatever diversion offered itself. Any excuse to escape the tensions at Rhosllyn for a little while sufficed. And on these excursions he was a different man, the wonderful man he could—would—have been if his blood had been free of the taint it carried.

One morning in late May as Bronwyn brushed my habit I opened the wardrobe and reached down to take out my riding boots. Something cool and swift touched my fingers. Drawing back in surprise, I accidentally knocked the left boot off the rack. It fell out, one buckle clinking sharply as it struck the edge of the wardrobe. And then I saw the dangling fringe on the sash of my green wrapper. I laughed at myself and lifted out the other boot. Turning to speak to the Welsh girl, I broke off in mid-sentence as she dropped the habit and pointed in horror at my right hand. I looked down swiftly to see what could be wrong.

A snake was slithering out of the boot and upward toward my bare wrist. With a cry of revulsion I flung the boot and the snake from me as far as I could. Both hit the far wall and fell to the floor. Bronwyn, shrieking, ran for the door. And then Mrs. Powell came hurrying in, stopping stock still on the threshold.

I had not stirred, for the snake, lightly coiled, was watching me with its cool, unblinking eyes. Nearly two feet long,

brown with distinctive diamond markings, it was obscenely out of place in the delicate blue of my chamber.

The housekeeper stood where she was as the snake gracefully uncoiled. "*Do* something!" Bronwyn whispered. "'Tis a *viper!*"

A viper, whose bite brought sickness and nervous prostration, sometimes death. Even now it was rippling across the polished floor, with only a few feet of carpet between it and me. Still I couldn't move, rooted to the spot in fascination and terror. Behind me Bronwyn was shouting to me to get out of its way.

Suddenly Mark was there, shoving me aside and raising the fire tongs in his other hand. I cried out, for I didn't want the snake killed here, on my floor, before my very eyes.

"Yes, all right," he said, and caught it deftly between the tongs and flicked it out the opened window, calling down to one of the gardeners. And then he turned furiously on the startled, silent housekeeper. "How did that come to be here?"

"I—I don't know, my lord! Indeed—it must have come in with the woodbox, and looking for somewhere dark—"

I shuddered. "It was in the wardrobe." Stumbling, I crossed to a chair and sat down quickly.

Mark turned swiftly to me. "Did it strike you? Are you hurt?"

I shook my head, and he rounded on the housekeeper again. "My orders were that the woodboxes were never to be left where snakes might crawl into them."

"Yes, my lord, and one of the grooms sees to it that they are brought in as soon as the boy fills them. They never sit by the kitchen door!"

One of the grooms. Morgan. I heard no more as I considered that. Had the viper been placed in the woodbox on purpose? Or even slipped into my room, with the certain knowledge that the woodbox would be blamed? For everyone was aware that I preferred wood to coal in the grate in my bedchamber. What if I had put my foot into that boot—worse still, if I had found the snake in my bed or coiled among my gowns! I felt sick at the thought.

Mark was bending over me, asking if I preferred to postpone our ride. I shook my head again, managed a weak smile, and promised to meet him at the stables in ten minutes.

He left, taking the chastened housekeeper with him, and I barely heard Bronwyn's excited chatter as she described in lurid detail every case of snake bite she had ever heard of.

When I crossed the courtyard toward Deirdre, Morgan met me halfway. With his back to Mark, he said, "I'll see that the woodbox is never left by the door again, my lady." Whether he meant his words as an apology or a confirmation of his guilt was impossible to determine. But the dark eyes challenged me to denounce him.

I couldn't begin to guess why this man was my sworn enemy—because I was English, because I was the Devil Baron's wife, because of some twisted explanation in his own brain? But I knew that I must guard myself as best I could, and find my own way to deal with him, or else run to Mark and admit that he *had* been wrong to bring me to this strange borderland where eight hundred years of prejudice and misunderstanding could run to cruelty and madness.

With a curt nod of acknowledgment I brushed past the groom to where Mark waited to give me his hand in mounting.

We came that day to a small village that was celebrating a local festival of some sort, and I saw here another side of the Welsh character. The streets were crowded with people, and booths were set up in the widest stretch across from an old stone inn. There was laughter, and as always where the Welsh gather, music. A young man sat on the steps of the inn accompanying himself on a small harp as he sang whatever the passersby requested. A cap full of coins lay before him, and his dark eyes were brimming with laughter even as he sang the saddest ballads. A girl in the peaked, lace-edged black hat and woolen shawl of the traditional dress stopped to listen, and at once he switched to a mock-mournful version of "Drink to Me Only with Thine Eyes." She blushed and turned away, but not before I had caught sight of her green

eyes beneath her dark lashes, set in a dimpled, heart-shaped face. The singer winked humorously at Mark and then inclined his head gracefully as several coins were tossed into the collection at his feet.

We sat beneath the spreading limbs of a tall oak, enjoying the pageantry before us, listening to the singing, mostly glee —simple, unaccompanied melody that provided its own music. There were tarts and cakes and hot meat pies for sale, beer in the shade of the inn wall, the kegs resting on wooden horses, trinkets and peddler's goods of every sort, and a tinker who had set up his wagon at the side of a tilted magpie house. I thought wistfully how happy we might be, Mark and I, if we were an ordinary couple like the boy and girl shyly holding hands as they wandered about the street enjoying the excitement and color of their holiday. No fears, no worries, not even the faintest shadow of secrecy between them. Only a sunlit afternoon of pleasure and each other's company. I watched them stroll along, her fair head nearly as high as his dark one, stopping now and then to point out something of interest or stare at a display of goods. Would Mark and I ever be so close?

My thoughts were interrupted by a thin man who carried a tray of cheap jewelry across his chest. He bowed to us and gestured to the scene we had been watching. "Not likely to end before moonrise, but end then it will. Chapel folk don't take kindly to the old ways."

"What are they celebrating?" I asked.

"You wouldn't be the only one to want to know that, ma'am! 'Twas the end of the Great Plague in the village. The last victim was buried nearly five hundred years ago today, and never again did it strike here, so they say. Something to do with everlasting prayers to chase away the evil. Once there used to be a man in black who would go dancing about the streets, shouting and taunting the people until the householders came roaring out with brooms of new straw to chase him away—him representing the Plague, you understand, and nimble-footed at that, for they took the broom-slamming seriously, d'ye see. My grandfather remembered it as a boy,

but then the chapel folk did away with the broom chase, being more sober-minded and not given to papish ceremony. And so we have a fair in its place and do a good day's business at that, and all tucked away by the morrow."

Mark laughed. "Good sense, in its own way."

"Aye, business is business." The man adjusted his tray. "Is there anything the lady would care to see? Good ware, none stolen, fine workmanship!"

"Choose what you like," Mark said good-humoredly. He inspected the trinkets and pointed to a small heart-shaped locket on a slender chain. "That is the best crafted, I should say. Or the bracelet, perhaps."

"The locket, if you please," I said, smiling at the man.

He lifted the locket with a flamboyant sweep of his hand, laid it carefully in a square of silver tissue, twisted the ends into an artistic peak, and handed it to me with a quaint bow.

I held it gently, for it was a gift to *me* and not an heirloom that had belonged to someone else. No matter that it was a fairing, it captured the charm of the moment, and that was priceless enough.

"To remember your outing and a day as fair as yourself," he said gracefully to me as Mark paid him for the locket, and then, with a last bow to both of us, walked away to find another likely buyer.

Mark watched him go. "That man is happy. Few people can say as much and be honest." He turned to me. "You needn't keep the locket if you don't care for it—I hadn't the heart to refuse him."

"I shall treasure it," I replied, keeping my voice light as I tucked the wisp of silver paper into my reticule. "A souvenir, as he said."

We did not wait for moonrise; by teatime we had turned our horses toward Rhosllyn and left the little village of Carregfan behind.

I don't know when I began to fall in love with Mark Trecourt. It grew slowly, quietly, without my knowledge or will, until one day it could be ignored no longer.

In spite of everything, perhaps it was inevitable, Mark and I were so often in one another's company. Because no one visited us other than the Trecourts, we were very much alone. Thus, except for the one secretive corner of his life where madness lurked, a relationship developed that might not have existed under other circumstances. It was to me that Mark talked of his plans for the stud farm or about a problem with the tenants, any aspect of his day that came home with him.

His uncle shared an interest in the dairy and of course worked with the farm and cattle, but Mark was not close enough to Rhys to discuss his thoughts and ideas. It was sometimes painful to watch Rhys try to bridge the gaping void between them. Though he never complained to me, it was obvious that Mark's coldness hurt him. Noel was interested in the estate, though he preferred the stud farm, especially the breaking and training of two-year-olds, and I had heard Morgan praise his ability. Even so, Noel and Mark avoided each other as much as possible, and the only conversation between them consisted of polite banalities or subtle insults. I often wondered why Noel didn't leave. Of course he, too, loved Rhosllyn deeply. He had said to me one evening as twilight fell across the park where we strolled, "Everything I care about is here," then abruptly changed the subject as if he had immediately regretted this glimpse of what lay beneath the charm.

Still, he must have found his life here confining, and sometimes impossible. He gave the impression that he was waiting for something to happen, but there was an underlying emotion of—bitterness, possibly, certainly not eagerness and excitement. I couldn't begin to define Noel. Only his antagonism for Mark seemed to bring him to life. The rest of the time the still waters of the surface covered unknown depths. Was he waiting for the day when he could take Mark's place as lord of Rhosllyn?

Cecily, for all her reserve, always warmed to Mark, but he made no effort to treat her with anything more than the

courtesy and friendliness that often exist between cousins. He teased her about tagging at his heels in their childhood or having to be fished out of the pond beyond the woods, but he never confided in her, much as she might wish him to. I sometimes believed that she felt I had come between them, that in time Mark would have turned to her if it had not been for his marriage to me!

And so, at our meals and on our rides and during our quiet evenings, he came to me with his pent-up words, and I listened.

I said nothing. Love had been no part of our bargain, and Mark was in no way interested in me beyond the companionship I supplied. His detachment was absolute and unyielding.

Might as well stop the winds that swept across Rhosllyn from Wales as stop the change in my feelings. Slowly, insidiously, they had grown to maturity, catching me unawares, defenseless.

Sometimes there seemed to be a conspiracy to see how far Mark could be driven before he lost his temper. There was endless provocation—from tenants, servants, even from Noel —and at times it flared up with sudden, explosive force. But if he could, he would turn on his heel and walk away, even from Morgan, rather than lash out.

And then, one day, I myself bore the brunt of his wrath, though I had believed he would never turn on me, his wife. That was no protection.

It all began innocently enough. Mark was at the home farm to supervise a foaling, and I had enjoyed an afternoon in the gardens with Bryn, cutting flowers for the house. My basket was full of roses and marguerites and peonies, iris carefully set upon the top. Bryn was the only person on the staff or among the tenants who seemed to take me at face value. His flowers and shrubs were his life, and there was no place left in his world for grudges, old or new. I took an interest in his efforts, and that was sufficient passport to grace in his eyes. After five years of loneliness, since the death of

Rhys's beloved wife, he was satisfied to have a mistress once more, someone who could sympathize over an infestation of slugs or marvel at his skill in growing a perfect rose. And so I was rewarded with the bounty of his gardens for arrangements in the house.

Making the rounds with him, I stopped by Letitia Trecourt's little Alpine garden. Bryn never cared for it especially, but I liked the grace and beauty of these strange mountain blossoms. On that day I saw a star-shaped bloom of rose and white next to one of gentian blue. These had never before been plentiful enough to cut. Remembering a chased silver bowl I had found in the cupboard of the plant room, I stooped to pick the best of the blue and several of the rose and white for accent. In the small bowl they would be lovely on Mark's desk.

Pleased with the idea, I made a point of having the arrangement there for his return. He always appreciated the pleasing touch of flowers in the house. It was the first thing Mark noticed as he crossed to his desk, and I happily awaited his word of approval.

Instead, he stopped in mid-stride, his face parchment white. "Where did these come from?" he asked in a strangled voice. "Who put them here?"

For a dreadful instant I couldn't speak. "I did," I managed at last. "They are from your aunt's favorite garden."

In a single movement he was at the desk and had sent the bowl flying through the air to crash into the paneled wall. The silver rang hollowly as it struck the floor, and the flowers lay strewn on the water-splotched carpet. His face was livid as he wheeled toward me.

"Don't ever touch those again," he said through clenched teeth. "Don't cut them, bring them into my house, or go near them in the garden, do you understand? *I hate the sight of them!*"

Without waiting for an explanation or an apology, he stormed out of the room, slamming the door behind him. He did not come home for tea or for dinner, but late in the

night I heard the stallion, galloping madly, cross the park toward the stables. I turned my head into the pillow and for no reason that I could think of began to cry.

The next morning I walked down to the breakfast room with butterflies in my stomach. I had been awake since dawn worrying about whether he would even be there, and what he might say. Most of all I dreaded a cold blank silence as he completely ignored my presence. But Mark smiled and asked if I had rested well, as though the terrible scene in the library had never occurred. Trembling with mingled relief and happiness, I never considered why this might be so, but later in the day a chance remark by Cecily brought me sharply out of my euphoria.

Mark had been searching for a book of records from the stud farm as his cousins and I rode into the courtyard. He called a query to Noel, who denied all knowledge of its whereabouts.

And then Cecily said, "Don't be silly, Noel, it is lying on Father's desk—you saw it there after lunch! He said you had let him borrow it for a few days, Mark. Or have you forgotten?"

Mark frowned and replied, "I suppose I must have. Never mind, then."

As he turned to walk away I remembered what he had told me about his madness—the symptoms included lapses of memory. Had he been kind at breakfast because he had recovered his good humor? Or had he completely forgotten the angry words he had flung at me? And he never spoke of his nightmares afterward either, or admitted that his Aunt Margaret's room was more than it appeared to be. What *else* slipped his mind, I wondered uneasily as Noel gave me his hand to dismount.

I tried to discover more about the nightmares he endured, but Mark refused to discuss them with me. That they were horrifyingly real while they lasted was clear enough. But they had grown worse in the last few years, which was why Mark had in desperation turned to marriage with me. He was de-

termined to hold his madness at bay for as long as possible, and whatever crept out of his mind in the darkness of the night, these dreams remained his own. I was allowed to soothe his torment but not to share it.

I myself slept well, though occasionally the creaking of the house woke me. But that was because I always half-listened for Mark's tap at my door or his steps going down the passage to the library or drawing room, where he would sit until he was calmer. One night I slipped out of bed to go after him and saw him unlock the door of his Aunt Margaret's room and step inside. I had been right, I thought, suddenly chilled. Something drew him to that room and shut me out—but what? After hesitating, undecided whether to wait for him, I finally returned the way I had come. I lay in the darkness, eyes wide, nearly two hours before I heard him pass my bedchamber again.

If I had been the superstitious sort I might have fabricated ghostly movements in the rooms overhead as the floorboards squeaked and stirred. Instead, next morning I brought in the barn cat, a great black beast with green eyes and an independent air, to hunt for mice. He caught three, but with the endless wainscoting and chimneys and attics, it was not to be expected that Tom would remove the lot. Enough to put the fear of God into the rest, though, for we heard nothing for several nights thereafter. Mrs. Powell was upset, however, and had the maids turning out the closets and cupboards. Rhys Trecourt laughed and asked if the mice or the cat had disturbed the housekeeper more.

"Mark keeps no dogs," I said, accustomed to the sight of several spaniels asleep on the hearth rugs or paddling about Tilmer Hall.

"No, he hasn't had one since his own died—oh, some seven or eight years ago, I believe. A handsome hound he'd raised from a pup. I gave Gelert to him when he was ten in an effort to encourage him to exercise more. They tramped the hills together, and my poor wife lived in dread of Mark's becoming ill from exposure. Oddly enough, he never did. Oh, colds and such, but nothing as serious as she expected."

He smiled. "If you would enjoy a dog of your own, you may take your pick of Joslyn's next litter."

I shook my head, though sorely tempted. I loved animals, and they always responded to me, but I must consult Mark first. "Thank you. Perhaps later," I said, then added, "You would never think, looking at Mark now, that he had endured such a sickly childhood. He is never ill."

"Well, I suppose I took a grave risk, but I couldn't bear to see the boy an invalid, watching other children run and play and longing to be like them. It seemed more cruel to allow that to happen than to push him as far as his strength and will would permit." He frowned, remembering. "If he had died as a result I would have blamed myself for the rest of my days. Still, *was* it living to be pale and weak and miserable, unable to enjoy anything and forever feeling left out? I don't know. All I could think was, if I *don't* try, then it will be my fault, not Mark's, if that is all he ever experiences."

"Yes, I can understand that. And you were right, weren't you?"

He shook his head. "In hindsight. I look back and wonder how I ever came by the courage, especially with a child not my own but in my keeping. And it was doubly difficult in face of my wife's deep concern for him. Letitia and I were devoted, and it distressed me to add to her worries." With a sigh he rose to go. "Don't forget, you both are coming to dinner on Wednesday."

"I'm looking forward to a pleasant evening," I said.

And it was, if rather quiet. A meal chosen to please the eye as well as the palate. In the bright, lemon-yellow-and-white dining room, the linen and silver and huge vases of golden roses were matched by poached salmon encircled with lemon wedges and early peas, hens baked to a crisp brown and set among saffron rice and broiled plums, a leg of spring lamb roasted in mint conserve and decorated with rosettes of pastry.

Afterward we sat on the terrace and watched the sky change colors with the setting of the sun, drinking liqueurs from

delicate crystal glasses shaped like just-opening tulips on slender stems. Mark had brought them home from Venice for Cecily. Later she played the harp and sang for us, but Mark was growing restless, and we left as soon as the coffee had been drunk, though Noel had asked to show me the gardens.

In contrast to that evening, two nights later the Trecourts entertained lavishly, and as I strolled in the early twilight through the gardens and into the park, I heard laughter and the music of a small orchestra. Drawn by the sounds, I leaned against the rough bark of a tree and listened. I recognized Liszt and Mendelssohn, a Haydn sonata, and then a selection from Michael Balfe's *Bohemian Girl*. Later there would be dancing, but as "I Dreamt I Dwelt in Marble Halls" faded into the still air, I turned back the way I had come. It was shameful to stand in the darkness and watch the pleasures of others even when there was no envy in one's heart. I did not begrudge them their parties, it was simply that I would like to attend with Mark at my side, chatting and joining in the gaiety with the other young people. To dance the night away and return to Rhosllyn in the dawn mists, laughter spilling over as we tried not to wake the servants.

Lost in my wistful thoughts, I nearly stepped out of the shadow of the park into the path of Morgan, the groom.

He was some yards away, looking back over his shoulder as if to be certain that he had not been observed from the house. Edging swiftly into the shelter of the shrubbery that bordered the drive, I thanked God for my dark gown, for he had not seen me. I should have been mortified to have been found spying upon the Trecourts—and that would have been Morgan's interpretation of it, surely. His knowing smile, covered by his outward pretense of respect, would have been more than my pride could endure. And more than that, I was afraid to be alone with him here in the isolated darkness of the woods.

Half-holding my breath, I stood stock-still and allowed him to walk past the spot where I was hidden. It was not until

he had turned the bend of the drive that I felt safe—and suddenly began to wonder why he came this way, half-stealthily as if he were not here by right. Surely if he simply wished to talk with the coachmen and grooms of Rhys Trecourt's guests, he was free to do so openly. As far as I knew, Mark made no effort to prevent his staff from mixing with villagers and the neighbors' servants.

Why, then, if his purpose was honest, had he looked back carefully and moved quietly over the loose chippings?

Curious, I decided to follow him. In the gathering darkness I was nearly invisible. There was a risk that I might run into him, or the carriages of the Dower House guests drawn up nearby. With this caution in mind, I walked behind the shrubbery, well out of the drive, yet within hearing and sight of it.

Morgan himself had avoided the carriages clustered near the gatehouse. For of course the Rhosllyn stables could not be used by these visitors, and the vehicles came no farther than the first fork. From the silence—save for the occasional stamping of a horse, the jingle of harness, and other normal noises of animals and equipages left standing on their own—I gathered that the coachmen had stepped around to the Trecourt kitchen for a mug of beer and a gossip with the servants. Morgan was briefly outlined by the lights from the Dower House windows and then lost for several seconds until the gatehouse windows pinpointed him once more. Someone was standing in the road, just outside the Rhosllyn gates but clearly waiting for the groom, for he took a step forward to meet Morgan. They stood talking quietly, heads close together, and I strained to see the other man. Slipping closer, I inadvertently stepped on a dry twig which broke with a loud snap. Both men turned guiltily to see who was there, but I was already frozen against a tree. After a moment they resumed their conversation, but I had no need to remain. As the stranger had lifted his head to look up the drive I could see the outline of the beard and the set of the shoulders. The blacksmith, Owen Evans.

With infinite care I retraced my steps and then cut across the drive to circle around the park, going past the back lawn of the Dower House but completely safe from an encounter with Morgan before I reached the terraces of Rhosllyn.

The music had not resumed, and as I passed the lawns I saw people gathered by the French windows and along the garden walks. They were framed in the glow of candles from indoors while I was in darkness, so I continued on my way, feeling reasonably safe.

Not for long. A shrill whistle split the air and sent me headlong into the trees as a skyrocket burst into brilliant colors overhead. The darkness took on a greenish cast as the display continued, and heart thudding, I suddenly realized that the center of attraction was a clever scene contrived on the ornamental pool near the rose arbor. Small ships, sails stretched and cannon belching fire, moved in a mock battle across the dark surface of the water.

There were loud exclamations of surprise, pleasure, and amazement from the gathered guests as the tiny fleets tacked and turned in unison. The fireworks, oddly enough, added a touch of reality to the battle and in that strange light made the ships seem larger than they actually were.

It was quite well done. Old Mrs. Tilmer had enjoyed describing spectacles of this sort one might see in London, and I knew that the Battle of Trafalgar had been very popular even five years ago. Noel had provided a very successful diversion for the entertainment of their guests. Even from my place far across the lawns in the edge of the park I could appreciate his skill.

The light died, and the candles in the tiny fleets winked out one by one until only the largest of the ships sailed on in brightness. From the burst of applause and cheers I gathered that the White Ensign could still be seen at the mainmast. Conversation began as servants moved about lighting the colored lanterns, and I hurried on my way.

Later in the week, as Noel was on his way to the Home Farm, he found me on my knees by the drive.

"Melanie—!" he began.

"Hush! There's a young bird beneath the shrub. I've been coaxing it out. I think it fell from a nest in that beech."

"And what on earth will you do with it if it comes to you?" he asked.

I glanced up from under the brim of my straw peasant hat. "Put it back," I said indignantly. "What else?"

He chuckled and helped me capture the young robin while its parent scolded from a nearby hawthorn. I held the trembling ball of feathers and smoothed its head with my fingers until Noel found a ladder and quickly restored it to its less adventurous brothers and sisters.

Drawing out his handkerchief, he said with a grin, "How long were you crawling about? There's a smear of mud on your nose and leaves all over your skirt."

Standing meekly while he cleaned my face, I said defensively, "Not long. But, you see, at first it was caught in that tangle of rhododendron."

He mechanically refolded his handkerchief into a neat square and replaced it in his pocket, his dark eyes still on my face. And then abruptly he turned to retrieve the ladder, saying brusquely over his shoulder, "We ought to go so the mother can come back to the nest."

With a quick word of thanks I hurried away, leaving him there alone.

Several days later I thought to ask Mark whether he would mind if we had a dog.

"No," he said abruptly, "not again."

"But you used to have one?" I asked, curious to know why he was so adamant. If he had been deeply attached, I would understand and not press.

"Yes, I had one. He was deliberately poisoned."

"Poisoned! Mark, surely not!" I exclaimed, shocked. Rhys Trecourt had left the impression that Gelert had died of old age.

"I would wager it was Morgan. Noel wouldn't have struck at me through the dog." He moved restlessly about the library.

"But why? I mean, one doesn't poison a dog simply because

one dislikes the master!" And yet I had suspected Morgan of far worse intentions toward me, simply because he disliked my English blood and my husband. If he could harm a person, why not a dog?

Mark said irritably, "If there had been proof, I'd have sacked the man. As it is, I can only guess."

"Mark, why would Morgan or Noel—or anyone else—dislike you enough to do such a dreadful thing?" I asked earnestly.

His back was to me as he stared out the window across the sunlit gardens. "I have told you, Melanie, I lived the devil's own life before I met you. They feel they have reason enough, God knows—" He broke off, wheeling to face me, his eyes pleading but his lips grim. "Don't ask me, Melanie, for God's sake leave it alone!" He took a deep, shuddering breath. "You would be easy to confide in, but I dare not. I'd not have *you* turn from me in disgust and horror as the others have done. Not yet! Not while I'm sane enough to read your thoughts in your eyes!"

"Your uncle and your cousin Cecily have not turned from you," I said gently. "Why should I?"

"You don't understand," he said heavily. "Rhys would stand by me if necessary until doomsday. Sheer duty! It's one of the reasons I hate him. As for Cecily—she refuses to see or believe anything that is contrary to her own view of life. Try arguing with her if you don't believe me. Her world is ordered in her own fashion. I've got to look in at the Home Farm. Will you walk over with me or stay here?"

I went with him of course, but it was tacitly understood between us that the painful subject was closed, at least for the present.

We met Mrs. Powell in the hall as we came out of the library that day, but I couldn't judge from her face whether she had heard our conversation or not. The vase of wilted flowers in her hand had come from the drawing room, and she might easily have been merely passing.

One afternoon Cecily and I went riding together.

Noel had arranged the outing and then at the last moment had been called to the stables to look in at a sick mare. And so for the first time the two of us were alone. There was a protracted silence, for she was not talkative at the best of times, and I felt certain she would not have come with me at all if there had been a plausible excuse for her to offer. And then I had the happy thought of mentioning Mark to her. After that she talked of the years when she and her family had lived in the main house with him.

"How long were you there?" I asked to keep the conversation going, though Mark had already told me.

"I was born there—so was Noel of course. It was my father who decided we must move when Mark came of age. My mother felt it was silly to maintain two separate households when one would do, but he insisted that Mark should have his own home to run as he pleased. It was painful for all of us. My parents had been living in the Dower House when Mark's father died, but they hadn't been married for very long—a year or so, I suppose—and so most of their associations as well as Noel's and mine were with Rhosllyn."

"What did Mark think about it?" I asked, for I liked to hear about his childhood.

"He had only just come down from university, and he was

different, somehow. He made no objections at all." There was disappointment in her voice even now. She had clearly not expected Mark to agree with her father. "I was almost sixteen, and it was like tearing out old roots. But my father was right, I suppose. We had no reason to remain—Mark was a grown man, nearly twenty-one."

We had circled the orchard, climbed the ridge, and were now in a meadow above the village. The church tower rose above the trees and a dozen swallows were darting and skimming the air about it.

Suddenly she said, "I'd like to ride down to the church. Would you mind?"

"No, of course not," I replied. Mark and I had never attended church services, though I knew he had donated a large sum for repairs to the church roof. It would be interesting, I thought, to go in.

Cecily led the way along a track that brought us to a ford just before the churchyard. We splashed across and then stopped briefly to allow the horses to drink. Afterward, tethering them in the shade of trees near the gate, we walked up the beaten path to the door.

Two other women were there replacing the altar cloth, though I had not seen their horses until we reached the porch. They looked up as we entered and then stared in open surprise as they realized who I was. Immediately afterward they turned their backs on me. Flushing with embarrassment, I pretended to be interested in a memorial plaque on the nearest wall, then quietly moved away from the chancel. It must have been coincidence—I couldn't believe Cecily had deliberately brought me here to be cut.

It was as plain a church on the inside as it was on the outside. Accustomed to the rich carvings and ornate design of the Chilterns, I found the interior of St. Giles almost severe. The stone flags, slender columns, carved wooden arches of the ceiling, and open rood screen were saved from cold Norman simplicity by fine lancet windows that brought in the sunlight and warmed the barrenness with the blues and reds of stained glass. There was a crusader's tomb, worn but

strongly carved, bearing the name of Trecourt, and other monuments to the family as well. While Cecily spoke to the women and found the vase she wanted, I searched out the memorials to Mark's parents, and just beyond, that of Rhys Trecourt's mother, with an incised Celtic cross, beautifully ornamented, marking her resting place.

Here were Mark's people, stretching back in time, a heritage as real as Rhosllyn itself. I would have liked to come with him, to hear him describe each one as we paused beside the tombs, giving brief, exciting life to his ancestors. But he had never brought me here, or suggested that I visit the church on my own. I now knew why. We were not welcome here either.

Cecily called to me and we left, riding back through the village as the shortest way home. A family driving by in a crested carriage nodded to her but did not stop, and Cecily made no effort to identify them. Because they had covertly stared at me, I assumed they were neighbors. As we passed the smithy, the man Owen Evans was at his forge, the fires roaring about his heavy frame as he stoked the blaze.

Turning to my companion, I said, "Why is the smith so unfriendly? He positively glared at Mark and me one day."

Cecily shrugged. "He isn't the friendly sort."

"But," I said, persisting, "I have seen him speak pleasantly enough to other villagers. Why should he glare at us?"

"He blames Mark for something, I suppose."

"What?" I asked bluntly.

"Nonsense, really. His daughter Gwenneth was wild and not especially particular in her behavior. When she ran off with an itinerant peddler he was beside himself."

Immensely relieved for some reason, I laughed. The smith's words had bothered me for a very long time. "What on earth did Mark have to do with that?"

"Oh, Evans claimed that Gwenneth had been Mark's mistress and that he had gotten rid of her when she bored him. I suppose he couldn't believe that his daughter was what she was."

Rhosllyn was in sight now, high up the slope. I hadn't even

noticed that we had come so far. "*Was* she his mistress?" I asked, feeling cold.

It was Cecily's turn to laugh. "She was any man's. Oh, beautiful enough, if you care for the wild gypsy type. Mark had just come down from university, he was certainly no monk, but I'm sure his interest in the girl was merely casual."

She sounded so certain that I longed to believe her, but both Mark and Noel had said that Cecily saw life as she wanted to see it. I was silent, afraid to hear more.

After a moment she added calmly, "The inquest was held because Evans would give the magistrate no peace. There was a search for the peddler, but of course the man denied any knowledge of the girl. She had probably moved on to someone else by that time, and he wanted no trouble with the law. Morgan nearly killed him, but he wouldn't change his tale. And so the inquest came to no conclusions at all."

"Morgan? But what has he to do with it?" I asked blankly.

"He was engaged to marry the girl—so he said. Frankly, Gwenneth wasn't the sort to marry and settle down, not while she was young and enjoying life. After all, Mark was lord of Rhosllyn, and his passing attentions went to her head. I suspect she was leading Morgan on. Certainly she made his life miserable enough. Even Noel was infatuated with her for a time. The village could talk of nothing else."

I tried to sort out all she was saying in that calmly disinterested voice. We turned in at the gates and waved to Mrs. Jones, clipping the dead blooms from a bed of marguerites. After a deep breath I managed to ask, "Why were there no conclusions at the inquest?"

"Well, they couldn't find Gwenneth—or her body. What other choice had they?"

"And that—that is why Mark isn't received anywhere?"

"Silly, isn't it? But, then, he had always led a wild and turbulent life—my father encouraged that—and because of the other things he had done he wasn't precisely above suspicion in narrow minds. Drinking and gambling and reckless driving scarcely prepare a man for murder, do they?" She

might have been discussing the weather. "Still, when scandal topped the list of his escapades, the line was drawn."

I was glad when we reached the stables that she excused herself from joining me at tea. I wanted desperately to be alone with my thoughts.

Of all the sins Mark might have had upon his conscience, I had not dreamed of murder, and even now I could not bring myself to think the word in connection with him. He was not cold-blooded. As I changed from my riding habit to a yellow silk gown for tea, I tried to recall Cecily's remarks. It was Owen Evans—the smith whose daughter had not come home—who had accused Mark. Had she flaunted her titled lover in her father's face to make him hate Mark so? Or had he truly preferred a daughter dead at her lover's hands to one who had run off with a peddler and soon afterward taken up with someone else?

I understood now. Jessica Tilmer's probing to see how far Mark had confided in me, the drunken accusation of the man in Worcester, the reticence I met with everywhere, even among the staff and tenants. I had been made welcome at Rhosllyn, but never wished happiness in my marriage, for how could I expect to find happiness with a man facing madness and suspected of murder? No wonder Edward Tilmer was so certain I would soon return to Tilmer Hall!

And I knew why Morgan hated Mark. I suddenly remembered his taunt: "An eye for an eye, a tooth for a tooth—a life for a life." Was I to be the way to the groom's vengeance on my husband? A twisted mind might be capable of anything.

Fastening a gold chain at my throat, I stood back to stare at the reflection of the outward me—cool, serene, rather pretty. Inside I was in turmoil. But there was no reason to doubt Mark if a court of inquiry had failed to find him guilty. I had stupidly allowed myself to be upset by Cecily's words. Perhaps she had even meant me to be, just as she had intended me to be humiliated by the snubs in the church; jealousy could drive people to stranger lengths. She had cru-

elly used her opportunity all too well, but I wasn't so easily frightened away. Mark needed me, and Cecily would have to find far more effective weapons than words. Slightly ashamed of myself for being gullible, I went downstairs to wait for him.

Several days later Rhys walked into the small dining room where we sat over luncheon. There was a letter in his hand and a rueful smile on his face.

"Margaret is dying again," he announced calmly, and then added quickly as I exclaimed in concern, "No, no, don't be alarmed. It's a habit of hers. She becomes lonely and depressed and writes to everyone that she is on her deathbed. It has been so for a good many years. I wouldn't be surprised if she outlasted every one of us."

"Shall I go up to Chester?" Mark asked with a sigh.

"I'll go this time," Rhys replied with a grimace. "Penance for the soul. She won't see me—she never will—but I reassure her that the family cares. Her stepsons have shown her every kindness—I don't believe she is as martyred as she thinks."

"I heard that Stephen was in Italy," Mark said. "He is her favorite, and she may simply be lonely without him. I suppose being tied to a bed most of one's life isn't pleasant." There was sympathy in his voice. "Small wonder she indulges in fantasies for attention."

"'Healthy mind, healthy body,'" Rhys quoted. "Yes, there's much to that. And rheumatism *is* damnably painful. I'll leave tomorrow." He turned to me. "Melanie, would you care to visit Chester? I can't promise you excitement, but you might wish to shop while I cool my heels in Margaret's drawing room."

I turned to Mark, but he answered Rhys for me. "No. Melanie would be a stranger to the town and find it lonely and boring," he said, not even asking if I would care to go or not. "Another time."

His curtness left Rhys no choice. He smiled apologetically at me and echoed pleasantly, "Another time, perhaps."

"Yes, thank you," I said. "It was kind of you to ask."

He left soon after and Mark said at once, "I don't trust him to take care of you." He rose from the table. "At best he visits my aunt in the hope of being included in her will. She never liked him."

It was a hateful accusation to make. Distressed, I shifted the subject. "We have had some difficulties with mice again. Have you by any chance seen signs of them in your aunt's room, the one that is locked?"

Mark shook his head. "I haven't been in there in years," he said as he held my chair. "I wouldn't begin to know."

It was on the tip of my tongue to remind him that he had gone in there only recently, but I caught myself in time. If he didn't remember . . .

"It's odd that she would write to Rhys rather than to me," he went on as we crossed the hall. "Or she may wish to make up their quarrel. It was before my time, I haven't an idea what it was about, but it has given her a permanent dislike of him. It's one thing Aunt Margaret and I share."

"Perhaps she didn't care for her father's second marriage. It often happens," I replied absently, my thoughts still on the locked room.

"Very likely. Or her mind may be playing tricks on her and she has forgotten. Illness has a way of twisting reality after a while. One starts to wonder where fact ceases and fiction begins. I know from my own experience." He stopped at the foot of the stairs. "I'll be late this afternoon. Don't wait for me." With a smile, he was gone, leaving me standing there.

Should I have told Mark the truth, I debated, or was it unwise to confront him with his lapses of memory? Yet I had *seen* him enter Aunt Margaret's room, and there was no way of knowing how many other times he had shut himself in there. Perhaps when he returned from Chester I ought to talk to Rhys, if only to find out how to deal with this question.

Noel came to tea that day, and I almost suspected that he knew Mark was not planning to be at home. He cajoled Williams into bringing it out on the terrace, where a cool wind

tempered the day's heat, and we had a gay party as the table
linen threatened to blow away and take the cucumber sand-
wiches with it. I caught a glimpse of Mrs. Powell as she passed
the tall windows, and there was an odd smile on her face, as if
she approved of our laughter. Or thought Mark would not.

I liked Noel. He was much like Mark, though less swept
by moods and yet somehow more intense. Had he indeed
been in love with the bewitching Gwenneth, or merely jealous of Mark's success there as in everything else? I now suspected Noel had been on the point of telling me that story
one evening just as his father interrupted us. It would have
been easier to hear it from him rather than from Cecily.

Thinking of his sister, I asked if she planned to accompany
her father to Chester.

"I doubt it. But, then, you never know."

"If she does, perhaps she would bring me a selection of
silks and patterns. I've thought of recovering that ghastly
tapestry chair in the East bedchamber."

"The one with the odd tree on it?" As I nodded, he said,
"I don't blame you. It gave me nightmares as a child. I
thought the figures were *hanging* from the tree. I wasn't to
know until later that it was a family genealogy going back to
the first baron. Mark's mother embroidered it, you know, between the time his father died and he himself was born. I
often wondered if her husband's loss turned her mind. But
there was talk of her father too. It wasn't a cheerful occupation, I'm damned sure of that. My mother wouldn't toss the
chair into the attics, where it belonged, because of Mark, but
at least she had the sense to put it out of sight."

"I'll bury the cover in a trunk somewhere, then, in case it's
ever wanted," I said quickly, "but something more cheerful
goes on that chair."

He laughed. "Cecily will be relieved."

"She didn't care for it either?"

"I wouldn't know. But she has been predicting that it
wouldn't take you long to begin making changes at Rhosllyn.
Now she'll have the satisfaction of telling us she was right."

"Mark said he wouldn't mind," I began diffidently.

"Who has a better right?" Noel asked with a shrug. "Cecily has made a fetish of preserving everything. I can't think why —improvements never do any harm so far as I can see."

"Perhaps because she lived here as a child—" I suggested.

"Or expected to live here as a woman," he finished. His dark eyes suddenly held mine. "She isn't the only one to feel that it was a mistake for you to marry my cousin! A waste, a damnable waste," he said roughly, abruptly getting to his feet. "You'll take a chill if you stay out here without a wrap of some sort."

He held the door for me and I gave Williams the signal to clear away the tea things. Noel and I were silent as we crossed to the hall. There he took my hand briefly and said goodbye, giving as an excuse the need to help his father prepare for the journey to Chester. But I knew as well as he that it was the scene on the terrace that had driven him away. My heart ached for Noel, because I knew how he felt. I, too, cared for someone who treated me with every courtesy but never with affection.

With a sigh I walked to the morning room to prepare a list of colors for the silks I would need from Chester.

The next week was rather quiet. Rhys had gone to Chester and Mark chose the same time to drive to Hereford to look at another mare. Naturally he could not take me with him, for he was not received socially and I had therefore not been invited to accompany him. But with infinite tact he had merely said, "You'd find it dull, I fear. Shall I take you to London later? You would enjoy that, I think!"

Pleased with his thoughtfulness, I smiled. "Yes, it would be very nice, Mark! Thank you! I should like to go to the theaters and see the sights—and yes, the museums as well." I, too, knew that we would not be attending parties or giving them, but the pleasure of Mark's company would be enough, more than enough for me.

"You should have no problems while I am away. If there's any question about the estate, refer it to Noel. He'll manage. I'll be here before Rhys returns, you may be sure."

It was the second time he had indicated his mistrust of his uncle. And I was nearly certain that he had postponed going to Hereford, even at the risk of losing the mare to another buyer, until Rhys had luckily been summoned to Chester. Why should I not be left alone with Rhys Trecourt? It was Morgan who had tried to harm me! Rhys had shown me every kindness since I had come to Rhosllyn—indeed, treated me with the same affection he showed Cecily. Stranger that I was, he had taken me into the family without hesitation, smoothing over Mark's refusal to have him at the wedding. Then what was the fear that drove Mark into refusing me the visit to Chester and making certain that Rhys did not return to find me here alone?

Chilled, I thought suddenly that Mark must be afraid for himself and not for me, for what Rhys might purposely or inadvertently tell me about my husband that Mark did not want me to hear. Whatever it was that Rhys knew, his son and daughter must not, for Mark had no qualms about my seeing them during his absence.

Gathering my courage, I was on the point of asking him outright for his reasons, but at that moment Williams entered to collect Mark's letters for the post, and I fell silent.

Noel never came to the house while Mark was away, not even to ride with me, and I knew why. It was one thing to come to tea alone, but he did not trust himself continually in my company with Mark absent, he had already been too near confessing his feelings. Besides, there might even have been talk, for Mrs. Powell was watching me closely, I felt sure. Given time, I hoped Noel would come to himself again and we could go on as before.

Cecily visited only once—at her father's instigation, I was certain, for she showed no inclination to linger. Her eyes swept the drawing room as she rose to leave, as if to discover what else besides the chair covering I had seen fit to change. As she straightened an ornament on one of the small tables, I said I hoped Rhys would not find Chester as warm as it was here.

"I don't know why he bothers to go," she said. "He and his sister never got along."

Remembering what Mark had said about his uncle, I made no reply.

Cecily turned to me. "I suppose she thought Mark ought to be clapped up, simply because his grandfather was a lunatic and his mother was . . . peculiar, if not actually mad. That's why she left Rhosllyn and won't ever return. She's frightened to death of him—did you know that?"

I heard an echo of Rhys's voice, and the unfinished sentence, "Whatever my sister Margaret may say—" And he had been referring to Mark's acts of violence. "But Mark sees her in Chester, he told me so!"

"Naturally. Aunt Margaret hates open scandal. But she is always attended by nurses, servants, or her doctor—never alone." She crossed to the door and paused to add, "*You* needn't fear being murdered in your bed!" And with that barbed bit of reassurance she was gone.

I stood where I was, gripped by a chill feeling of horror. Then I sternly reminded myself that Cecily had every reason to frighten me away, that it was foolish to let her words weigh with me at all.

Left to my own devices, I took Deirdre out for a run once or twice and walked in the gardens or park.

Seeking the cool shelter of the trees on the second afternoon, I suddenly became aware of sounds behind me. It was as if someone followed me, moving stealthily just out of my sight. I stopped to look, but no one was there. Yet the sounds followed me again as I began walking once more. And then I felt watched, as if eyes bored into my back.

Uneasy, for I was out of hearing of Rhosllyn and the Dower House, I began to hurry toward the path leading to the Home Farm. Almost as if my unseen companion guessed my thoughts, I heard the steps hasten to cut me off. Turning, I fled back the way I had come, but he was there too, fleet and certain in his movements.

Morgan—it could only be Morgan—and I was alone here

at his mercy. Frightened, I left the paths and ran through the underbrush, heedless of my skirts. But it was as if I had done exactly what he had expected me to do. Behind me I could almost hear his laughter at the ease with which he cornered me, driving me first this way and that among the trees toward—what?

And then the slim trunk of a long-dead chestnut, delicately balanced to lean against its nearest neighbor, slipped and crashed down. I screamed and tried to throw myself aside, but it was too late.

The wood was half-rotten from the spring rains, and as the trunk scraped past a clump of oak saplings, it splintered into three sections. One struck my back and shoulder, knocking me down—a heavy blow that left me breathless and stunned. But I had not been killed. By the sheerest accident the tree had broken up before it reached me and I had not been killed.

For precious seconds I lay helpless and still, sobbing with unspeakable relief. Then with a gasp I remembered, and sat up to face my attacker, wherever he was. He would not find me in a whimpering huddle waiting for him to strike again! But the park was silent. The trees stretched in empty ranks as far as I could see. Without even stopping to discover if I had lived or died, Morgan had vanished. I was completely alone.

With a painful effort I got to my feet, brushing off the chunks of wood and the damp leaves that clung to my hair and gown. My shoulder ached, but nothing was broken. Only a fast-darkening bruise would mark the place where the section of rotting wood had struck. Making myself as presentable as possible, I turned and stumbled toward the house.

Whatever Morgan thought Mark had done, it was cowardly to strike at a man through a defenseless woman. I was angry, though still badly frightened. But I told no one. How could I hope to prove that I had not been alone in the park, panicked by my own nervousness? Or that someone had left that tree trunk ready to fall as I was forced to run between it and

its neighbor? Though I knew the groom roamed the grounds, there was not one shred of evidence linking him to my headlong flight from an unseen pursuer or to that dislodged chestnut. He had been very careful in his plans—as he always was.

In the end I resolved to stay safely indoors until Mark returned. And so Mrs. Powell and I took advantage of the time to give the house a thorough cleaning and airing. Not that it needed either, but she was a perfectionist where her work was concerned. I felt more certain than ever that she strove to make herself indispensable in the running of Rhosllyn as a constant reminder to Mark that he was dependent on the very people he had wronged.

Morgan was her younger brother and the only family she had left, according to Bronwyn. So it was not surprising that she was deeply attached to him and his interests. Would she also close her eyes to his attempts to harm me?

As we went about our work—for I had pinned on an apron and shielded my hair with a kerchief, preferring to stay occupied and miss Mark less—she was deferential but always watchful. We kept the maids exhausted, though they never dared to complain in her presence, and would have sent the dust flying had there been any to send. I brought in the stable cat once more, but he found no mice this time and retired to his more usual hunting grounds.

It was Mrs. Powell who suggested that we clean Aunt Margaret's room while we were about it, but I shook my head.

" 'Tis of little use, as well you know, to clean the whole and leave a part, my lady! A disgrace it is, and Miss Margaret not being one to allow her things to go to wrack and ruin in such a fashion," she pressed.

"I'm sure she isn't. But so long as she has her belongings stored there, I must respect her wishes in the matter."

"I daresay she has forgotten that they are here, much less left to the mice. It has been so many years, and she being old and ill."

"How long?" I asked in spite of myself.

"She left and vowed never to return when his lordship was but a boy. Sickly he was, as you would be knowing, and she had a row with Mr. Rhys about him. I was parlor maid then and frightened silly when they began shouting at each other, forgetting that I was polishing the passage floor just beyond."

"Why did they quarrel?" I asked against my better judgment, for it was wrong to gossip with her. Still, I wanted to know if Cecily was right.

"About his lordship," she said quietly enough, but there was a satisfied smile in her voice, if not on her face. I thought she would say no more, but after a moment she added, "Miss Margaret feared for him, as they all did. Better for Mr. Rhys if his lordship had died, but he wouldn't allow it. Miss Margaret thought his methods wrong, most particularly with his lordship's grandfather and mother—like they were. Mr. Rhys wouldn't hear a word against him."

"And so she left, locking her room as she went," I said briskly, resolutely ignoring the insinuation as I helped to turn the mattress in the East bedchamber.

"Oh, no, my lady, it wasn't locked until Mr. Rhys and his family left Rhosllyn for the Dower House. His lordship locked it himself that very day, and no one has been inside since."

Except Mark, I thought. Except Mark, who denied it. "Well, he has the only key, so I'm afraid we must leave the room as it is," I replied, feigning indifference I was far from feeling. "Have that chair taken downstairs, if you please. I'm going to recover it, I think."

"Yes, my lady," she replied, accepting the snub without demur.

But that evening while the servants were having their meal I walked outside and found the windows that marked Aunt Margaret's bedroom. There were two double windows; French doors had been set in the place of a third to allow the invalid to reach the terrace without mounting steps. From here she might walk in the gardens, leaning on her stick or the elbow of a maid, enjoying the sunlight that brought relief to her

aching joints. After a brief look around to be certain that no one was watching, I came closer and tried to peer inside the room.

But the heavy, lined draperies were tightly closed across the windows and the curtains on the slender doors were impenetrable. I was drawn to that closed, locked room as a moth is drawn to a flame, yet at the same time I was repelled by a dread I could not put into words. For though I realized that whatever answer I found in it would be unbearably painful to me, the desire to know was greater than the fear of knowing.

Was this his sanctuary—or his prison? Did he come here to escape his nightmares or to lock himself away until he was sane again? No, I mustn't let myself dwell on such things. I couldn't bear it!

Suddenly, as I stood there in the twilight, I found myself thinking of Gwenneth. *Had* she been Mark's mistress? Beautiful as she was said to be, wanton as she might have been, Mark's dark attraction had called to her. No matter that she had been promised to Morgan, the groom. No matter that Noel desired her too. It was Mark who had turned her head, Mark, lord of Rhosllyn, down from Oxford and excitingly handsome, trailing the whispers of wildness that had already grown about him. How could Gwenneth resist being swept into loving him?

So much of Mark's past had come to me in bits and pieces—the temper, the threat of madness, the strange relationships that surrounded him. I put out my hand and touched the cool knob of the French doors. If only I could know the whole and stop my wild imagination from building its own version of the truth. If only I could talk to someone, or see through these glass panes and into the secret recesses of his life.

Or was it better to cherish hopes for a future that wasn't there at all? I jerked back my hand as if the knob were red hot. How long before madness swallowed him, left him a raving, frightful thing in place of the man I loved? That was one answer I didn't want to hear. I was afraid for him and of

him, of what lurked in the corners of his mind and at night roamed free in this room, of the dark side of his nature that lashed out in blind fury. But I loved the charming, laughing man who had shared the midnight meal in the kitchen and walked by my side at the fair at Carregfan and sometimes touched my hand in gratitude when I had soothed away his horror.

An owl's cry in the home wood startled me, and I turned guiltily away from the door of the locked room. Inside myself I felt the unshed tears burning my eyes and throat as I hurried away from the terrace and shut out my own racing thoughts.

But the silent, lonely house closed about me and I wished desperately for Mark's return.

THE EVENING HE ARRIVED from Chester, Rhys Trecourt came directly to Rhosllyn to see Mark. We were sitting on the terrace, lingering over our coffee as the last colors of sunset faded from the sky. A peaceful hour, the two of us in companionable silence as the opalescent rose shaded into pearl. I sighed as the sounds of carriage wheels echoed across the quiet and then footsteps approached along the hall toward the garden doors.

Mark rose regretfully and went to meet his uncle as he stepped out into the gloom.

"Good evening, Mark, Melanie," he said, moving with his usual quick grace. "I thought I might find you here. A lovely sunset, wasn't it? I had a spectacular view from the carriage. But Jones at the lodge vows there'll be rain before morning." He took the chair opposite to mine and refused the offer of coffee. "For I must be off to the Dower House. Cecily will have my dinner on the table."

"How were matters in Chester?" Mark asked.

Rhys frowned. "Not very well, I'm sorry to say. Margaret is indeed fading. The doctor says that her illness has been a strain on her heart. You remember old Cromie? Well, this is his son, and a good man. And you were right, Stephen is in Italy, and she thinks she won't last until his return. Of course he might brighten her considerably, but I would wager this

is more than one of her flights of self-pity."

"You saw her?" Mark asked in surprise.

"Yes, I did. She wanted to speak to me about family affairs and so on." His eyes flickered toward me and back to Mark. "Her mind is fading as well. Age, illness, isolation—it isn't surprising she has a few . . . quirks. Nothing serious, I'm certain of that!" There was false heartiness in his tone for my benefit.

"What does she say?" Mark asked.

"Well, I'm not going to distress Melanie with the sad details. She merely wanders in the past, reliving old quarrels and—other events. But her mind was clear enough for her to decide she wants to be buried with her husband rather than with the Trecourts," he replied.

"That isn't new," Mark said shortly. "Stephen told me it was all arranged."

Rhys lifted a hand in a deprecating gesture. "I haven't been in her confidence, of course. I found her little changed, actually, except for this heart condition, and I daresay her memory problems are a part of it. Young Cromie tells me she doesn't take enough exercise to keep her circulation in good order. Otherwise—thin, pale, and ramrod-straight as she has always been. And," he added ruefully, "as sharp-tongued."

"So Cromie agrees that this time it is serious?"

"No, no. Just that her heart is not what it used to be, which makes a difference. I told her about Melanie, and she was quite pleased. In fact, you are to bring her along the next time you go to Chester." He turned to me. "In my traps I have your silks and a pattern you should find to your liking. The young lady in the shop assures me that it is the latest rage in Paris." With an attractive smile he added, "I can't imagine how she would know! Still, it's a floral design, and I know you like flowers."

"How nice! Thank you for running my errand. I hope it didn't take time from your duties," I added, knowing full well that Rhys would have made a special effort on my behalf. "I look forward to seeing it."

"No trouble at all, my dear! I simply relied on the advice of the young lady in charge. If you don't like it, tell me so honestly!" He rose. "Cecily will be wondering what has kept me. But I knew you would wish to hear about Margaret."

"Yes, thank you for coming at once. I'll go to Chester myself as soon as possible."

"As you like. But Cromie promised to keep us informed, so there's no hurry at the moment, I should think." With a wave, he left by way of the gardens, and the darkness swallowed him.

Mark rose. "I'll write to Stephen tonight. Shall we go inside? You haven't a wrap. And we might stop in Chester on our way to London," he added, holding the door for me.

"I'd like that," I said, smiling up at him as I passed.

As I walked across the park one morning I could hear the dogs barking wildly from the direction of the pond. Idle curiosity led me along the left fork to see what had disturbed them, and I soon began to pick up other sounds.

Coming into the open, I saw at the water's edge a great gray gander, wings spread stiffly and neck lowered in an angry arch, holding three excited hounds at bay. The dogs, favorites of Rhys Trecourt, were making a frantic effort to reach the gander, first one and then the other darting across the gentle slope of grass to snap at a wing or a foot, then dodging back out of reach of the savage thrust of a beak.

I thought at first he might be defending his family, but the pond at his back was empty, as were the surrounding beds of water iris. He was alone, refusing to take to the water and flee, determined to stand off the intruders in what he considered his domain.

He was tiring, yet his gallant defense had taught the dogs a wary respect, and they were growing more cautious in their attacks. I didn't care for the odds of three to one, my sporting instincts quickly siding with the gander. Walking briskly toward the noisy quartet, I called to the dogs.

They were too intent on their quarry to heed me, and I

had to catch at their collars and shake them before dragging them back. One liver-colored hound, a young male, growled at me, and I hesitated only a fraction of a second before jerking him around and flinging him into the shallows to cool his temper. The hissing goose, ungrateful, bore down on me as his earlier antagonists held their distance, still barking desultorily. The sport had gone out of the affair, but their pride demanded a last effort.

His beak struck at my skirts as I whirled and stepped quickly out of reach. "Here!" I cried angrily. "Don't you recognize a friend?"

He settled back and watched me coldly from red-rimmed eyes.

"Go home!" I called sharply to the dogs, and as they turned to trot away, tongues lolling, I added to the goose, "And you too!" For he was a newcomer to the pond and had no business to remain.

He ruffled his heavy wings, settling them in place again in a smooth gray line, then answered with an impertinent honk.

"Well, you may defend yourself in future." I turned on my heel and walked away, angling back to the house by way of the lodge at the gates. Mrs. Jones, the gatekeeper's wife, kept fowl in a run out of sight of the drive, and I thought perhaps the gander might have escaped from there.

But she shook her head firmly as I told her about the incident. "Not mine, my lady, no, not that wild thing! Nobody owns him, so far as I do know, excepting maybe the rector. He was one of old Janie's goslings two years ago, and got himself lost one stormy day. Grew up wild, he did, and not quite right in the head either. I'm surprised the dogs set on him—most everything and everybody leaves him be. Tough as saddle leather, anyway, I'd swear!" She shook out the shirt in her hands and pinned it to the wash line. It was as close to turning her back as a tenant's wife dared to come.

Refusing to be daunted, I said, "How is Tommy today?" A cheerful lad of seven, he was recovering from the measles. I had missed him whenever I rode up the drive.

"Much better, my lady. He was hungry for his breakfast, and that's a good sign in a growing boy."

"Indeed it is. I must be on my way. Send to the house if there is anything special he might fancy to tempt his appetite —fruit or whatever."

With a clumsy curtsy as I turned to go, she said neutrally, "Thank you, my lady. I'll remember that." But I knew she would never accept such a favor from me. From Cecily, perhaps, but not from the Devil Baron's wife.

The gander was standing in the drive as I walked up the last curve, blocking the way and weaving his head about in a half-threatening gesture.

"Oh, stop that!" I said shortly. "You are as foolish as you look. Behave yourself and mind your own affairs."

He sidestepped awkwardly, and I saw that there was blood on the smooth gray feathers of his left wing. One of the dogs had been more successful than I thought.

To my surprise the gander stood still as I came slowly toward him and warily allowed me to examine his wing. There was a long gash just above the shoulder joint, bleeding freely now but not dangerously so. "Poor old fellow," I said soothingly as I worked, half an eye on the beak so close to my face. "Gently, now!" The cut needed attention before the gander was weakened by it or other dogs were attracted to the scent.

Moving carefully, I got to my feet. "Come along, we'll do what we can for you."

He hesitated, then followed me at a safe distance. The grooms stared at the strange sight as I came into the stable yard with the huge gander trailing behind me. Although Morgan was by the tackroom door, I called to one of the undergrooms to bring water and bandages and the pot of special ointment used for the horses.

The gander would allow no one else near him, hissing angrily at the curious stable lads who gathered around. But he stood still as I knelt on the cobblestones and spread a thick smear of the yellow ointment across the wound. He wanted no part of the bandages, however, and I abandoned the at-

tempt at once, using them instead to sponge away the blood on his feathers. While I worked he shifted restlessly under my hands, and when I stood back at last, turned away immediately and waddled off down the drive.

Morgan had watched the proceedings in silence. As I turned to hand someone the pot and basin, he said, "You have a way with the wild things, there's no gainsaying it." There was a measuring expression in his eyes.

"Perhaps it is a sense of compassion," I replied briskly, not wishing to stand talking to him.

"Aye," he added softly as I walked on toward the house. "And the devil's own luck." I made no sign of having heard, but he knew that I had.

Thereafter when the gander saw me walking alone about the grounds he followed me at a short distance, never inviting friendship but in his own way acknowledging the debt between us. I found it amusing and at the same time touching. Mark teased me about him, and the old gardener, Bryn, built a small shelter for him by the pond's edge. I sometimes carried dried bread crumbs down to him, which he ate rather disdainfully. The gash on his wing healed, but he continued to greet me when we met, and took up residence at Rhosllyn with the air of a victor possessing conquered territory. Which, in a sense, was his right.

When Noel returned from a brief visit with friends in Shrewsbury I was sorting through embroidery silks in the morning room. He walked in, greeted me, and laid a small parcel on my work table. Surprised, I glanced up at him, but he said only, "I brought music for Cecily, and felt you might enjoy this more."

Inside the silver tissue and blue ribbon I found a beautifully bound two-volume edition of *Poems* by Mr. Tennyson. It was a perfectly acceptable gift.

"Noel—how very thoughtful! Thank you," I said with a smile, and opened the gilt-edged pages to look over the titles.

"My pleasure," he said, smiling in return.

The door of the morning room crashed open and Mark, in a towering rage, stood on the threshold.

"What the hell are you doing here?" he demanded.

Noel had wheeled toward the door, his face tight with shock and an answering anger. "What do you mean by that?" he retorted.

Suddenly frightened by the tension between them, I stepped forward, but Noel thrust out his arm to hold me back.

"I rode in to find John Harrison waiting to take the three-year-old he bought, and the horse is still out in the north pasture. And you are dawdling here. I thought you were attending to that sale."

"So I was. But I can't read your mind. How else am I supposed to know when the man is coming?"

"I told you a week ago, before you left for Shrewsbury—"

"You told me nothing," Noel interrupted. "Not one word."

Mark stared at him. "Have you run mad? I even sent over the damned letter!"

"You may think you did, but I never saw it. It is *you* who have run mad—"

"Stop it!" I forced my way past Noel and stood between them. "Noel, Mr. Harrison is still waiting. Mark, he simply called to leave a book for me."

"So I was told when I went to the Dower House," Mark snapped as his cousin stalked past him. The two tall men stared at each other for a long, taut moment, and then Noel was gone.

I could have shaken Cecily for making such mischief. She had expected to cause trouble for me and instead had nearly succeeded in bringing her brother and her cousin to blows.

"He brought Mr. Tennyson's latest book," I said, trying to soothe Mark. "May I keep it?"

"Of course you may," he said frowning, and then brushed a hand across his eyes. "I could have sworn— My God, I wish I could *remember*—"

I closed the door and then touched his arm, feeling the tension in the hard muscles beneath my hand. "Mark—"

He jerked away. "No, I'm all right. I'm sorry to come crashing in here. I was furious, and—" He stopped, then smiled suddenly, ruefully. "Perhaps we both need a change. Rhys can cope without me—the tenants will be just as glad. London it is, then, and the sooner the better."

Mark and I began to plan the journey to London, and I neglected the embroidery for the new chair covering in compiling lists of places to see and purchases to make. It was intoxicating to dream of a fortnight spent in Mark's company and forget, for a space, all that Rhosllyn had come to stand for in my mind.

Was Morgan right, that I had a way with wild creatures? And could I still find a way with Mark, as wild as they in his own way? I held that hope before me like a guiding lamp as I made preparations for the journey, for it eased the ache in my heart and the jealousy that gnawed at me whenever I thought of the Welsh girl I had never known.

But fate stepped in and took a hand in my dreams. Aunt Margaret, who seemingly had recovered at the news that her beloved Stephen was on his way back to England, died suddenly in Chester, even as the doctor sent for Mark. She had asked repeatedly for him at the end.

"I'm sorry," he said, taking my hand as he told me the news. "It was bound to come, but I hadn't expected it to be now. We'll go to London in the autumn, I promise you. This is merely a postponement, no more."

I smiled, hiding the chill feeling that we would not be going to London at all. "Of course I don't mind—how could I? Yes, I'd like to go in the autumn, it will be much pleasanter then. For now, you must attend to your aunt's affairs and do all that is necessary for her. Shall I go with you?"

He shook his head. "Rhys, Noel, and I will represent the Trecourts."

I felt better that Cecily would not be going either. "Then I shall see to your packing. How long do you expect to be away?"

"For a week, no more. There's the funeral and the reading of the will, possibly immediate household matters to settle as well." He stopped to wind the library clock. "I wish I knew what she had wanted to say to me."

"Should you take any of the things she has stored here at Rhosllyn?" I asked in spite of myself. "Perhaps she intended for Stephen to have them, and tried to tell you?"

"Here?" he asked blankly, turning to face me where I sat with my sewing strewn about me.

"Yes—in the room your grandfather prepared for her. You said she had stored a few of her possessions in there."

"Did I? I daresay they belong to the Trecourts now, since they were from our family originally." He finished winding the clock and put away the key. "If the mare from Hereford arrives in my absence, see that she is stabled here and not at the home farm. I want to try her paces again, and, frankly, I believe we have another winner."

"I'm looking forward to seeing her," I replied, trying to ignore his change of subject. I was more certain than ever that it was something else and not his aunt's possessions that made the locked room sacrosanct.

He went on with his instructions, and I listened carefully, ready to serve in any way. But another part of my mind taunted me with questions even as he spoke.

At their departure the next morning I stood beside the carriage talking with Rhys and Noel while Mark saw to the bestowal of their luggage. He was quite handsome in his mourning black, and I watched the glint of sunlight on his dark head as he bent to check the straps. Noel stirred restlessly at my side, impatient to be off, but his father was as thoughtful as ever.

"Are you certain there are no further colors you wish, my dear?" he asked. "Though our errand is a sad one, there will be time and to spare to visit the shop again. The Rows are not so far from Margaret's town house."

"I have everything I need," I said, "but it is kind of you to ask."

"Not kind, Melanie, just happy to be of service," he said with a smile. "I say, Mark, we'll be late if we don't start."

"We'll be even later if this strap should break," Mark replied tersely. He finished at last and came around to us. Noel had already made his farewell and taken his seat inside, and Rhys followed. Mark paused to take my hand and say gently, "We'll be home as soon as possible."

I smiled up into his eyes. "I shall manage very well," I replied lightly, though, indeed, I was already worrying about what Morgan would try next. "Take care—and have a good journey, all of you."

With an answering smile he was gone, and the carriage rolled down the drive into the trees and out of sight. With a sigh I turned to go inside, feeling my loneliness already.

The first two days I wandered about the gardens or rode for a short distance accompanied by one of the undergrooms. I was very careful never to venture into the park or anywhere else that Morgan—or his clever snares—might be waiting for me. With all three of the Trecourt men away, the groom had all the freedom he could wish for in dealing with me. I had even asked Mark to take Morgan with him to Chester, but the expected arrival of the mare made that impossible, and I could not insist without explaining *why* I did not want to be left alone with him. And so I took what precautions I could.

Cecily came to dinner but was as poor company as I was myself, so she left shortly after the coffee tray had been removed. Because it was a lovely night and I was restless, I walked with her to the door and stepped out onto the dew-wet lawn.

She stood for a moment looking up at Rhosllyn, longing in her shadowed blue eyes. And then she said, almost to herself, "I wonder if Mark still loves Gwenneth."

"I thought—" I began, and paused to still the tremor in my voice. "I thought you said it was only infatuation."

"So it was at the time. Afterward, after she had gone away, he couldn't put her out of his mind as I thought he would. Morgan is haunted by her, and Noel—I've heard Noel call out her name in his sleep."

"Why should a village blacksmith's daughter bewitch three men long after she has run away with another?" I asked scornfully, refusing this time to let her low voice cast its wicked spell.

Cecily shrugged. "How should I know? But Gwenneth left her mark on them as surely as a brand. Perhaps because *she* tired of them first. Well, good night." She walked away down the drive, leaving me prey to despair.

Was it true, or only Cecily's way of tormenting me? Lifting my silk skirts out of the dew, I moved farther out into the lawn until I could see the wing where Aunt Margaret's room stared with dark windows out into the night.

Was this where they met? Had Mark locked this room when the house was his to order as he pleased because his memories were too much to bear? And did he come here in the loneliness of the night, wishing for the past to be restored to him, for Gwenneth to come home again? Were his nightmares only the terrible longings for lost love that gave him no peace?

Mark had tired of Gwenneth, and she had run away rather than stay to marry the Rhosllyn groom. Afterward—too late —Mark might have realized how much he cared for Gwenneth. How bitter it must have been to find himself accused of murdering her!

What had he said to me about that strange proposal of marriage at Tilmer Hall after I had in desperation told him of my life there? "An answer—for both of us." Had he rescued me to pay for an unpayable debt, as he hoped someone, somewhere, had been kind enough to do for Gwenneth after her rash flight?

A faint crunch, like a step, on the gravel of the drive brought me out of my thoughts. Whirling, I fled headlong for the open front door before Morgan could find me wandering alone and unprotected.

I often fed the gander by the pond, talking to him to ease my own emptiness, and finally, on the afternoon of the third day, found myself standing in Mark's impersonal room trying to find something of him there. His brushes were gone

from the dressing table, leaving even the space they had occupied barren. For a time I tarried by the window and looked down to the edge of the grass and the flower beds beyond. Wales stood out clearly in the distance, the hills a sharp blue in the afternoon sun, and I thought of Mark as a boy staring out even as I now did. What had he been thinking as he parted the curtains and leaned his palms on the sill? Happy thoughts or sad ones? Thoughts of Gwenneth as he grew older, perhaps, stirrings of desire and then of surfeit. And now of heartache. No, I refused to believe that Mark's love was hers forever. He would soon cease to grieve for the smith's daughter and find me, patiently waiting.

I let the draperies fall into place and turned to go. But on the bedside table something caught my eye and I stopped to see what was there.

It was a ring of keys, Mark's keys, and he had left them behind. For an instant I toyed with the idea of sending them to Chester by one of the grooms, then realized that he would not need them there. Somehow they had fallen between a book and the nightstick, nearly out of sight. I set them back into place, then decided to keep them for him. The maids were trustworthy, so far as I knew, but the key to the strongbox, to his desk, and to other personal possessions were on this ring. It might be as well to remove temptation from anyone's path.

But the temptation became mine. The keys seemed to burn a hole in my pocket, reminding me with every musical clink that I could now satisfy my curiosity about that locked room.

Mark trusted me, and rightly so. I could not behind his back do something that I knew he would not permit. My own conscience would have to live with my deceit even if Mark never found me out!

For another two days I struggled with myself, fought the gathering urge to take *one* look into that room, to satisfy once and for all my unhealthy desire to know what it represented in Mark's eyes. *Was* it his sanctuary from his night-

mares—or the place where he had waited for Gwenneth? And even if I unlocked that forbidden door, what could the musty room tell me after so long a time?

It was an unfair battle, unfair from the beginning. Where Mark was concerned, I knew no honor. I loved him, wished to see him the happy, untainted man he could be. If there was a possibility of freeing him from his obsession, I would accept any risk. And to free myself from Gwenneth's spell was nearly as great a need.

While the servants were at tea on Friday and I knew myself safe from observation, I took the keys and slipped down the stairs to the passage leading to Aunt Margaret's room. With the stealth of a housebreaker I made my way to the door, and fumbling with nervousness, inserted keys into the lock until I found one that fitted.

For an instant I paused, almost afraid of the answers I was so desperate to find. And then with a deep breath I turned the key and swung wide the door.

I don't know what I had expected. I sometimes think, looking back on that day, that I would not have been shocked to find Gwenneth herself seated there in the darkness, either alive and mocking or skeletal and accusing. Living or dead, she was no less terrifying to me.

Instead, I found a room.

Pale light, barely filtering through the draperies, marked the windows. The rest was in darkness, a musty darkness that spoke of long airlessness and disuse. It was simply furnished —a large bed with hangings drawn back, their blue nearly white now with dust, a nightstand and bureau, a wardrobe against a far wall, chairs by the hearth, and a table beneath one of the windows. And no body. Nor even a living woman, imprisoned here by choice or force.

Letting go the breath I had held in fear, I stepped across the threshold and into the room, shutting the door carefully behind me. My eyes adjusted to the darkness rapidly, and after a moment I walked across to the French doors and unbarred them to let in the sunlight.

An empty room.

So far as I could tell, Mark's aunt had not stored anything here, unless it fitted into the drawers or the wardrobe. There were no cases, no chests or trunks, save for a blanket box in cedar at the foot of the bed, half-hidden in the shadows of the hangings.

With some trepidation I lifted the lid of the blanket box, but there were two folded, moth-gnawed blankets in the bottom, nothing more. Crossing to the wardrobe, I found only a few articles of clothing—a pair of worn shoes that belonged to an older, not a younger woman, and unimportant odds and ends of the sort that one leaves behind when one travels between several homes.

There was no carpet on the floor, but with her rheumatism, Mark's aunt would have preferred bare boards to the possibility of tripping.

Above all, the room had the untouched, dusty look of a place seldom used and long uncleaned. There was no indication of careful preservation, as of a shrine of love. Nor any sign that this was his prison.

For a time I stood perplexed, staring about me. What brought Mark here, then? Why, in the torment of his nightmares, did he seek some sort of solace in this room? Surely, if it had meant so much to him at one time, he would have made an effort to keep it cleaned, if not by Mrs. Powell's hand, then most assuredly by his own! He could find no peace in this dusty, long-deserted chamber, no memory of love won and then tossed aside too soon.

Why, then, did he come in here and yet afterward deny it, saying that he hadn't entered in years? What did he see here that I did not, try as I would?

A sound at the passage door startled me. Whirling about, I found Mrs. Powell standing there in the opened door, staring about her in avid curiosity.

"What are you doing here?" I demanded angrily, shamed by my own actions as much as by hers.

"The door was ajar—" she began.

"The door was closed. I left it so," I replied coldly.

"No, my lady, the outer door. Morgan saw it open and came to me in the servants' hall," she said primly.

I wheeled in fright to see if the groom had dared to enter from the terrace, cornering me here, but there was no one in the sunlit opening. My heartbeat slowed again.

"It is in need of a cleaning and an airing," she said, still looking about as if to miss nothing that might be seen. Or had she also suspected a connection between this room and Gwenneth Evans? Had Morgan, lurking in the shadows of the drive, followed the girl he loved to a meeting here with his master? Watched her slip soundlessly across the moonlit lawns and tap lightly at the terrace doors, where Mark waited for her?

Struggling to throw off my morbid thoughts, I said sharply, "I have come to see if Mark's aunt left anything here that ought to be sent on to Chester." It was a feeble lie and we both recognized it as such. Only Mark could know what disposition should be made of his aunt's belongings.

"Yes, my lady, and is there anything you wish me to pack?"

"No. Nothing."

"Shall I set the maids to cleaning up, then?"

"No. The room is to be left as it is until my husband decides to open it," I replied, defending Mark's privacy as best I could.

She had not come into the room, but I could feel her invading presence in every corner, and I was angry with myself as well as with the housekeeper. Whatever justification I had found for my actions, I had betrayed Mark by coming here, betrayed him by allowing other eyes to inspect his innermost feelings and fears—for the locked door sealed off part of Mark as surely as if he had been inside. It was wrong of me to have allowed my curiosity to probe where he had forbidden me to enter, whether into this room or into his soul. That he had accidentally left his keys in my keeping made the intrusion all the worse. It was wrong, and the guilt was mine alone, but in my shame I was ready to lash out at Mrs. Powell.

She stood staring at me, clearly disappointed that the room

had nothing to offer her in the way of information or sensation, hoping to read in my face what she had not found in the bare walls. Determined not to satisfy her curiosity any further, I said curtly, "You may go. And you might remind the groom in future that his place is in the stables, not on the terrace lawns. See that he remembers."

Her lids dropped over her eyes in a gesture of mute humility, but I had seen the blaze of resentment at my order. Without a word she turned on her heel and ran straight into Mark, white-faced and angry, behind her. Neither of us had seen him come or heard the sound of the carriage on the drive. But he had found us here, unarguably and unforgivably trespassing.

With a cry of alarm she scuttled past him into the passage, and left me face-to-face with him, torn by my guilt and the anguish in his eyes.

And then he stepped across the threshold and gently shut the door behind him, turning the key as he did so.

I WAS BADLY FRIGHTENED. His deliberate locking of the door had left me speechless, half-sentences whirling through my head but finding no access to my tongue. Without haste Mark walked across the width of the room and closed the terrace doors, shutting us into the musty darkness and silence.

Finding my voice at last, I faced him resolutely and said, "I have done a terrible thing. I can apologize for it, but not undo it." Swallowing to ease the dryness in my throat, I added, "Your keys were left here, and the temptation was more than I could bear."

He looked down at the ring in his hand as if seeing it for the first time. "Why did you bring Mrs. Powell in here?"

"I didn't. Morgan saw the terrace doors open and told her. She came to investigate. I can't say why he was on the lawns. I thought they were at their tea—the servants."

Mark nodded and moved to the hearth to light a candle in the holder there. The dancing flame threw grotesque shadows about the room, and I clutched the back of a chair to steady myself, for the ordinary furnishings and the great bedstead took on an ominous appearance in the dimness.

"It had to come sooner or later," he said bleakly. "I accepted that. Yet I had hoped that I could spare you—for my sake as well as yours." His gray eyes held mine, pale lights in his dark face.

"Mark, please—" I whispered, but he seemed not to hear.

"How much do you know? How much have they told you?"

I shook my head, unable to answer him, scarcely understanding what he had asked, except to realize that my trespass was graver than I had dreamed. Desperately I wished myself outside this room, away from the evil here that rose like dust motes from the floor. I wished myself innocent of offense, innocent of knowledge I shouldn't possess, innocent of wrongdoing and curiosity satisfied.

"Shall I tell you what happened?" Mark was saying. "Shall I tell you the whole of it, or have you heard enough from others to guess?" His voice was tired, as if he were at the end of a long race.

We stood facing each other across the empty hearth, silence and the past stretching between us like some vast river without bridges.

Did I *want* to know anything? I couldn't be certain of my own feelings now, torn between the torment of wondering and the horror of hearing the truth. And then I remembered that I had precipitated this scene with my inquisitive poking into his affairs. Now I owed it to Mark to listen to him, whether I cared to do so or not.

"Tell me," I said at last. "Please tell me."

He smiled a little, an unhappy smile, and gestured to the chair before me. "You have always shown spirit, Melanie. It is a trait I have respected in you." Weak, I sat down.

Pacing the floor, slowly at first and then with increasing agitation as his story unfolded, Mark began to talk. His deep voice filled the room, peopling it with faces and events long past, vividly recreated before my eyes as if resurrected from the shadows and dust.

"I don't know where it began. I suppose I resented the constant pressures on me to try harder and harder. When I was sent away from Rhosllyn to school I finally began to grow stronger, as Rhys had predicted I would, and out of spite strove toward excelling beyond my uncle's wildest

dreams. If he would have me ride, I would become the most bruising rider in the field. If he would have me drive a carriage, I would drive it within an inch of disaster. If he would have me learn to hold my own at any man's game, I would beat him at it. I can drink anyone I know under the table, stake any sum on any wager and win, ride anything with four legs, handle any team— It isn't boasting to say this, Melanie, it is quite true. I can fence, I am an excellent shot and superb swimmer— Whatever Rhys urged me to try, I didn't stop until I had risen to the top. I must have frightened poor Aunt Letitia out of her wits, worried her incessantly, and I was sorry for it, but a demon drove me where Rhys was concerned, and I knew no peace."

He stopped before me. "Ironic, isn't it? His only purpose was to restore my health, and my sole aim was to confound him if I could. And so today I have Rhys to thank for what I am—and damnably galling it is to live with that fact."

"Surely it is normal to resent others deciding what is best for one."

"I wonder." He was off again, striding across the bare floor as if to outdistance himself. "I was equally good at my studies, surprisingly enough, and when I came down from Oxford I suppose I was puffed up in my own conceit—lord of Rhosllyn, successful at anything to which I set myself, already courted by eager mothers with marriageable daughters, only months from my twenty-first birthday. The world was mine, and I was determined to have it." He paused for the briefest moment.

"And then, for the first time since I could remember, I met with defeat. Utter, bewildering defeat," Mark said heavily.

"Gwenneth," I breathed, divining the direction of his thoughts.

"Gwenneth," Mark agreed. "Can I make you see her, Melanie? The blacksmith's daughter, fair beyond words to tell, dark hair that unbound would tumble down her back like a cascade of black water, eyes of sea green on a sum-

mer's day, with depths that glinted gold when she laughed, a fringe of dark lashes that hid her thoughts or dared the devil himself. A face and form that stunned a man, and a wildness that taunted him. Small wonder that when I came home I fell head over heels in love with Gwenneth."

His words tore at my heart, for I knew that I could not compete with such a memory. Even Gwenneth's ghost was more fair than I. Across my mind's eye I saw the Welsh girl at the fair in the village of Carregfan, where Mark had bought the peddler's trinket for me. She had the same heritage of beauty and spirit, yet possessed virtue, whereas the blacksmith's daughter was wanton. Such a girl had been Mark's first love—and his last.

"Noel was home that spring as well, and we fought over her time and again. I always won, and Noel hated me for that. And yet Gwenneth would lead the three of us—Noel, Morgan and I—a merry dance, smiling on first one and then another, with neither rhyme nor reason to her choice. The village could talk of nothing else. I was nearly demented, I tell you, elated one moment and in the depths of despair the next! For all I know, half the county shared her favors, yet she had a way of making each man seem special and set apart. And then," he said roughly, "and then I discovered, by the merest chance, that she had a *lover*."

He passed a hand over his eyes as if to brush away the memory. "Twice I found her slipping to a rendezvous—once through the park and once by the rose gardens. I knew well enough that she had not come to meet me—it had to be Morgan or Noel—yet she cajoled me into believing what I wanted to believe. But not the third time."

I could feel the cold gripping my heart now as I sat mesmerized by his words. A man such as Mark would not take betrayal easily, would not suffer the humiliation to his pride without striking out in mad fury.

"It was here that I found her," he said softly, a hand moving in a vague gesture toward the massive bed. "I had taken to walking the grounds at night, hoping to surprise her

with her lover, confronting them both once and for all. As I tramped the dark lawns I saw a sliver of light at the French doors there. No one used Aunt Margaret's room, no one had for years. But it was always kept in readiness for her coming and never locked in those days. I crept to the terrace and tried to look in, but the draperies were drawn to a mere slit. Still, that knife's edge of light told me enough. It was *here* that Gwenneth met her lover, and that was why I had never caught them on the grounds anywhere, try as I would. She must have had a key to the terrace doors, coming late after the family and the servants had gone upstairs to bed. And that meant Noel, though I wouldn't have put it beyond Morgan to steal the key and flaunt his victory here under my very roof. Somehow I kept my temper under control and gently tried the latch, but it had been locked behind her. So I raced inside through the front door and came quietly down the passage to this room."

I couldn't have stopped the flow of words now if I had tried. Mark had forgotten me as he poured out the painful story that had haunted him for so many years, eating into his mind and soul. I would have liked to cover my ears and shut out his voice, but that was not possible either. All I could do was sit like a carved statue in my chair, every sense and nerve ending in my body concentrated on the man before me.

"I listened at the door, and she was humming softly to herself, an old Welsh song that was a favorite of hers. I recognized it at once. For a time I waited, hoping Noel would soon come, but my patience ran out and I couldn't bear it any longer. I opened the door and walked in.

"She looked up from the bed with a smile of welcome that faded almost at once. But she didn't move from where she was, half-reclining on one elbow, her dark hair in clouds about her face, firelight and one branch of candles brightening the room and her green eyes. I don't remember all I said—I know I demanded the name of her lover, and when she wouldn't answer, shouted angrily that it was Noel and

that I should kill him when he came." His voice was husky now, his face drawn with fatigue and strain. "She told me to stop playing at dog in the manger, that she would choose for herself any man who caught her fancy. I told her I loved her and would marry her tomorrow, but she laughed in my face. To prove it, I flung down on the bed a jewel box with an emerald ring in it. I had bought it for her in Shrewsbury that afternoon and carried it in hope of a meeting with her. She picked it up, opened it, and slipped the ring on her finger. And then she tilted her head and said airily, ' 'Tis kind of you, my lord, but I don't care for loving words one minute and bad temper the next.' Then she admitted that she had found someone more to her taste than the whole of Rhosllyn, a man with Welsh blood in his veins to match her own fire. I suppose she was taunting me in the hope that I would leave before Noel came, but I was beside myself and beyond all reason. I can hear her voice even now, low and musical and tormentingly exciting. Once more I demanded a name, but she laughed and tossed her head and refused to answer.

"I was out of my mind with fury and jealousy. I caught her shoulders and began to shake her violently—whether to get at the truth or stop her laughter, I don't know to this day. And then she laughed again, low in her throat, and her face went red and black before my eyes, and I can't remember anything after that." He stumbled to the chair across from mine and sat down, his eyes closed and his mouth in a grim line of anguish.

"Mark," I said, frantically shutting out the sight of Gwenneth struggling with him on the rumpled blue coverlet, "Mark, don't—"

But he couldn't hear me at all. "When I came to my senses again we were sprawled here on the floor, before the hearth. Gwenneth was beneath me, my hands about her throat. It wasn't until I had spoken twice to her that I realized she was dead." He swung to his feet again, pacing the room like a trapped animal. "She had put up a struggle of sorts. A chair

was overturned, the bedclothes dragged across the floor, and the wood rack scattered all over the hearth. We must have fallen there, for later I found a cut on the side of my head. But it was too late for Gwenneth. In a fit of madness I had killed her, and I wasn't even aware—" He broke off, and then, after a silence, went on in a tortured voice, "Do you know my first thought when I realized that I was her murderer?"

I shook my head numbly. Nothing could touch me now.

With his hands gripping the chair before me until the knuckles gleamed white in the candlelight, he leaned forward and said in anguish, "My first thought was that when I died on the scaffold, Rhys would inherit Rhosllyn. Not a flicker of concern for the girl lying there dead, and by my hand. Nor for her family or mine. Not even a thought for my immortal soul, *merely the fact that my uncle would step into my shoes!*"

"You were still in shock—it doesn't mean anything! At such a time you weren't responsible—"

He shook his head angrily. "Don't find excuses for me, Melanie. God knows, I've done that well enough on my own! It was a madman's cold-blooded, selfish desire to thwart my uncle, and I must accept the truth of that. Damn it, whatever I manage to hide from others, I will not lie to myself!" He lifted a hand toward me as if in supplication and then dropped it quickly to his side. "You are married to a murderer, a madman and a murderer. I thought you might never know, that I might somehow make amends for what I had done by giving you a new life and making you happy. I believed that through you I might find myself again, and one day, when my uncle was dead, go to the authorities of my own free will and admit to my crime. Or use a pistol on myself to spare Noel and Cecily the further shame of my hanging. I owe them that much."

"Oh, Mark—" The tears welled in my throat and shut off the words. I didn't dare allow my thoughts to dwell on his confession. Not yet. Struggling for control, I sought for

something, anything, to postpone the full horror a little longer. "How—how did you manage to cover up your crime?" I asked at last.

"Somehow—I was still groggy from angry passion and my fall amongst the logs—I got to my feet and made doubly certain that Gwenneth was dead. And then I set the room in order, forced myself to straighten the bedclothes, wrapped her body in a blanket from that box, and took her outside. I was desperately afraid that Noel would arrive before I had finished, but when at last I closed the French doors, there was no sign that Gwenneth had kept her assignation or that I had found her there. What had seemed like a lifetime to me since I had first opened the door and walked into this room must have been less than half an hour." He shook his dark head. "I didn't know what to do with her, only that I must cover my guilt in some way. I suppose the devil looks after his own, though, for I suddenly remembered my aunt's rock garden. She had been planting a collection of wild flowers, varieties sent to her from Switzerland by friends traveling there. In the center was a great rock, a monolithic slab of granite that local superstition claimed was a villager who was caught out watching Merlin build the original house at Rhosllyn and turned into stone. There are a number of prehistoric remains along the Marches here, and this was one of them. My Aunt Letitia liked its shape and color and had planned her garden around it purposely, but I knew no one else would dare go near it."

The Alpine garden, from which I had blithely picked flowers to set upon Mark's desk in the library. Small wonder he had lashed out at me when he recognized them! A reminder of his guilt that sent him out into the night to ride the wild stallion at breakneck speed.

"God knows how I managed. Somehow I excavated a pit of sorts, finding superhuman strength from fear and panic, and buried the body beneath the stone. There were only a few plants on one side—the rest were still in the potting shed—and I was infinitely careful not to disarrange them.

The soil I raked out smoothly again, frantically working against the lightening sky and the risk of being seen by the servants who rose to lay the fires. But when the first golden streaks touched the clouds the garden was exactly as I had found it, the great stone slab appearing as immobile as it had for centuries. To this day I don't know how I managed to dig that grave, to scoop out enough earth to make room for Gwenneth's body, but I carried away the extra soil in my shirt and scattered it under the hedgerows by the highroad. A light rain shortly after six took care of the last traces for me. And then, aware that I was filthy, I went to the river, as I had often done, washed the earth from my trousers and shirt, spread them to dry on the rocks, and swam until breakfast. By that time I was calm enough to face people."

He shrugged. "That's all there is to tell. When Evans raised the alarm for his daughter two days later, search parties combed the village, the grounds, the river itself for seven miles downstream. Whatever they suspected, they found nothing, could prove nothing." He sank into the chair, drained now of all energy and emotion. "Nothing."

"They?"

"The villagers. Her father. My uncle. The coroner's inquest. Evans swore she had been meeting me secretly, that she had thrown into his face the fact that she came to me at Rhosllyn. But there was no proof of it. Finally, months later, it was ruled that she had run off, presumably with an itinerant peddler who had passed through the village. Two or three women—including my cousin Cecily—were certain that she had shown an inordinate interest in the fellow. Despite her father's vehement objections, the case was closed. My aunt and uncle moved into the Dower House after a decent interval, and I locked that bedroom door forever."

I sat in silence, trying to comprehend the magnitude of his crime—murder of the girl he had longed to love, secret burial in the garden already protected by superstition, years of remorse and hidden guilt. Rhys had always found excuses for Mark's black temper, but even he would be unable to

offer any defense in the face of Gwenneth's tragic death. Yet she had foolishly taunted Mark into blind rage; small wonder those who knew her best felt so certain she had met with foul play at his hands. Both of them willful, arrogant, spoiled—and too young to realize the danger. My throat ached with the unshed tears of shock and sorrow.

He looked across at me, his face guarded against hurt and prepared for my rejection. "You will want to leave—I can't blame you. And I shall make it as easy as possible for you to go."

To my utter astonishment I heard myself saying, "Not yet. No." The man I had married, whom I had come to love so deeply, was guilty of murder. I needed time to think, to feel again, to accept in my own mind what his quiet voice had confessed. Then I would have to leave. But not yet.

Once more he reached out his hand to touch mine and then withdrew it quickly. "Dear Melanie!" he said gently, "I would not willingly have hurt you so. You know that!"

And suddenly he was gone, leaving me to the echoing silence of that tragic room.

A patter of rain against the windows roused me finally, and I blew out the guttering candle before walking to the door and closing it behind me. The house was quiet about me, the nightsticks already placed on the small marble table by the stairs. A clock chimed somewhere in one of the rooms, but I neglected to count the strokes. In something like a daze I climbed the steps to my room and was glad to meet no one on my way.

The candles were lit, the bed turned back, and hot water waited on the hearth. A small tray on the table by the window held an assortment of delicacies and a decanter of wine. I realized that I had missed my dinner and knew that Mark had ordered this light meal in its place. It was a gesture so like him that I tried to swallow a few mouthfuls of cold chicken and one of the little tarts that Mrs. Davies made so well. The wine gave me strength. Crossing to the draperies,

I pulled them aside and looked out into the rain-washed night. Those slender, powerful hands that had so gently flicked the snow from my hood at Tilmer Hall had choked the life out of Gwenneth.

Turning away, I undressed mechanically, preparing for bed. But I slept ill that night, tossing and turning in restless misery until the sheets felt hot and uncomfortable. Finally I threw back the covers, thrust my feet into slippers and went again to stand by the window.

Mark had confessed his guilt to me and ought to be brought to justice for what he had done. But I couldn't betray him. And my heart was heavy at the thought of having to leave him. The hot tears burned my lids and I brushed them away wretchedly. I might go on my whole life through loving the man Mark might have been, but surely it was unthinkable to continue living here with him—a murderer! And he himself had provided for me with this very day in mind. I must go, but certainly *never* back to Tilmer Hall, where Edward and his wife were waiting to gloat over the failure of my marriage!

If I left, I thought, watching the moon's brightness pick out familiar landmarks across the hillside, what excuse could I give? How could I explain walking out of Rhosllyn after less than six months of marriage, especially now, just after I had entered the locked room? There would be wild speculation about what I had discovered, and Mark would be condemned in every mind for what he was—a murderer. What would Rhys think of me as scandal enveloped the Trecourts once more—Rhys, who loved him too and had always stood by him?

Could I simply abandon him to insanity and the empty years ahead? Who would talk him out of his moods, his fits of depression and despair, sit with him when the devils rode too freely or the haunted past spilled over into the present? Between his bouts of madness he was still the man I had come to love.

Mark and I had made a bargain, and he had kept his part.

Could I do less? Perhaps he could even be brought to see that a life spent in serving others was not wholly wasted, though he could never atone for what he had done.

Drowsy at last with moonlight and the rain-cooled breeze, I turned back to my bed and smoothed the sheets. As I kicked off my slippers and climbed in, somewhere in the darkness a nightingale began to sing.

Awakening early the next morning, I dressed swiftly without waiting to summon Bronwyn, and hurried to knock on Mark's door before he had gone down to breakfast. I wanted to tell him my decision without fear of Williams' ear pressed to the pantry door.

"Come," he called, and with a heavily beating heart, I turned the knob and entered.

He stood by his desk, dressed but wearing a dressing gown over his shirt sleeves. I wondered if he had even gone to bed. His brows rose in wary surprise as he saw me in the doorway, and his body tensed as if to ward off a physical blow.

"I have reached a decision," I said swiftly before he could speak.

"Come in and shut the door," he said, not moving from where he stood. "The maids may be about."

"Yes." I did as I was told and then faced him down the length of the room. Somehow his presence filled the emptiness with light and color and warmth, making the cool blue and silver seem vividly alive and a fitting backdrop for the man. "I have decided to stay at Rhosllyn a little longer. I can't change the past and I can't betray you. What I *can* do is help you accept your guilt and somehow make amends for it." In my nervousness I feared I had put it badly.

"I would rather have you go than see disgust in your face and distrust in your eyes, Melanie. It would be kinder," he said quietly.

I shook my head, striving to hold back the tears at the hopelessness in his voice. His face was haggard from lack of sleep and the open wound of remembering, and I longed to go to him and comfort him. But I had less right now than

I had had before. "It happened eight years ago. Why should I fear you now? Why should I feel anything but sadness?"

His eyes searched my face for a long, long moment.

"We had made a bargain, after all," I said. "How has my learning the truth changed it?"

"You don't know—can't imagine—the relief of coming home each day to find you waiting, not the faintest shadow of suspicion in your smile," he said heavily. "*That* has changed, Melanie."

"I can't judge you, Mark, if that's what you are afraid of. I haven't the right. Will you at least let us *try,* while we find a plausible excuse for my departure? Then I shall leave if I must, but not now."

A wintry smile crossed his lips but did not touch his gray eyes. Grasping at the reprieve even as I had done, he nodded at last. "We'll try, then. For your sake. And mine."

Afraid to trust myself any longer, I murmured a disjointed reply and fled from the room.

The next few days were difficult for us. Gwenneth's ghost stood between us like a living person. Mark spent most of his time overseeing an addition to the barn at the home farm and I concentrated on the embroidery of the floral design for the chair. The scowling Norman barons in their arrogant pride, dominating the immense family tree, would soon be displaced by old-fashioned roses wreathed in ribbon. As my fingers flew, the bright silks filled the pattern, bringing the golden glory of the roses to life against the cream background. In the evenings Mark and I learned all over again to talk to each other, avoiding any painful reference and sometimes stumbling over unintended allusions. It was slow, careful, heartbreaking work.

But I could take no further joy in the Alpine garden.

Though Mrs. Powell avoided me when she could, I knew she watched me covertly, and I often saw her whispering with Morgan. I thanked God that there had been nothing in that room to betray Mark, and she had been far too frightened to listen at the door. Morgan was still ignorant of

Gwenneth's fate; I knew he would be capable of anything if he ever learned the truth.

Noel, sensitive to the change in me, asked bluntly if Mark and I had quarreled. We were watching the horses graze in the north pasture.

"No. Certainly not." I managed a smile.

"Then what's wrong?" he demanded. "Are you unhappy —or ill?"

"I—I suspect this unaccustomed heat has made me feel unwell. Mark has suggested a visit to London in the autumn, but perhaps a change now would be more beneficial."

He glanced sharply at me but said nothing more. Yet he must have spoken to his father, for Rhys planned a picnic jaunt for the five of us and was quite solicitous for my welfare. No one could have been kinder.

It was Bronwyn who first spoke of my paleness, and frightened that I might give Mark away, I rode in the sun and tried to coax color into my cheeks with the wind. In the glass I saw my face staring soberly back at me and knew what Mark had meant about reading his guilt in my eyes. With a determined effort I got myself in hand. When Mrs. Powell commented spitefully on the improvement in my health, I shrugged and said I was glad that the spell of heat had broken.

Somewhere I found the strength I needed—not the hot-blooded rashness that had sent me into marriage with a stranger rather than submit to my aunt and uncle at Tilmer Hall, but a maturer sort that enabled me to face the truth about Mark. Perhaps it was a growing-up from girl to woman, swift and painful but nevertheless inevitable. I even found the courage from time to time to pluck blossoms from the plants in the Alpine garden when Bryn pointed out an especially fine specimen, though I took care to set that bowl in seldom-used rooms where neither Mark nor I had to look at them.

I was more afraid of Morgan than ever now. "A life for a life," he had said, and I knew he meant it. Mark had un-

wittingly given him the perfect weapon for revenge; Morgan would make him suffer through me as he had suffered through Gwenneth. The time had come, I decided, to find a way to tell Mark what had happened and ask him to dismiss the groom. Meanwhile my knowledge was another spur to my watchfulness. Nothing more happened, and I began to hope that I had outwitted the groom.

Then, on one of Mark's night rides, a poacher, frightened perhaps by the great ghostly stallion pounding down on him in the darkness, fired at Mark before fleeing in the undergrowth along the river lanes. The ball grazed his cheek close by the temple—a bloody wound but not as dangerous as it so easily might have been.

He came ruefully to me, his coat and shirt dark with blood, when he failed to staunch the flow himself. Though he tried to make light of the situation, I was shocked wide awake at the sight of him.

Holding cold compresses to his face, I listened while he told me what had happened. A chill crept over my heart and I asked with a calmness I didn't feel, "Are you certain that this man was a poacher?" For I would not have put an attempt on Mark's life past the groom, though the shooting had been closer to the village than to Rhosllyn.

"Who else at such a time of night?" he asked, restless under my fingers. "If the gray hadn't shied I'd have caught him."

"I can think of more than one person who might wish you harm," I replied carefully, keeping the anxiety out of my voice.

"Morgan?" he asked contemptuously. "How would he know to find me by the river?"

"It might have been luck."

"To find me there, yes. But how would he come to have a gun in his hand?"

"You have a point," I conceded. "Still . . ."

Mark shook his head, wincing as the towel scraped across the raw flesh. "This was an accident."

"There is Evans, the smith," I persisted. "He might have heard you ride through the village. Of anyone there, he would have reason to know your horse."

"And he would be the first person anyone thought of if I had been found lying dead by the river in the morning. Why should he take such a risk—and now, after so long a time?"

"It isn't so long a time to him. I think he may be a little mad when it comes to—this subject."

"Possibly," Mark said consideringly. "Even if it *is* true, don't you see that I can't make an issue of it? I daren't be the first to ask questions, not on so little evidence. If this was Owen Evans' work, he didn't succeed, and I can't believe he'd be fool enough to try again. There is nothing to be gained by either of us in dragging this into the open. Let it rest, Melanie."

But I was thoroughly frightened. For his own sake as well as mine, he must be told about Morgan. If nothing else, he might take this attempt more seriously. "Mark . . . about Morgan . . . and the smith. You know how they feel. And now it appears—"

"Don't!" he said harshly. "Don't read conspiracy and danger where there are none, or we're finished. This is one reason why I dreaded telling you about Gwenneth. I can't fight back—I'm guilty! For God's sake, say no more about it."

I bit my lip and did as I was told, removing the last compress. "It has stopped bleeding finally. I'll dress it—"

"No. I don't want attention called to it. I have a meeting at the rectory tomorrow—today. Leave it to heal on its own."

"At least let me use an ointment to protect it against infection." Very gently I applied a coating of the salve Mrs. Powell used for cuts and burns among the servants. There were deep lines of tension about Mark's eyes and in the grim set of his mouth. "Go to bed and sleep," I said as I straightened up and set the pot on the desk top. "I'll clear away here."

At first I thought he hadn't heard me, for his thoughts

seemed far away from the library for a moment. And then he came back to me, frowned as if trying to remember what I had said, and finally replied obediently, "Yes. I'll try."

I watched him walk out of the room. If his assailant *had* fired deliberately at Mark, would he try again?

From that moment on, I knew I would have no peace when Mark was out of my sight.

Rhys was the one who made the most of Mark's accident. Angry and concerned, he tried to talk Mark into finding the poacher and teaching him a much needed lesson. To pot a hare or a bird was one thing, to fire at a man was something else again. "For you were lucky, you know. And the next man who stumbles across that fool might not fare as well!"

"I'm sure the poacher, whoever he was, got the fright of his life. I daresay he is quaking in his boots even now, and has already learned a lesson. He won't be likely to fire again when someone startles him."

Unsatisfied, Rhys turned to me. "Talk sense into him, Melanie!"

I smiled. "I agree with Mark. It's over. Let's be thankful that he suffered so little harm and leave it at that."

Rhys stared at me for an instant, taken completely aback. Noel, rising to set his cup upon the tea tray, said irritably, "Leave it, Father."

Fleetingly I wondered if Noel could have shot at Mark, and then dismissed the idea as shameful. It was not even his style. Whatever taunts he might fling in Mark's face, any grudge would be settled openly, not by lurking in the dark along the river's edge, gun in hand. But would he protect Gwenneth's father? Or Morgan?

Cecily, her gown of palest lavender complementing the gray stone of the terrace and the rose of the geraniums set in urns along the edge, spoke then. "You really ought to call Dr. Thomas, Mark. There's going to be a scar if the wound isn't seen to *properly*."

"Melanie took care of it last night," he said, polite still but out of patience with the subject.

"Of course," Cecily replied smoothly. "Still, it would do no harm to seek *professional* advice."

"Except for an abominable headache afterward, I scarcely knew it had happened," he said testily.

Ignoring Cecily's taunts and trying to ward off the explosion I knew was coming, I turned and smiled at her. "Rhys tells me he brought new music for you from Chester. Could you play something for us? If the music-room windows are opened, I think we could enjoy your performance from here."

She rose gracefully to the bait. "There's a new piece by Liszt, actually. Definitely not for the amateur, but I'll try not to disgrace myself." She smiled at Mark. "Would you turn for me? I'll send one of the maids for the music."

"Tell me where it is and I'll fetch it myself," he replied, casting a swift and grateful glance toward me.

They walked inside, a handsome couple, with her fairness set off by his dark coloring. Would Mark have come to love his cousin if Gwenneth had indeed run away with a peddler, or would his madness still have stood in their way?

As I turned back to my remaining guests I found their eyes on me, one in longing and the other in speculation.

For a fortnight I was filled with anxiety whenever Mark was away on estate business, riding alone at night, or in any way vulnerable to attack. There were numberless places where a man might lie in wait, unseen, unsuspected until it was too late—places where Mark might bleed to death long before he was discovered. I suffered endless torments as I waited for sounds of his return, pretending to be occupied and cheerful. Whatever busied my hands, my mind traveled with Mark, willing him safely home. I even forgot my own fears of Morgan in my concern for him.

And nothing more happened.

Perhaps it had indeed been a frightened poacher, I thought at last. Perhaps in our own guilty knowledge we had made more of the incident than it truly warranted. I began to breathe more easily again.

Meanwhile I tried to interest Mark in the small village school. I had never dared go there myself, but Cecily spoke of it from time to time and considered it one of her most successful charitable efforts. She had contributed books for a small library, arranged simple outings for the younger pupils, and provided the materials for improving the appearance of the plain, whitewashed classroom—fabric for bright curtains, a globe, and so on. Now there was need for a piano—the elderly instrument contributed years before by

a neighbor had finally succumbed to damp, age, and children's enthusiasm. The great cast-iron stove that served to heat the room in winter was also far from efficient.

And so, in keeping with my hope of repaying Mark's debt to society, I suggested that he might care to give the school funds for a new piano and a new stove.

"Why should I?" he asked me bluntly. "Rhys supports village charities. Ask him to supply the school's needs."

"But Mark—as the major landholder—"

"No, I tell you!" he said bitterly. "There has been nothing but dislike between these people and myself. Why should I now begin to court their favor? Even as a child I received only cold service and implacable reserve from them. It has nothing to do with Gwenneth, she merely gave them a better excuse to dislike me. Rhys—and his family—have crossed the barrier, perhaps because of his Welsh mother, and they respond to him in a way that you or I shall never see. If I suddenly provided a piano or anything else, they would look on my gift with suspicion and very likely set it down to a guilty conscience."

"But you contribute funds for St. Giles and no one minds," I pointed out. "Indeed, the rector *depends* on you for such projects as repairing the roof or raising the sunken flags or shoring up the tower—whatever strains the ordinary resources. Why is the school different?"

We were walking to the home farm together, and he stopped to watch the horses grazing beneath the shade of the trees. "There's a difference," he said heavily. "My people are buried in St. Giles. We have always supported it, and it would be thought strange if I didn't do as my father before me and supply the means for major repairs. The school is part of the chapel. It takes every village child now, but it was begun so that chapel-goers could read the Scriptures for themselves. Now there are only youngsters in the school, but in the beginning a dozen adults were on the front benches, one a man of seventy-two. Morgan does most of the repairs there. Though he doesn't think I know it, he's actually quite skilled with his hands. The Trecourts, except for

Rhys and Cecily, naturally, have had nothing to do with the school."

"I begin to understand," I said slowly. "But I just can't accept the chasm between your family and these people of the village. Mark, you know as well as I that the Trecourts have been here nearly eight hundred years! Surely in that length of time the old rivalries could have been forgotten."

Mark turned to walk on. "Not here. My ancestors carved out of this land an estate to match their pride, setting aside Saxons and Welsh alike. They made enemies, and they kept them because they kept the land. Merlin built the first house on this site, but a Norman set his castle in its place. There was a Celtic church and a small monastery just beyond where the Home Farm is today. I've seen the foundations, like bones, protruding here and there from the earth. Both were replaced by French priests and monks, the old ways set aside for the new. When the Celtic monks rebelled, they were hanged out of hand. During the Reformation, history repeated itself—the Catholic monks were hanged, and the monastery was torn down altogether. From the beginning the wishes of the people were ignored and the Trecourts made the decisions for the valley. Now most of the villagers are chapel-goers, and because we are more civilized we turn a blind eye to them, but we don't in any way support them. Yes, we have been here for nearly eight hundred years, but what in all that time have we had in common? Not one thing."

"There are other landowners," I said hurriedly, watching the groom approaching us with the new mare on a lead. "They seem to be accepted."

"They are latecomers," Mark said briefly. "It isn't at all the same situation. No, Melanie, don't ask me to support the school or any other part of the village. It would do no good and might conceivably do a great deal of harm."

In spite of my disappointment I had to agree with him. The last thing I intended was to stir curiosity in anyone, least of all Owen Evans. He would pounce on such an extraordinary action and play with it like a cat until he had

found an explanation for it. I dared take no chances with Mark's life. Yet it was here, at Rhosllyn, that his guilt was incurred; it had seemed fitting that he should begin to re-pay here.

It was difficult to explain later to Cecily that I had failed. We were by the pond, watching the gander, while Noel sat reading in the shade of a tree.

She shrugged lightly. "I'm used to Mark's feelings on that subject. It doesn't matter. I'll find someone else to under-take the project." She looked at me closely. "You seem to have recovered your health."

Taken aback, I said, "Yes, I feel quite well, thank you. It was a passing indisposition, nothing to speak of."

She turned away and snapped the blossom from a wilted water iris. "Mrs. Powell thought that . . . congratulations might shortly be in order. So did my father."

Completely at a loss for words, I gaped at her. And then the meaning became clear and I knew I was blushing deeply, much to my horror. "No," I said through a constricted throat. "No." To cover my acute embarrassment I added quickly, "Tell me, do the villagers and the people on the estate feel differently toward Mark because he is a descen-dant of those Norman barons?"

Cecily moved on along the bank toward the lawns. "The Welsh have long memories for an injury, my father says. And there was much that couldn't be forgiven on both sides, I suppose. Noel doesn't care for that chair you are so busily re-covering, but I find it rather interesting. If you take the time to *look* at it, you'll note how many Trecourts fell in battle, sometimes against the French, but most often in Welsh uprisings."

This was not the first time that Cecily had indicated that she did not care for my changing anything at Rhosllyn. "Were Mark's parents also disliked?"

She shrugged and said indifferently, "Probably. Ask my father." As Noel caught up with us she excused herself gracefully and went home.

He escorted me as far as the terrace, saying as soon as his sister was out of earshot, "What difference does it make whether Mark's parents were liked or not? Mark carries the worst blood from both sides of his family, and everyone knows it except you. Stop trying to find excuses for him."

"What about his concern for the estate, his courtesy to me—"

We had stopped by the steps, in the shadow of the house, and he interrupted with an angry gesture. "How do you know what Mark is really like? Don't you understand that he takes *care* to present a calm and smiling front to you? This is only one face of the man. And the other is secretive, evil, dangerous."

"That's a terrible accusation to make," I said coldly, and then remembered how true it was. I added defensively, "He has never harmed *me!*"

Noel raised his brows. "Not openly. Not knowingly, perhaps. But even you can't be sure what goes on in his mind when he's riding that gray monster through the night. And neither can he. Look at the way he treats my father—the innocent people he has injured with his mad temper. Because he loves you now, do you think it will prevent him from turning on you sometime?"

I shook my head. "No. I don't believe you!" But a small voice reminded me bitterly that I didn't have the protection of Mark's love, had never had it. Furious with myself and with Noel, I turned on my heel and left him standing there, on the terrace steps, worry still deeply etched on his face.

That night Mark suffered one of the worst of his nightmares, and once more we sat in the library until dawn lightened the eastern sky. Exhausted, Mark turned to smile wryly at me. He had walked to the window and was staring out at the pale streaks above the hill for several minutes before he spoke.

"I had thought that once I confessed to someone, the worst would be over—that a burden shared, as they say, is a burden halved. And all I have done, Melanie, is complicate

your life. You should have left me, you know. It would have been better for you."

"Left you? I couldn't have faced myself, Mark. It sounds pompous, I know, but I feel, somehow, that by staying I am more useful. Don't ask me how or why—I can't begin to explain."

"I'm very grateful," he said softly after a moment. "I told you at Tilmer Hall that you could make the difference, and you have. But promise me one thing, Melanie. It has worried me for some time, and I won't be satisfied until I have your word. If one day the truth comes out, promise me that you will deny all knowledge of it and leave at once. *At once!* Whatever happens to me after that, I'll have the peace of knowing that you are safe and untainted."

"Mark, I couldn't run! It would be *cowardly!*" I cried indignantly.

"Cowardly or not," he said firmly, "I want that promise! Do you think your Tilmer cousins will miss the opportunity to enjoy your misfortunes? No, the court must discover that you are ignorant and in no way connected with my misdeeds. Wealthy in your own right, you can go where you please, properly horrified by the revelation of my past. And people will never turn their backs on you as they have on me."

"Do you think I *care*—" I began, but he cut me short.

"Hush! Of course you don't care! But life is damned harsh enough without being cut off from the society of your peers, and there's not one thing you can do for me by staying, except to damage your future far more than you can imagine. No, you'll go, and never look back. Do I have your word on that?" He came forward to stand before me.

"Mark—"

"Promise me," he demanded savagely. "I can't stand in the prisoner's dock and endure the ordeal of public trial knowing what each word spoken does to you!" His eyes held mine. "Your word is as good as any man's."

Torn, knowing that I couldn't bear to leave him at such a time, yet yearning to give him this assurance at least, I

stared into his haggard face. And then I knew I must give my word, and keep it. Whatever I felt, no matter how difficult it might be for me, I owed Mark that final dignity.

"Yes," I whispered finally. "Yes, I promise, Mark."

Relief washed across his face. "Thank you. That at least is one horror I shall be spared." He gestured toward the window. "The sun is up, and the maids won't be far behind it. Go upstairs and sleep. I'll follow you as soon as I have taken a turn on the terrace. Fresh air will relax me, I think."

I would have walked with him, but had no desire to meet the maids in my nightdress and wrapper. "You'll come soon? You need to rest more than I do," I said, hesitating.

"Yes. No more than fifteen minutes."

I nodded, and with a smile, went out of the library and up the stairs. Pray God, I thought, my mind still on our conversation and my promise, pray God it never comes to that. I would not willingly leave him to face—

Something turned under the toe of my slipper and I was pitched head first into the banister, the wind almost knocked out of me. Whatever it was, it fell bouncing and dully ringing to the hall floor below. Steadying myself, I peered down to see what was there, but I could find nothing. Mark was standing in the library door.

"What's wrong?" he asked quickly. "Are you hurt?"

"No—there was something on the steps and I lost my footing. Luckily I was thrown forward, not backward. Do you see anything?"

Mark glanced about, drew a blank, and then walked out into the hall to look further. After a moment he stooped to retrieve a small object from beneath a chair, turning it in his fingers as he examined it closely. "A marble. How in God's name did it come to be on the stairs?"

"Perhaps Mrs. Powell has been cleaning the nurseries—" I broke off and stared down at the small colored glass ball in his fingers. I tried to picture myself walking up the stairs. How had I come? Not holding onto the railing, but lightly hurrying up the steps, almost in the center of the treads. Yet when Mark and I had come down together, side by side,

we were on the edges of the steps. Who usually came down alone in the dark, to pace or ride or sit in Aunt Margaret's room? Mark. Though I accompanied him occasionally, I rarely left my room on my own after retiring. But he wandered the house at night, his mind on other things as he came down these steps, as often as not without a candle when moonlight brightened his way. He couldn't have seen the marble in time—he would have lost his balance and fallen. Not to his death, perhaps, but certainly to serious injury. Going up, I had been less vulnerable, though my ribs ached from striking the banister.

Looking around, I found first one and then another of the marbles scattered in a line on other steps, and passed them down to Mark.

"Do you suppose these were *purposely* left here?" I asked.

"Good God, no! One of the maids might have broken her neck," Mark said crisply.

"Yes," I replied dubiously, but added silently, The maids would not have been the first down these stairs. Mrs. Powell was always up betimes and could easily have removed the marbles before anyone else had come this way. How often had they lain on the steps waiting to catch Mark's unwary feet?

"I don't like the idea of carrying the dustpans down the main stairs. You might tell Mrs. Powell." He slipped the marbles into his pocket. "Sleep if you can," he added, and I turned to go up once more.

Not for the first time I wondered if someone had tried to listen outside the door of Aunt Margaret's room while Mark made his confession. But Mrs. Powell had been far too frightened to linger, and besides, if she had been in possession of the truth, she would have gone straight to her brother and Owen Evans.

And I couldn't see how such an accident could have been meant to injure me.

I didn't mention the marbles to Mrs. Powell at all. She would deny all knowledge of them, smiling with her eyes and not with her lips as she turned away from me, and there

would be nothing to connect her or her brother with the incident. Instead, why not let them wonder? The marbles had been taken away and no one had been hurt. Anyone might have discovered them; she could not, would not dare ask. And for the same reason no one would attempt it again. Mark might be better served by silence.

But my anxiety returned. What had stirred this sudden spurt of activity? The unlocking of the door and the realization that Gwenneth's body was not hidden in that sealed room? Surely Morgan and Evans didn't expect Mark to be frightened into confessing at long last—or had I guarded myself so well that Morgan had turned to a more accessible target? Mark was guilty of murder, undeniably—but this was vengeance!

The following afternoon I tried to speak to Mark about the groom, but once more he refused to hear me out.

"I can't start at my own shadow, Melanie. The poacher—yes, that could have been Evans, I grant you. But wild horses couldn't drag Mrs. Powell away from Rhosllyn until Gwenneth's body is found. She wouldn't risk dismissal just to make me fall down the stairs."

"What of Morgan?" I persisted. "It might have been Morgan."

Mark frowned as he set down his cup. "There is nothing to be done about Morgan. Not yet. Not until he gives himself away."

"And then it might be too late," I replied bitterly, my eyes on the dishes before me, afraid Mark might read too much in them. Angry at my helplessness, torn by love and despair, it hurt to think that he might welcome the peace of death. "And Rhys will step into your shoes."

That roused him to say, "Yes, all right. I'll be on my guard."

I told myself it would be enough.

It wasn't. Morgan struck in the small hours of darkness, when the mind is drugged with sleep and suspicion is lulled. The first warning was a shout below the windows of our

wing, and then Mark's feet racing down the passage.

I fumbled for my wrapper, thrusting my arms into the sleeves even as my feet groped for my slippers beneath the bed. There was not time to consider my hair, tumbling free down my back. I caught up a ribbon from the dressing table on my way to the door, and found myself in darkness as I emerged into the passage. Mark had already disappeared, his candle's glow flickering up the stairwell for an instant, like an insubstantial butterfly, and then suddenly vanishing. Feeling my way with outstretched hands, I hurried after him.

Already there was noise from the stable block to guide me—men shouting, horses screaming—and then, as I reached the hall and flew to the wide-open terrace doors, I smelled smoke and heard the ominous crackle of flames.

"Fire!" I whispered, still dazed and uncomprehending.

I ran toward the rear courtyard and saw smoke billowing in heavy black clouds from the stable block, occasional tinges of flame brightening the darkness. The grooms and tenants were calling hoarsely as they brought water in the great wooden fire buckets, and someone was rigging a hand pump at the well. Several round-eyed, frightened boys were leading the horses away, struggling to hold the plunging, frenzied animals as they made their way toward the paddock at the Home Farm. Stumbling toward them, I stepped into the circle of light from the first lantern.

"Where is Lord Teville?" I asked the lantern bearer. He stood stock still and stared at me in wonder, as if some apparition had suddenly come to cast a spell on him. "Lord Teville," I repeated sharply. "Where is he?"

Gulping once as he recognized me, the boy jerked his head toward the building. "In there, my lady. The stallion—"

I waited to hear no more. The carriage horses and the riding horses had been removed to safety already. Only the stallion remained in jeopardy. And everyone knew that Mark would risk his life for the ghostly dappled gray rather than leave him trapped to die in his stall.

Even as my mind flew ahead of me I was racing across the

stableyard to the nearest group of men. "Lord Teville," I shouted over the noise and chaos. "Where is he? Has he come out yet?"

Noel's voice answered me from the darkness to my left. "He's in the stable still." He came forward to catch my arm. "What the hell are you doing here? Go back to the house, Melanie—you are in the way and might be hurt!"

"No! Noel, you must get him out of there—the smoke—"

"—is worse than it looks. He went after the stallion. It was a foolish thing to do, and I'll not risk another life sending after him!"

"He'll die—he may be trapped, hurt—"

Morgan appeared behind Noel, his face grimed with black but his eyes seeming to reflect the lanterns with an unholy gleam. I wheeled toward him. "Why was the stallion left inside?" I demanded furiously. "You know how valuable he is!"

"It was not our choice, my lady," Morgan replied with suppressed triumph. "He fought like the demon he is."

"Then get Lord Teville out—now! That's an *order*, Morgan, and by God, I'll have your place if he—"

"I'll go after him," someone called from behind me. "Where is he? With the gray?"

"Father—no!" Noel shouted, releasing me as he lunged forward.

I whirled in time to see Rhys running toward the smoke-obscured door. He was inside, a wet cloth over his face, before Noel or I could reach him. Noel was swearing in a steady stream of unrecognizable words, invective masking his anger and his fear for his father. I caught at his arm and held him with all my strength to keep him from plunging into the stable after Rhys. As Noel fought to shake me off, Morgan was cursing the men on the buckets and pumps, forcing every one of them into redoubled effort as if suddenly bereft of his own senses. The din was deafening, the stableyard a maelstrom of activity and men and equipment.

A jagged streak of lightning crossed the sky above us, and

I flinched, crazily certain that the stable had somehow blown up. The thunder was a rumble that shook the earth as Noel broke free and dashed toward the doors. A storm was nearly upon us, and I prayed desperately for torrents of rain to fall as I screamed to Noel to turn back. Just inside the doors he met Mark half-guiding, half-dragging the raging stallion out of the smoke. A rag was bound over the fire-crazed animal's eyes, and his plunging feet nearly struck Noel as he jerked swiftly to one side.

"My father!" Noel yelled to Mark.

"He's coming behind me now—" Mark broke off to cough harshly, his smoke-filled lungs choking him.

Noel dragged him out of the way and reached for his father, but Rhys was on his feet and smiling. "I nearly missed him in that hellhole," I heard him say. "I had already turned back when the stallion brushed against me. Thank God!"

Weak with relief, I waited until Mark had relinquished the shaking horse to two grooms and stumbled farther into the fresh air. Then, unable to restrain myself, I ran forward to grasp his arm. I needed to touch him, to feel for myself that he was safe and alive and out of danger. I longed to throw my arms about him and hold him close, but dared not make such a display of myself before the gaping grooms and tenants and the small cluster of house servants on the rim of the light.

"Hay—it was the hay," Mark said, and choked again.

"Don't try to talk," I urged, but he shook his head.

"I'm all right now, I've got to take charge. The gray is safe, thank God for that!" He turned away, his breath still rasping harshly in his throat, and began to supervise the pumps.

A few sprinkles of rain touched my face and then were gone as the thunder echoed again. The wind gusted, sending black smoke billowing. In his white shirt and dark trousers Mark was clearly visible in the sheet lightning that flashed almost directly overhead, and then the rain came down in

earnest. The house servants crowded into the kitchen passage and I stepped below the eaves, drawing my thin wrapper more tightly about me. Using soaked blankets to protect themselves, the men continued to fight the blaze, and already the smoke seemed to be less thick about the doors and windows. After a time I could see most of the passage into the interior, and Mark dashed in with a pitchfork three times, each time bringing back a charred and smoking bale of hay to toss it hissing on the rain-drenched cobbles. I scarcely noticed how wet I was, my eyes following Mark wherever he went.

In half an hour more the fire was out. Noel, beside me for a moment, said tiredly, "The stable block is stone, and there's oak inside, so the damage is relatively small. A half-dozen bales of hay, improperly stored—but the smoke alone would have killed those poor animals. God, what a night!"

"Why wouldn't you go after Mark?" I asked coldly. "Why were you willing to let him die?"

"I wasn't *willing* to let him die!" Noel said, suddenly angry. "He knew what he was about. I saw no reason to risk my life or order someone else into that death trap so long as we didn't feel he was in danger."

"And yet when your father went in—"

"My father went to rescue Mark without a thought of himself. He is nearly twice our age—I had no choice. Melanie, believe me, Mark knew what he was about!"

"I don't believe you," I said, turning away.

He caught my arm, swinging me to face him. "That fire—" he began, but Rhys was there beside us, tired and wet and streaked with black grime.

"Melanie, my dear, you will be ill! Go at once and change to dry clothing! There's nothing more to keep you here."

I was suddenly aware of myself, my wrapper clinging to me in sodden, revealing lines, my long hair plastered about my neck and shoulders. "Yes—yes, I'm going just now. I'll ask Mrs. Davies to make tea and sandwiches for the men."

"That would be most kind," he replied.

"Good night," I said to Rhys, and left Noel to decide for himself whether he was included in my farewell.

After a brief word with Mrs. Davies, who was standing in the shelter of the servants' door, I slipped away, hurrying up to my room, with drops of water marking my progress.

Stripping off my drenched nightclothes, I dropped them on the stone hearth, rubbing myself down with a heavy towel before putting on a fresh nightdress and matching wrapper in apricot silk. My hair was another matter. I brushed it briskly before twisting it into a knot to keep my shoulders dry. And all the while my mind raced through the events of the night. Morgan, of course. Morgan alone would have the opportunity to stack that hay in the far end of the stable, to drop a candle stub there and wait until the flames had caught well and the gray was unmanageable before sounding the alarm. Who else had the freedom of movement, the *right* to be in the stables, shifting hay, working late on some bit of harness, changing the compress on a pulled tendon or bruised hock. Any of a hundred pretexts.

And once again Mark had been spared. The question was, would there be more of these terrifying attempts against us, on and on, until Mark or I broke from sheer exhaustion and stress? Gwenneth had left a legacy of hatred that had disrupted half a dozen lives, and it would be ironic justice if she now brought Mark to retribution after he had escaped the hangman.

There was a tap at the door and I crossed to open it, unwilling to be disturbed by Bronwyn or Mrs. Powell in my present mood. But it was Mark, standing there in his torn and blackened clothes, his face streaked, his eyes red-rimmed from smoke and fatigue. He found a smile for me, and I longed for him to hold me close and soothe away the horror of the night.

"I thought you would want to know—the fire is out and all is well. Some damage in the loose boxes of course, and the place needs a good cleaning and a number of repairs. All the horses got out, and no one was hurt." He lifted a hand to brush his hair out of his eyes.

"No one except you," I said, catching his wrist and turning his hand to the light. It was crisscrossed with angry welts, and on the other forearm was a long scratch.

He looked down in surprise. "I must have got them working with the stallion. Nothing serious."

"They might have been. Come in," I said, taking his arm and leading him to a chair.

"I'm filthy—" he protested.

"So you are." Pouring fresh water into the basin, I gently washed and bound his hands while he lay back in the chair, his eyes closed and his breathing growing more and more even. As I finished, I debated waking him and decided against it. Sleep was what he needed desperately, and though he would rest better in his own bed, there was no assurance that he would fall asleep again there. Very gently, I tucked a blanket about him and felt the stab of pain in my heart at the memory of what he was. For a time I stood watching him, and then blew out the candles and quietly went to bed, listening to his steady breathing from across the room even as I myself drifted into sleep.

Mark was gone when I awoke the next morning, and it was over luncheon that I had the first opportunity to speak with him alone.

"It was Morgan who set that fire," I began.

"I searched the stables myself. If the fire was deliberately started, it was cleverly done. There's no proof, Melanie. I can't accuse him," Mark said, his voice grim but resigned.

"Who else had the opportunity?" I demanded.

"Suppose we are right? Suppose he set that fire. Without proof I have no cause to suspect arson, you know, and I can't present my own guilty conscience as evidence." He shook his head. "We must leave it."

"And so they try again, the three of them?" I asked harshly.

Mark rose and came past my chair on his way to the door. "I have no right," he said softly, "to fight back. I am what I am, Melanie, and I have no *right*."

Standing to face him, I fought back the tears. "Nor have

they the privilege of judging and executing you. Only the law can do that."

He touched my cheek with his bandaged hand. "It is an impasse, isn't it? But I tell you this: they haven't the discipline to kill me. Not unless they face me in anger—and they won't, not after all these years. Try to believe this, and don't be afraid."

I nodded, not trusting my voice. And then he was gone, leaving me prey to mixed emotions while deep within me a small whisper repeated, "Noel? What about Noel?" His emotions ran deep, his hatred deeper still.

Ten days later Mark was brought home on a makeshift stretcher.

I was at the top of the staircase, talking with Cecily, who had been sorting through several boxes stored in the attics. She was laughing over drawings she and Noel had made as children when the servants' door into the hall swung open and four men carefully edged through it. Suddenly the laugh froze into a grotesque grimace, and then, the drawings fluttering from her hand, she was pushing past me to fly down the steps.

Turning swiftly, I saw Mark for the first time, and my blood ran cold. His face was ashen and there was a dark bruise across his cheek. Grasping at the ornate banister, I watched in horror as the men clumsily came down the hall toward the stairs. Cecily had already reached them, bending frantically over Mark as she cried his name. He lay still except for the slight jarring of the stretcher, and I could not bring myself to call to the grooms to ask if he was alive— or dead. It was Cecily who demanded in a voice quite unlike her own if he had broken his neck.

"No, Miss Cecily, Mr. Noel said he was knocked unconscious as he fell. Your father has gone for the doctor, and Mr. Noel said to bring him home while he stayed with the horse."

"The gray?" she asked in foreboding.

"No, Miss Cecily, 'twas the young black we were having the trouble over. Mr. Noel hadn't been able to break him to the saddle, and after some words with his lordship over it—" he paused as they cautiously rounded the newel-post —"Mr. Trecourt interrupted and said it was no casting of doubt on Mr. Noel's skill, and Mr. Noel got that mad that he dared his lordship to ride the black for himself. Mr. Trecourt, he begged his lordship not to do it, but the horse was ordered saddled anyhow."

My breathing slowly returned to normal as I listened to their tale of Mark's ride and the fall as the spirited black lost his footing on the bruised grass. Mark had tried to throw himself clear, and in so doing, collided with the stone watering trough.

While Cecily, fussing over Mark, accompanied the stretcher up the steps, I turned and hurried to Mark's room to ready his bed.

He was alive, that was all that mattered to me. He was alive! Let Cecily fling herself over his inert body in a bald display of emotion. I couldn't have cared less. It was enough to know that he had survived.

And all the while my mind raced through the scene as the groom had described it. Noel might very well have created, in his subtle way, a stratagem of that sort, knowing Mark would never refuse his challenge or heed Rhys's pleading not to ride. It *might* have been an accident, a coincidence that my distraught mind turned into a threat, but I didn't think so. No, Noel had attempted to kill Mark, I was certain of it, and the scheme had failed. Mark's skill as a rider was unsurpassed.

Almost in echo of my thought, the groom was saying as he entered the open chamber door, "But he rode that black demon, rode him to a standstill, for all they fell. The black won't never fight the saddle again."

And there was grudging respect in his voice for the limp man they carefully laid down on the turned-back sheets.

ALTHOUGH MARK was not severely injured by his fall, he was ordered to bed for a day or two as a precaution. He had remained unconscious for well over an hour and when he awoke was rather vague for a time—symptoms of a concussion, according to the doctor.

"It can do no harm," Rhys told him, worry showing clearly on his face, "to remain in bed. After all, you gave us quite a fright, you know, and for our peace of mind—"

"I'm fine, I tell you!" Mark snapped irritably.

I was watching Rhys, well aware that Noel had not come to the house to inquire after his cousin and wondering if his father suspected any intentional attempt to harm Mark. There was a frown between his eyes and a pained expression in them, as if Rhys were torn between the two boys he had raised. It could not be easy for him to watch in silence a rivalry that flared up so violently between Mark and Noel, and yet what could he do?

It was rather like chaining an irritable, half-tamed bear to keep Mark in his room, much less resting in his bed, for the remainder of that day and a part of the next.

In the evening we walked in the gardens before dinner, and Mark apologized for his crossness. "I can't bear to be still," he added, as if to explain. "So long as I am occupied I don't think about the past or the future."

"I understand." For I, too, preferred to stay busy. We

turned away from the vicinity of the wild-flower garden and wandered among the roses. There was a sudden racket in the shrubbery, and the wild gander came dashing out, wings spread in fury, nipping at the heels of one of Rhys's young dogs. Our laughter must have caught his attention, for the gander turned on us until he recognized me, then came forward less belligerently.

"I'm surprised to see him here," Mark was saying, warily eyeing the gander's approach. "I thought he lived by the pond."

"He does," I replied guiltily. "I'm afraid I've rather neglected him. I usually take him a handful of grain or crusts each day."

"Instead of which you were minding me. Here—stop that!" he added, swiftly retreating in face of the gander's unexpected attack on his leg. "You would think he understood me!"

Smothering a laugh, I sank to my knees and held out a hand to the smooth gray head. After a last hiss in Mark's direction, the gander consented to a brief caress. "I'm sure it isn't personal, Mark—he seems not to like people at all. He tolerates me because I protected him once and bring him delicacies he can't find by the pond."

"I think I prefer that arrogant black mouser from the stables," Mark replied, taking care to remain out of reach. "Stay here and I'll fetch something for him—a burnt offering to his displeasure." With a smile he was gone.

Murmuring to the restive fowl, I held his attention while Mark was away. When he ruffled his feathers and hissed ominously I turned toward the approaching footsteps and found myself face-to-face with Noel. Rising quickly, I waited for him to speak.

"Don't stand there glaring at me. I've heard enough from my father," he said roughly.

"Was I glaring?" I asked coldly.

"I assure you, my dear Melanie, I had no intention of cracking Mark's skull. The fool was merely showing off and

got what he asked for." He sidestepped the gander's vicious attack. "You misbegotten Christmas dinner!" he swore, keeping his distance, and then laughed ruefully. "My temper is foul—envy, I suppose. My father has always worried more about my cousin than he has about his own son. Why are you so certain I'd want to harm him?" He frowned suddenly. "Or has he said something to you—"

"What could he say to me?" I parried, grateful for the fading light that kept my shocked, betraying expression from his quick eyes.

"Never mind. Even Mark wouldn't— Shall I walk with you to the pond?"

My heart began beating again. How often Mark had warned me not to show guilt or suspicion to watchful eyes, and I had nearly done just that. The shortest way to the gallows for Mark might very easily come through me.

Forcing a smile, I said, "Mark has gone for crusts. The gander was hungry and came in search of me. He's spoiled, a little." And then I added, "I'm sorry, Noel. Three frights in a row . . . I'm not accustomed to Mark's love of danger, and it unsettles me."

"Yes, I can appreciate that. God knows why he hasn't broken his neck long since. It's not for want of trying. Melanie, did it ever occur to you that Mark contrived what appears to be the poacher's attack, and even the fire in the stable? For your sympathy?"

"I don't want to discuss Mark again," I retorted coldly.

He lifted a hand. "Yes, I know, you believe in him. But I tell you, he doesn't always remember, and I wonder sometimes— If you are ever frightened of him, go to my father, if you can't come to me." He glanced over his shoulder. "I'll be on my way. I'm not in the mood for a family reunion." He turned and strode briskly down the path as Mark came into view. I didn't believe him, but my pleasure in the evening was tainted and I was glad that the gander was there to mask my lack of spirit.

As I sat alone in the library after dinner, waiting for Mark to return from an errand to the stables, I found myself

thinking about Noel's odd warning. It was not the first time he had tried to say that Mark was dangerous, and a threat to me. It couldn't be true. And yet Mark had no memory at all of Gwenneth's death. Could *he* have been my tormentor all these months, and not Morgan? In periods of insanity had he turned on me as he never would in his right mind?

I swallowed to ease the dryness in my throat. My own imagination might have magnified the poacher, the fire in the stables, and the fall with the horse into a deliberate attack on Mark simply because he had each time been injured. There *was* no real proof either way. As for the marbles on the steps, they might just as easily have been meant for me.

But Mark had been in *Hereford* when the tree trunk fell —or so he said. Had I been too ready to find Morgan guilty because he so obviously hated me, Mark's wife, instead of looking deeper into each attempt?

In my agitation I started up from my chair, scattering my embroidery silks across the carpet. What did I know of madness, I asked myself desperately as I paced the floor. Or of Mark when he was in its grip?

The door opened and Mark came in. He stared in surprise at the rainbow of colors spilling around my chair. "What happened?" he asked quickly, his eyes scanning my face.

"I—have lost my thimble," I improvised, pretending to search.

"It's here, on your cushion," he said, giving it to me.

As I took it from him I looked up into the tired, somber eyes. Noel as well as Cecily would rejoice in the end of my marriage. They each had personal reasons for wanting me to doubt Mark. What had he said in Ludlow? "You have nothing to fear from me. I'll see to that." And he had meant every word, I told myself fiercely, stooping to gather up the tangled silks. I trusted him still. I had to.

Late one night in the following week Mark burst into my bedchamber, the sound of the door flying back on its hinges bringing me out of sleep with a wild start.

"Melanie—" he cried in a strangled voice. "Oh, *God*—!"

"Mark, what's wrong?" I fumbled for the candle as he flung himself on his knees by the bed, his face buried in the embroidered coverlet. As the light flared and the wick caught, I saw his hands clenched in the sheets until the knuckles were white and rigid beneath the skin.

Stilling the tremor in my fingers, I set the candle in the night dish. "What has happened?" I asked, touching his dark head lightly. "Mark, what's wrong?"

His face as he looked up at me was stark white, his eyes burning darkly in the candle's feeble glow. "It's worse than it has ever been—she gives me no peace! And now *this!*" He lifted his hand and turned it over, staring at his palm.

I could see nothing except the long tanned fingers, the callused palm, the strong wrist. "What is it?" I asked gently and reached out to touch him.

He jerked his hand away. "*No!*" Then, controlling himself with a tremendous effort, he said, "It's her blood. Don't touch it."

"But, Mark, there's nothing on your hand!" I managed to say, fighting down my own fright. "It was a dream—here, look for yourself!"

"No, I tell you—Melanie, I can't go on, I'm so very *tired*. There is only one answer left. You'll be well provided for, and I can only say I'm sorry." He rose and turned toward the door.

"Mark—" I threw back the bedclothes and ran after him, catching his arm. "Where are you going?"

"To the gun room. Stay here, Melanie. I'll leave the house. Don't come down until they send for you." His step was firm, his voice steady now.

"Mark, no, please!" I cried frantically, trying to stop him. "You are wrong, there's nothing to fear, there's nothing on your hand! Mark, it was a dream, only a *dream,* I won't let you do this!"

"Can't you *see?*" He held out his hand again, and I caught his wrist. "It is no use, Melanie. Let Rhys have Rhosllyn— I'm too tired to fight any longer."

I held tightly to his wrist. "Mark, there is nothing here, please look at your hand in the candle's light."

Mark stared at his palm. "I tell you, her blood is on my hands. I could almost feel it—warm, sticky, horrible—"

"Mark, it was a dream! They can be terrifyingly real sometimes, and perhaps the blow on the head— Come to bed, and I shall sit by you until you have gone to sleep again. Don't be rash—at this time of night everything *seems* worse than it is."

He shook his head. "I'll not go back in there. I can't."

"Take my bed, then, and I'll sleep in your room. Please, for my sake, *try* to sleep. And in the morning we'll discuss this sensibly and decide what must be done. A visit to London, perhaps, or Paris—I'd like to see Paris, or even Florence." I was talking swiftly, earnestly, putting every ounce of persuasion I could muster into my voice and face.

He stared at me for a moment longer and then pressed his fingers into his eyes. "God knows, I'm half out of my mind with lack of rest, but when I sleep, they start again. You can't imagine, Melanie, what it is like. Your conscience is clear, and you can't imagine such horrors. She's there, dancing before my eyes, slowly twirling about the room like a shadow. Or struggling with me. Or running to meet *him*— One night I saw her outside my window searching for a way to come in, and once I heard her laughter, low and taunting and inviting." He dropped his hands. "Do you wonder I can't sleep?"

Listening to him, I put myself into his place, adding up the years of haunting, guilty dreams that gave him no peace, making his nights a sleepless torment. And I understood now why death seemed a merciful release.

"Lie down, and I'll sit with you. Perhaps I can hold the nightmare at bay, at least for a little while."

For the first time he smiled sadly. "Dear Melanie! Was I wrong to bring you into my own private hell? I wish I knew!"

"I would not go back to Tilmer Hall for anything in this world," I said, my voice ringing in my sincerity.

Taking his arm, I led him to the bed. He was wearing a white shirt and dark trousers, for he seldom undressed for the night, often pacing the floor or walking in the gardens until he was exhausted, and then flinging himself down as he was to fall into a troubled sleep at last.

"Just for an hour or so," he said, stretching out on top of the sheets. His voice was already thick with fatigue and reaction. "No longer."

"Yes, just a little while," I said soothingly, drawing a blanket over his shoulders. "I'll blow out the candle and sit here near the bed."

But I had no more than snuffed the flame and drawn up a chair when his deep breathing told me he was asleep. Slipping my wrapper about my shoulders, I sat for a time watching him, his dark head clearly visible on the pillow, his lashes and the shadow across the plane of his cheek marking his features. "Thank God," I breathed, gratitude and relief equally mixed in that brief prayer. It had been a near thing, and I was still trembling with fright and distress. Still, I had won. The question was, would there ever come a night when I would fail to win? Shoving that dreadful thought aside, I prepared myself for my vigil.

Perhaps half an hour passed before I found myself fighting sleep. Stiff and chilled though I was from sitting for so long, I caught myself nodding off. Mark's breathing was unchanged and he had not stirred since his head had touched the bed. He would sleep until morning, I was quite sure.

The temptation to close my eyes was nearly irresistible. Surely, I told myself, it would do no harm now to leave him here and finish the night in his bedchamber. For a minute or two more I debated with myself, and then rising softly, slipped from the room and closed the door carefully behind me. There was no sound. Relieved, I walked down the passage to Mark's room and went inside. Without bothering to light a candle, I smoothed the tumbled bedclothes and then lay down, sighing as I pulled a sheet over me. Too tired to feel restless in a strange bed, I let my eyelids fall and drifted into sleep.

Perhaps my troubled mind was unable to relax with my exhausted body. Or possibly Mark's feverish words had poisoned my peace. Suddenly, as if I were awake and watching, I saw the dancing figure of a girl, her long hair swirling about her shoulders as she slowly, gracefully, moved across the room. Smothering a cry of terror, I lay bewitched, unable to take my eyes from the dancer until she had faded from sight. And then in her place, someone walking, and then two struggling forms, swaying together in a macabre ballet of their own.

It was Gwenneth. And now she had come to haunt me.

The dream went on, slowly, silently, repeating itself in endless variety. On and on and on, until I was hypnotized, seeing the dark figure as clearly as if she were actually in the room. Clutching the sheets to my throat, I dared not move, though every nerve in my body screamed to me to run to Mark and safety. Whatever was with me was so vivid, so *real*, that I felt it would reach me before I reached the door.

This was what Mark had known, had endured for years, what invaded his sleep, filled his nights, scarred his mind. And because I had shared the knowledge of his guilt, I now shared his nightmare.

A face appeared dimly, the mouth opened in a wild, silent cry of fear and pain that had no end, the features contorted, the long dark hair unmistakable. And then the two bodies, almost indistinguishable in the dark, struggling together for an eternity. My imagination colored them with flesh and identity; I had no doubt who they were. That night in Aunt Margaret's candlelit room was vividly recreated, the horror repeating itself again and again.

It was unendurable, and I tried to force myself into blessed wakefulness, but the dream would not dissolve at my command. Struggling desperately, I tore at the bedclothes, but, as in most nightmares, it was useless. My tired body could not cope with my tortured mind.

And on she danced, seductively, tormentingly, irresistibly, the ghost of a girl who had laughed at Mark's love, taunted him into murder, and left me with only the empty shell of

the man. As her face flickered before me I cried out in anguish, and from the darkness about me came a low, breathless laugh, as if she knew.

Burying my face in the pillows to shut out the sound, I must have awakened and broken the thread of the dream, for it was gone. How long it had lasted I couldn't begin to guess. Minutes? Hours? Suddenly it was not there, either in the empty room or behind my eyelids, and I sank limply beneath the sheet, exhausted.

After a time I slept again, dreamlessly, and woke early to the patter of rain against the windows. For a moment I couldn't remember where I was, staring around the blue-and-silver room in bewilderment. The gray light touched the furniture and windows with only shadowy familiarity, but slowly the night's harrowing events came back to me.

Lying where I was, I shivered at the memory. Small wonder Mark had come to hate his room, for it held the oppressive remnants of nightmare within its very walls! Unwilling to stay here, I rose and made my way down the chill passage to my own chamber, opening the door quietly and taking the chair by the bed.

Mark lay as I had left him, and I sat for a time staring down at his face. Sleep had smoothed out the grim lines of stress and torment, leaving it rather defenseless and young. But the strength of the jawline, the resolute set of the lips defined the character of the man as clearly as the graceful hands and broad shoulders suggested his latent strength. In his fury he had choked the life out of the girl he loved. He may even have tried to hurt me. And yet, in spite of myself, I still loved him in his quieter moments, miserably torn between his two temperaments.

How much longer could a man endure such horror and not crack beneath the strain, mentally if not physically? Mark was slowly going out of his mind, and the wonder was that he had survived these many years. And all because a wanton girl, in the arrogance of her beauty, had taunted him to murder. It was then that I began to hate Gwenneth

with a fierceness that was unreasonable and abiding.

Mark stirred, and after several minutes, opened his eyes. I smiled at him but said nothing, expecting him to drift into sleep again. Instead, he sat up and rubbed his eyes, his hands grating over the night's growth of dark beard.

"God, I must have slept after all. What time is it?"

"Something after six, I should think. I hear the servants moving about."

He lifted his head to stare at me. "Did you sit there all night?" he demanded, frowning.

I was on the verge of telling him the truth, and then decided against it. Knowing Mark as I did, I was certain it would precipitate a quarrel about leaving him if he even guessed what I had suffered.

"I've rested," I said. "I couldn't really sleep."

He swore, then got to his feet. "Why didn't you wake me?"

"Don't be silly," I said, smiling again. "You needed to sleep, and you did. I'll nap in the afternoon if I feel tired. You can't."

"I shouldn't have made a nuisance of myself. I'm sorry, Melanie. It won't happen again." He strode toward the door, then stopped and turned back to me, his hand on the knob. "I couldn't go back in there. Dream or no, it was too real."

"Yes," I said gently. "I understand."

"You can't begin to understand," he said grimly, and was gone.

I stood for a time by the window watching the rain slanting in a gray sheet across the hills. And I couldn't stop myself from wondering if I would have that nightmare again.

I had decided that the only answer for both of us was to go away from Rhosllyn, either to the Continent, or at the very least to London, the journey we had postponed once before. But it was impossible to make plans after all. A French mare, purchased before our marriage, finally arrived that same morning—lame. A shipboard accident had been aggravated by the slow progress to Rhosllyn, and the mare

could scarcely bear to touch her hoof to the ground. Mark was livid, and Noel cursed the French grooms until they fled white-faced and shaking. How could I ask to go abroad at such a time? I stood with Rhys and watched Morgan run gentle hands over the swollen leg while Mark and his cousin discussed what must be done. She was a beautiful, spirited creature with impeccable bloodlines, and her fleetness was proven on the track. Her price had been high, but Mark had great expectations of improving his own stock through her.

How could I ask? With a sigh I turned away and Rhys followed me.

"Don't worry," he said kindly. "It will take time, but she'll recover."

He had misinterpreted my sigh, and I let it go. "Yes, I'm sure she will," I answered, trying to sound enthusiastic.

"Can we hope to see you both at dinner tonight?" he asked with a smile. "Once they are occupied with a new horse, I never know what those two will do. Forget to eat, and then sleep in the stable, likely enough. And Cecily was counting so on this occasion. I shouldn't tell, you know, but she has a new frock from London and looks forward to showing it off."

I had completely forgotten that we were promised to dinner. "And only you and I will notice," I said, diverted by the thought, then added quickly, "It does wonders for the spirits all the same."

"What do you need for your spirits, my dear Melanie?" he asked gently. "You seem quite cast down today."

"I have a mild headache," I lied, avoiding the puddles by the stile. "It is the dreariness of the rain, I suppose."

He looked at me closely. "I'm old enough to be your father, my dear. And I'm the only father Mark has known. Surely you can confide in me?"

The drizzle began again, and I pulled the hood of my cloak tighter. "There's nothing to confide. I worry about Mark, that's all—his wild ways, his lack of fear."

"He has changed considerably since his marriage. I have

you to thank for that, I know! Give him time, Melanie. And you'll forgive me for asking this, but have you considered setting up your nursery? There's nothing like a family to teach a man prudence and responsibility. To be truthful, I long for my grandchildren, and Noel and Cecily don't seem to be in any hurry to oblige me!"

Somehow I could not imagine handsome, impeccable, sophisticated Rhys Trecourt romping in a nursery with small children. The thought brought a smile to my lips.

"Ah," he said, nodding, "children will give you an interest in life, too—filling your days, your thoughts, brightening everything."

I said, with some difficulty, "We plan to wait a while. We hope to travel a little, perhaps this autumn—"

"There's plenty of time, my dear! There's much to be said for a year or so alone together, getting to know each other. It cements the marriage, gives it lasting closeness. Yes, you are very wise!" He held the garden door for me. "Go along and rest before luncheon. It will do you good. We hope to see you cheerful and feeling well tonight!"

I thanked him and hurried inside, glad to be away from his probing eyes. Did he guess that Mark and I were married in name only? Or was he merely comforting me for failing thus far to produce an heir? One couldn't be certain with Rhys Trecourt, for his warmth and courtesy were often an exhibition of sympathy. And he had treated me, since my arrival, as a beloved daughter-in-law rather than a niece.

Mark didn't come to Cecily's dinner that night. He sent word that he and Morgan would take turns sitting with the mare, changing the compresses and making certain that she did no further injury to her leg. I knew that he had no desire to sleep in the house, that any excuse to keep him from his bed was welcome. But I made his apologies to Cecily and gave no hint of my suspicions.

It was Noel who came to Rhosllyn to escort me to dinner. He was in evening clothes, handsome and charming and in a mood for laughter. I thought fleetingly that I might have

been attracted to him if I had not fallen in love with Mark. As he guided me down the steps he noticed my satin slippers, dyed a soft rose to match my gown.

"You aren't walking to the Dower House in those?" he demanded, stopping on the last steps. "The drive is awash from the rain."

"I can't very well appear in my gardening shoes," I replied, glancing down at the slippers. "Unless I carry these in my hand."

"Better still, I shall carry you," he said, and stooped to swing me into his arms.

"Noel, put me down!" I whispered angrily. "Williams will see you."

"Let him see. Keep still or I shall drop you and muddy your skirts," he warned, striding briskly down the drive. "And beware you don't overeat at dinner or I shall have to send for a groom to share your weight on the return journey."

My hood slipped back and I caught at my reticule to prevent it from snapping its slender silver chain. "Noel!"

He laughed. "Sir Walter Raleigh tossed his cloak in a puddle to allow the queen to pass dry-shod. Do you suppose *she* made such a fuss?"

"If I know anything about Elizabeth, she scolded him for wasteful extravagance!" I snapped. It was undignified to struggle and I stopped, treating him to silence for the rest of the distance.

Holding me with no more concern than he might have given to his sister, he continued to tease. "You can't appear muddied, you know. Cecily is wearing the most expensive gown imaginable, and it is only polite to offer her competition. Sea green, with trimmings of dark green—quite splendid with her fair coloring, as I'm sure she planned it to be. Here we are." He set me on my feet at the door and it swung open to reveal Cecily and her father in the light of the brass chandelier above the curving stairs. They greeted us warmly as we entered.

And Cecily was wearing a gown of blue trimmed in white —elegant, new, but not the sea-green creation. Mark was not coming, and she had no intention of wasting her weapons on me.

It was a pleasant meal, and I found myself laughing and talking with the Trecourts while the servants silently and competently served us from the array of well-prepared dishes. Light French sauces, a perfectly broiled fish surrounded with tiny onions and mushrooms, a selection of dainty side dishes, a lobster pâté in crisp pastry shells—Cecily had chosen with her usual care and eye for color. Her father smiled proudly across the candles, lifting his glass in a gallant gesture to acknowledge her success as a hostess, but there was no answering smile in her eyes. Mark had not come, and the party was a failure for her.

Afterward we lingered over coffee in the Georgian drawing room listening to Cecily play for us. Occasionally she sang the words of an old ballad or popular music-hall piece as her mood vacillated between disappointment at Mark's absence and remembrance of her duties as hostess. Noel sat beside me, relaxed in one corner of the brocade sofa. Rhys, enjoying the music as he always did, leaned against the mantel, a faint smile lifting the corners of his mouth.

"You belong here," Noel said softly under cover of the songs. "In a house like this one, not a great empty mansion like Rhosllyn. You are at your best in brightness and beauty, with laughter and music about you, surrounded by admirers. Why can't Mark see that?"

"I'm happy where I am," I replied firmly.

"Are you? Sometimes I wonder. Your eyes betray you, Melanie."

I turned to face him. "Or do you choose to read in them only what you wish to see?" I asked quietly.

He was silent, frowning angrily. As Cecily finished her selection and rose from the piano he set his cup upon the tray. Holding out his hand to me, he turned to his father.

"I must be up early if I'm to spell Mark with the mare. If

Melanie is ready, I'll escort her to the house."

"Yes, thank you," I said at once, and we made our farewells.

The moon was struggling to find a gap in the clouds as we stepped out the door. Noel took my arm to guide me, saying not a word. Somewhere in the home wood an owl hooted mournfully, and our shoes crunched loudly over the gravel. The moon came out briefly as we turned the bend in the drive, and I started back in alarm at the barely glimpsed figure of a man standing well into the shadow of a great beech.

"There's someone in the wood," I whispered to Noel. "Did you see him?" For the moon had hidden itself again.

"There is no one," Noel replied, barely glancing in that direction. "Only the shadows of the trees. Mind your skirts, that puddle is deep."

But I had recognized the man. The great wide shoulders, faintly outlined even in this poor light, belonged unmistakably to the blacksmith Evans. I said nothing more to Noel, following him to the door of Rhosllyn in silence. It would be as well not to draw attention to the blacksmith's presence, I thought, or hint at a conspiracy against Mark. Once again I wished desperately that we could go away, out of this suspicion and danger and endless fear.

As we stopped at the foot of the steps Noel said contritely, "Melanie—"

The owl called from the woods again, closer this time. And at my back Williams opened the great door.

"Never mind," Noel finished, and after an abrupt good night, turned on his heel.

I stood in the open door watching his swift stride down the drive, wondering what he might have said before we were interrupted. An apology, probably, for his fit of sullen temper. I smiled sadly, wishing the emotional turmoil that unsettled all of us could be brought into the open and dealt with rather than carried inside us like a gnawing canker. Turning toward the hall, I glanced once more in Noel's

direction just in time to see him swing away from the drive into the wood where it approached the bend. The owl called softly a third time.

Had Noel indeed believed me and gone to investigate the lurking figure I had seen? Surely it was too wet a night to choose to walk off his mood in the wood. Or had he planned to meet someone there, summoned by the owl's cry to confer with Evans the smith?

Hiding my sudden flare of interest, I said good night to the waiting butler and made my way upstairs.

I slept without dreams that night, though I lingered over my undressing for fear of what lay in wait for me once the candles were snuffed and I closed my eyes. Indeed, I rested well, and awoke feeling refreshed. Yet because of my reluctance to succumb to sleep, I could understand Mark's casual remark the next evening that he thought he'd read in the library for a time before going up to bed. He was haggard from two nights without rest.

The mare was slowly improving and Morgan was perfectly capable of managing her alone now. There was no reason or excuse to remain in the stables, and his body was crying out for sleep, but he refused to acknowledge the need, forcing himself with an iron will to stay awake.

I shut the library door and walked back to the hearth. "I'll sit with you, then," I said.

"Go on to bed, Melanie. I'll not read long."

"You won't read at all," I said quietly. "You will merely sit here and wait until dawn."

His gray eyes were angry suddenly. "I'll do as I please," he snapped. "I don't require a keeper—yet."

"Of course you don't," I answered soothingly, unfolding my embroidery. "I'm simply not tired." Selecting a matching thread, I began to work the ribbon that encircled the bouquet of flowers. "I mean to finish this before autumn," I went on, refusing to notice his black look, "but I'm not sure I have all the colors I need. If someone rides into Chester, perhaps I might send a list and some samples?"

"Yes. Let me have it next week," he answered grudgingly. And then, "Damn it, put that away!" He was on his feet. "I've decided not to read after all." He drained his brandy glass as he waited for me, and together we climbed the stairs.

"Mark," I said gently, "if you like, I'll have Mrs. Powell make up a bed for you in the library."

"And have the servants talking about the fact that I can't sleep? Thank you, no!" he said grimly. "I can scarcely force myself to cross that threshold, but better that than to stir up gossip and conjecture!"

"Then after Bronwyn has gone, take my room and I'll sleep in yours. No one will know—"

"Good God, I'll not stoop to hiding behind petticoats!"

"Is it that?" I demanded, angry myself now. "Or is it common sense? You can't go on like this, and you know it! And it needn't be a permanent arrangement—just until the horror has worn off a little. Or until we can go away for a time. At least *try*."

He stopped before my door. "I'm too tired to think, Melanie, I'm sorry. Yes, all right, I'll try it tonight. If you will unlock the dressing room door when you are ready, I'll come that way."

And so, half an hour later, when Bronwyn had wished me good night and closed the door behind her, I waited until her footsteps had disappeared and locked it. Then, blowing out the candle, I called softly to Mark. We met in the dressing room and I was glad of the darkness to hide my own apprehension as we said good night. I locked his passage door, resolutely crossed to the bed, and slipped between the sheets. I had not dreamed last night, and I would not tonight, I told myself firmly.

After a time I fell asleep, only to wake with a start some hours later. Muffling a cry of revulsion as something seemed to touch me, I realized I was dreaming again, not truly awake. Too frightened to move or call out, I stared at the advancing figure of a girl, silhouetted in a glow of orange light as she came nearer. And then she began slowly to twirl

in her graceful, macabre dance, the floating hair long and thick and dark. Unable to stop it, I watched the dream unfold in all its horror until I thought I should smother from the constriction in my throat. Struggling frantically to end the dream, I gasped for breath and fought against the sheets that covered me.

Suddenly I was free of the bedclothes, stumbling wildly across the room toward the windows. Even in my sleep-ridden daze I knew I must not cry out for Mark. He must not know that I, too, was haunted and frightened. It would be the last straw, the final shame, sending him racing for the gun room and the loaded pistol I knew he kept there. Somehow I must manage to fight my own way clear—or leave Rhosllyn tomorrow.

Reaching the window, I flung aside the curtains, and with the strength of the desperate, unlatched and opened the sash. Cool night wind struck me across the face, and I gulped the precious air deep into my tortured lungs. There was the smell of rain-wet earth and a trace of fragrance from the gardens, faintly sweet and refreshing. I dropped to my knees, my back to the room, and slowly steadied my breathing. My mind was too numb to think, could only feel the blessed release from the dream.

For an endless, uncounted measure of time I knelt by the window with my face upturned to the cloudy sky, waiting for the courage to return to bed.

And then, swooping out of the trees as if she knew I was there, came a dark-haired *thing* in black, directly toward the window, where I was transfixed in terror. Throwing my hands out before me to ward off the approaching horror, I scrambled wildly to my feet and fled to the sanctuary of the bed, expecting at any moment to feel the cold touch of her pale hands against my back. I must have fainted then, for when I awoke, the room was dark and empty, the window framing only the night sky.

Collapsed in a huddle against the pillows, I lay still. I must go away, my mind repeated like a litany. I must go

away from Rhosllyn. Before *both* of us lost our sanity, we must go away!

Mark's tainted conscience had become mine. The dancing figure, the screaming face, the struggling pair, even as he had described them. And now this great shapeless swooping abhorrence that grew out of the night air to seek an entrance to this very room—

But surely I had seen that before! When I first arrived and had found myself sleepless, there had been something—a nightbird, I thought at the time—flying out of the trees toward Mark's window.

Mark's window. I sat up sharply, staring at the rectangle of gray light. Except for once, on horseback as he came through the park, Mark had never experienced his nightmare outside this room. Nor had I! He had slept in my bed as peacefully as a child, and so had I! Only here in this blue-and-silver room had Gwenneth haunted his dreams, threatened his rest. And my nightmare had been a duplicate of his, almost *exactly* as he had described it.

With a flood of anger that surged through me like a hot wave, I knew the answer. There was no nightmare, there were no tormented dreams that gave Mark no peace even in his sleep.

Someone, somehow, was trying methodically and mercilessly to drive Mark Trecourt out of his mind—or into his grave.

I SAID NOTHING to anyone about my discovery. As I had suspected, Mark had slept the night through undisturbed, and he looked better than I had seen him for some time.

Later in the morning he suggested a picnic lunch in the hills on the Welsh side of the border, and we spent a relaxed hour or two away from Rhosllyn. The mare was much on his mind, but except for that, Mark was pleasant company indeed. In a secluded nook shaded by a wind-gnarled tree we found a tiny spring and sat among the moss and ferns to spread our cloth and eat the delicacies Mrs. Davies had packed for us. Mark had included a bottle of wine, and we finished it as we talked about the racing stable. Or he talked and I listened, content to watch his face and envy the light in his gray eyes.

Suddenly he laughed bitterly. "I speak of my plans as if there's time for them. Rhys said only last evening that in ten years we'll be taking the French mare's descendants back to Paris to win a cup. In ten years—" He broke off and shrugged. "I live day to day. That's all I can do."

"It could be enough," I replied, looking out across the valley. "If you let it." And if these dreams really are fabricated, I added silently. His madness could not be cured, but no one would *use* it again, if my theory was correct.

"Yes. You have taught me that." He held out his hand to help me rise. "You make me forget," he added lightly, and

then turned briskly to clear away the picnic basket. We rode home in good spirits, and I left him to check on the mare.

Telling Mrs. Powell that I had a slight headache from the sun, I went to my room on the pretense of lying down. Instead, I locked my door, and then, slipping through the dressing room, locked Mark's as well. There was no chance that he would return before I had finished my search, but I had no desire to be caught in here by the housekeeper.

That done, I set to work. But search as I would, I could find no secret entrance to the bedchamber, no hidden devices that could account for the dream. Not even behind the wardrobe or the heavy draperies. Perplexed, I began again, using every ounce of ingenuity I possessed to think where something or someone might lie hidden.

"Not even a mouse could escape unnoticed," I said angrily, trying to prevent the slow creeping of doubt into my mind.

"Mice!" I stopped stock-still in the middle of the room. I had complained several times to the housekeeper about mice in the woodwork, and she had taken offense at the suggestion that we bring in the stable cat. The black monster, as Mark called him, found very little to interest him in spite of the noises I had heard!

If I were to play at such tricks, I thought swiftly, would I keep my gear, whatever it was, where others might stumble over it accidentally? Certainly not, if I intended to go undetected for as long as possible! And these nightmares had lasted for years. Upstairs would be the safest place.

Unlocking doors as I went, I hurried back to my room and carefully stole out into the passage. No one was about. Moving swiftly and silently, I slipped up the stairs to the floor above.

This had been the nursery quarters, with smaller bedrooms nearby for less distinguished guests or penniless relatives, and a few larger chambers at the front of the house. One of these last lay directly above Mark's room.

Though my heart was in my mouth, I turned the knob, and moving silently, entered the room.

It was empty, just as it always had been, the bed turned back and the chairs under holland covers. A bright, pleasant chamber, with a view across the Welsh hills as well as a glimpse of the pond through the trees to the far left. Mrs. Powell made certain that there was no dust, not even in the closed rooms, and this one was no exception. There was no danger of leaving signs that I had searched here.

After a time I found what I was looking for.

It was diabolically clever. Outside the window were two fine, strong wires, precisely the sort of thing one might use to run a flimsy cloth figure between the sill and the nearest tree. Beneath the faded Aubusson carpet a floorboard had been loosened and then reset carefully in place. Directly below it, in the molded ceiling of Mark's room, was the plate that held his chandelier. There were small holes on each side of it. There was also a hole drilled directly above Mark's bed, and several sections of woodwork that were removable, with hollowed-out areas reaching down into the very fabric of the walls. Except for the wires, nothing was stored here to lend the least color to my theory, but I was certain now that someone had used this room to create Mark's nightmares—and, inadvertently, mine. *What* he had used, I couldn't begin to guess—he was too clever for me. And the holes, even the wires, might have been contrived any time in the last fifty years, for all anyone could prove to the contrary. Thus the sounds of the mice had indeed been man-made, and no one had ever suspected.

Fearing to stay too long, I carefully restored every object I had touched to its rightful place and left, shutting the door behind me.

On my way back to my room I met Mrs. Powell. Fortunately I was in the passage by the steps as she came out of a guest room. I smiled at her and said hurriedly, "The rest was all I needed. I shall be in the gardens if you want me."

"Aren't you forgetting your hat, my lady?" she asked, her eyes going to my bare head.

"Oh—yes, of course." I turned and continued down the

passage to my bedchamber, feeling her speculative stare on my back. And then, to avoid arousing her curiosity further, I went on to the gardens, stopping first in the kitchen to fill a small basket with bread crusts for the gander.

Seated by the pond, I began to think through the meaning of my discovery.

Who was deliberately tormenting Mark, using Gwenneth's death in such a diabolical way? Noel, for one? Or Morgan and his sister. Or even the blacksmith. Twice I had seen him prowling about Rhosllyn at night. Who was to say that he had not entered the house after everyone had retired, hoping to force Mark into a confession or else to suicide? Four people believed that Mark was involved in Gwenneth's disappearance; which one had devised such a scheme and coldly carried it out year after year? It was a simple enough matter to copy a key. Mrs. Powell held the household ring and would deny her brother nothing. Even the smith might have gotten possession of the ring for one night, long enough to duplicate the lot at the forge.

For an hour or more I turned the matter over in my mind, reaching the same cul-de-sac in the end. Which one? Did I dare to lay a trap? No, it was far too dangerous to attempt alone, and I was not ready to confide in Mark.

Feeding the last of the crusts to the gander, I got to my feet. I had a headache in earnest now, yet I felt immensely relieved to know that I could sleep this night in Mark's bed without fear. Indeed, by watching carefully I might even learn more about who was behind the nightmares.

But there were no dreams for either of us. I lay awake until I could scarcely hold my eyelids open, and nothing happened. Someone had discovered the switch in bedchambers and had been frightened away! Or had Mrs. Powell somehow learned which room I had entered when I was supposedly napping?

No, to work best, the nightmares must be unpredictable. Fear of them alone would be enough to numb the spirit and mar one's rest. And each night it would grow worse until the

coming of the dream would seem the lesser of evils. Or bring in its wake natural ones nearly as bad.

And so for the next several days I watched Morgan and Noel and Mrs. Powell. I listened at night for the distant hoot of an owl. And I waited for the dream that didn't come.

In the darkness of the third night, as I mulled over the evidence against each possible tormentor, I was suddenly struck with a new thought.

How could the silent scream and the struggle drive Mark to desperation if they hadn't happened just that way? The nightmare was horrifying because it was *true*. It recaptured the events of that night in flickering, half-seen forms that found flesh and blood in Mark's memory. And because he had described the girl's death so vividly I, too, had been prepared to accept what I saw in the darkened bedchamber as a dream. Even the cloth figure, which I had thought to be a night bird my first evening at Rhosllyn, had seemed a living apparition to a mind dazed by fear and guilty knowledge.

Had the dream-maker made a very clever guess, or had he or she been a witness to murder?

It was a chilling possibility.

Mark had to be told as soon as possible. Although there was nothing he could do without betraying himself, at least he could have the protection of knowing his enemy was watching. And he would be freed from the tormenting dreams and the dreadful suicidal mood they caused.

The next morning I waited for an opportunity to speak privately with Mark. He was on his way to the Home Farm and I walked part of the way with him. In the open there was no risk of being overheard.

"Mark, if someone had *seen* you kill Gwenneth, what do you suppose he would have done?" It was a roundabout approach, but I was afraid he would refuse to listen if he knew I had shared his nightmare.

He turned abruptly to face me. "Why do you ask me such a question?"

"Because these—accidents worry me," I said evasively.

He laughed harshly. "You may be certain that any witness would have reported me at once. I told you, I wasn't especially popular even then."

"No one would keep such a secret? For—for blackmail, perhaps?"

"Gwenneth's father did his best to see me hanged. Morgan, even Mrs. Powell, felt the same. They were certain that Gwenneth was my mistress and they hated me. Noel—as for Noel, why should he want to blackmail me? Or better still, why has he waited all these years to begin?"

Mark had come unwittingly to the same conclusion I had been unable to face. Noel had the best reasons—and the skills—to fabricate the dreams. "Would Mrs. Powell or her brother have been afraid to give evidence against you?" I asked desperately.

"You don't know the Welsh, Melanie. Or the chapel-goers. Sin must be rooted out at the source. No, they would have feared their consciences before me. If there *had* been a witness, I'd have gone to the gallows. Feelings ran high at the time, and these people don't forget."

I toyed with a blade of grass, despondent. It must be Noel. For revenge? Or because he had stood so long in Mark's shadow that any weapon would have answered his purpose? Possibly a little of both, I thought. The others would have been too eager to see Mark hang, just as he said.

Mark touched my arm gently. "Give it up, Melanie. Even if someone had come in while I lay unconscious, why should that person have gone away again and never spoken of what had been seen? You are grasping at straws. These attempts on my life— Melanie, what's wrong?"

For I had stopped short and clutched at Mark's hand as the universe tilted wildly before my eyes. My heart seemed to stop beating and my knees would not support my weight.

"Melanie!" Mark caught my shoulders and lowered me to the ground.

Unable to stop myself, I began to laugh and cry at the same moment, verging on hysteria in my utter relief. Mark's face, white and shocked, bent over me in concern.

"Oh, Mark—oh, my dear—" I gasped, and shook my head as words failed me. "Please, could you fetch the horses? I'll wait here. I must talk to you."

"What's wrong? For God's sake, Melanie, tell me!"

I shook my head again. "Not here, Mark—away from prying eyes."

He rose, and with a last worried glance in my direction, walked swiftly back the way we had come.

I waited until we were high above the valley, sitting our horses on the ridge where England sloped down the hillside to the stream and the border with Wales. Even to myself I had not yet dared to consider the enormous possibility that had come to me like a cold shock, and so we had ridden in a tense silence. Now I turned to the watchful man at my side.

"Mark, twice—three times, if you count what occurred the night we arrived—I had the same dream you have lived with these many years. I thought at first it was compassion, or my own guilty knowledge of your confession." Before he could speak I hurried on, describing the nights I had slept in his bed, the terror I had known as the dream's realism filled the room with Gwenneth's ghost, and the dread of falling asleep that had held me wide-eyed and trembling even when the dream had *not* come. His face was grim as I tried to put into words the chilling horror I had felt as the creature swooped out of the night toward the window, where I had clung, helpless, to the sill. Finally I told him I had recalled seeing such a figure flying toward the eaves long before I had heard of Gwenneth or his nightmares. "And then I discovered that it was *not* a dream at all, merely a contrived means of tormenting you—"

"Are you *certain* of that?" he interrupted sharply, drawing in his horse as his eyes searched my face. At my nod he swore savagely.

"I don't know how it was done, but I found that someone has used the room above your bedchamber to make the trick work. There are some holes and two wires, but no one could prove what they were for."

"Such a possibility had never crossed my mind! I don't remember when or how the dreams began. I had just been through the inquest and a riot, Rhys and his family were planning to move to the Dower House, and I expected at any moment that someone would find Gwenneth's body. God knows, I was in no state to think logically—I was already sleeping raggedly and sometimes even drinking myself into oblivion. It seemed natural to have nightmares, I suppose. Or perhaps they were real enough to begin with. All I know is, they've gotten worse—more vivid—over the years, and I believed that they were an outgrowth of madness as well as guilt." He took a deep breath to bring his anger under control. "Damn him! I'd like to catch him at his clever tricks, whoever he is, and thrash him soundly! It may even be precisely what he hopes I will do one day—lose my temper, confront him, and in the process betray my guilt. Or kill myself, as I so nearly did. Well, I too can be patient," he ended grimly. "He has no proof of murder and no idea what became of the body. Let him go on wondering—and playing at hobgoblins!"

"Do you know who might have done this to you?"

"Does it matter? At least, thanks to you, I can sleep once more."

"But, Mark, don't you see—"

He wheeled to face me again, his eyes flashing. "Stay out of it, Melanie! Do you hear me? I don't want to know. That's his safeguard, not mine! I've killed before in a blind rage, and if he drives me too far, I could do it again. How do you suppose I *feel,* knowing that someone has tormented me for years on end, very nearly to suicide, if not closer to insanity?"

"I understand, but—"

"Do you? Do you know what it is like to feel your grasp on sanity slipping from you—already knowing madness is the only future you have? What else *could* I believe? You say you saw the dreams. They were damnably convincing, weren't they? Even to you? I could almost justify murder for that!"

"But don't you see? The dreams mean someone guessed—or had witnessed—your part in Gwenneth's death! Yet in all these years no one has come forward to accuse you. And that would mean Noel is the dream-maker. Unless—" I turned my eyes from the placid scene of sheep grazing below us and faced him resolutely. "Has it never occurred to you, Mark, that *someone else* came into that room while you were unconscious and killed Gwenneth, leaving you to take the blame?"

His face twisting in anguish, he put out a hand as if to ward off a blow. "Melanie—don't—I beg of you!"

"Please, at least think about it for a moment! Do you recall actually placing your hands about her throat and choking her to death? *Do you?*"

"My dear, I have told you, I was so lost in fury that I was easily capable of such an act. No, I don't remember, you know that. But when I came to myself again, my hands were at her throat and Gwenneth was dead. I am well aware that the truth is harsh and unacceptable, but I must live with it. So must you."

"Mark—!" I cried, but he cut me short.

"*No!* We shall never speak of this again. Do you believe I enjoy seeing hope in your face when I know there is *none?* I haven't told you that, in a similar fit of madness, my grandfather killed his younger brother, and never knew what he had done. In later years he was sometimes seized by the notion that his wife was unfaithful, and would lay small traps for her that he afterward swore, and sincerely believed, were none of his devising. Melanie, I don't want to send you away, but I shall be forced to do just that if you persist in this misguided effort to find excuses for the inexcusable!"

"But the dreams—" I managed, doggedly fighting through shock.

"I grant you, they may be contrived. God knows, several people hate me enough to torment me that way. For delivering me from their snares I am grateful to you. But don't ever again turn away from the truth. I killed Gwenneth. To my

everlasting sorrow, she will always stand between us, and nothing can change that, nothing!" He touched the great gray with his heel and the eager stallion raced away, tail flying in a graceful arch as if he delighted in his own strength.

I sat where I was, numb and frightened. I had been so certain that Mark was innocent. I had expected excitement, happiness, even praise—not this violent reaction or the story of his grandfather flung in my face like a slap. And yet his last words cut through my heart like a knife. "Gwenneth, I hate you!" I cried as the tears spilled over and ran unheeded down my cheeks. "I hate you, I hate you, I hate you!"

For more than an hour I rode aimlessly, lost in misery and despair.

Had Mark, like his grandfather before him, devised accidents for me? Had the man-trap, for one, been left at his favorite view to catch me as we rode that way? Only Morgan had taken me there first, and I had misread his elation for guilt because he disliked me so openly. Instead, had he been jubilant that the man who had killed Gwenneth had now turned on his own wife, just like his grandfather before him? A fitting vengeance indeed, for whether it was Mark or Morgan who plotted against me, I was still a pawn in the deadly battle between these two men.

Perhaps Noel was right. Because I saw only one side of Mark, I wanted to believe it was the only side. He *admitted* killing Gwenneth, and yet I weighed only the qualities of his sane moments.

Then, as the pain dulled, a spark of anger came to my rescue.

Mark had lived so long with the past that he had no room left for doubt. Hope had been a will-o'-the-wisp and he wanted no part of it now. But what if I could find proof of some sort, anything that might serve to open his eyes to the truth! Or was I simply so desperate that I blinded myself?

Distasteful as it was to pry, dangerous as it was to draw attention to Gwenneth, I had to know who the dream-maker

was, and why he took such pleasure in vengeance when he might have had justice. It was the last chance for my marriage, and would either wrench the smith's daughter from my husband's heart or prove irrevocably that he was the monstrous madman he appeared to be.

Wheeling the mare, I turned back the way I had come, determined to try. There were four other people involved with Gwenneth—her father, her lover, her betrothed and his adoring sister. I wanted to go to Rhys Trecourt with my suspicions, but I couldn't, even for Mark's sake, ask him to stand in judgment of his own son. He might be faced with that soon enough anyway.

Once the blacksmith had told me caustically to come to him when I wished to know the truth about his daughter. Perhaps the time had come to take him at his word, much as I disliked the task. There was danger in it too, though he might be led to think my interest was jealousy.

I guided the mare toward the village and found the smith at his forge. At this time of day no one else was about, and I dismounted at the stone block with a resolution that trembled a little at his forbidding aspect. For Owen Evans glowered once in my direction and then ignored my approach, hammering at the plowshare on the anvil.

Waiting silently until he stopped to hold it once more over the flame, I said, "I have come to speak to you about your daughter."

"I have nothing to say to you, my lady," he replied gruffly.

"You told me once to come to you for the truth when I was ready to hear it."

He looked at me then, a long, measuring glance. "Can you bring her back to me, my lady?" he asked coldly.

"No." I waited a moment, and because my determination wavered in face of his implacability, added, "Was it merely a taunt, then? Your promise?"

His face flushed angrily. Setting aside the plowshare, he looked up and down the empty street, then motioned me to follow him into his house. A breath of fear touched me, for

he was an exceptionally strong man and no one knew that I had come here. Even with my riding crop in my hand, I was no match for him. Gathering my courage, I stepped across the stone threshold and into the dim room. The Welsh dresser gleamed with brass and a blue-and-white patterned china, but there was a film of dust on the furnishings because the house lacked a woman's hand.

"Why do you want to know?" Evans asked. "Who sent you here?"

"No one sent me," I answered. "I am here because everyone tells me that Gwenneth Evans was a beauty and that my husband loved her once."

"What does your husband say?"

I dropped my eyes before his probing glance and made no reply. I was not here to discuss Mark or, inadvertently, to betray him.

Pointing to a heavy oak chair, he said, "Sit, my lady," and leaned against the wall facing me. I sat down and waited.

"She was always a beauty, my girl," he began suddenly. "Even at thirteen the boys followed her with their eyes. And once I broke Tom Meredith's nose for speaking about her in common fashion. She was a *good* girl then, laughing and gay but never overstepping the boundaries. It wasn't until the young men in the big houses began to pay her court that she had her head turned and took to tempting 'em with her walk and her ways. I was glad and all when she accepted young Morgan. A dour man he is, but strong enough to hold the line with her. And then Master Noel and the Devil Baron came home from school and began fighting over her favors. 'Twas then I knew that she was slipping up to that house to see one of the three, though I could never catch her at it. Morgan swore it wasn't him, and he was a chapel man and I believed him. I locked her in, but she was wild to keep her word and found ways to get out. I accused her of seeing one of the Trecourts, and she laughed and said he was more a man than any she had met before and she thought that she would keep him. Well, I tried to tell her

he'd tire of her, but she'd not hear of it." He shook his heavy, dark head. "Morgan was told off for his pains when *he* tried to talk sense into her. He believed her innocent until the Devil Baron lured her to sin with a rich man's trinkets. I'd have *beaten* sense into her, but she looked too much like her mother—I couldn't lift a hand. And then one night she slipped out to meet the Devil Baron and never came back. Mistress Cecily swore she'd seen my girl with a traveling tinker, but I knew it wasn't so. Gwenneth had no eyes for any man save the lord of Rhosllyn. She told me so herself, laughing in that way she had, tilting back her head and her green eyes dancing with mischief. 'I'll have the lord of Rhosllyn or no man at all,' she said."

He rubbed his eyes with his forge-blackened fingers. "When she didn't come home the second night I knew she was dead. We searched the hills, dragged the streams and ponds, even dug up Seven Brothers' Field and sent lines down the old wells. We never found my girl, but I knew she was dead. She had always come home before, whatever she had done—she knew I would wait for her. He had killed her and *there was no way I could prove it!*"

Except by dreams that were uncannily close to the truth because he knew his daughter so well? "My husband says she was not meeting him," I replied quietly. "He thought she was seeing his cousin."

He laughed then, a cracked and bitter sound. "Do you suppose the Devil Baron would tell *you* that she was carrying his child?"

I was on my feet. "Is that true? Was Gwenneth with child?" For one terrifying moment the room seemed to spin before my eyes and I was torn by shock and doubt, doubt of Mark himself. Had he lied to me? Was his story of Gwenneth's death a fabrication to conceal his panic-stricken reaction to her news? I could only stare at the anguished face of the smith.

"You wanted the truth, my lady! Well, it is as bitter for me as it is for you. I've never told another living soul what I

suspected, not even Morgan, for all that he had a right to know. Why else would his lordship have killed her that night, crazy as he was over her? Aye, he had wanted her, but not for marriage, not when half the fine ladies in the county were parading their daughters before him. And she was set to make trouble. The last words she spoke to me as she left, standing there in the doorway with the glowing light of the forge behind her, were, 'He can't send me away, for I'll have the child to hold him. And I *won't* be bought off with fine jewels! Aye, he'll take care of me or I'll go to his family, to that haughty Cecily who thinks her precious cousin too good for me. If needs must, I'll bargain with the devil to keep him. I'll yet count for something at Rhosllyn—or have a house of my own. Wait and see!' And I cursed her when she'd say no more than that, only laughing as she walked away, as if she had a secret of her own. Do you suppose I'd ever forget?"

"No," I said, my throat constricted so that the single word was harsh and grating to my ears.

"I'll find her yet," he said grimly. "You can tell the Devil Baron that. And when I do, I'll see him hang till he rots!"

"Thank you for the story, Mr. Evans," I said, going blindly to the door. "It doesn't make pleasant telling for you or pleasant hearing for me, but I thank you for the truth."

He nodded with a peculiar grace of his own, and I left him standing there in the dimly lit room, his face grimly set and his eyes almost fanatically alight.

Retrieving the mare, I rode slowly homeward. The ache in my heart nearly suffocated me. Mark was indeed a murderer, and he had lied to me about Gwenneth's taunt. Whether he recalled the actual killing or not, he had a far better reason for her death than the one he had given to me. Inspired by my love, tormented by hope, I had thought there was still a chance the evidence would lead to someone else. The time had come to stop deluding myself and accept the unacceptable.

And the time had come to go away, for my sake as well as

Mark's. Noel was right—how little I knew about the violent, driven man behind the civilized facade of sanity. It was frightening to realize how trusting I had been, how often I had placed my life in his keeping, and how near I had come to disaster. For appearances, we would leave here together, and once away from Rhosllyn, part forever. Only then would I feel safe.

Meanwhile I would pay the remainder of my debt to Mark and do what I could to safeguard him. Because I loved what he might have been, and must use a small part of the money he had so generously settled on me until I could make plans for the future, I could not betray him. And for my own peace of mind I had to find out how and why Noel had made the nightmares.

As I dismounted in the stable yard Morgan came forward to take the mare. I stared for a moment at his mocking, secretive face, still torn by my earlier fear of him and the certainty that he hated Mark and me. Was it Mark's seduction of Gwenneth, I wondered suddenly, more than her death, that goaded the groom into revenging himself where and how he could? For he took a twisted pleasure in anything that endangered us.

On impulse I spoke to him as he led the mare toward the watering trough. He touched his cap and came back to stand before me.

"I understand you are something of a craftsman," I said casually, though I was nervously drawing my riding crop through my hands.

A closed look came over his face. "Aye, my lady?"

"I'm thinking of making a pen for the gander, something sturdy for his safety while Lord Teville and I are away. Perhaps a door double-hinged somehow, so he will be free to come and go, yet have protection from the weather?" I gestured helplessly. "Surely this sort of thing is possible?"

"I shoe horses, my lady, and that is all my skill. Go to old Tom at the farm—he mends the gates and plows and hinges. I know naught of them." With a brazen smile he touched his cap again and turned back to the mare. But I had seen the

baleful gleam in his eyes. Was he reminding me in his odd fashion that once he had loosened my mare's shoe? It was outright insolence. *Did* he know Mark's secrets and therefore have no fear of dismissal? And then I reminded myself that he had every right to feel as he did toward us, even if he was only guessing at the truth.

I said quickly, "But I've heard you do repairs at the village school . . ." My voice trailed off as he glanced across at me.

"Aye—mend the stove and benches, rig the water pump, and keep the old piano working. No more."

Irritated by his manner, I nodded and walked away. Bronwyn might know more, and I was determined to find out if he was lying to me or not.

Waiting until evening when Bronwyn was finishing my hair, I asked as if at random, "Do the staff at Rhosllyn attend chapel regularly?"

"Oh, yes, my lady, all of us that are free of our duties, the minister being that strict about it!"

"Even Mrs. Powell? She always seems to be here whenever I want her."

"I haven't known her to miss a Sunday, ever." All at once she giggled and added quickly in a low voice as if she expected to be overheard, "My da says the roof is supported by her head, she's that dependable. *Very* devout, she is."

Devout—or penitent, I wondered silently. Her conscience appeared to be rather flexible, at least where the inhabitants of Rhosllyn were concerned. Choosing a diamond spray to set in the curls Bronwyn had arranged, I waited a moment before saying, "I imagine Morgan drives her in—that they attend together?"

"*Morgan?*" Bronwyn repeated, round-eyed. "Oh, no, my lady, he hasn't been in chapel for ever so long! Takes his sister whenever it is raining, but never steps across the threshold, so to speak. And him once a pillar of the church." Once again she lowered her voice. "Not since his betrothed ran away and left him without a word has he come into the services."

For an instant I forgot all about my original purpose in talking to her. Had I been wrong about Noel? Was Morgan afraid of facing his God because of the dreams, or was he guilty of something far worse? And then Bronwyn added innocently, "No, he vowed he'd not come to chapel again until old Mr. Meredith apologized for calling her—what he did. Something terrible it was too, for my da won't tell me."

"Yes," I replied, hiding my swift disappointment. And yet in a way it answered my real question too. Morgan was the sort of man to carry grudges and indulge in bitter feuds. Skilled craftsman he might—or might not—be. It was the temperament he lacked to be the dream-maker, to find satisfaction in subtle torture of his victim. "Well, I'm glad to know the staff is free to worship as they wish. Thank you, Bronwyn—my hair looks very nice this evening."

Mark was rather preoccupied through dinner, and excused himself afterward to look in on one of the tenants. As he reached the door he stopped and said briefly, "I'll sleep in my own room tonight. Don't wait up for me. And—it might be as well for you to reconsider your decision to stay at Rhosllyn."

Nodding in response because I was too hurt to speak, I preceded him into the hall and crossed to the empty library. I felt strangely drained.

Although I knew Mark no longer needed me, even this slender thread between us was broken. There was nothing left of the marriage I had faced with such high hopes that first night at Rhosllyn after we had raided the kitchen and laughed over our daring. I would take away with me only bitter memories to fill the years ahead.

Wishing I could cry to ease the tight lump in my throat, I fumbled for my embroidery and sat before the fire listening to the clock tick the silence away.

Mark was distant, almost cold, after that. I thought he might have regretted confiding so completely in me, or resented the way I had interfered in his affairs—almost as if

by right, whereas I had none. It was less painful than facing the truth, that he had never cared for me at all, only for the solace I could bring when the nightmares and madness swept away his rigid self-control.

I had postponed talking with Noel, for it would not be a simple task. But when we went riding alone several days later, I knew the time had come, and tried to allay any suspicions by approaching the subject obliquely. As we trotted along the stream I asked, "Tell me about growing up at Rhosllyn. Did you and Mark fish along here when you were boys?"

"When he was considered well enough for outings. There isn't a great deal of sport to be had, but it can be a pleasant way of spending an hour."

"You were competitors all the same," I said, smiling.

"Oh, yes," he replied somewhat grimly. "We still are."

Ignoring the bitterness, I said, "It can be beneficial, you know, this competition. In riding, for example—both of you ride superbly. Or other sports, studies, that sort of thing." I laughed, trying to make my tone light. "Of course competition ends and rivalry begins when a girl steps into the picture."

"Melanie, if you want to know something about Gwenneth, ask me. You needn't rattle on in the hope I'll stumble over the subject myself." He had raised an eyebrow in mock reproof, but his eyes were wary.

"What makes you think I want to hear about her?" I asked haughtily.

"Because you are Mark's wife and she was in his past. And because you are usually more direct with me."

"Well, then," I said, making the best of a bad situation and hoping he would put it down to wifely curiosity or even jealousy, "tell me. Everyone says she was beautiful—I already know that. What sort of person was she?"

"Clever, aware of her beauty, wild and untamable—all the things that drive a man out of his senses. If you are afraid she overshadows you, you're wrong. There's no comparison, unless a man's a fool."

"Why did she run off with a peddler when she was betrothed to Morgan?" I asked, watching his face from under my lashes.

He shrugged, his eyes on the distant hills and hidden from me. "Your guess is as good as mine. The excitement of new places, perhaps, or he may have had money. It was an odd thing to do, and I've always had my doubts. Cecily swore to seeing them together, and because she was so young and presented her evidence in a very affecting manner, they believed her. And then several other women also recalled the peddler paying marked attention to Gwenneth. Cecily was devoted to Mark even then. My father couldn't shake her testimony or stop her from giving it, though he was afraid she'd be held for perjury."

"But if the girl didn't go away . . ." I paused and waited for him to finish the sentence.

"Then she is still here, isn't she?" he replied enigmatically, and turned his horse toward Rhosllyn. "Mind the thorns there as you pass."

Taking a firm grip on myself I said steadily, "Which means that she would be dead."

"Women like Gwenneth are born to be killed, aren't they?" he asked harshly, an echo of regret in his voice. "Perhaps it is a part of their fascination, this undercurrent of violence that makes seduction a challenge and a torment all at once. I hated her sometimes in spite of the madness in my blood, and yet I'd have pawned my soul for her favors. In the end, if Mark hadn't killed her, I suppose I would have."

Suddenly afraid to hear any more, I let the silence lengthen, and we rode the rest of the way in rather uneasy company.

It began to rain that night, one of the steady, unpleasant drizzles that sometimes worked itself into a downpour but more often than not simply made the ground a morass and the house quite chill. I busied myself with several projects, and then, restless, I longed for an excuse to leave my thoughts behind and talk to someone. Mark and Noel had ridden to Stretton Barrow, but Rhys was at home.

Catching up my cloak, I asked Mrs. Davies for a crock of

her excellent rhubarb preserves, which Cecily was known to be fond of, and with this as my excuse, made my muddy way to the Dower House.

Cecily was writing invitations when I was announced, and she slipped them gracefully into a pigeonhole of her elegant cherry desk. Smiling coolly, she said, "Father is searching for a leak in the roof. The kitchen maid awoke in a pool of water this morning."

"I brought a crock of your favorite preserves," I said, crossing to warm my hands by the fire. "There may be rhubarb tarts for tea, to coax him into a better mood."

"How kind of you," she replied mechanically as she took the chair opposite mine and gestured toward the window. "Miserable, isn't it? But we have had our share of sun this summer, I shouldn't complain."

We talked at random for a few minutes, and I began to regret my impulse to come here, wondering what excuse I might offer for leaving.

"Mark is sleeping better, isn't he?" Cecily asked so abruptly that I was not prepared for the change in subject.

"Why—yes—I believe he is," I said, too surprised to evade the question.

"I thought so. Something about the eyes, a relaxation of the tenseness there. In time I knew it would wear off—his obsession with Gwenneth, I mean. She wasn't worth such devotion—not all these years. But there was nothing I could do about it."

"In time, as you say—" I began, uncertain what answer to make.

Her clear blue eyes searched my face. "Now he is in love with you. For your sake I hope it is real, and not merely rebound affection."

"In love with me—" I began in astonishment, and then recalled in some agitation that, after all, I was his wife, it was only natural for Cecily to suppose that he cared for me. "Do you believe that's the reason he is putting the memory of Gwenneth aside?" I asked carefully.

"Don't *you?*" Her eyes, boring into mine as if to read my very thoughts, never wavered.

"Yes, it must be so," I murmured, uncomfortable beneath her scrutiny. Surely she was unaware of Mark's nightmares or that they had ceased to trouble him?

"I didn't quite know what to do about Gwenneth," she said slowly. "If I had been older I'd have managed better. As it was . . . I never dreamed Mark would marry someone else as long as he was haunted by her. In time I thought he would turn to—us," she finished lamely, then added with a thin smile that sent cold chills through my nerves, "I can deal with you more—easily."

Before I could interpret that strange remark Rhys came into the room, and there was not another chance to talk to Cecily alone before I left.

Was her comment a veiled threat to me or merely an acknowledgment that she had accepted me in Mark's life as she had never been able to do with the blacksmith's daughter?

LIKE MY MOOD, the dreary rain continued. Gray, heavy skies seemed to brush the ridge tops, and the smell of wet earth permeated the house. Only Bryn was pleased with the weather, busily dividing plants and rearranging crowded borders. I saw very little of Mark. He seemed to have no time for me and was stiffly formal when we did meet over meals.

I had come to a standstill in my attempts to find Mark's persecutor, and began to feel that it was safer to leave well enough alone. My prying and probing had solved nothing, though it had brought me heartache and emptiness.

Afraid that Noel would read too much in my face and suspect the reasons behind my curiosity, I made excuses to avoid seeing him alone. If he was the dream-maker, let him continue in ignorance of my discovery rather than turn to something more diabolical. Mark had been wiser than I knew when he refused to consider who might have fabricated the nightmares.

Three days later, as I finished reviewing menus with Mrs. Davies, there was a tap on the morning room door and Mrs. Powell entered.

"There's a message for you, my lady. One of the lads brought it. You're wanted at the new barn."

"By Lord Teville?" I asked hopefully. He had never suggested that I visit the newly completed building, and I hadn't

wanted to intrude in his present frame of mind.

"I couldn't say, my lady. But he was going there half an hour since."

I thanked her and left by the terrace. Avoiding Morgan as I angled across the stable yard, I took the longer path because the pasture shortcut was soggy from rain. Beyond the dairy, where gossiping maids were scrubbing down, I thought I heard Cecily's voice somewhere in the distance, and hurried directly to the freshly painted doors of the great stone barn.

The interior was dim and cool. I stood for a moment, letting my eyes adjust. There were dust motes floating in a pale shaft of light from the high window of the hayloft, otherwise the barn seemed empty. "Mark?" I called, moving past the stalls toward the opening to the loft. Somewhere a dove mourned softly, but no one answered. I walked on, nearly to the far door and the stairs to the loft, stopping now and then to look about me. The barn was empty.

He must have been called away before I got here, I thought, and turned to retrace my steps. The smell of mortar and paint and new wood filled the dimness.

It was the sudden flapping of the dove's wings that saved me, for I was startled and halted abruptly to look upward toward the sound. The pitchfork, hurtling from the loft opening high above me, struck the ground at my feet, the prongs burying themselves deep in the packed earthen floor. The handle, quivering not six inches from my face, flickered in the half-light. There had not even been time to cry out.

Overhead I could see no one, hear nothing, but the loft felt alive with menace. Terrified, feeling helpless and all too vulnerable in the empty aisle, I fled for the doors. Shoving them open, I flung myself into bright sunlight as the clouds parted. Half-blinded, I didn't see Noel until I had stumbled into him.

He steadied me, staring down into my face. "What's wrong?" he demanded, his eyes going past me toward the barn. "What has frightened you?"

Gathering my scattered wits, I said quickly, "Nothing! A—

a dove in the loft, that's all." My knees seemed too weak to support me, and I clung to his arm while I tried to steady my ragged breathing.

"I think I shall see for myself," he said, turning toward the doors.

"No!" I said, thinking of the pitchfork still standing there, mute evidence against Mark, but he led me firmly back inside over my protests.

The aisle was empty. Whoever had been lurking in the stillness high above my head had taken his weapon—and my proof—as he left. Only the dove, cooing sadly, remained.

Noel listened to its call and then turned to me. "Melanie, what's going on? You shun me as if I had the plague, Mark is as surly as a bear and doesn't come near you if he can find work to do anywhere else on the estate, a *dove* sends you racing headlong out of here, your face as white as death, and Cecily is uncommunicative except to hint that you and he have quarreled over the Tennyson volumes. Is it true?"

Surprised, I said, "No. Why should we?"

"Mark is a violently jealous man. He might resent gifts to his wife. If it isn't that, tell me what is bothering you." Angry, his hands reached out and grasped my shoulders in a grip that hurt. "Why don't you trust me? Don't you *know* I—"

"Know what?" Mark asked, standing quietly in the barn doorway, a cold smile touching his lips but not his eyes.

Noel released me and stepped back. "If you had eavesdropped a little longer, you might have heard," he replied curtly.

"Possibly. Well, go on, man, if you haven't lost your tongue —or your courage."

His cousin flushed. "I was about to tell her," he said between clenched teeth, "that I'm not a fool. I can see that she's worried, frightened even. And I want to know why."

I didn't believe for an instant that that was what he had intended to say. But Noel was not a man to back away from a challenge. And he had no way of guessing how Mark would take such a charge—or had he?

Mark's eyes turned to me, dark gray, cold and speculating. "*Are* you afraid, Melanie?" he asked directly.

"N-no!" I said, but in my confusion I stammered over the word. I had nothing to fear from Mark sane. It was when his madness blotted out the man I knew so well that I was afraid. How could I explain that, even if Noel were not present?

He studied me a moment longer, then turned back to his cousin. "I hope that satisfies your chivalrous urge to interfere. I suggest you leave."

Noel swung toward me. "Melanie? May I escort you back to the house?"

From somewhere I found the strength to smile. "It's all right."

"We'll ride later if the rain permits," he answered, and without a glance at Mark, strode to the barn door, shutting it so quietly behind him that it had all the impact of a slam.

"He's right, you know. You look tired, worried, on edge. The sooner you leave Rhosllyn, the better. For your own sake." He took a deep breath and added bitterly, "I thought the marriage would work, Melanie. Instead, it has brought you pain. I didn't foresee the harm I've done you—I thought I could protect you even from myself."

Tears were streaming unheeded down my face. "You won't be afraid to sleep," I said stupidly, the way one blurts out the first thing that crosses one's mind to cover deeper emotion. "I tried very hard to find out who was doing it. I believe it is Noel, though there's no proof."

He crossed to a stall, his back to me. "Very likely it is Noel. I suspected as much myself." His hands gripping the wooden frame, he said over his shoulder, "You have given me more than I deserve. God knows what I have done to you."

I thought of the accidents that had befallen me and the deliberate lie about Gwenneth's death. My throat closed over any words I could say.

When I didn't speak he went on, "We'll leave as soon as we can, and make whatever arrangements you wish when

we reach London. If," he added harshly, "you aren't afraid to travel that far with me." And then he was gone, leaving me standing there, miserable and alone.

It was sprinkling again as I left the barn. I made my way blindly back to Rhosllyn. And then, because I couldn't face going into the house, I looked into the plant room for an old pair of boots and a cloak and went to walk in the gardens. Bryn was puttering about in the flower beds, mourning the pansies that were splashed with earth and the stock beaten down by the hard showers. I tried to avoid him, but could not hurt the old man by turning aside once he had seen me.

"Fair breaks the heart and all," he said, stooping to touch a muddied pansy face. "'Twill be days before they stand again, and even so the colors will be faded and bruised."

"It is a shame after all your work," I said, "but there will be more blooms. In a week or two you'll never know this happened."

"Aye," he said doubtfully, and gently lifted a clump of stock to lean against its fellows.

"I expect it will end tonight," I added in encouragement, but he shook his head.

"My hip says not, begging your pardon, my lady! It's the rheumatism, and I've not known it to be wrong in twenty years." He got stiffly to his feet. "I'll fetch a bit of string for these and a stake."

"Yes, that's a very good idea," I replied and watched him shuffle away in his heavy boots. How simple his problems were in comparison with mine, I thought, and yet to him they seemed just as enormous.

I wandered about for a while longer and finally turned back, sick with the bitter knowledge that my marriage was in ruins. I had come to love Mark so deeply, and now I must put him out of my heart.

But what if I were wrong, what if in my ignorance and my fear I had somehow missed the truth? Or was I desperately following the fox fire of hope to ease the heartache of departure?

I trudged on through the rain to the garden door. Shaking the moisture from my cloak, I hung it on the hook and went on into the library to warm my hands by the fire. The door opened and Mark came in, unsmiling.

"The French mare is all but recovered," he said, pouring himself a glass of wine. "I'm ready to wager she hasn't lost an ounce of her speed."

"That's marvelous," I said, trying to infuse enthusiasm into my voice.

He glanced up sharply, sensitive as always to my moods, and then came to lift my chin with his fingers, searching my face in the candlelight. I steeled myself against his touch, but too late to stop the tremor that swept me. He must have thought I flinched, for whatever he was about to say, he changed his mind. His mouth tightened as he moved away, and then he said, "Can you be ready to leave within the week?"

"Yes," I replied, keeping my voice under control, my head high. "I shall send Bronwyn for the cases now." I waited several seconds, but he made no reply, and I hurried from the room.

Ignoring the rain, I spent the next several days sorting through my wardrobe and packing my trunks with clothing I would not need until I had found a place to live. Italy, perhaps? England seemed too small for both of us; I wanted to get as far away as possible.

Noel and Cecily were not pleased with our travel plans, and when we made our announcement over tea one afternoon, they wished us a pleasant journey in noticeably luke-warm fashion.

As I passed him a tray of thin sandwiches, Noel said in a low voice, "Florence is unbearably hot this time of year. Why not wait for the autumn or early spring?" For I had expressed a vague interest in Italy when pressed for our destination.

"Mark has time to spare from the estate at the moment. There might not be an opportunity later," I said evasively.

"Nonsense! Mark has always done as he pleased."

With a forced smile I said, "Perhaps he is doing so now."

He turned away with a gesture of irritation. Cecily had nothing to say to me, but I saw her speaking earnestly to Mark in low tones, and his answer was a curt shake of the head. From a word caught here and there I suspected she was trying to persuade him not to leave Rhosllyn.

Rhys Trecourt was the only one who seemed genuinely pleased. He smiled down at me and promised the loan of a guidebook on Italy. "Not too many years out of date," he went on, "and a pleasant way to pass the dreary days of travel. Mark has been to Italy, of course, and can tell you about what you see, but you may prefer more details."

"Yes, thank you, I should enjoy that," I said gratefully, for Mark would not be there to explain the journey. And then I impulsively added, "I shall miss you. You have made me feel so welcome here, as if I had always belonged."

"My dear child! Of course you belong! As Mark's wife certainly, but as yourself as well. If only Letitia could have known you! Like most doting parents, we were afraid Mark might not find a wife to match our hopes and dreams for him, but he has succeeded beyond our expectations. Hurry back to us, Melanie—we shall miss your brightness and charm."

Flushed with pleasure at his praise, I thanked him and promised not to stay away too long, completely forgetting that I would never return.

As they left, Cecily paused in the drawing room door, her eyes going from Mark to me, and I inadvertently stepped back before the strange expression in them that, for a split second, showed through her mask of serenity. With a shock, I recognized it for what it was—a hopelessness so deep and so bitter that I shivered and turned away from the force of it.

And as I did, my mind grappled with a question so overwhelming that I was breathless. I scarcely heard Mark make some excuse to leave; for once I was almost glad to have him go.

Could it be? Could Cecily have murdered Gwenneth? She had the best of reasons! From her bedchamber windows she

might have watched Mark prowl the grounds each night in search of Gwenneth. Had she followed him to Aunt Margaret's room, and stood in the dark passage beyond the door, listening to Gwenneth's demands for herself and the child she carried? I could see her opening the door as the sounds of struggle reached her, perhaps even praying that Mark's temper would rid them both of Gwenneth. But he had fallen by the hearth and struck his head. Cecily knew how to make the most of an opportunity. The Welsh girl, already dazed by her ordeal, would have been no match for her. Jealousy, driving her like a spur, would have given Cecily the strength for murder. Afterward, frightened and perhaps even shocked by what she had done, had she crept away, leaving Mark, still unconscious, to deal with the body? It could have happened that way. And Cecily's testimony about the peddler might have been a desperate invention to save both Mark and herself. The question was, did the Trecourts—Mark, Noel, or even Rhys—guess? Had Mark turned from her because he thought himself guilty—or suspected she was?

I sat very suddenly in the nearest chair and stared at the fire.

While Mark spent our last afternoon leaving his instructions at the stable and the Home Farm, I worked on my embroidery. It was nearly finished. Like Mark's mother, who had for so brief a time been mistress of Rhosllyn, I was leaving behind only a chair's cover to be remembered by. Though the rain had stopped, the chill gray day felt more like September than summer, and I was content to sit by the fire, my mind wrestling with my doubts while my fingers flew. I had said nothing about Cecily, half from uncertainty and half from the intuitive knowledge that I should wait until we reached London before broaching such an explosive subject. Later . . .

Williams entered the room and bowed. "My lady, I hesitate to disturb you for such a paltry reason," he began in tones of deep disapproval, "but the gardener, Bryn, wishes

to speak with you. He is in distress and refuses to explain his business."

Feeling a wave of alarm for the gander, whom the dogs still occasionally attacked, I put aside my sewing and said, "Thank you, Williams. I shall put on my boots and meet him outside."

His lips set in a grim line of forebearance, the butler bowed again and left the room in a speaking silence.

Hurrying after him, I pulled out my boots and caught up a cloak. Leaving by the side door, I cut across the lawns in the direction of the pond, and instead found Bryn waiting by the garden arbor.

His cap wadded between his hands and his face haggard, he made no effort to come forward. My heart lurched in my chest.

"What has happened?" I called.

"Mistress, I didn't know where to turn! Awful—awful!"

"Is it the gander?" I said hastily as I came up to him.

"Nay, Mistress, I was set on dividing those plants, and there were roots all through the bed from that specimen maple. Thick they were! I pulled and chopped most of them out, and when the rains came hard in the night, they softened the earth by the rock and I dug out the rest. Then I saw something white off by itself, and pulled at it . . . it were a *hand,* Mistress!"

"A hand!" I repeated in bewilderment, staring at his pale face and glazed eyes. And then I understood. It was Gwenneth, risen from her grave. "Oh, God!" I whispered before I could stop myself. And then with a composure that was rapidly slipping from my control, I said sharply, "I'm sure you must be mistaken. Where was this?"

"In the foreign garden, my lady, near the great stone."

"Take me there," I ordered resolutely. "The dogs may have buried a bone among the plants. Or it may have come from long ago—doesn't legend say Merlin turned someone into a stone there? Though I'm quite sure it is only a root!"

"I know roots when I touch them, my lady," he chided

216

gently. "I've lived with plants all my days. Are you sure you want to see? 'Tisn't a spectacle fit for a lady's eyes!"

"We mustn't create an uproar over nothing," I said firmly. "You did well to come to me, Bryn."

We hurried in silence to the Alpine garden. I found what I feared would be there—a skeletal hand with the long, slender finger bones of a woman. And caught on one white joint was the tarnished, earth-smeared circlet of a ring.

With a will of iron I stilled the shudder that racked me and tried to seem unperturbed by the dreadful sight. But there was nothing I could do to help Mark now. Bryn, in the way of his kind, stubbornly refused to believe that this was some resurrection from prehistory whose remains should be left undisturbed where they were. We stood together above the rock and stared at the white loathsome thing as I tried to make a case for superstition and the long-dead past, while Bryn watched me in compassion.

"Nay, my lady," he said, finally. "It is the smith's daughter, I've no doubt of it. But what do I do, my lady? Fetch the constable or tell his lordship?" And left unspoken was the fear of Mark's wrath and the uncertainty whether he would see fit to inform the authorities himself.

"Tell his lordship, by all means, Bryn," I said, keeping my head. "It is his place to send for the constable." I paused, thinking rapidly. "He's at the Home Farm. I shall wait until he comes in. If she has lain here all these years, an hour won't matter now. We don't want the servants milling about in curiosity before this is reported. After all, it may not be the Evans girl—we are merely guessing, and it would create unpleasantness if we are wrong."

He nodded in understanding, and I left him there on guard after a final glance at the terrible thing lying in the wet earth.

I had bought time for Mark. I could tell him in privacy, screened from hostile stares as he heard the news. He had dreaded this day, and when I thought we might have been on our way to London in less than twenty-four hours, I felt

the hot tears sting my eyes. Another day, two at most, and we would not have been at Rhosllyn!

Sending one of the grooms to the Home Farm with a message, I waited miserably in the library for Mark to return. When he came in, it was difficult to tell him what had occurred, but I kept the recital brief and to the point. After the first abrupt movement of shock he simply stood there and listened. At the end I fell silent, my throat constricted.

He remained motionless for a time, staring into space beyond me, saying nothing. And then, with infinite relief, he lifted his head and met my eyes. "Except for you, I'm glad. I'm tired of the lies and the suspicion and the unutterable loneliness. God knows— You must go on to Italy. I'll ask Noel to escort you. You'll be in good hands. Later, perhaps, you may choose to return to England. The scandal will pass, and you have the means to live comfortably. I'm sorry—"

"Mark," I said, fighting for control, "I'm going nowhere. My place is here, beside you! How will it look! Indeed, unless you confess, there's nothing to *prove* you were with her that night. I know you don't want me to speak of it, but you might *not* be guilty. At least we can give them a battle before the—the verdict is brought in!"

He shook his head sadly. "My dear, I admire your spirit— I always have. It is one of the reasons I decided to marry you. But you are wrong. Inside the emerald ring are our linked initials, and Evans will swear she didn't have it when she left his cottage. The jeweler's records will confirm his testimony." He frowned, as if remembering. "I thought I could meet her price with that ring. Instead, it will hang me." He lifted a hand to brush my hair gently, and then was gone, on his way to the gardens.

My thoughts followed him to that muddy grave, and a small voice somewhere in a corner of my mind whispered, "Her price for silence in place of marriage and a name for her child, or an expensive trinket to lure her from her last lover? Was Mark guilty—or Cecily?" But at least he did not tell me again to leave.

218

And I did not go. Mark sent for the constable, a middle-aged man of calm, almost phlegmatic disposition, who looked at the exposed bones and ordered the rock removed. Bryn protested for the sake of his rare plants, and finally, in compromise, the earth beneath was carefully excavated to lay bare the rest of the body.

Mark stood watching the proceedings with a detached somberness, refusing to be drawn on the identity of the skeleton. But in the minds of most of the spectators that was a foregone conclusion.

Morgan had placed himself to one side, his arms folded, his eyes unwaveringly on the earth. Owen Evans had been sent for and waited nearby, his face bleak and unreadable. Mrs. Powell, a shawl about her head, was white and drawn, glancing often and nervously at her brother. Noel and Rhys stood on either side of Mark, one scowling and the other deeply concerned. Bryn crouched close by, guarding his precious plants.

Cecily remained at home, and so did I, for it was unseemly to appear. But I had the advantage of an upstairs window that offered a glimpse of the scene, though not of the rock itself. It seemed to take an eternity before the workmen stepped back and the village doctor moved into view, kneeling to examine the remains. After a time he rose to consult in a whisper with the constable, before both stepped over the shovels and approached Mark. Something was held out in the constable's hand. I saw Mark nod briefly, and the doctor passed on to the smith, who seemed to crumple as the little man spoke a few words to him.

And then, almost as an anticlimax, the scene broke up, leaving the doctor and the constable to remove the body. Mark, his cousin and his uncle came in and went directly to the library, closing the door behind them. From where I watched I saw the smith turn away and walk slowly in the direction of the drive. Morgan made a move as if to stop him, stood staring for a long moment at the remains of his betrothed, and then took his sister by the arm to lead her

toward the house. Mrs. Powell was weeping. Gwenneth had come home at last, and there was no shadow of a doubt that her death would be laid at Mark's door.

If he was not guilty, how could he save himself without sacrificing Cecily? In the fading gray light I could find no answer to that, and no way to defend Mark from the vindictive jubilation of those who had waited so long for his downfall.

The next twenty-four hours were dreadful. Mrs. Powell retired to her room with the excuse of illness. No one knew —or so they said—where Morgan had gone. The servants carried out their duties in a wary silence that strained the nerves. And Mark went on as if nothing had happened, refusing to speak of the case even to me. I had been excluded from that male conference in the library as I was excluded when the constable paid an official visit the next morning. It was Mark's way, I knew, of protecting me from the scandal that engulfed him, but I would have preferred to stand by his side. At least nothing more had been said about my going to Italy, either alone or with Noel, and Bronwyn had begun to unpack my luggage.

Even the Trecourts stayed away except when it was necessary to have a conference with Mark. Whether it was out of kindness for my distress or to protect Cecily, it didn't matter. I couldn't have borne their sympathy in silence while every fiber of my being cried out to them to consider Mark's innocence as well as his guilt.

It was clear that the old evidence against Mark had been brought up in light of the new findings, and that while a perfunctory investigation would be carried out, there was only one conclusion that it could point to. Once I caught Rhys going out the door and made him tell me that much. His face tired and worried, he tried to spare me as much as he could, but there was no way to hide the truth.

"I must talk to you," I began resolutely, prepared to confide in him in the hope of working out some plan that might save Mark without involving Cecily, but Rhys shook his head.

"I must leave, my dear," he said, pressing my hand gently.

"There are some rather—well, nasty rumors floating about the village, and I'd like to do what I can to scotch them. If there is any trouble—and I'm sure there won't be, of course —do promise to come to the Dower House. Mark has enough on his mind without worrying about your safety as well!" Without waiting for a reply he was gone, leaving me prey to all manner of fears.

Did he have any suspicions at all about his daughter? If Noel had been guilty, I thought sadly, Mark might have had a chance. But Rhys, much as he loved his nephew—more perhaps than his own son—would never willingly send a gently bred girl to prison, or worse still, condemn her to the horrors of transportation to a penal colony, guilty or not.

Bronwyn's mother sent for her, not wishing her daughter to spend one more night in such a—her phrase—den of iniquity. The girl was apologetic but reluctant to disobey her mother. I was actually relieved to see her go. It was becoming impossible to sustain my pretense of optimism as she served me. Two of the younger kitchen maids and one of the upstairs maids were also ordered home by their parents. The remaining servants took on an air of righteous martyrdom, though I suspected that they were waiting until Mark was arrested before giving their notice, a hardheaded precaution.

And I waited for the knock on the door that signaled the end of waiting.

I slept poorly that night, hearing the noise of shouting and calling from the direction of the gates. Not until later did I learn that Rhys had finally persuaded the unruly mob to disperse to their homes. In the darkness I had expected the rampaging villagers to rush up the drive at any moment, and for a long time lay wide-eyed in my bed, wondering what was going through Mark's mind now. He had not wished to spend the evening with me, going to the estate office immediately after dinner and from there to his bedchamber, so I dared not disturb him with my own fears or chance waking him if he had somehow managed to sleep.

The next day passed, and the next, each in a kind of limbo

of fear and uncertainty. I even considered going to Cecily myself and begging her to speak up if she was guilty, but couldn't find the courage. Mark would never forgive me.

It appeared that Mark was no more than a suspect, however, for he still came and went quite freely. No one would tell me what was happening, and I was exhausted from the false front of self-confidence I presented to the remaining staff.

By Thursday morning I was too restless to sit still. Mark was away, and I wandered aimlessly from room to room, and finally found myself at the pond feeding the gander. But nothing kept me occupied for long. The day was hot and sultry, which didn't help. Rhys brought Mark home shortly before luncheon, but neither had much to say.

And then, later that afternoon, the constable came for Mark.

He was given time to speak privately with me, and taking me into the library, he said quietly, "This is a mere formality. I shall be home for dinner. There is no danger of them locking me up until after the trial. The inquest has found cause to try me, that's all."

"The inquest! But I knew nothing about it! When—?" I felt numb.

"Today. I thought you would worry less if you weren't told."

"Why wasn't I called? I had a right to testify! It was to me that Bryn came when he found the—Gwenneth." Suddenly I was angry, for there had been a conspiracy of silence while Mark was in jeopardy. They—Mark, Rhys, and Noel— through some misguided sense of sparing me, had ignored my need to know and help. "It was my right!" I cried.

"Shhh," he said, taking my hands. For a moment the coldness had gone, and the tension. He was the man I had known at Tilmer Hall. "Hush, my dear. What could you have told them? That you have convinced yourself that someone else killed her? You weren't even here when Gwenneth died! You would only involve yourself to no purpose."

"But, Mark, you may not be guilty. And I know who could be! Please let me speak to them, let me tell them what *might* have happened when you were unconscious and she was helpless!"

The distance had returned, like an iron door slammed between us. "I hit my head *after* I killed her, for my hands were still about her throat. We've been through this before —don't make it harder for me than it is. I must go. Promise me you'll stay with Rhys until I return. Will you do that for me?" His eyes held mine, and I nodded, agreeing so that he might leave in peace. But I vowed to myself that I would not be kept in the dark between now and the trial, that I would take my suspicions to Mark's solicitor before he had prepared the case. Surely he would find a way to circumvent the difficulty of Cecily!

Suddenly Mark bent his head and kissed me; then, without a word, he left the room. For a long time I remained, staring at the closed door.

Was Mark *afraid* to listen to me? Would he shield Cecily with his own life? If only Cecily would betray herself, then no one would be sacrificed for her sake!

If he was innocent, I couldn't lose Mark to the hangman. Once he was my happiness, and I had held before me like a lamp in darkness the hope that one day, before madness struck him down, he might come to care for me, not perhaps as I loved him but enough to build a life together. That was over. Still, I could find an existence of sorts in the ruins of my hopes if only Mark was spared that appalling death!

Yet what could I do? Because Mark had taught himself a brutal honesty and refused to evade the question of his guilt in Gwenneth's death—or shift the burden to Cecily's shoulders—I was powerless. There was nowhere I could turn. For years Noel had tried to protect her by making Mark believe he was guilty; I was sure of it. Even Rhys, fond as he was of me, would not put my happiness before his daughter's life. I would have to fight him too. The Trecourts would despise me ever after. It wouldn't matter—what was there in

my future except bleak loneliness until I was too old to remember what I had lost!

Rousing myself at last, I rang for Williams and waited to tell him that Mark would not be home to tea. But no one came to answer my summons. After a time I went down to the kitchen and found the room empty, the fire on the great hearth banked. No one was in the pantry or in the servants' hall, and I could not find the maids about their duties in the house.

Rhosllyn was empty. For a moment I knew a touch of fear, and then decided that the servants had attended the inquest and stayed to discuss the outcome with their friends. It was a breach of duty, but understandable in the circumstances. I made myself a pot of tea and ate one of Mrs. Davies' small tarts.

Feeling better afterward, I returned to my embroidery. The chair covering was quite beautiful, though I wished there had been time to place a wreath in the seat to match the one in the center of the back. Sewing quietly, I glanced up to find the sun had gone in and the room was dim.

I lit the candles, rang the bell again, and waited. No one answered. I was still alone in the house. Should I go to the Dower House, as Mark had requested me to do? Yet I couldn't bear to sit across from Cecily and her family believing that she had held her tongue and left Mark to carry the blame.

Uneasy alone in the house, I set about closing windows and locking doors, lighting candles in the hall and on the stairs, drawing draperies across the early twilight. Heavy clouds obscured the sunset, and a shadowy gray light in the echoing rooms seemed to hold a sinister quality.

Another hour passed slowly, and then I heard the far-off rumble of thunder. At first I didn't notice that there was no break in the sound, as there would have been with real thunder. My ears were too preoccupied with the noises of the empty house. And then the slow dawning of the truth brought me to my feet in terror.

What I heard was not thunder but the approaching roar of a crowd of angry people.

Hurrying to an upstairs window, I saw a carriage pass beyond the trees of the park and swing the last curve into the broad sweep of the drive. I had not even heard its approach for the noise of the mob. As the vehicle drew to a halt by the steps, I was relieved to see Mark spring out. The worried face of the constable leaned out of the open door to say something, but Mark shook his head and turned away to the steps. Out beyond the gates, invisible from where I stood, there was a pale glow in the sky as if from fire, and the constable's driver knew what was drawing nearer, for he raised his whip and sent his team forward at a gallop.

Flying out of the room and down the stairs, I met Mark as he came in the door. There was a dark smudge high on one cheek and a lock of hair fell across his forehead.

"What has happened to you!" I cried.

"Melanie! Good God, why are you *here?* I thought you were at the Dower House."

"The servants—" I began.

"Yes, I know, I saw a few of them in the village. Melanie, there is an angry mob out for my blood coming down the road. They will be here at any moment. For God's sake, get out of here while you can!"

"I'm not afraid of a mob! I won't leave you!"

"False bravado, my dear. They are in no mood to be generous. You must go."

"But you will come with me?"

He shook his head. "I must stay and deal with them or they'll burn Rhosllyn. A mob is an ugly thing, Melanie. I know—I've faced one before."

"The last time?"

"Yes. When there was no body to provide proof of my guilt, Evans and Morgan drove the villagers into a frenzy. But Rhys and my aunt were living here in the house with me, and that was all that stopped them. Now will you go?"

"No," I said stubbornly. What was wrong with Cecily?

Was she going to let him *die* because she couldn't have him? "I can talk to—"

I broke off as the angry roar swarmed up the drive. We could hear distinct voices now, shouts and curses, and once, quite clearly, "Hang him!"

Mark caught my arm. "Out the back door—now, while there's time!"

"No, I tell you!" But I was deathly afraid. There was an orange glow in the windows, sending dancing black shadows about the walls. And then the first rock broke a glass pane. Mark pulled me back out of the way.

"Stay clear of the windows—I don't want them to see you. And for God's sake, if they break in, get out of here as quickly as you can."

Still gripping my arm, his face grimly set, he led the way up the stairs and to a window in a bedchamber overlooking the front lawns but not directly above the hall and the door. I could sense him beside me, tense and resolute. Carefully parting the heavy drapes, he made it possible for us to look down on the scattered crowd, clearly visible in the light of their torches. In the lead I recognized Morgan and Evans, and behind them several faces I remembered from the village. Shouting angrily, they were denouncing Mark for a seducer and a murderer. I noticed a coil of heavy rope in the hands of one man and wondered if they meant to mete out a rough justice of their own. It was a frightening, uncontrolled mob, moving restlessly and wrathfully, needing only a spark to set it aflame. Another rock crashed through a window, followed by a roar of approval, and another struck the solid gray wall of the house. There was a surge forward, Morgan shaking a fist and calling for Mark to dare show his face. And then into the torchlight walked Rhys, bareheaded and pale. Mark swore, furious at his uncle's intervention.

"Think before you act!" I heard him call. "Don't live to regret this night's work. Since my nephew is accused of murder, he shall stand his trial. I give you my word on that. Don't let your emotions play tricks with your judgment! Go home and let the law speak your will!"

I could have applauded, for he had carefully said nothing about innocence and right to a trial, things these inflamed men did not want to hear. He merely promised them legal vengeance to soothe their fever.

Mark stood tight-lipped and silent beside me, listening impatiently as his uncle went on. "Would you commit murder yourselves in order to punish murder? To satisfy your lust for vengeance, will you sin too?"

There was a defiant shout that putting down a mad dog was no sin.

"This is a *man,* and for all we know, he is not even guilty of the crime for which he is blamed! It is for a jury to decide, as it should be for any man accused of breaking the law!"

"He isn't any man—he's a devil, and his people before him! Burn him out, I say!" another voice called.

"This is my home too," Rhys replied. "I love every stone, every beam and nail. Will you attack me and my house in your blind rage?"

"Haul him out here, then," Morgan cried, and there was a roar of agreement at his back. "We'll spare the house."

"He will not come out to meet a mob. I won't let him be murdered before my very eyes, do you hear? He is safe from your revenge and your reckless fury! *I will not let him face you!* Go home—now!"

"Coward!" Several voices cried at once. "He's a coward!"

"Call it cowardly in your ignorance! *I* call it good sense."

There was a savage oath beside me and then Mark was gone, racing for the stairs. I flew after him, at his heels but unable to stop him as he took the steps in twos and threes to jerk open the door and stand, breathing hard, on the top step. "No man calls me coward," he shouted.

The mob turned as one and surged forward. Rhys was swept roughly aside, and a single cry of rage rose from dozens of throats as the villagers bore down upon the defenseless man framed in the door. He tried to speak, but they drowned out his words, and then were upon him. Mark struggled like a demon, but even he was no match for so many hands.

I ran to the gun room for the pistol Mark kept loaded in the rack. I had no key for the cabinet door but didn't hesitate to shatter the glass with my hand, pausing only long enough to wipe the blood from a cut onto my skirts. And then I was flying down the length of the hall, searching the heaving pile of arms and legs for Mark, for he had gone down now. Reaching the door, I pointed the pistol into the air and fired. It would have given me great pleasure to point it in the direction of the grinning, gloating Morgan, but I didn't dare risk hitting anyone else.

In the aftermath of silence following the sharp report of the pistol everyone was transfixed in a grim tableau, the orange glare of the torches sending distortions of light and shadow across the upturned faces.

"Are you *animals,* to set upon one unarmed man? Or afraid to let him speak for fear he will tell the truth to your faces? What man of you will *dare* set foot in chapel this Sabbath day with murder on your conscience?" I took a deep breath to stop shaking. "Let that man go, *in the name of God!*"

They stared for an instant longer, held by my voice. And then before I could know if my appeal had stopped them, a figure in white stepped out of the shadows and raised a hand as if in benediction.

INTO THE TORCHLIGHT stepped the slim figure of a girl, and the men nearest her fell back abruptly, stunned by her appearance. For Cecily wore a loosely fitting white gown and her long fair hair hung down her back in shimmering waves. To the crowd of flustered men it must have seemed that she had dropped from heaven.

She had raised her hand for silence, but there was no sound in the night air save the heavy breathing of those who had subdued Mark. Speaking in a clear and carrying voice, she said, "If you have come to hang a murderer, be done with it and leave this man alone. *I* killed Gwenneth Evans, for she had stolen the man I loved with her wild gypsy ways!" The words were out before anyone could stop her.

"Cecily, be silent!" Mark shouted. "Rhys, get her out of here!"

Her father, white and staring, had not moved since she began to speak, paralyzed by fear and horror until it was too late. Mark struggled furiously in the grip of those who had borne him to the ground, but it was Noel, sprinting up the drive, who reached his sister first, flinging her behind him. I knew then that he had stayed behind to guard her and somehow she had slipped away from him.

Rhys, recovering himself with monumental effort, turned to the mob. "She has been made ill by her cousin's arrest.

Indeed, you see for yourselves that she has come from her bed! You must not believe her confession, for it is given to save this man from your vengeance. Because of her devotion to her cousin, she would trade her life for his!"

"It *is* true," Cecily said then, her voice strangely calm and all the more effective because of her lack of emotion in this emotionally charged atmosphere. "I killed her, and he has protected me all these years by taking the blame for her disappearance. I shall not let him hang on my account! Do what you will with me, but set him free."

"She's wrong," Mark shouted. "Damn it, can't you see—"

As Noel wheeled to sweep Cecily in his arms and carry her away, she eluded his grasp. Rhys dashed to stop her, but she had seen the coil of rope in a villager's hand and had flown to take it from him before any of us realized what she was about. Holding it high above her shining head, her taut body almost frail in the flare of the torches, she cried, "Here is your murderer! If there must be a hanging, hang *me!*"

And then, in unbelievably slow motion, her head fell back and she sank unconscious to the ground.

Noel reached her almost as she touched the grass, scooping her up and rising defiantly to his feet again. Rhys was on one side of him. Mark, savagely breaking the loosened grip of his captors, stood grimly on his left, the three tall men in a united front above Cecily's limp body.

The mob, badly shaken, shocked into sober awareness by the startling turn of events, became a group of embarrassed individuals wishing fervently that they were safely home in their beds. As they edged away from the wall of defiance before them, Morgan and the smith, sensing the defection of their followers, stood their ground.

Morgan shouted to them to finish what they had begun, cursing them fiercely, while the silent smith stared implacably at Mark and his family. But the villagers had had enough. Simple men, law-abiding for the most part, momentarily inflamed by old hatreds and swayed by the cry of vengeance into letting their passions rule their consciences,

they wanted no part of cold-blooded murder. They might well have hanged Mark in their fury, seeing it as a rough justice, but now it seemed evil and shameful even to contemplate such an act. Heads lowered, eyes averted, they dropped their torches and slipped away, eager to be lost in the protective anonymity of the surrounding darkness.

I was still holding the pistol in my nerveless hand, standing in the doorway, completely forgotten by those on the lawn beyond the drive. As Morgan stepped forward, shaking his fist in Mark's face, urging the smith to avenge Gwenneth while he could, I raised the weapon and pointed it directly at the groom's chest. He stopped short.

Morgan had no way of knowing whether the pistol was reloaded or not. My feelings must have shown plainly in my face, however, for he did not put me to the test.

"It isn't over," he flung at Mark, his voice low, "I don't believe the girl, and, by God, somehow I'll *finish* what we started this night!" He spun on his heel and walked away without looking back.

"My daughter has come home now," the smith said, his eyes never leaving Mark. There was no direct threat, not even the implication of one, but I shivered suddenly at the man's voice. And then he was gone, leaving a strained and empty silence behind.

"Bring Cecily inside," Mark ordered, but his cousin shook his head.

"She's been through enough on your account," Noel replied harshly, staring down at the girl in his arms. "I wish to hell they had killed you!"

Rhys, tired and drained, could find no more words to heal the breach in his family. The solidarity was over, and neither he nor his son would allow Cecily to suffer in her cousin's place. In spite of his deep love for Mark, he couldn't make this final, heart-rending sacrifice. It was exactly as I had foreseen it, and the two men strode down the drive, leaving Mark where he was without a word, as if they held him responsible for Cecily's actions.

Dropping the pistol as I ran, I came to Mark and put my

hands on his arms, needing to touch him to assure myself that he was safe.

His clothes were torn, grass-stained, bloodied. There were cuts on his face, scrapes across his knuckles, and the dark smudge on his cheek was now a massive bruise. Dirty, disheveled, swaying on his feet, nearing exhaustion, he was still in my eyes the only man in the world.

He tried to smile, but because of the bruise managed only a one-sided grin that quickly became a grimace. "It was close," was all he said, and then took me into his arms, holding me for a moment in the failing light of the torches. Then, with an arm still about my shoulders, he led me inside and shut the door. The empty house, dark and echoing, nevertheless seemed to offer us shelter. We went into the library by common consent, and Mark poured both of us a glass of brandy.

Drinking his down, he knelt stiffly to build up the fire and bring warmth to the room, for reaction had set in and I was shaking in spite of the brandy.

Neither of us spoke for a long time, unwilling to relive what had happened or look ahead to the future. And then I said, "I think we ought to eat. Tea, perhaps, and the rest of the chicken we had for luncheon. I'll wash those cuts first, then see what I can find in the kitchen."

He shook his head. "They'll keep. I'll go with you."

"Stay by the fire and rest."

"No. I don't want you alone anywhere in the house. It may not be over." Refilling his glass, he took up a candle and lighted it from the branch over the mantel. "We'll have a tray here by the hearth."

"The mob won't gather again, I'm sure of that! Do you think Morgan or Evans will attack you by themselves?" I asked doubtfully. "It seems foolhardy. Everyone would know who had done it—they couldn't take refuge in a crowd now!" But I felt the chill of returning fear. A man driven by hate wouldn't care about the consequences.

Mark shrugged. "Who can say? But I intend to be pre-

232

pared." He lifted my hand and kissed it. "You were very brave, Melanie. So small and alone there in the door and yet ready to fight all of them." He smiled. "I was proud of you!"

His praise warmed me and filled the empty void in my heart, but I had to give Cecily the credit due her. "It was Cecily who was courageous, not I. To go in the midst of those men and *confess!*"

"Very dramatic, but not very sensible! They might have believed her." And it was obvious from his voice that he had not. Rhys, too, had been completely unprepared. Noel had been too far away—I hadn't seen his face. How many others had heard the truth this night and failed to recognize it, refused to see in it even a remote grain of fact?

"But Mark—" I began and quickly stopped myself. This was no time to try and convince him, to have him turn from me in anger. Later, when this terrible night was over, not now. "Surely they wouldn't have harmed her," I finished lamely.

"A mob is unpredictable," he said, taking up the candle and leading the way into the hall. "That's its greatest danger."

We walked to the kitchen in silence, busying ourselves there with a pot of tea and cold chicken, several of the tarts and a dish of fruit. Mark cut thick slices of bread and smeared them with butter, but I couldn't touch them. Neither of us had an appetite, though we tried to eat. He was still tense, withdrawn into his own thoughts. The strong, sweet tea revived us more than anything else, and I made up a tray to take back to the library for later.

Suddenly there was a sound from above, as if a shutter or a door had slammed in the wind. We started, and then relaxed as a gust of rain spattered against the kitchen panes and somewhere in the distance thunder rumbled, real this time.

"The storm," Mark said, and gathered the dishes to set in the sink. "Leave these. I'll carry your tray." He led the

way up the passage to the servants' door into the hall, and I followed with a candle, wishing this frightful night would end.

Mark put his shoulder to the swinging door, his hands holding the tray before him. As it opened, the darkened hall gaped before us, though we had lit candles in the sconces there when we had gone down to the kitchen. The library door was closed. And then the single light I carried wavered and was snuffed out as if by a draft of air. The tea tray clattered to the stone flags and Mark's arm, like a bar of iron, thrust me back into the passageway. In the darkness I could see nothing, and my heart pounded with such force that I could scarcely breathe. Above us I thought something stirred.

Never moving or making the slightest sound, Mark whispered into my ear, "Someone is on the stairs. Get out of here *now*. Send help if you can find it, but *don't come back*."

I clutched his arm, terrified to leave him alone. How many had returned? Who was there, silent in the darkness above us? Perhaps only Morgan, or even the smith, determined to finish what the mob had begun, but for all I knew, the blackness was peopled with deadly intent.

"*Go!*" he whispered again fiercely as lightning bathed the length of the hall in a peculiar green. And I knew he was right. I could do nothing to help, but others might.

Pressing his arm in answer, I felt my way backward into the passage, and, holding to the wall, hurried toward the kitchen. Something scraped lightly in the hall, as if Mark had brushed against the stately Tudor chair that stood to one side of the music room door. He was making his careful way toward the stairs, and danger. Reckless of the consequences, he was going to deal with the intruders alone. I was in the kitchen now, and fear lent wings to my feet.

I unbarred the kitchen door with feverish hands, determined to summon help. Rhys would come back with me. The Trecourts might not let Cecily take Mark's place in the prisoner's dock, but surely they would stop an innocent

man's murder! Thunder rolled as I stepped into the cobbled stable yard, and something rose near my feet so suddenly that I cried out in fear. But it was not a man—only the gray gander sheltering beneath the eaves. The mob had frightened him, I thought fleetingly, and now he was caught out in the storm. There was no time to spare for him, and I ran on, angling across the terrace to the drive. As I passed the library windows lightning flashed again, and the thunder was closer this time. Then, on the heels of it came a second sound. Muffled and distant, I barely recognized it for a pistol shot, and when I had left him, Mark had been unarmed. Perhaps he had reached the gun room and was now holding his attackers at bay. Or else they had brought pistols in place of rope, no longer pretending to mete out justice in their thirst for vengeance.

Torn by conflicting emotions, I stood poised, undecided. What if there had been no intruder at all? What if the storm-driven wind had snuffed the hall candles and slammed the library door, and Mark had seized upon my fear of the mob ringleaders to send me away? What if, even as I ran from the house, he had taken a pistol from the rack and at long last turned it upon himself, in a mistaken notion of protecting Cecily and ending his own bitter life? *I should never have left.*

Turning, I raced back the way I had come, blind with fear and the desperate need to hurry. Picturing the kitchen in my mind, I pulled open the door and strove to avoid the furnishings as I crossed the room. If there *were* intruders, surprise was the only weapon I had. Skirting the table as my hands brushed past a chair, I reached the servants' passage at last. Only minutes had passed, but time had slowed for me and each step seemed to drag.

At the servants' door into the hall I stopped to steady myself and then very gently edged it open a crack.

There was light now, pouring out of the library, but nothing moved. My heart thudding, I carefully widened the crack until I could see the length of the great hall. No one

was there, either on the stairs or lying on the flagstone floor. I crept to the door of the gun room. It was dark, but the faint shaft of light from the hall was enough to tell me that Mark was not here.

Stealing to the open library door, I peered in, but it was empty, just as we had left it when we went down to prepare our dinner. The candelabra had been snuffed, but a single candle burned on the table nearest the door.

And on the stone flag by the jamb, at the very edge of the carpet, I found a dark drop of blood.

Thoroughly frightened, I listened, but the house was still. Yet in the silence was menace, lurking somewhere in the darkness, waiting to spring at a wounded man—or searching grimly for a dead one. I could feel eyes all about me pinning me to this bright circle of candlelight, and in sudden panic, blew out the dancing flame, only to catch my breath in terror as I was plunged, blinded, into darkness. I had wasted precious time in returning.

The great front door was the shortest way to the Dower House, and with my pulse pounding in my throat, I found my way across the lightning-blurred hall to let myself out. I managed to unbar it, but before I could swing it wide the stairs creaked behind me. I didn't wait to see if anyone was there. Stricken at the thought of being outlined, even briefly, in the open door, I turned under cover of the thunder and sped toward Aunt Margaret's room with its tall French doors.

"Dear God, let it be unlocked," I whispered as my hand reached for the knob. I had never again dared to touch the handle since Mrs. Powell and I had trespassed there. But the knob turned easily beneath my fingers, and I slipped silently into the room, carefully closing the passage door behind me. I had reached the terrace doors and was turning the key softly when the merest breath of sound stopped me. Freezing where I was, I listened. Thunder rolled overhead, blotting out any other noise, but I knew with chilling certainty that the room behind me was occupied.

Was it Mark—or someone else? Remembering suddenly

how often danger had stalked me and caught me unprepared, I hesitated. Was Mark dead, and my turn to come? Or had he already disposed of the intruder, and, swept by madness, cornered me at long last. Steeling myself I spoke softly. "Who's there?"

And the muffled reply drifted across to me like an echo in my own mind. "Why did you come back?" Something in his voice released me.

Turning to the sound, I found the hangings of the bed with my outstretched hands and then knelt where Mark sat in an armchair facing the passage door. My fingers brushed his face. "I heard the shot—I was so afraid! Why didn't you leave?"

"I can't," he whispered, "—bleeding heavily—my side."

"Dear God!" Scrambling to my feet, I felt something beneath my heel and realized that it was Mark's key ring. Catching it up, I crossed to the corridor door and silently locked it, then felt carefully for the bedside table, where I found matches and a candle. As the match flared and the wick caught, I flew back to Mark. Setting the candlestick away from the bed hangings, I knelt once more. His right side was dark with blood.

Mark didn't stir, his eyes shut in pain as I gently lifted his coat out of the way and opened his shirt. There was a torn and bloody wound low on his right side. I felt my head swim for an instant and thought I would lose the little dinner I had managed to swallow. And then the nausea passed and I tried to determine what damage had been done. For all I could see, the ball was still in the wound; as for its having struck a vital organ, since I hadn't a very sound idea of anatomy, I couldn't tell.

Despairing, I tore strips from my petticoats, pressing them against the ugly wound and binding longer ones about his body to hold the makeshift bandage in place. He had winced as I worked and choked back a cry when my shaking fingers pressed too hard, but somehow he had held onto his senses.

"I told you to go," he chided.

"How could I? Mark, you need help desperately, and I don't know where to turn! I don't want to leave you, not like this. What shall I do?"

Thunder rumbled as he shook his head slightly. "Get out while you can! This is a better death than hanging. But I want you safe!"

"Did you see who it was?"

"No. A cloak—wore a cloak. Morgan, I think. He's still here, waiting—"

Morgan, who would take vicious pleasure in including me in his revenge because I was Mark's wife, as Gwenneth should have been his—Morgan, who savagely promised to return and finish what the mob had begun.

"You knew he would come back," I cried accusingly, "and yet you stayed here!"

"He—or Evans. That's why I wanted you out of Rhosllyn!" He caught his breath and then added faintly, "There must be nothing vital involved or I'd not have lasted this long."

I hoped—pretended—that he was judging honestly, not trying to mislead me. And then, because it might be the last opportunity I would ever have to learn the truth, I said, "You went to look at a mare while Rhys was in Chester. Tell me—*did* you leave for Hereford when you *said* you did? Or return earlier than we knew?" To stalk me in the home wood.

He smiled slightly. "What an odd question! Ask the Carrisfords if you like. I was there exactly five days, as I said I would be. What does it matter now?"

"It matters—more than you know!" I said tremulously. "Can you manage if I go to the Dower House? I won't be long!" He was so white that I was frightened, and there was bright blood on the strips of cloth now.

"Take no chances on my account, Melanie!" he murmured.

"I promise I won't!" For if I were to die saving Mark now, it would be in vain—he would still hang. I was the only person who could deliberately send Cecily Trecourt to the

gallows in his place. But was it Morgan—or Cecily—who had tried to harm me?

His fingers sought for and found mine. "Melanie. I love you. I have loved you for a very long time. There's no future for us, but I want you to know."

"Oh, Mark—" I sank to my knees by the chair, brushing away the quick tears of joy. "We'll survive somehow. I mustn't lose you now!" And then, before my resolution failed me completely, I kissed his bruised cheek and stumbled to my feet.

Unbarring the French doors, I opened them quietly in the next rumble of thunder and stepped out into the wind-lashed rain. Mark would be safe—for how long? Running now, I headed for the trees, and then stopped to glance back at the house.

At that moment someone twitched the dining room draperies and I saw a flicker of light as if he had looked behind them. In the shadow of the trees I was invisible. The light moved to the next of the tall windows. The intruder was meticulously searching the house and would find Mark long before I could rouse anyone at the Dower House. The morning room, the library, the music room—and then the passage leading to Aunt Margaret's locked bedchamber, and Mark, wounded, in the chair.

Without a thought or a plan, I wheeled and ran back to the house, my breath caught in my throat. Flying over the wet grass, I angled toward the stable yard, the only certainty in my paralyzed mind the knowledge that Morgan must not reach that room and force his way in.

The kitchen door was barred now. To prevent help from arriving before he had finished what he had come to do? The gander, still huddled outside, hissed angrily at me, his beak striking hard against my ankle. Frantic, I tried the windows and found them latched. In a last effort, I pushed hard against the small pantry panes, and, miraculously, the casement swung open. It was a struggle to lift myself high and swing my body over the sill, but fear brought a wild strength

with it, and I went tumbling through headfirst, by the merest chance missing the crocks of preserves on the shelf below. I had torn my gown and scraped my ribs in the process, but barely noticed the sting.

Moving swiftly, I made my way into the kitchen, pausing only long enough to unbar the door and let the gander inside for fear his noise would attract attention to *me* too soon to help Mark. Then I felt my way to the back stairs, kicking off my shoes to run lightly up to the first floor. Mark's danger drove me like a spur. Was I already too late?

Entering the first bedchamber I came to, I let myself bump against anything in my way, as if a wounded man had staggered blindly through the darkness. When a small table fell with a crash I nearly cried out from the loudness of the sound.

Hurrying again, I left the room, reached the shelter of the stairs, and hid beneath a table just beside the servants' door. Its long cloth covered me completely, and I waited in growing alarm to see if my scheme had worked.

The house was silent, and after a time I knew I must try again, terrified that the intruder had found his quarry long before I had created the first distraction. And then, before I could stir, the glow of a shielded lantern moved soundlessly out of the stairs and into the passage. I dared not lift so much as a corner of the cloth to watch, but I could follow his progress by the pool of light and knew he was stealthily seeking the source of the noise.

Mark was safe for a little longer. But I couldn't hope to play this deadly game of hide-and-seek hour after endless hour without the risk of betraying it for what it was or being trapped in my turn. Not with a man who had, I suspected, plotted my destruction several times over. Even as a hostage I was a fine weapon to draw out Mark. If only I could somehow convince him that Mark was indeed dead! Otherwise he would search Rhosllyn until dawn, and I dared not leave either to seek help or summon the doctor.

When the shadowy figure had entered a second bedroom

in search of his prey, I stole from my place and made my way to the stairs, the back of my neck crawling with fear as I slipped up the carpeted treads. Perhaps if I could barricade myself somewhere— But no, he had only to force the door or even wait outside, pinning me there while Mark slowly bled to death in Aunt Margaret's room. He could trick me as easily as I could trick him. Then, how—

With my mind in a frenzy of activity that nearly blotted out my terror, I made my way first to the Nursery for the cricket bat that the Trecourt boys had hung upon the wall long years before, and then down to the East bedroom on the next floor, the large airy one where Mark's mother had awaited his birth and mourned the death of her husband. It was far enough from Aunt Margaret's room and yet near enough to the stairs to serve. Entering silently, I felt among the sheet-shrouded furnishings for the large wing chair. Thunder rumbled in the distance as I carefully dragged it toward the window, its back to the door. There was a heavy coverlet on the bed, and I caught it up and draped it from the seat of the chair to the floor, as if I had wrapped it about the lower half of Mark's body for warmth. And there must be a candle, a single candle, so Morgan could just barely see what was happening. But I also needed a distraction, something so startling that he would be thrown off balance, unable to think clearly or force his way to that chair.

I remembered the gander. Was there time to reach the kitchen, bring him this far in silence, and then somehow draw the groom up to this floor? I had to chance it. The shattering surprise of the gander's attack might even, with my help, send Morgan in full retreat. But it took almost more courage than I had to leave the security of the East bedchamber for the terror-filled blackness of the passage.

With every sense aware of my surroundings, I slipped out the door, found my way to the servants' stairs and started down. Alert as I was, I nearly missed the sound of breathing somewhere in the stillness below me. He was waiting for me! Without a second's hesitation, I began frantically to climb

straight up two flights. Reaching the floor above the East bedchamber, I raced headlong for the other stairs at the far end of the corridor. Thunder rumbled again as the storm circled the ridge, and it masked my stumbling fall as I tripped over a table leg. Though I wrenched my knee painfully, I caught myself in time to protect my head. Back on my feet, I reached the shelter of the stairway just as the lantern's pale glow flashed into view. He hadn't seen me dart in here, didn't know where I had disappeared. He would have to search every room on this floor. I had the time I needed, if I was careful.

Praying feverishly, I hurried down the steps, clinging to the handrail to guide my bare, flying feet. Flight after flight, until I was dizzy and out of breath, my knee throbbing. But the gander was still in the kitchen where I had left him, his head under his wing. To prevent a furious outburst I began talking softly to him as I crossed the floor. He was near the door, a darker mass in the graying light, barely discernible until a flicker of lightning showed me the way. Glad to be dry and out of the tumult of the storm, he had gone to sleep.

Never before had I tried to lift him. Ripping my skirt to use the cloth folds as a hood, I touched him briefly on the head as he stiffened his neck to attack. Perhaps because he was already drowsy and recognized my low voice, he offered no further resistance as I dropped the dark fabric over his eyes and then gently lifted him. He was large and bulky to carry, and I couldn't hurry for fear of startling him into indignant honking. Ever so slowly, crying with sheer frustration at the loss of precious seconds, I made my way up the curving steps. The gander struggled briefly and I stopped to find a better grip. Then we began to move once more.

It seemed that hours had passed since I left the east room. Where was Morgan now? Still searching the floor above, or had he realized that his prey had eluded him once more? Dear God, I prayed, don't let him grow suspicious! Not yet! Don't let him realize that I, not Mark, had led him on this wild chase through the dark house!

At last I reached the room and let myself inside, setting the gander carefully between the bed and the door. He hissed angrily, but in the blackness made no real effort to attack me. Searching first the bedside table and then the mantel, I found a candle and matches. Lighting it, I set it carefully in one corner behind the draped French commode. There it would be safe from drafts, and its light was barely sufficient to pick out the details of the room. Ripping the lace from the front of my gown, I tied one end to the leg of the winged chair and the other to a bedpost. My tired, numb mind surveyed my scheme. It would work. It had to work!

Forcing my thoughts away from Mark and the peril that separated us, I ventured out once more. It must not appear too easy, I reminded myself nervously, closing the door behind me. I must not seem to lead him anywhere; *he* must find *me*. Three doors away I entered another bedchamber, and feeling my way to the mantel, knocked a candlestick to the floor with a shattering explosion of noise. Only later did I discover that it had struck the hearth broom and tongs as it fell. On the heels of the crash, I was out the door.

Too late I realized that my enemy had outguessed me. He was waiting in the corridor, between me and the East bedchamber.

I ran. Headlong and blindly, I ran for the far stairs, expecting any moment to feel a pistol ball tearing through my back. But he held his fire, his heavy boots thudding down the passage as he followed me.

He did not intend to lose me this time. As clearly as if he had spoken, I knew now what he had been doing. He must have recognized me on the servants' stairs, possibly heard the whisper of my gown. Certain that I would never be far from Mark, he had long since given up the fruitless search for his victim and had instead used me as a stalking horse, letting me lead him, ultimately, to his goal. Perhaps he was totally unaware that I had ever left the house! With Mark wounded, possibly dying, I would never be far from him. And so in following me, he had only to wait.

I was on the narrow stairs leading up to the servants' quarters now, tears of panic on my cheeks and my mind in turmoil. There was no time to plan or even to think clearly as I gained the corridor. He was still there behind me, giving me a head start to lull me into his trap but never letting me get quite out of sight—or range. Had he seen me coming from that east room, Mark's mother's room? Or could I still spring a trap of my own? Down, now, down, and then along the passage, one more door—I jerked at the knob and flung it open, letting it slam behind me. All the while I babbled wildly, as if Mark were indeed seated in the chair, his back to the door.

Startled, the gander thrust out his neck and lifted his wings, ready to attack whatever had caused the sudden commotion. I flung myself on my knees by the chair, burying my face in the musty coverlet. There was a distant clatter on the stairs, and then silence.

I lifted my head to listen, but he was being cautious now, stalking his victims and rejoicing that we were cornered. Savoring, perhaps, the vengeance to come. For I was still babbling wildly, and then I broke off sharply as if someone had suddenly hushed me. Staring at the back of the chair, I strained my ears to hear any sound indicating his nearness, but there was nothing. In the flickering candlelight the figures on the genealogical tree indeed seemed to hang from the limbs, jerking and swaying as if in the throes of death. Costumed and caricatured, the long line of Teville barons, from the rapacious Norman invader to a bewigged eighteenth-century courtier, danced before my eyes, all with the same face carefully picked out in black silk thread. Somehow familiar, well enough sketched to be a portrait rather than a stylized ancestral figure, as I had always thought it. Or was it simply the freakish light that threw the features into bold relief and gave them a strangely vivid reality? I could have sworn they all looked like Rhys! How odd!

Time stood still. As if all the pieces of a puzzle had abruptly fallen into place, I stared, mesmerized, at the faces.

Apparently kind and considerate, yet warped beyond comprehension—Rhys had never entered my mind. His charm had blinded me, just as it had seduced Gwenneth. Rhys, whom she had facetiously called the lord of Rhosllyn because of his single-minded ambition. Yet somehow Mark's mother had suspected the potential evil in his heart, for she had given his features to each of the cruel, covetous ancestors on the family tree, all her unspoken fears and mistrust carefully worked into a lasting accusation that the worst of the Trecourt blood ran in Rhys Trecourt's veins. Was he even now stalking this bedchamber, disguised as a vengeful Morgan? Or had madness warped her judgment?

The gray gander's arched neck stiffened and he hissed once. The fowl's keener senses had heard something in the passage. My heart pounding and my mind in a whirl, I waited.

The knob turned ever so slightly, without a sound to betray it. The gander, wide awake and eager for battle, was poised to strike. And the door swung open. I glimpsed a muffled figure in the darkness, recognized the cloak I had often seen on a nail in the stables, and then screamed as the hissing gander darted forward to nip the leg of the intruder.

"Mark, look out!" I cried, throwing myself away from the chair and into the lace tied to the bedpost. "It's Morgan!"

The chair jerked and a corner of the coverlet fell back just as the figure in the doorway fired. Even in the chaos his aim had been true, for there was a hole among the dangling figures on the tree, straight through the back of anyone seated there. I flung myself toward the chair and exclaimed, "You've killed him—Oh, God, he's dead!"

The frightened gander, frantic from the noise, attacked in earnest, his piercing clamor reverberating through the room. The figure fought off the darting neck and retreated to the passage. As I raced for the door I caught up the cricket bat lying on the bed. "You've killed him!" I shouted again. He had turned to run down the corridor toward the stairs, and I was not far behind. I knew the risk I was taking, but he

must believe he had succeeded in killing Mark and that I had not guessed his identity. It was the only hope left to Mark and me now.

As he reached the main staircase he hesitated, and I knew a moment of doubt, for he *was* very like Morgan in the dimness of the lantern he carried beneath his cloak. Yet I had to take the chance.

"I'll see you *hang,* Morgan!" I cried, as if completely distraught from Mark's death. Then, before he could change his mind and turn back, I hurled the cricket bat down the passage with all my strength. Miraculously my aim was good. It caught him heavily on the shoulder, and the lantern fell from his hand, tumbling, to shatter and snuff itself out on the stairs. The man swore, and I saw him fumble angrily with a second pistol. Ducking instinctively as I cursed my own stupidity, I was crouching behind a heavy oak chest when he fired, the sudden blazing flash of light blinding both of us. The heavy ball thudded into the wall just above me.

I couldn't stop now, shaken though I was. He must not have an opportunity to circle back through the darkness! I picked myself up and ran in the direction of the stairs, stumbling hard as I caught the newel-post in my chest. Already his feet were pounding down the steps, and I fought to catch my breath and follow. My vision slowly returned as I hurried on. Not until he was out of the house would we be completely safe. We were nearly to the great hall, and my breath was short as my heart pumped madly to serve my flying feet.

He reached the stone-flagged hall just as the massive front door, unbarred, swung open. I saw the broad shoulders of the smith outlined against the graying sky. Here was help at last, if only Evans would listen to me.

"Stop him!" I cried. "*He* killed your daughter!"

The muffled figure flung an empty pistol in Evans' face, but the smith sidestepped it lightly. With an explosive grunt he launched himself in a great leap that brought the two of them crashing to the floor in a heap of legs and cloak. There

was a tremendous struggle and then the pale flash of a knife. The smith threw himself to one side and clutched his arm.

Panting now, his muffler gone, Rhys Trecourt got to his feet, the smith forgotten. "Damn you, Melanie!" he panted heavily. "I never wanted to harm you, but you insist on getting in my way! Wherever I turn, there you are. I tried over and over to frighten you away, and you wouldn't go. Well, then, I shall finish you and let this fool take the blame for tonight's work." He was reloading the remaining pistol as he spoke.

Evans, struggling to rise, swayed and put out an arm to catch himself. Rhys laughed. "Yes, I killed your daughter. She was threatening to tell my wife about our affair—claiming she carried my child! Passionate, beautiful—and scheming. When I saw Mark struggling with her I struck him over the head and killed her with my bare hands. That's what became of your daughter—and I was as surprised as any of you when her body vanished. Mark's dead and I'll have Rhosllyn at long last!" He steadied the pistol at the smith's chest.

"You were the dream-maker," I said rapidly, desperately trying to give the smith time to collect himself and act. "How did you do it?"

"Oh, you know about those? An oil lamp, a pair of lenses, and various strips of silhouettes. An ingenious trick I learned from one of my theatrical friends in Paris. Imagination did the rest. Of course I continually varied my effects to prevent exposure, and tried to take advantage of Mark's real dreams whenever possible. Ventriloquism proved very successful last winter. The cloth puppet I devised in time for your arrival. It was macabre, if simple, though I used it quite sparingly—only four or five times. But for you I'd have driven Mark to suicide!" There was a low chuckle as he enjoyed his brilliance. And at his back in the graying light I saw a flicker of movement.

"Did you scheme to kill Mark all through the years?" I asked, my voice unsteady.

"Not at first. The doctor said he wouldn't live. Later, when the doctor proved wrong, I did what I could to bring about a natural death. And I spread rumors wherever possible to discredit him and his English ancestry. Margaret always suspected they were my doing, and before she died she tried to warn him. I thought perhaps he had confided in you, and contrived a few 'accidents' to him, expecting to frighten you into turning to me. Unfortunately, you were not as easily influenced as you appeared."

"How could I turn to you? I was convinced Cecily was Gwenneth's murderer." The flicker had become an outline. Mark!

"Cecily!" Rhys repeated, shocked. "Good God, the child was scarcely sixteen at the time! No, Mark should never have lived at all, and I simply did what I could to rectify nature's mistake in allowing him to survive. I belong here, I'm half Welsh, half English, and this is properly *my* heritage."

My heart was in my throat as I watched the blurred shape of a figure at Rhys's back. In spite of his wound, Mark had come.

I made a last effort. "But why didn't you merely wait until he was locked away, mad. You'd have had Rhosllyn anyway then."

Rhys threw back his head and laughed. "He wasn't *mad!*"

"His grandfather—and the murdered brother—" I stammered, too stunned to frame my thoughts into words.

"Oh, his grandfather was as mad as a March hare in later years, but there is no hereditary insanity in that family. And there wasn't any murder—it was a tragic accident, actually. I've enjoyed embroidering their history over the years and creating little incidents to make Mark believe he really was losing his mind. His bad temper was a godsend! Since he was old enough to understand, he'd been warned about his mother and his grandfather and what was waiting for him, inevitable and inescapable. You see, there were no close relatives on his mother's side to refute my inventions. Even

Margaret accepted it." He spoke casually, as if the premeditated destruction of a mind was commonplace. All the evil at Rhosllyn had come from this one man.

I tried frantically to shut out his voice and concentrate. The pistol was still pointing at the silent smith, but Rhys's reflexes were superb. Mark was going to try for his uncle, but I feared that he had neither the strength nor the co-ordination left for a struggle. Our best hope lay in the smith, who was still holding his left arm near the shoulder. In the increasing light I could see dark blood spilling over his fingers and down his sleeve as he flexed the torn muscles. *Had* Evans seen Mark there, and could he make his move if I somehow gave him his chance?

"Mark is your nemesis," I said quietly, striving to alert Evans. "He won't die. His shadow is at your back even now, waiting."

Rhys smiled. "You are a delightful girl, Melanie. I admire your courage and your persistence. It is really a shame you must die."

The smith's head had moved almost imperceptibly. "I'm speaking the truth, Rhys. Look behind you—if you dare!" I goaded.

He shook his head. "Evans is waiting to jump me the moment I turn. I'm not a fool, Melanie, as you discovered earlier. I knew I'd find Mark by stalking you. And he is quite dead. Your time has come, my dear."

"Rhys—" The word was a muted whisper, a breath of sound, but Rhys Trecourt stiffened, his face a mask of horror.

"I'm here, Rhys," the voice went on, steadily and softly. Mark was poised to attack.

Rhys whirled, his pistol ready to fire as soon as it came to bear, but the smith was on him even as he turned, roaring ferociously as they went down. Avoiding their thrashing bodies, I ran blindly toward Mark, who, white and spent, stood ready to block Rhys's escape. He shouted a warning, but I paid no heed. His good arm lifted to gather me to him just as the shot rang out, deafening in the confines of the hall.

For an instant we were frozen in a tableau of terror, Mark and I leaning against the paneled wall, his body shielding mine, the smith and Rhys Trecourt sprawled on the flags at our feet. And then Mark sank heavily against my shoulder and I cried out in helpless disbelief.

BUT THE PISTOL BALL had not traveled so far. As the smith rose clumsily to his feet, Rhys Trecourt rolled limply against the stairs and lay still, a dark stain spreading rapidly across his throat and down the ruffled white front of his shirt.

"Trecourt's dead," Evans said gruffly, helping me to lower Mark into a Queen Anne chair nearest us. "And in hell, for all I care. This one's in a bad way. You'll get the doctor at once, Mistress."

"Yes—I'm going. Oh, please, don't let him die!" I cried.

"No. Gwenneth's death is paid for. We'll not lose his lordship now."

"Melanie?" Mark whispered.

"Yes, Mark, I'm going for help—"

"I love you," he said for the second time this terrible night. "Don't ever forget—"

It was nearly an hour later that I jumped down from the doctor's carriage and hurried ahead of him into the house. Ragged, bruised, tear-streaked, I had ridden bareback into the village to his pleasant little cottage beyond the inn and roused him from his bed with an incoherent tale that had brought him wide awake and full of questions.

The windows of Rhosllyn streamed light now, and Morgan opened the door to us, his face a shocked mask.

"In there." He gestured toward the library and we went quickly into the bright room. Rhys Trecourt's body was gone from the hall, I noticed as we passed the stairs, and someone had made an effort to straighten the furniture and scrub the bloodstains from the flagstone floor. And then I could see the massive form of the blacksmith seated in a chair by the fire, his arm being cleaned by a white and drawn Mrs. Powell.

Noel met us on the threshold, his expression grim, and I couldn't form the words that trembled on my lips. And then I saw Mark, lying on the library sofa, his face pale and strained but his eyes open and aware as I fell to my knees at his side.

Clucking his tongue, the doctor lifted the blanket and set to work. Mrs. Powell had already brought in hot water and bandages and a nearby table had been prepared for his use. I don't know how I endured that endless time as he cleaned and sewed and bandaged the ghastly wound in Mark's side. All the while Mark's hand held tightly to mine, and his eyes never left my face.

"There," the little man said, stepping back at last to smile down at me. "It was close, but nothing vital is damaged. If there is no infection he will be on his feet in a week. Loss of blood is his greatest danger, but a careful diet will set that to rights."

I smiled back through my tears but could not find any words to say. The doctor moved on to examine the smith's shoulder and then glanced curiously about the room, clearly wondering what had happened here.

"My father is upstairs," Noel said then. "You'll need to make a report on his death."

Disconcerted, for I had refused to make any explanation for my summons other than the briefest description of the wounds he must attend to, the doctor nodded and reached again for his case.

"I'm sorry," I said gently to Noel as he passed me.

He put a hand on my shoulder. "I never guessed—" he began, then glanced in Mark's direction. "At least Cecily is

well out of it." His fingers tightened briefly and then he was gone.

I was grateful that my suspicions about Cecily had seemed merely a ruse to distract her father, that no one would ever know what I had really believed. There would be many wounds to heal at Rhosllyn besides those made with gun and knife, but without Rhys's subtle poisoning of our minds we would find our way to a peaceful future.

Mrs. Powell, her hands full of bandages and basins, lingered by the door, and I saw Morgan in the hall. Ashamed and uncertain, they were prepared for dismissal—or worse. In the experiences of this night I had seen the depth of human passions, and for the first time understood who lashed the groom to such bitterness and destruction. We could never forgive his leadership of that dreadful mob nor forget the hate-filled service that had delighted in our suffering. There was no need to punish him, but he and his sister would never again work at Rhosllyn.

Owen Evans, rolling down his slit sleeve and easing it over the bulky bandage, smiled briefly at me. "He'll live, Mistress," he said quietly and stepped to the foot of the sofa where Mark could see him. "I came back tonight because what we had done didn't sit right, somehow. The riot—" He stopped, not wishing to go back over that nightmare.

"I'm glad you did," Mark replied with a faint smile.

"Aye. You and your lady, you faced them squarely, and then the lass, your cousin— Well, it was the truth I was wanting, if I had to beat it out of you. I was wrong. As for your uncle, he was an evil man and I find no regret in me for what I did."

"It was self-defense," I said quickly. "Mark and I are witnesses to that!"

Owen Evans looked at me enigmatically. " 'Vengeance is mine, saith the Lord. I will repay.' But a mite of help is never amiss."

"I'm sorry—about Gwenneth," Mark said. "It caused you suffering, and I had no way to know—"

"She was what she was," the man said heavily. "I'll not

hold it to your door. 'Twas as well you didn't speak out. They'd have hanged an innocent man, else. We've let the past blind us too long. 'Tis time the Welsh and the English stopped feuding and put a man's worth before his blood."

"Yes," Mark said quietly. "I've learned that tonight. You are a good man to have at one's back in a fight, Owen Evans. Thank you."

"We're quit, then, you and I."

"Quit," Mark repeated, and tried to lift his hand. The smith, suddenly red in the face, bent to grasp it firmly, and then with a nod toward me, walked out, closing the door in Mrs. Powell's anxious face.

"It's over," I said, holding tightly to Mark's hand and fighting back the tears. Aching and exhausted, I could nevertheless have sat by him for hours more, grateful to be near him.

"My dear—" His eyes searched my face. "We've not had much of a marriage, have we?" He paused to steady his voice. "I have loved you for a very long time and I thought I had no right to speak of it. Now, at last, I can offer you my heart and hope that in time—"

"Oh, Mark, I loved you even when I believed you had killed her and were trying to harm me. I was so terribly jealous of that poor girl!" I cried and threw my arms about his shoulders.

Mark gulped in pain and then laughed softly. "She was a fever in my blood, nothing more, a boy's dream. Give me a week, Melanie, and I'll show you that there's no other woman in my life and never will be!" The vibrancy in his voice shook me, and I buried my face against his throat as he whispered promises against my tumbled hair.

S